American Apartheid

Segregation and the Making of the Underclass

DOUGLAS S. MASSEY

NANCY A. DENTON

Harvard University Press
Cambridge, Massachusetts
London, England

Printed in the United States of America

Library of Congress Cataloging-in-Publication Data

Massey, Douglas S.
American apartheid: segregation and the making of the underclass
/ Douglas S. Massey, Nancy A. Denton.
p. cm.
Includes index.
ISBN 0-674-01820-6 (acid-free) (cloth)
ISBN 0-674-01821-4 (pbk.)
1. Race discrimination—United States—History–20th century.
2. Segregation—United States—History—20th century. 3. Afro-Americans—Social conditions. 4. Inner cities—United States—History—20th century. 5. United States—Race relations.
6. United States—Social policy.
I. Denton, Nancy A. II. Title.
E185.61.M373 1993
305.8'00973—dc20 92-13889
CIP

To
Dr. Kenneth B. Clark
an inspiration to a generation

Contents

Preface

This book grew out of research that was originally funded by the National Institute of Child Health and Human Development in June 1984 (grant number R01-HD-18594) to undertake a systematic study of racial and ethnic segregation based on the 1980 Census. A follow-up project to examine the consequences of residential segregation was funded by the same agency in June 1987 (grant number R01-HD-22992). As work progressed on these projects, the unique segregation of black Americans stood out in ever-sharper relief, and the deleterious consequences they suffered as a result of this spatial isolation became painfully obvious.

Equally obvious was that these facts were ignored in ongoing debates about the relative importance of race in American society and the origins of the urban underclass. It seemed to us amazing that people were even debating whether race was declining in importance when levels of residential segregation were so high and so structured along racial lines, and we did not understand how the volumes of material written on the underclass could gloss over the persisting reality of racial segregation as if it were irrelevant to the creation and maintenance of urban poverty. Our research indicates that racial residential segregation is the principal structural feature of American society responsible for the perpetuation of urban poverty and represents a primary cause of racial inequality in the United States.

The book and its underlying research are really a collaborative effort of many people and institutions. First and foremost, we owe a debt of thanks to the National Institute of Child Health and Human Development (and hence to U.S. taxpayers) for sponsoring most of the research underlying this book, and we are particularly indebted to Dr. V. Jeffery Evans of that institute for his constant help and encouragement. The National Opinion Research Center administered the research project and we acknowledge the dedicated efforts of its outstanding staff. We also thank the Guggenheim Foundation for a fellowship awarded to Douglas Massey during 1990–91 that granted him a sabbatical year in which to prepare the manuscript, and we thank the University of Chicago and its Division of the Social Sciences for providing additional salary and research support during this leave. Thanks are also owed to the New York State United University Professors for a New Faculty Development Award to Nancy Denton in 1990–91.

The project also benefited greatly from a host of students and colleagues who contributed their expertise and knowledge to research during various phases of the project. Isabel García and Adelle Hinojosa were responsible for day-to-day administration and project support. Stuart Bogom, Mark Keintz, Michael Strong, and Stephen Taber provided invaluable assistance in creating the computerized data files used in later investigations, and we also benefited from the hard work of Brendan Mullan and Felipe García. Gretchen Condran compiled a special data set covering Philadelphia and collaborated in a study of segregation's social, economic, and health consequences in that city, and Eric Fong helped extend this analysis to San Francisco. Mitchell Eggers worked intensively with us to understand the determinants of urban poverty and its spatial concentration. Andrew Gross carried out research on methodological issues and contributed to studies of the causes and consequences of black segregation. Adam Bickford collaborated in a study of racial segregation within U.S. public housing, and Shawn Kanaiaupuni carried out additional research to determine the effect of project location on poverty concentration. Richard Sander worked with us on a theoretical and empirical analysis of neighborhood racial transition.

Andrew Cherlin, Katharine Donato, George Galster, Hector Cordero Guzmán, Harvey Molotch, and several anonymous reviewers gave generously of their time in reading all or some of the manuscript, and Elizabeth Gretz improved its prose through her careful editing. The comments and suggestions of these individuals greatly improved the manuscript, and they cannot be faulted for the shortcomings that no doubt remain. The book also reflects the patience and support of many friends and family members, particularly Susan Ross and John Pipkin.

We are grateful to several authors and institutions for permission to cite or quote their published materials. We thank Stanley Lieberson and the University of California Press for permission to use indices originally reported in *Piece of the Pie: Blacks and White Immigrants since 1880,* © 1980 by the Regents of the University of California. We also thank Reynolds Farley, Suzanne Bianchi, Diane Colasanto, and the American Academy of Political and Social Science for permission to reprint data from "Barriers to the Racial Integration of Neighborhoods: The Detroit Case," from volume 441 of *The Annals of the American Academy of Political and Social Science*, © 1979 by the American Academy of Political and Social Science. We again thank Reynolds Farley, Suzanne Bianchi, and Diane Colasanto as well as Howard Schuman, Shirley Hatchett, and Academic Press for permission to reproduce data from "'Chocolate City, Vanilla Suburbs': Will the Trend toward Racially Separate Communities Continue?" published in volume 7 of *Social Science Research*, © 1978 by Academic Press. Finally, we express our gratitude to Roderick J. Harrison and Daniel J. Weinberg of the U.S. Bureau of the Census for sending us preliminary calculations of 1990 segregation indices prior to their presentation in "Racial and Ethnic Residential Segregation in 1990" at the April 13, 1992, meetings of the Population Association of America in Denver, Colorado.

To all these people and institutions we extend our deep and heartfelt thanks, and hope that the end result justifies the sacrifices that they made on our behalf.

Chicago, Illinois
March 1992

Racial segregation, like all other forms of cruelty and tyranny, debases all human beings—those who are its victims, those who victimize, and in quite subtle ways those who are mere accessories.

Kenneth B. Clark

1

The Missing Link

It is quite simple. As soon as there is a group area then all your uncertainties are removed and that is, after all, the primary purpose of this Bill [requiring racial segregation in housing].

Minister of the Interior,
Union of South Africa
legislative debate on the
the Group Areas Act of 1950

During the 1970s and 1980s a word disappeared from the American vocabulary.[1] It was not in the speeches of politicians decrying the multiple ills besetting American cities. It was not spoken by government officials responsible for administering the nation's social programs. It was not mentioned by journalists reporting on the rising tide of homelessness, drugs, and violence in urban America. It was not discussed by foundation executives and think-tank experts proposing new programs for unemployed parents and unwed mothers. It was not articulated by civil rights leaders speaking out against the persistence of racial inequality; and it was nowhere to be found in the thousands of pages written by social scientists on the urban underclass. The word was segregation.

Most Americans vaguely realize that urban America is still a residentially segregated society, but few appreciate the depth of black segregation or the degree to which it is maintained by ongoing institutional arrangements and contemporary individual actions. They view segregation as an unfortunate holdover from a racist past, one that is fading progressively over time. If racial residential segregation persists, they reason, it is only because civil rights laws passed during the 1960s have not had enough time to work or because many blacks still prefer to live in black neighborhoods. The residential segregation of blacks is viewed charitably as a "natural" outcome of impersonal social and economic forces, the same forces that produced Italian and Polish neighborhoods in the past and that yield Mexican and Korean areas today.

But black segregation is not comparable to the limited and transient segregation experienced by other racial and ethnic groups, now or in the past. No group in the history of the United States has ever experienced the sustained high level of residential segregation that has been imposed on blacks in large American cities for the past fifty years. This extreme racial isolation did not just happen; it was manufactured by whites through a series of self-conscious actions and purposeful institutional arrangements that continue today. Not only is the depth of black segregation unprecedented and utterly unique compared with that of other groups, but it shows little sign of change with the passage of time or improvements in socioeconomic status.

If policymakers, scholars, and the public have been reluctant to acknowledge segregation's persistence, they have likewise been blind to its consequences for American blacks. Residential segregation is not a neutral fact; it systematically undermines the social and economic well-being of blacks in the United States. Because of racial segregation, a significant share of black America is condemned to experience a social environment where poverty and joblessness are the norm, where a majority of children are born out of wedlock, where most families are on welfare, where educational failure prevails, and where social and physical deterioration abound. Through prolonged exposure to such an environment, black chances for social and economic success are drastically reduced.

Deleterious neighborhood conditions are built into the structure of the black community. They occur because segregation concentrates poverty to build a set of mutually reinforcing and self-feeding spirals of decline into black neighborhoods. When economic dislocations deprive a segregated group of employment and increase its rate of poverty, socioeconomic deprivation inevitably becomes more concentrated in neighborhoods where that group lives. The damaging social consequences that follow from increased poverty are spatially concentrated as well, creating uniquely disadvantaged environments that become progressively isolated—geographically, socially, and economically—from the rest of society.

The effect of segregation on black well-being is structural, not individual. Residential segregation lies beyond the ability of any individual to change; it constrains black life chances irrespective of personal traits, individual motivations, or private achievements. For the past twenty years this fundamental fact has been swept under the rug by policymakers, scholars, and theorists of the urban underclass. Segregation is the missing link in prior attempts to understand the plight of the urban poor. As long as blacks continue to be segregated in American cities, the United States cannot be called a race-blind society.

The Forgotten Factor

The present myopia regarding segregation is all the more startling because it once figured prominently in theories of racial inequality. Indeed, the ghetto was once seen as central to black subjugation in the United States. In 1944 Gunnar Myrdal wrote in *An American Dilemma* that residential segregation "is basic in a mechanical sense. It exerts its influence in an indirect and impersonal way: because Negro people do not live near white people, they cannot . . . associate with each other in the many activities founded on common neighborhood. Residential segregation . . . becomes reflected in uni-racial schools, hospitals, and other institutions" and creates "an artificial city . . . that permits any prejudice on the part of public officials to be freely vented on Negroes without hurting whites."[2]

Kenneth B. Clark, who worked with Gunnar Myrdal as a student and later applied his research skills in the landmark *Brown v. Topeka* school integration case, placed residential segregation at the heart of the U.S. system of racial oppression. In *Dark Ghetto,* written in 1965, he argued that "the dark ghetto's invisible walls have been erected by the white society, by those who have power, both to confine those who have *no* power and to perpetuate their powerlessness. The dark ghettos are social, political, educational, and—above all—economic colonies. Their inhabitants are subject peoples, victims of the greed, cruelty, insensitivity, guilt, and fear of their masters."[3]

Public recognition of segregation's role in perpetuating racial inequality was galvanized in the late 1960s by the riots that erupted in the nation's ghettos. In their aftermath, President Lyndon B. Johnson appointed a commission chaired by Governor Otto Kerner of Illinois to identify the causes of the violence and to propose policies to prevent its recurrence. The Kerner Commission released its report in March 1968 with the shocking admonition that the United States was "moving toward two societies, one black, one white—separate and unequal."[4] Prominent among the causes that the commission identified for this growing racial inequality was residential segregation.

In stark, blunt language, the Kerner Commission informed white Americans that "discrimination and segregation have long permeated much of American life; they now threaten the future of every American."[5] "Segregation and poverty have created in the racial ghetto a destructive environment totally unknown to most white Americans. What white Americans have never fully understood—but what the Negro can never forget—is that white society is deeply implicated in the ghetto. White institutions created it, white institutions maintain it, and white society condones it."[6]

The report argued that to continue present policies was "to make permanent the division of our country into two societies; one, largely Negro and poor, located in the central cities; the other, predominantly white and affluent, located in the suburbs."[7] Commission members rejected a strategy of ghetto enrichment coupled with abandonment of efforts to integrate, an approach they saw "as another way of choosing a permanently divided country."[8] Rather, they insisted that the only reasonable choice for America was "a policy which combines ghetto enrichment with programs designed to encourage integration of substantial numbers of Negroes into the society outside the ghetto."[9]

America chose differently. Following the passage of the Fair Housing Act in 1968, the problem of housing discrimination was declared solved, and residential segregation dropped off the national agenda. Civil rights leaders stopped pressing for the enforcement of open housing, political leaders increasingly debated employment and educational policies rather than housing integration, and academicians focused their theoretical scrutiny on everything from culture to family structure, to institutional racism, to federal welfare systems. Few people spoke of racial segregation as a problem or acknowledged its persisting consequences. By the end of the 1970s residential segregation became the forgotten factor in American race relations.[10]

While public discourse on race and poverty became more acrimonious and more focused on divisive issues such as school busing, racial quotas, welfare, and affirmative action, conditions in the nation's ghettos steadily deteriorated.[11] By the end of the 1970s, the image of poor minority families mired in an endless cycle of unemployment, unwed childbearing, illiteracy, and dependency had coalesced into a compelling and powerful concept: the urban underclass.[12] In the view of many middle-class whites, inner cities had come to house a large population of poorly educated single mothers and jobless men—mostly black and Puerto Rican—who were unlikely to exit poverty and become self-sufficient. In the ensuing national debate on the causes for this persistent poverty, four theoretical explanations gradually emerged: culture, racism, economics, and welfare.

Cultural explanations for the underclass can be traced to the work of Oscar Lewis, who identified a "culture of poverty" that he felt promoted patterns of behavior inconsistent with socioeconomic advancement.[13] According to Lewis, this culture originated in endemic unemployment and chronic social immobility, and provided an ideology that allowed poor people to cope with feelings of hopelessness and despair that arose because their chances for socioeconomic success were remote. In individuals, this culture was typified by a lack of impulse control, a strong present-time orientation, and little ability to defer gratification. Among families, it yielded an absence of childhood, an early initiation into sex, a prevalence of free marital unions, and a high incidence of abandonment of mothers and children.

Although Lewis explicitly connected the emergence of these cultural patterns to structural conditions in society, he argued that once the culture of poverty was established, it became an independent cause of persistent poverty. This idea was further elaborated in 1965 by the Harvard sociologist and then Assistant Secretary of Labor Daniel Patrick Moynihan, who in a confidential report to the President focused on the relationship between male unemployment, family instability, and the intergenerational transmission of poverty, a process he labeled a "tangle of pathology."[14] He warned that because of the structural absence of employment in the ghetto, the black family was disintegrating in a way that threatened the fabric of community life.

When these ideas were transmitted through the press, both popular and scholarly, the connection between culture and economic structure was somehow lost, and the argument was popularly perceived to be that "people were poor because they had a defective culture." This position was later explicitly adopted by the conservative theorist Edward Banfield, who argued that lower-class culture—with its limited time horizon, impulsive need for gratification, and psychological self-doubt—was primarily responsible for persistent urban poverty.[15] He believed that these cultural traits were largely imported, arising primarily because cities attracted lower-class migrants.

The culture-of-poverty argument was strongly criticized by liberal theorists as a self-serving ideology that "blamed the victim."[16] In the ensuing wave of reaction, black families were viewed not as weak but, on the contrary, as resilient and well adapted survivors in an oppressive and racially prejudiced society.[17] Black disadvantages were attributed not to a defective culture but to the persistence of institutional racism in the United States. According to theorists of the underclass such as Douglas Glasgow and Alphonso Pinkney, the black urban underclass came about because deeply imbedded racist practices within American institutions—particularly schools and the economy—effectively kept blacks poor and dependent.[18]

As the debate on culture versus racism ground to a halt during the late 1970s, conservative theorists increasingly captured public attention by focusing on a third possible cause of poverty: government welfare policy. According to Charles Murray, the creation of the underclass was rooted in the liberal welfare state.[19] Federal antipoverty programs altered the incentives governing the behavior of poor men and women, reducing the desirability of marriage, increasing the benefits of unwed childbearing, lowering the attractiveness of menial labor, and ultimately resulted in greater poverty.

A slightly different attack on the welfare state was launched by Lawrence Mead, who argued that it was not the generosity but the permissiveness of the U.S. welfare system that was at fault.[20] Jobless men and unwed mothers should be required to display "good citizenship" before being supported by the state. By not requiring anything of the poor, Mead argued, the welfare state undermined their independence and competence, thereby perpetuating their poverty.

This conservative reasoning was subsequently attacked by liberal social scientists, led principally by the sociologist William Julius Wilson, who had long been arguing for the increasing importance of class over race in understanding the social and economic problems facing blacks.[21] In his 1987 book *The Truly Disadvantaged,* Wilson argued that persistent urban poverty stemmed primarily from the structural transformation of the inner-city economy.[22] The decline of manufacturing, the suburbanization of employment, and the rise of a low-wage service sector dramatically reduced the number of city jobs that paid wages sufficient to support a family, which led to high rates of joblessness among minorities and a shrinking pool of "marriageable" men (those financially able to support a family). Marriage thus became less attractive to poor women, unwed childbearing increased, and female-headed families proliferated. Blacks suffered disproportionately from these trends because, owing to past discrimination, they were concentrated in locations and occupations particularly affected by economic restructuring.

Wilson argued that these economic changes were accompanied by an increase in the spatial concentration of poverty within black neighborhoods. This new geography of poverty, he felt, was enabled by the civil rights revolution of the 1960s, which provided middle-class blacks with new opportunities outside the ghetto.[23] The out-migration of middle-class families from ghetto areas left behind a destitute community lacking the institutions, resources, and values necessary for success in post-industrial society. The urban underclass thus arose from a complex interplay of civil rights policy, economic restructuring, and a historical legacy of discrimination.

Theoretical concepts such as the culture of poverty, institutional racism, welfare disincentives, and structural economic change have all been widely debated. None of these explanations, however, considers residential segregation to be an important contributing cause of urban poverty and the underclass. In their principal works, Murray and Mead do not mention segregation at all;[24] and Wilson refers to racial segregation only as a historical legacy from the past, not as an outcome that is institutionally supported and actively created today.[25] Although Lewis mentions segregation sporadically in his writings, it is not assigned a central role in the set of structural factors responsible for the culture of poverty, and Banfield ignores it entirely. Glasgow, Pinkney, and other theorists of institutional racism mention the ghetto frequently, but generally call not for residential desegregation but for race-specific policies to combat the effects of discrimination in the schools and labor markets. In general, then, contemporary theorists of urban poverty do not see high levels of black-white segregation as particularly relevant to understanding the underclass or alleviating urban poverty.[26]

The purpose of this book is to redirect the focus of public debate back to issues of race and racial segregation, and to suggest that they should be fundamental to thinking about the status of black Americans and the origins of the urban underclass. Our quarrel is less with any of the prevailing theories of urban poverty than with their systematic failure to consider the important role that segregation has played in mediating, exacerbating, and ultimately amplifying the harmful social and economic processes they treat.

We join earlier scholars in rejecting the view that poor urban blacks have an autonomous "culture of poverty" that explains their failure to achieve socioeconomic success in American society. We argue instead that residential segregation has been instrumental in creating a structural niche within which a deleterious set of attitudes and behaviors—a culture of segregation—has arisen and flourished. Segregation created the structural conditions for the emergence of an oppositional culture that devalues work, schooling, and marriage and that stresses attitudes and behaviors that are antithetical and often hostile to success in the larger economy. Although poor black neighborhoods still contain many people who lead conventional, productive lives, their example has been overshadowed in recent years by a growing concentration of poor, welfare-dependent families that is an inevitable result of residential segregation.

We readily agree with Glasgow, Pinkney, and others that racial discrimination is widespread and may even be institutionalized within large sectors of American society, including the labor market, the educational system, and the welfare bureaucracy. We argue, however, that this view of black subjugation is incomplete without understanding the special role that residential segregation plays in enabling all other forms of racial oppression. Residential segregation is the institutional apparatus that supports other racially discriminatory processes and binds them together into a coherent and uniquely effective system of racial subordination. Until the black ghetto is dismantled as a basic institution of American urban life, progress ameliorating racial inequality in other arenas will be slow, fitful, and incomplete.

We also agree with William Wilson's basic argument that the structural transformation of the urban economy undermined economic supports for the black community during the 1970s and 1980s.[27] We argue, however, that in the absence of segregation, these structural changes would not have produced the disastrous social and economic outcomes observed in inner cities during these decades. Although rates of black poverty were driven up by the economic dislocations Wilson identifies, it was segregation that confined the increased deprivation to a small number of densely settled, tightly packed, and geographically isolated areas.

Wilson also argues that concentrated poverty arose because the civil rights revolution allowed middle-class blacks to move out of the ghetto. Although we remain open to the possibility that class-selective migration did occur,[28] we argue that concentrated poverty would have happened during the 1970s with or without black middle-class migration. Our principal objection to Wilson's focus on middle-class out-migration is not that it did not occur, but that it is misdirected: focusing on the flight of the black middle class deflects attention from the real issue, which is the limitation of black residential options through segregation.

Middle-class households—whether they are black, Mexican, Italian, Jewish, or Polish—always try to escape the poor. But only blacks must attempt their escape within a highly segregated, racially segmented housing market. Because of segregation, middle-class blacks are less able to escape than other groups, and as a result are exposed to more poverty. At the same time, because of segregation no one will move into a poor black neighborhood except other poor blacks. Thus both middle-class blacks and poor blacks lose compared with the poor and middle class of other groups: poor blacks live under unrivaled concentrations of poverty and affluent blacks live in neighborhoods that are far less advantageous than those experienced by the middle class of other groups.

Finally, we concede Murray's general point that federal welfare policies are linked to the rise of the urban underclass, but we disagree with his specific hypothesis that generous welfare payments, by themselves, discouraged employment, encouraged unwed childbearing, undermined the strength of the family, and thereby caused persistent poverty.[29] We argue instead that welfare payments were only harmful to the socioeconomic well-being of groups that were residentially segregated. As poverty rates rose among blacks in response to the economic dislocations of the 1970s and 1980s, so did the use of welfare programs. Because of racial segregation, however, the higher levels of welfare receipt were confined to a small number of isolated, all-black neighborhoods. By promoting the spatial concentration of welfare use, therefore, segregation created a residential environment within which welfare dependency was the norm, leading to the intergenerational transmission and broader perpetuation of urban poverty.

Coming to Terms with American Apartheid

Our fundamental argument is that racial segregation—and its characteristic institutional form, the black ghetto—are the key structural factors responsible for the perpetuation of black poverty in the United States. Residential segregation is the principal organizational feature of American society that is responsible for the creation of the urban underclass. Because this view is so alien to public and academic theorizing, and because beliefs about the voluntary and "natural" origins of black segregation are so deeply ingrained in popular thinking, we build our case step by step, grounding each assertion on a base of empirical evidence.

In Chapter 2 we trace the historical construction of the black ghetto during the nineteenth and twentieth centuries. We show that high levels of black-white segregation were not always characteristic of American urban areas. Until the end of the nineteenth century blacks and whites were relatively integrated in both northern and southern cities; as late as 1900, the typical black urbanite still lived in a neighborhood that was predominantly white. The evolution of segregated, all-black neighborhoods occurred later and was not the result of impersonal market forces. It did not reflect the desires of African Americans themselves. On the contrary, the black ghetto was constructed through a series of well-defined institutional practices, private behaviors, and public policies by which whites sought to contain growing urban black populations.

The manner in which blacks were residentially incorporated into American cities differed fundamentally from the path of spatial assimilation followed by other ethnic groups. Even at the height of immigration from Europe, most Italians, Poles, and Jews lived in neighborhoods where members of their own group did not predominate, and as their socioeconomic status and generations spent in the United States rose, each group was progressively integrated into American society. In contrast, after the construction of the black ghetto the vast majority of blacks were forced to live in neighborhoods that were all black, yielding an extreme level of social isolation.

In Chapter 3 we show that high levels of black-white segregation had become universal in American cities by 1970, and despite the passage of the Fair Housing Act in 1968, this situation had not changed much in the nation's largest black communities by 1980. In these large urban areas black-white segregation persisted at very high levels, and the extent of black suburbanization lagged far behind that of other groups. Even within suburbs, levels of racial segregation remained exceptionally high, and in many urban areas the degree of racial separation between blacks and whites was profound. Within sixteen large metropolitan areas—containing one-third of all blacks in the United States—the extent of racial segregation was so intense and occurred on so many dimensions simultaneously that we label the pattern "hypersegregation."

Chapter 4 examines why black segregation continues to be so extreme. One possibility that we rule out is that high levels of racial segregation reflect socioeconomic differences between blacks and whites. Segregation cannot be attributed to income differences, because blacks are equally highly segregated at all levels of income. Whereas segregation declines steadily for most minority groups as socioeconomic status rises, levels of black-white segregation do not vary significantly by social class. Because segregation reflects the effects of white prejudice rather than objective market forces, blacks are segregated no matter how much money they earn.

Although whites now accept open housing in principle, they remain prejudiced against black neighbors in practice. Despite whites' endorsement of the ideal that people should be able to live wherever they can afford to regardless of race, a majority still feel uncomfortable in any neighborhood that contains more than a few black residents; and as the percentage of blacks rises, the number of whites who say they would refuse to enter or would try to move out increases sharply.

These patterns of white prejudice fuel a pattern of neighborhood resegregation because racially mixed neighborhoods are strongly desired by blacks. As the percentage of blacks in a neighborhood rises, white demand for homes within it falls sharply while black demand rises. The surge in black demand and the withering of white demand yield a process of racial turnover. As a result, the only urban areas where significant desegregation occurred during the 1970s were those where the black population was so small that integration could take place without threatening white preferences for limited contact with blacks.

Prejudice alone cannot account for high levels of black segregation, however, because whites seeking to avoid contact with blacks must have somewhere to go. That is, some all-white neighborhoods must be perpetuated and maintained, which requires the erection of systematic barriers to black residential mobility. In most urban housing markets, therefore, the effects of white prejudice are typically reinforced by direct discrimination against black homeseekers. Housing audits carried out over the past two decades have documented the persistence of widespread discrimination against black renters and homebuyers, and a recent comprehensive study carried out by the U.S. Department of Housing and Urban Development suggests that prior work has understated both the incidence and the severity of this racial bias. Evidence also suggests that blacks can expect to experience significant discrimination in the allocation of home mortgages as well.

In Chapter 5 we demonstrate theoretically how segregation creates underclass communities and systematically builds deprivation into the residential structure of black communities. We show how any increase in the poverty rate of a residentially segregated group leads to an immediate and automatic increase in the geographic concentration of poverty. When the rate of minority poverty is increased under conditions of high segregation, all of the increase is absorbed by a small number of neighborhoods. When the same increase in poverty occurs in an integrated group, the added poverty is spread evenly throughout the urban area, and the neighborhood environment that group members face does not change much.

During the 1970s and 1980s, therefore, when urban economic restructuring and inflation drove up rates of black and Hispanic poverty in many urban areas, underclass communities were created only where increased minority poverty coincided with a high degree of segregation—principally in older metropolitan areas of the northeast and the midwest. Among Hispanics, only Puerto Ricans developed underclass communities, because only they were highly segregated; and this high degree of segregation is directly attributable to the fact that a large proportion of Puerto Ricans are of African origin.

The interaction of intense segregation and high poverty leaves black neighborhoods extremely vulnerable to fluctuations in the urban economy, because any dislocation that causes an upward shift in black poverty rates will also produce a rapid change in the concentration of poverty and, hence, a dramatic shift in the social and economic composition of black neighborhoods. The concentration of poverty, for example, is associated with the wholesale withdrawal of commercial institutions and the deterioration or elimination of goods and services distributed through the market.

Neighborhoods, of course, are dynamic and constantly changing, and given the high rates of residential turnover characteristic of contemporary American cities, their well-being depends to a great extent on the characteristics and actions of their residents. Decisions taken by one actor affect the subsequent decisions of others in the neighborhood. In this way isolated actions affect the well-being of the community and alter the stability of the neighborhood.

Because of this feedback between individual and collective behavior, neighborhood stability is characterized by a series of thresholds, beyond which various self-perpetuating processes of decay take hold. Above these thresholds, each actor who makes a decision that undermines neighborhood well-being makes it increasingly likely that other actors will do the same. Each property owner who decides not to invest in upkeep and maintenance, for example, lowers the incentive for others to maintain their properties. Likewise, each new crime promotes psychological and physical withdrawal from public life, which reduces vigilance within the neighborhood and undermines the capacity for collective organization, making additional criminal activity more likely.

Segregation increases the susceptibility of neighborhoods to these spirals of decline. During periods of economic dislocation, a rising concentration of black poverty is associated with the simultaneous concentration of other negative social and economic conditions. Given the high levels of racial segregation characteristic of American urban areas, increases in black poverty such as those observed during the 1970s can only lead to a concentration of housing abandonment, crime, and social disorder, pushing poor black neighborhoods beyond the threshold of stability.

By building physical decay, crime, and social disorder into the residential structure of black communities, segregation creates a harsh and extremely disadvantaged environment to which ghetto blacks must adapt. In concentrating poverty, moreover, segregation also concentrates conditions such as drug use, joblessness, welfare dependency, teenage childbearing, and unwed parenthood, producing a social context where these conditions are not only common but the norm. Chapter 6 argues that in adapting to this social environment, ghetto dwellers evolve a set of behaviors, attitudes, and expectations that are sharply at variance with those common in the rest of American society.

As a direct result of the high degree of racial and class isolation created by segregation, for example, Black English has become progressively more distant from Standard American English, and its speakers are at a clear disadvantage in U.S. schools and labor markets. Moreover, the isolation and intense poverty of the ghetto provides a supportive structural niche for the emergence of an "oppositional culture" that inverts the values of middle-class society. Anthropologists have found that young people in the ghetto experience strong peer pressure not to succeed in school, which severely limits their prospects for social mobility in the larger society. Quantitative research shows that growing up in a ghetto neighborhood increases the likelihood of dropping out of high school, reduces the probability of attending college, lowers the likelihood of employment, reduces income earned as an adult, and increases the risk of teenage childbearing and unwed pregnancy.

Segregation also has profound political consequences for blacks, because it so isolates them geographically that they are the only ones who benefit from public expenditures in their neighborhoods. The relative integration of most ethnic groups means that jobs or services allocated to them will generally benefit several other groups at the same time. Integration thus creates a basis for political coalitions and pluralist politics, and most ethnic groups that seek public resources are able to find coalition partners because other groups can anticipate sharing the benefits. That blacks are the only ones to benefit from resources allocated to the ghetto—and are the only ones harmed when resources are removed—makes it difficult for them to find partners for political coalitions. Although segregation paradoxically makes it easier for blacks to elect representatives, it limits their political influence and marginalizes them within the American polity. Segregation prevents blacks from participating in pluralist politics based on mutual self-interest.

Because of the close connection between social and spatial mobility, segregation also perpetuates poverty. One of the primary means by which individuals improve their life chances—and those of their children—is by moving to neighborhoods with higher home values, safer streets, higher-quality schools, and better services. As groups move up the socioeconomic ladder, they typically move up the residential hierarchy as well, and in doing so they not only improve their standard of living but also enhance their chances for future success. Barriers to spatial mobility are barriers to social mobility, and by confining blacks to a small set of relatively disadvantaged neighborhoods, segregation constitutes a very powerful impediment to black socioeconomic progress.

Despite the obvious deleterious consequences of black spatial isolation, policymakers have not paid much attention to segregation as a contributing cause of urban poverty and have not taken effective steps to dismantle the ghetto. Indeed, as Chapter 7 documents, for most of the past two decades public policies tolerated and even supported the perpetuation of segregation in American urban areas. Although many political initiatives were launched to combat discrimination and prejudice in the housing and banking industries, each legislative or judicial act was fought tenaciously by a powerful array of people who believed in or benefited from the status quo.

Although a comprehensive open housing bill finally passed Congress under unusual circumstances in 1968, it was stripped of its enforcement provisions as its price of enactment, yielding a Fair Housing Act that was structurally flawed and all but doomed to fail. As documentation of the law's defects accumulated in multiple Congressional hearings, government reports, and scholarly studies, little was done to repair the situation until 1988, when a series of scandals and political errors by the Reagan Administration finally enabled a significant strengthening of federal antidiscrimination law.

Yet even more must be done to prevent the permanent bifurcation of the United States into black and white societies that are separate and unequal. As of 1990, levels of racial segregation were still extraordinarily high in the nation's large urban areas, particularly those of the north. Segregation has remained high because fair housing enforcement relies too heavily on the private efforts of individual victims of discrimination. Whereas the processes that perpetuate segregation are entrenched and institutionalized, fair housing enforcement is individual, sporadic, and confined to a small number of isolated cases.

As long as the Fair Housing Act is enforced individually rather than systemically, it is unlikely to be effective in overcoming the structural arrangements that support segregation and sustain the ghetto. Until the government throws its considerable institutional weight behind efforts to dismantle the ghetto, racial segregation will persist. In Chapter 8 we propose a variety of specific actions that the federal government will need to take to end the residential segregation of blacks in American society.

Ultimately, however, dismantling the ghetto and ending the long reign of racial segregation will require more than specific bureaucratic reforms; it requires a moral commitment that white America has historically lacked. The segregation of American blacks was no historical accident; it was brought about by actions and practices that had the passive acceptance, if not the active support, of most whites in the United States. Although America's apartheid may not be rooted in the legal strictures of its South African relative, it is no less effective in perpetuating racial inequality, and whites are no less culpable for the socioeconomic deprivation that results.

As in South Africa, residential segregation in the United States provides a firm basis for a broader system of racial injustice. The geographic isolation of Africans within a narrowly circumscribed portion of the urban environment—whether African townships or American ghettos—forces blacks to live under extraordinarily harsh conditions and to endure a social world where poverty is endemic, infrastructure is inadequate, education is lacking, families are fragmented, and crime and violence are rampant.[30] Moreover, segregation confines these unpleasant by-products of racial oppression to an isolated portion of the urban geography far removed from the experience of most whites. Resting on a foundation of segregation, apartheid not only denies blacks their rights as citizens but forces them to bear the social costs of their own victimization.

Although Americans have been quick to criticize the apartheid system of South Africa, they have been reluctant to acknowledge the consequences of their own institutionalized system of racial separation. The topic of segregation has virtually disappeared from public policy debates; it has vanished from the list of issues on the civil rights agenda; and it has been ignored by social scientists spinning endless theories of the underclass. Residential segregation has become the forgotten factor of American race relations, a minor footnote in the ongoing debate on the urban underclass. Until policymakers, social scientists, and private citizens recognize the crucial role of America's own apartheid in perpetuating urban poverty and racial injustice, the United States will remain a deeply divided and very troubled society.[31]

2

The Construction of the Ghetto

The problem of the 20th Century is the problem of the color line.

W. E. B. Du Bois

Surveying the harsh black-and-white landscape of contemporary urban America, it is hard to imagine a time when people of European and African origin were not highly segregated from one another.[1] In an era when Watts, Harlem, and Roxbury are synonymous with black geographic and social isolation, it is easy to assume that U.S. cities have always been organized to achieve a physical separation of the races. The residential segregation of blacks and whites has been with us so long that it seems a natural part of the social order, a normal and unremarkable feature of America's urban landscape.

Yet it wasn't always so. There was a time, before 1900, when blacks and whites lived side by side in American cities. In the north, a small native black population was scattered widely throughout white neighborhoods. Even Chicago, Detroit, Cleveland, and Philadelphia—cities now well known for their large black ghettos—were not segregated then. In southern cities such as Charleston, New Orleans, and Savannah, black servants and laborers lived on alleys and side streets near the mansions of their white employers. In this lost urban world, blacks were more likely to share a neighborhood with whites than with other blacks.

In most cities, to be sure, certain neighborhoods could be identified as places where blacks lived; but before 1900 these areas were not predominantly black, and most blacks didn't live in them. No matter what other disadvantages urban blacks suffered in the aftermath of the Civil War, they were not residentially segregated from whites. The two racial groups moved in a common social world, spoke a common language, shared a common culture, and interacted personally on a regular basis. In the north, especially, leading African American citizens often enjoyed relations of considerable trust, respect, and friendship with whites of similar social standing.

Of course, most blacks did not live in northern cities, and didn't experience these benign conditions. In 1870, 80% of black Americans still lived in the rural south, where they were exploited by a sharecropping system that was created by white landowners to replace slavery; they were terrorized by physical violence and mired in an institutionalized cycle of ignorance and poverty. Over the next century, however, blacks in the rural south increasingly sought refuge and betterment in burgeoning cities of the south and north. By 1970, 80% of black Americans lived in urban areas, and nearly half were located outside the south.

This shift of blacks from south to north and from farm to city radically transformed the form, nature, and substance of African American life in the United States. As we shall see, the way in which blacks from the rural south were incorporated into the geographic structure of American cities in the years after 1900 proved to be decisive in determining the path of black social and economic development later in the twentieth century.

Southern blacks were not the only rural people migrating to American cities at the turn of the century. Between 1880 and 1920 millions of eastern and southern Europeans arrived as well, and after 1920 their place was taken by a growing number of Mexicans. For these groups, however, U.S. cities served as vehicles for integration, economic advancement, and, ultimately, assimilation into American life. For rural blacks, in contrast, cities became a trap—yet another mechanism of oppression and alienation. The urban ghetto, constructed during the first half of the twentieth century and successively reinforced thereafter, represents the key institutional arrangement ensuring the continued subordination of blacks in the United States.

The term "ghetto" means different things to different people. To some observers it simply means a black residential area; to others it connotes an area that is not only black but very poor and plagued by a host of social and economic problems. In order to distinguish clearly between race and class in discussing black residential patterns, our use of the term "ghetto" refers only to the racial make-up of a neighborhood; it is not intended to describe anything about a black neighborhood's class composition. For our purposes, a ghetto is a set of neighborhoods that are exclusively inhabited by members of one group, within which virtually all members of that group live. By this definition, no ethnic or racial group in the history of the United States, except one, has ever experienced ghettoization, even briefly. For urban blacks, the ghetto has been the paradigmatic residential configuration for at least eighty years.

The emergence of the black ghetto did not happen as a chance by-product of other socioeconomic processes. Rather, white Americans made a series of deliberate decisions to deny blacks access to urban housing markets and to reinforce their spatial segregation. Through its actions and inactions, white America built and maintained the residential structure of the ghetto. Sometimes the decisions were individual, at other times they were collective, and at still other times the powers and prerogatives of government were harnessed to maintain the residential color line; but at critical points between the end of the Civil War in 1865 and the passage of the Fair Housing Act in 1968, white America chose to strengthen the walls of the ghetto.

Before the Ghetto

At the close of the Civil War, American cities were just beginning to throw off the trappings of their pre-industrial past. Patterns of urban social and spatial organization still reflected the needs of commerce, trade, and small-scale manufacturing. Public transportation systems were crude or nonexistent, and production was largely organized and carried out by extended households or in small shops. People got around by walking, so there was little geographic differentiation between places of work and residence. Land use was not highly specialized, real estate prices were low, and socially distinctive residential areas had not yet emerged. In the absence of structural steel, electricity, and efficient mechanical systems, building densities were low and urban populations were distributed uniformly.[2]

Such an urban spatial structure is not conducive to high levels of segregation by class, race, or ethnicity, and the small African American population that inhabited northern cities before 1900 occupied a niche in the urban geography little different from that of other groups. Before 1900, blacks were not particularly segregated from whites, and although they were overrepresented in the poorest housing and the meanest streets, their residential status did not differ markedly from that of others in the same economic circumstances.[3]

If the disadvantaged residential condition of blacks in the nineteenth century can be attributed to racial prejudice and discrimination, it is to prejudice and discrimination in employment rather than in housing. Because blacks were systematically excluded from most skilled trades and nonmanual employment, they were consigned to a low economic status that translated directly into poor housing. Those few blacks who were able to overcome these obstacles and achieve success in some profession or trade were generally able to improve their housing conditions and acquire a residence befitting their status. Studies of black residential life in northern cities around the time of the Civil War reveal little systematic exclusion from white neighborhoods on the basis of skin color.[4]

Indeed, before 1900 African Americans could be found in most neighborhoods of northern cities. Although blacks at times clustered on certain streets or blocks, they rarely comprised more than 30% of the residents of the immediate area; and these clusters typically were not spatially contiguous. Maps from the period reveal a widely dispersed spatial pattern, with black households being unevenly but widely scattered around the urban landscape.[5] In no city of the nineteenth century is there anything resembling a black ghetto.

This view is verified by historical studies that report quantitative indices of racial segregation. The standard measure of segregation is the index of dissimilarity, which captures the degree to which blacks and whites are evenly spread among neighborhoods in a city.[6] Evenness is defined with respect to the racial composition of the city as a whole. If a city is 10% black, then an even residential pattern requires that every neighborhood be 10% black and 90% white. Thus, if a neighborhood is 20% black, the excess 10% of blacks must move to a neighborhood where the black percentage is under 10% to shift the residential configuration toward evenness. The index of dissimilarity gives the percentage of blacks who would have to move to achieve an "even" residential pattern—one where every neighborhood replicates the racial composition of the city.

Several studies have computed dissimilarity indices for American cities circa 1860, and their findings are summarized in the first column of Table 2.1. These numbers measure the extent of black-white segregation across city "wards," which are large spatial units of 6,000 to 12,000 people that are frequently used to approximate neighborhoods in historical data. A simple rule of thumb in interpreting these indices is that values under 30 are low, those between 30 and 60 are moderate, and anything above 60 is high.

According to these criteria, black-white segregation in northern cities

Table 2.1 Indices of black-white segregation (dissimilarity) in selected northern and southern cities: circa 1860–1870, 1910, and 1940

	Free blacks vs. whites, circa 1860	Blacks vs. native whites, 1910	Nonwhites vs. whites, 1940
Northern cities			
Boston	61.3	64.1	86.3
Chicago	50.0	66.8	95.0
Cincinnati	47.9	47.3	90.6
Cleveland	49.0	69.0	92.0
Indianapolis	57.2	—	90.4
Milwaukee	59.6	66.7	92.9
New York	40.6	—	86.8
Philadelphia	47.1	46.0	88.8
St. Louis	39.1	54.3	92.6
San Francisco	34.6	—	82.9
Wilmington	26.1	—	83.0
Average	45.7	59.2	89.2
Southern cities			
Augusta	—	58.8	86.9
Baltimore	22.1	—	90.1
Charleston	23.2	16.8	60.1
Jacksonville	—	39.4	94.3
Louisville	20.2	—	81.7
Mobile	29.8	—	86.6
Nashville	43.1	—	86.5
New Orleans	35.7	—	81.0
Average	29.0	38.3	81.0

Sources: For first column: Ira Berlin, *Slaves without Masters: The Free Negro in the Antebellum South* (New York: Pantheon, 1974), pp. 250–65; except Cleveland, which is Kenneth L. Kusmer, *A Ghetto Takes Shape: Black Cleveland, 1870–1930* (Urbana: University of Illinois Press, 1976), p. 43; and Milwaukee, which is Joe William Trotter, Jr., *Black Milwaukee: The Making of an Industrial Proletariat, 1915–45* (Urbana: University of Illinois Press, 1985), p. 23. Segregation is by wards and indices for Cleveland and Milwaukee are for 1870.

For second column: Stanley Lieberson, *Ethnic Patterns in American Cities* (New York: Free Press, 1963), p. 122; except Milwaukee, which is Trotter, *Black Milwaukee,* p. 23; and Augusta, Charleston, and Jacksonville, which are Karl Taeuber and Alma Taeuber, *Negroes in Cities: Residential Segregation and Neighborhood Change* (Chicago: Aldine Publishing, 1965), pp. 49–53. Segregation is by wards and index for Augusta is for 1909.

For third column: Taeuber and Taeuber, *Negroes in Cities,* pp. 39–41. Segregation is by blocks.

was quite moderate around 1860. The average index was 46, meaning that, on average, just under half of urban blacks would have to move to achieve an even, or "integrated," city. Wilmington, San Francisco, and St. Louis had especially modest indices of 26.1, 34.6, and 39.1, respectively. The only city that displayed a segregation index in the high range (barely) was Boston, with a value of 61.3. Boston's segregation, however, was much lower earlier in the century, with an index of only 44.4 in 1830. Moreover, even though segregation was relatively high in 1860, by 1890 it had gone back to a moderate level of 51, and racial segregation did not reach 60 again until 1910.[7]

Black-white segregation scores in the 30 to 60 range are not terribly different from those observed for European immigrant groups in the same period. Before 1880, immigrants to the United States came principally from Ireland and Germany. According to a variety of studies, the level of segregation between these two European groups and native whites ranged from 20 to 45 in northern cities in 1850 and 1860.[8] Thus black segregation scores were only slightly greater than those typical of European immigrant groups in the same era.

Such modest levels of segregation, combined with small black populations, led to substantial contact between blacks and whites in northern cities. This conclusion accords with historical studies of black communities in nineteenth-century northern cities. In places such as Cleveland, Chicago, Detroit, and Milwaukee, the small black communities were dominated by an elite of educated professionals, business owners, and successful tradespeople, most of whom were northern-born or migrants from border states.[9] Within the upper stratum, interracial contacts were frequent, cordial, and often intimate. Members of this elite were frequently of mixed racial origin and tended to be light-skinned. Although the black lower classes usually did not maintain such amicable interracial ties, they too interacted frequently with whites in their places of work and on the streets.

Typical of the northern black elite of the nineteenth century was John Jones, a mulatto who was the "undisputed leader of Chicago's Negro community until his death in 1879."[10] After his arrival in the city in 1845, he established a tailoring shop and built a successful business making clothes for wealthy whites. Before the Civil War, he was prominent in the abolitionist movement, where he had extensive contact with liberal whites, and after the war he ran for the Cook County Board of Commissioners and was elected with widespread white support.

Other members of Chicago's nineteenth-century African American elite included physicians, dentists, journalists, attorneys, and clergymen, all of whom relied substantially on the white community for economic and political support; and all maintained close social and professional relationships with individual whites. Like Jones, they supported the ideal of integration and opposed the formation of separate black community institutions. Above all they stressed the importance of economic self-improvement for racial progress.[11]

A similar picture of African American life emerges from other studies of nineteenth-century northern cities. In Cleveland, a light-skinned African American, Charles W. Chestnut, pursued a highly visible career as a court stenographer, lawyer, and writer, sending his children to integrated schools and maintaining a close circle of white associates. He argued that blacks could best overcome their disabilities by adopting the culture and values of the white middle class.[12] In Detroit, members of the black elite lived a similarly integrated existence and displayed their commitment to integration by attending predominantly white churches.[13] In Milwaukee, the nineteenth-century black elite included a number of successful professionals who catered to white clients, including a lawyer, William T. Green; a dentist, Clifton A. Johnson; and a physician, Allen L. Herron.[14]

A high degree of interracial contact in northern cities is confirmed by an analysis of the racial composition of the neighborhoods inhabited by nineteenth century blacks. Given racial breakdowns for ward populations, the percentage of blacks in the ward of the average black citizen can be computed. This average, known as the isolation index, measures the extent to which blacks live within neighborhoods that are predominantly black.[15] A value of 100% indicates complete ghettoization and means that all black people live in totally black areas; a value under 50% means that blacks are more likely to have whites than blacks as neighbors.

Stanley Lieberson made this calculation for black Americans in seventeen northern cities between 1890 and 1930,[16] and his results are reproduced in Table 2.2. We see from the first column that blacks in the north tended to live in predominantly white neighborhoods during the nineteenth century. The most "ghettoized" city in 1890 was Indianapolis, where the average black person lived in a neighborhood that was 13% black; in three-quarters of the cities, the percentage was under 10%. In other words, the typical black resident of a nineteenth-century northern city lived in a neighborhood that was close to 90% white. Even in cities

Table 2.2 Indices of black isolation within wards of selected northern cities, 1890–1930

	Isolation indices by year				
	1890	1900	1910	1920	1930
Boston	8.5	6.4	11.3	15.2	19.2
Buffalo	1.0	4.4	5.7	10.2	24.2
Chicago	8.1	10.4	15.1	38.1	70.4
Cincinnati	9.4	10.1	13.2	26.9	44.6
Cleveland	4.7	7.5	7.9	23.9	51.0
Detroit	5.6	6.4	6.8	14.7	31.2
Indianapolis	12.9	15.1	18.5	23.4	26.1
Kansas City	12.7	13.2	21.7	23.7	31.6
Los Angeles	3.3	3.2	3.8	7.8	25.6
Milwaukee	1.4	2.4	1.9	4.1	16.4
Minneapolis	1.6	1.6	1.7	2.1	1.7
Newark	4.1	5.5	5.4	7.0	22.8
New York	3.6	5.0	6.7	20.5	41.8
Philadelphia	11.7	16.4	15.7	20.8	27.3
Pittsburgh	8.1	12.0	12.0	16.5	26.8
St. Louis	10.9	12.6	17.2	29.5	46.6
San Francisco	1.4	1.1	0.7	1.0	1.7
Average	6.7	7.8	9.7	16.8	29.9

Source: Stanley Lieberson, *A Piece of the Pie: Blacks and White Immigrants since 1880* (Berkeley: University of California Press, 1980), pp. 266, 288. Isolation is measured by ward.

that later developed large black ghettos, such as Chicago, Cleveland, Detroit, Los Angeles, Newark, and New York, blacks were more likely to come into contact with whites than with other blacks.

There is also little evidence of ghettoization among southern blacks prior to 1900. Indeed, segregation levels in the south tend to be lower than those in the north. Prior to the Emancipation Proclamation, urban slaves were intentionally dispersed by whites in order to prevent the formation of a cohesive African American society.[17] Although this policy broke down in the years leading up to the Civil War—when free blacks and slaves who were "living out" gravitated toward black settlements on the urban periphery to escape white supervision[18]—historical studies are consistent in reporting a great deal of racial integration in housing prior to 1900.[19]

The bottom half of Table 2.1 presents black-white dissimilarity indices computed by several investigators to measure the extent of segregation between whites and free blacks in six southern cities circa 1860. Levels of racial segregation are considerably lower than those observed in the north. The average segregation score of 29 is some 17 points below the average for northern cities and, by the criteria set forth earlier, four of the six cities display indices in the low range (below 30). The most segregated southern city is Nashville, where 43% of free blacks would have had to leave their ward to achieve an even residential configuration.

No study has systematically examined the degree of black isolation within neighborhoods of southern cities in the nineteenth century, but published data on ward populations in Louisville in 1845 and Charleston in 1861 permit us to carry out this calculation ourselves.[20] In Louisville, the average free black lived in a neighborhood that was only 14% black, whereas in Charleston the figure was 45%. The higher figure in the latter city is attributable to the fact that blacks comprised 44% of Charleston's 1861 population, not to higher segregation per se; with an even distribution of blacks and whites in Charleston, every neighborhood would still be 44% black owing to the number of blacks alone. In any event, free blacks in both cities were more likely to share a ward with whites than with other blacks.

Free blacks, of course, were a minority of all African Americans in the antebellum south; most were slaves. The data from Louisville and Charleston reveal, however, that slaves were even less segregated from whites than were free blacks: the slave-white dissimilarity index was 14.2 in Louisville in 1845 and 11.4 in Charleston in 1861. Thus whether one considers slaves or free blacks, there is little evidence of a distinctive black ghetto in southern cities in the nineteenth century. Throughout the south, African Americans were scattered widely among urban neighborhoods and were more likely to share neighborhoods with whites than with members of their own group.

In contrast to the situation in the north, however, residential integration in the postbellum south was not accompanied by a relatively open set of race relations among elites. As the Reconstruction Era drew to a close, black-white relations came to be governed by the increasingly harsh realities of the Jim Crow system, a set of laws and informal expectations that subordinated blacks to whites in all areas of social and economic life.[21] The implementation of Jim Crow did not increase segregation, however, or reduce the frequency of black-white contact; it governed the terms under which integration occurred and strictly regulated the nature of interracial social contacts.

Neighborhoods in many southern cities evolved a residential structure characterized by broad avenues interspersed with small streets and alleys.[22] Large homes on the avenues contained white families, who employed black servants and laborers who lived on the smaller streets. The relationship of master and slave was supplanted by one of master and servant, or a paternalistic relationship between boss and worker. Despite their economic and social subjugation, however, blacks in southern cities continued to have direct personal contacts with whites, albeit on very unequal terms. As in the north, the social worlds of the races overlapped.

Creating the Ghetto, 1900–1940

The era of integrated living and widespread interracial contact was rapidly effaced in American cities after 1900 because of two developments: the industrialization of America and the concomitant movement of blacks from farms to cities. The pace of change was most rapid in the north, not only because industrialization was quicker and more complete there, but also because the south's Jim Crow system provided an effective alternative to the ghetto in bringing about the subjugation of blacks. Moreover, the interspersed pattern of black and white settlement in southern cities carried with it a physical inertia that retarded the construction of the ghetto.[23]

Industrialization in the north unleashed a set of social, economic, and technological changes that dramatically altered the urban environment in ways that promoted segregation between social groups. Before industrialization, production occurred primarily in the home or small shop, but by the turn of the century manufacturing had shifted decisively to large factories that employed hundreds of laborers. Individual plants clustered in extensive manufacturing districts together demanded thousands of workers. Dense clusters of tenements and row houses were constructed near these districts to house the burgeoning work force.[24]

The new demand for labor could not be met by native white urbanites alone, so employers turned to migrants of diverse origins. Before World War I, the demand for unskilled labor was met primarily by rural immigrants from southern and eastern Europe.[25] Their migration was guided and structured by social networks that connected them to relatives and friends who had arrived earlier. Drawing upon the ties of kinship and common community origin, the new migrants obtained jobs and housing in U.S. cities, and in this way members of specific ethnic groups were channeled to particular neighborhoods and factories.[26]

At the same time, the need to oversee industrial production—and to administer the wealth it created—brought about a new managerial class composed primarily of native white Americans. As their affluence increased, the retail sector also expanded dramatically. Both administration and retail sales depended on face-to-face interaction, which put a premium on spatial proximity and high population densities. The invention of structural steel and mechanical elevators allowed cities to expand upward in skyscrapers, which were grouped into central business districts that brought thousands of people into regular daily contact. The development of efficient urban rail systems permitted the city to expand outward, creating new residential districts in suburban areas to house the newly affluent class of middle-class managers and service workers.[27]

These developments brought about an unprecedented increase in urban social segregation. Not only was class segregation heightened, but the "new" immigrant groups—Jews, Poles, Italians, Czechs—experienced far more segregation from native whites than did the "old" immigrant groups of Irish and Germans. Whereas European immigrant segregation, as measured by the index of dissimilarity, rarely exceeded 50 before 1870, after the turn of the century values in the range of 50 to 65 were common.[28]

Southern blacks also formed part of the stream of migrants to American cities, but until 1890 the flow was relatively small; only 70,000 blacks left the south during the 1870s and 80,000 departed during the 1880s.[29] In contrast, the number of European immigrants ran into the millions in both decades. Immigration, however, was cyclical and strongly affected by economic conditions abroad. When the demand for labor in European cities was strong, migration to the United States fell, and when European demand flagged, immigration to the United States rose.[30]

This periodic ebb and flow of European immigration created serious structural problems for American employers, particularly when boom periods in Europe and America coincided. When this occurred, European migrants moved to their own industrial cities and U.S. factories had difficulty attracting new workers. Periodic labor shortages caused northern employers to turn to domestic sources of labor, especially migrants from American rural areas and particularly those in the south. Thus black migration to northern cities oscillated inversely with the ebb and flow of European immigration.[31]

But northern employers also found another reason to employ southern blacks, for by the turn of the century, they had discovered their utility as strikebreakers. Blacks were repeatedly employed in this capacity in northern labor disputes between 1890 and 1930: black strikebreakers were used seven times in New York between 1895 and 1916, and were employed in Cleveland in 1896, in Detroit in 1919, in Milwaukee in 1922, and in Chicago in 1904 and 1905.[32] Poor rural blacks with little understanding of industrial conditions and no experience with unions were recruited in the south and transported directly to northern factories, often on special trains arranged by factory owners.

The association of blacks with strikebreaking was bound to earn them the enmity of white workers, but discrimination against blacks by labor unions cannot be attributed to this animosity alone. European groups had also been used as strikebreakers, but labor leaders overcame these attempts at union-busting by incorporating each new wave of immigrants into the labor movement. Unions never employed this strategy with southern blacks, however. From the start, African Americans suffered unusually severe discrimination from white unions simply because they were black.[33]

Most of the skilled crafts unions within the American Federation of Labor, for example, excluded blacks until the 1930s; and the Congress of Industrial Organizations accepted blacks only grudgingly, typically within segregated Jim Crow locals that received poorer contracts and lower priorities in job assignments. Being denied access to the benefits of white unions, blacks had little to lose from crossing picket lines, thereby setting off a cycle of ongoing mutual hostility and distrust between black and white workers.[34]

Black out-migration from the south grew steadily from the end of the nineteenth century into the first decades of the new century. During the 1890s, some 174,000 blacks left the south, and this number rose to 197,000 between 1900 and 1910.[35] The event that transformed the stream into a flood, however, was the outbreak of World War I in 1914. The war both increased the demand for U.S. industrial production and cut off the flow of European immigrants, northern factories' traditional source of labor. In response, employers began a spirited recruitment of blacks from the rural south.[36]

The arrival of the recruiters in the south coincided with that of the Mexican boll weevil, which had devastated Louisiana's cotton crops in 1906 before moving on to Mississippi in 1913 and Alabama in 1916. The collapse of southern agriculture was aggravated by a series of disastrous floods in 1915 and 1916 and low cotton prices up to 1914. In response, southern planters shifted production from cotton to food crops and livestock, both of which required fewer workers. Thus the demand for black tenant farmers and day laborers fell just when the need for unskilled workers in northern cities skyrocketed.[37]

This coincidence of push and pull factors increased the level of black out-migration to new heights and greatly augmented the black populations of Chicago, Detroit, Cleveland, Philadelphia, and New York. Between 1910 and 1920, some 525,000 African Americans left their traditional homes in the south and took up life in the north, and during the 1920s the outflow reached 877,000.[38] This migration gradually acquired a dynamic of its own, as established migrants found jobs and housing for their friends and relatives back home. At the same time, northern black newspapers such as the *Chicago Defender*, which were widely read in the south, exhorted southern blacks to escape their oppression and move northward. As a result of this dynamic, black out-migration from the south continued at a substantial rate even during the Great Depression.[39]

Northern whites viewed this rising tide of black migration with increasing hostility and considerable alarm. Middle-class whites were repelled by what they saw as the uncouth manners, unclean habits, slothful appearance, and illicit behavior of poorly educated, poverty-stricken migrants who had only recently been sharecroppers, and a resurgence of white racist ideology during the 1920s provided a theoretical, "scientific" justification for these feelings. Working-class whites, for their part, feared economic competition from the newcomers; and being first- or second-generation immigrants who were themselves scorned by native whites, they reaffirmed their own "whiteness" by oppressing a people that was even lower in the racial hierarchy. Blacks in the early twentieth century frequently said that the first English word an immigrant learned was "nigger."

As the size of the urban black population rose steadily after 1900, white racial views hardened and the relatively fluid and open period of race relations in the north drew to a close. Northern newspapers increasingly used terms such as "nigger" and "darkey" in print and carried unflattering stories about black crimes and vice.[40] After decades of relatively integrated education, white parents increasingly refused to enroll their children in schools that included blacks.[41] Doors that had permitted extensive interracial contact among the elite suddenly slammed shut as black professionals lost white clients, associates, and friends.[42]

The most dramatic harbinger of the new regime in race relations was the upsurge in racial violence. In city after northern city, a series of communal riots broke out between 1900 and 1920 in the wake of massive black migration. Race riots struck New York City in 1900; Evansville, Indiana, in 1903; Springfield, Illinois, in 1908; East St. Louis, Illinois, in 1917; and Chicago in 1919.[43] In each case, individual blacks were attacked because of the color of their skin. Those living away from recognized "black" neighborhoods had their houses ransacked or burned. Those unlucky or unwise enough to be caught trespassing in "white" neighborhoods were beaten, shot, or lynched. Blacks on their way to work were pulled from trolleys and pummelled. Rampaging bands of whites roamed the streets for days, attacking blacks at will. Although most of the rioters were white, most of the arrests, and nearly all of the victims, were black.

As the tide of violence rose in northern cities, blacks were increasingly divided from whites by a hardening color line in employment, education, and especially housing. Whites became increasingly intolerant of black neighbors and fear of racial turnover and black "invasion" spread. Those blacks living away from recognized Negro areas were forced to move into expanding "black belts," "darkytowns," "Bronzevilles," or "Niggertowns." Well-educated, middle-class blacks of the old elite found themselves increasingly lumped together with poorly educated, impoverished migrants from the rural south; and well-to-do African Americans were progressively less able to find housing commensurate with their social status. In white eyes, black people belonged in black neighborhoods no matter what their social or economic standing; the color line grew increasingly impermeable.[44]

Thus levels of residential segregation between blacks and whites began a steady rise at the turn of the century that would last for sixty years. The indices shown in the second column of Table 2.1 reveal the extent of this increase. By 1910, the average level of racial segregation in seven northern cities was 59 (compared with 46 in 1860) and four cases fell clearly within the high range (with index scores above 60). The initial stages of ghetto formation are most clearly revealed in Chicago (where the index increased from 50 to 67), Cleveland (an increase from 49 to 69), Milwaukee (from 60 to 67), and St. Louis (from 39 to 54).

The progressive segregation of blacks continued in subsequent decades, and by World War II the foundations of the modern ghetto had been laid in virtually every northern city. The last column of Table 2.1 presents dissimilarity indices computed by Karl and Alma Taeuber for 1940.[45] Some caution must be exercised in interpreting these figures, because they are based on block statistics rather than on ward data. Blocks are substantially smaller than wards, and the degree of segregation that can be measured tends to increase as the geographic size of units falls: what may appear to be an "integrated" ward actually may be quite segregated on a block-by-block basis.[46]

The shift from wards to blocks adds at least 10 points to the dissimilarity indices (and probably more), but even making a liberal allowance for this artifact of the "neighborhood" unit used, it is clear that the level of black-white segregation rose substantially after 1910. At the block level, the degree of black-white segregation in northern cities reached an average value of 89 by 1940, with indices varying narrowly in the range from 80 to 100; this implies a range of about 70 to 90 using ward data, with an average around 80. It is safe to surmise, therefore, that by 1940 at least 70% of northern black city dwellers would have had to move to achieve an even residential configuration in northern cities (compared with a figure of only 46% in 1860).

With a rapidly growing black population being accommodated by an ever-smaller number of neighborhoods and an increasingly uneven residential configuration, the only possible outcome was an increase in the spatial isolation of blacks. As can be seen in Table 2.2, levels of racial isolation in northern cities began to move sharply upward after 1900, and especially after 1910. By 1930, African Americans were well on their way to experiencing a uniquely high degree of spatial isolation in American cities. Chicago led the way: its isolation index increased from only 10% in 1900 to 70% thirty years later. As of 1930 the typical black Chicagoan lived in a neighborhood that was over two-thirds black. That the level of black racial isolation also rose in other cities indicated the growth of more incipient ghettos: from 8% to 51% in Cleveland, from 5% to 42% in New York, and from 13% to 47% in St. Louis.

The increasing ghettoization of blacks was not simply a result of their growing numbers. Stanley Lieberson has clearly demonstrated that the segregation of blacks in the urban north increased after 1900 not only because their share of the population grew but because the same racial composition led to more isolation than it had during earlier periods.[47] As the new century wore on, areas of acceptable black residence became more and more narrowly circumscribed: the era of the ghetto had begun.

Migration and industrial development also segregated the "new" European immigrant groups, of course, but recent studies have made it clear that immigrant enclaves in the early twentieth century were in no way comparable to the black ghetto that formed in most northern cities by 1940.[48] To be sure, certain neighborhoods could be identified as "Italian," "Polish," or "Jewish"; but these ethnic enclaves differed from black ghettos in three fundamental ways.

First, unlike black ghettos, immigrant enclaves were never homogeneous and always contained a wide variety of nationalities, even if they were publicly associated with a particular national origin group. In Chicago's "Magyar district" of 1901, for example, twenty-two different ethnic groups were present and only 37% of all family heads were Magyar (26% were Polish).[49] Similarly, an 1893 color-coded block map of Chicago's West Side prepared by the U.S. Department of Labor showed the location of European ethnic groups using eighteen separate colors. The result was a huge rainbow in which no block contained a single color. The average number of colors per block was eight, and four out of five *lots* within blocks were mixed. In none of the "Little Italys" identified on the map was there an all-Italian block.[50]

The myth of the immigrant ghetto was perpetuated by Ernest Burgess, a founder of the "Chicago School" of urban sociology. In 1933 he published a well-known map showing the spatial location Chicago's various immigrant groups. On it, he identified specific German, Irish, Italian, Russian, Polish, Swedish, and Czech "ghettos." A closer examination of these data by Thomas Philpott, however, revealed that Burgess's immigrant "ghettos" were more fictive than real. The average number of nationalities per ghetto was twenty-two, ranging from twenty in ostensibly Italian and Czech neighborhoods to twenty-five in areas that were theoretically Irish, German, and Swedish. In none of these "ghettos" did the ghettoized group constitute even a bare majority of the population, with the sole exception of Poles, who comprised 54% of their enclave. In areas that Burgess identified as being part of the black ghetto, however, blacks comprised 82% of the population.[51]

A second crucial distinction is that most European ethnics did not live in immigrant "ghettos," as ethnically diluted as they were. Burgess's Irish ghetto contained only 3% of Chicago's Irish population, and only 50% of the city's Italian lived in the "Little Italys" he identified. Only among Poles did a majority, 61%, live in neighborhoods that were identified as being part of the Polish enclave. In contrast, 93% of Chicago's black population lived within the black ghetto.[52]

Thus even at the height of their segregation early in this century, European ethnic groups did not experience a particularly high degree of isolation from American society, even in 1910 at the end of the peak decade of European immigration. Among the 100 or so indices that Stanley Lieberson computed for seven European ethnic groups in seventeen cities in 1910, only seven cases had isolation indices above 25%, and all but two were under 40%. The highest recorded levels of spatial isolation were for Italians in Boston (44%), Buffalo (38%), and Milwaukee (56%), and for Russians (i.e., Jews) in New York (34%).[53] In contrast, black isolation exceeded 25% in eleven of the seventeen cities Lieberson examined in 1930 (see Table 2.2); and what is startling about this fact is that black ghettos were still in their formative stages in 1930 and had not yet begun to approach their maximum isolation.

The last difference between immigrant enclaves and black ghettos is that whereas ghettos became a permanent feature of black residential life, ethnic enclaves proved to be a fleeting, transitory stage in the process of immigrant assimilation. The degree of segregation and spatial isolation among European ethnic groups fell steadily after 1910, as native-born children of immigrants experienced less segregation than their parents and as spatial isolation decreased progressively with socioeconomic advancement.[54] For European immigrants, enclaves were places of absorption, adaptation, and adjustment to American society. They served as springboards for broader mobility in society, whereas blacks were trapped behind an increasingly impermeable color line.

The emergence of severe racial segregation in the north was not primarily a reflection of black housing preferences or a natural outcome of migration processes. On the contrary, as the ghetto walls grew thicker and higher, well-to-do class blacks complained bitterly and loudly about their increasing confinement within crowded, dilapidated neighborhoods inhabited by people well below their social and economic status.[55] Although they fought the construction of the ghetto as best they could, the forces arrayed against them proved to be overwhelming.

Foremost among the tools that whites used to construct the ghetto was violence. The initial impetus for ghetto formation came from a wave of racial violence, already noted, that swept over northern cities in the period between 1900 and 1920. These disturbances were communal in nature, and victims were singled out strictly on the basis of skin color. As history has repeatedly shown, during periods of communal strife, the only safety is in numbers. Blacks living in integrated or predominantly white areas—or even simply traveling through white areas to their own homes—proved to be extremely vulnerable.[56]

Blacks that survived these attacks were loath to return to their former dwellings where they feared (correctly) that they would be subject to further violence. Following the riots, there was an outflow of blacks from outlying neighborhoods into the emerging ghetto, as the old integrated elite resigned itself to the new realities of racial segregation. Blacks who had been contemplating a move to better housing in white areas before the riots thought better of the idea afterward.

Racial violence did not end when the riots ceased in 1920, however; it simply assumed new, more controlled forms. As the black settlement pattern imploded and scattered areas of black residence were eliminated or consolidated, a contiguous core of solidly black neighborhoods formed in most northern cities during the first decades of the century. By the time black migration quickened during the 1920s, new arrivals had to be accommodated within a very compact and spatially restricted area that was not open to easy expansion.

After 1920 the pattern of racial strife shifted from one of generalized communal violence aimed at driving blacks out of white neighborhoods to a new pattern of targeted violence concentrated along the periphery of an expanding ghetto. As migration continued and housing pressures within the ghetto became intolerable, and as health, sanitary, and social conditions deteriorated, middle-class black families were eventually driven across the color line into white neighborhoods adjacent to the ghetto. Their moves set off an escalating pattern of racial violence.[57]

The pattern typically began with threatening letters, personal harassment, and warnings of dire consequences to follow. Sometimes whites, through their churches, realtors, or neighborhood organizations, would take up a collection and offer to buy the black homeowner out, hinting of less civilized inducements to follow if the offer was refused. If these entreaties failed to dislodge the resident, spontaneous mobs would often grow out of neighborhood meetings or barroom discussions, and a pack of agitated, angry whites would surround the house, hurling rocks and insults and at times storming the home and ransacking it. Periodic outbursts of mob violence would be interspersed with sporadic incidents of rock-throwing, gunshots, cross burnings, and physical attack.

If the escalating violence still failed to produce the desired result, the last step was dramatic and guaranteed to attract the attention, not only of the homeowner, but of the entire black community: bombing. During and after World War I, a wave of bombings followed the expansion of black residential areas in cities throughout the north. In Chicago, fifty-eight black homes were bombed between 1917 and 1921, one every twenty days;[58] and one black real estate agent, Jesse Binga, had his home and office bombed seven times in one year.[59] In Cleveland, a wealthy black doctor who constructed a new home in an exclusive white suburb had his house surrounded by a violent mob, and when this attack failed to dislodge him, the home was dynamited twice.[60] Bombings were also reported to be a common means of combating the expansion of Detroit's ghetto.[61]

The wave of violence and bombings crested during the 1920s, although the sporadic use of these techniques has continued up to the present.[62] Violence, however, has its problems as a strategy for maintaining the residential color line. Although it was employed by whites of all classes at first, those in the middle and upper classes eventually realized its limitations. Not only did violent actions often destroy property within neighborhoods being "defended," but injuries or death could bring legal charges as well as unfavorable publicity that decreased an area's stability. After the 1920s, middle-class whites increasingly turned to more civilized and institutionalized methods to build the ghetto.

A typical organizational solution to the threat of black residential expansion was the formation of neighborhood "improvement associations." Although ostensibly chartered for the purpose of promoting neighborhood security and property values, their principal raison d'être was the prevention of black entry and the maintenance of the color line. On Chicago's South Side, for example, the Hyde Park Improvement and Protective Club and the Woodlawn Society were formed implicitly to rid their neighborhoods of unwanted black settlers and to prevent future black entry.[63] In New York, whites banded together in Harlem's Property Owners' Improvement Corporation and Brooklyn's Gates Avenue Association, again for the same reasons.[64] In other cities, similar organizations dedicated themselves to checking the expansion of black settlement along the ghetto's frontier.[65]

These voluntary associations employed a variety of tools in their efforts to preserve the racial homogeneity of threatened neighborhoods. They lobbied city councils for zoning restrictions and for the closing of hotels and rooming houses that attracted blacks; they threatened boycotts of real estate agents who sold homes to blacks; they withdrew their patronage from white businesses that catered to black clients; they agitated for public investments in the neighborhood in order to increase property values and keep blacks out by economic means; they collected money to create funds to buy property from black settlers or to purchase homes that remained vacant for too long; they offered cash bonuses to black renters who agreed to leave the neighborhood. In the exclusive Chicago suburb of Wilmette, a committee of citizens went so far as to ask wealthy homeowners to lodge all maids, servants, and gardeners on premises, or else to fire all Negroes in their employ.[66]

One of the most important functions of the neighborhood associations, however, was to implement restrictive covenants.[67] These documents were contractual agreements among property owners stating that they would not permit a black to own, occupy, or lease their property. Those signing the covenant bound themselves and their heirs to exclude blacks from the covered area for a specified period of time. In the event of the covenant's violation, any party to the agreement could call upon the courts for enforcement and could sue the transgressor for damages. As typically employed, covenants took effect when some fixed percentage of property owners in a given area had signed, whereupon the remaining nonsignatories were pressured to sign also. A typical covenant lasted twenty years and required the assent of 75% of the property owners to become enforceable.

Prior to 1900, such covenants did not exist. Legal restrictions on the transfer of property to blacks took the form of deed restrictions, which covered single parcels and did not solve the problem of massive black entry into white neighborhoods. Deed restrictions also did not lend themselves to forceful collective action. After 1910, the use of restrictive covenants spread widely throughout the United States, and they were employed frequently and with considerable effectiveness to maintain the color line until 1948, when the U.S. Supreme Court declared them unenforceable.[68]

Local real estate boards often took the lead in establishing restrictive covenants and arranging for their widespread use. In 1927, for example, the Chicago Real Estate Board devised a model covenant that neighborhood organizations could adapt for their own use; the board then organized a special drive to ensure its adoption by all of the "better" neighborhoods in the city.[69] Although Chicago's local board may have been unusually active in defending the color line, these actions were consistent with official policies of the National Association of Real Estate Brokers, which in 1924 adopted an article in its code of ethics stating that "a Realtor should never be instrumental in introducing into a neighborhood . . . members of any race or nationality . . . whose presence will clearly be detrimental to property values in that neighborhood," a provision that remained in effect until 1950.[70]

The maintenance of a rigid color line in housing through violence and institutionalized discrimination paradoxically also created the conditions for ghetto expansion. Rapid black migration into a confined residential area created an intense demand for housing within the ghetto, which led to a marked inflation of rents and home prices. The racially segmented market generated real estate values in black areas that far exceeded anything in white neighborhoods, and this simple economic fact created a great potential for profits along the color line, guaranteeing that some real estate agent would specialize in opening up new areas to black settlement.[71]

White real estate boards, of course, attempted to forestall such actions by threatening agents who violated the color line with expulsion, but because black agents were excluded from real estate boards anyway, this threat had little effect on them. Furthermore, the potential profits were great enough that many whites were willing to face public opprobrium for the sake of the money to be earned. In the end, the real estate industry settled on a practical compromise of keeping "blacks from moving into white residential areas haphazardly and to see to it that they filled a block solidly before being allowed to move into the next one."[72] Essentially this strategy represented a policy of containment and tactical retreat before an advancing color line. For some, it proved to be a very profitable compromise.

The methods that realtors used to open up neighborhoods to black entry and to reap profits during the transition came to be known as "blockbusting."[73] The expansion of the ghetto generally followed the path of least resistance, slowing or stopping at natural boundaries such as rivers, railroad tracks, or major thoroughfares, and moving toward low status rather than high status areas.[74] Blockbusting agents would select a promising area for racial turnover, most often an area adjacent to the ghetto that contained older housing, poorer families, aging households, and some apartment buildings. Agents would then quietly acquire a few homes or apartments in the area, and rent or sell them to carefully chosen black families.

The inevitable reaction of white violence and resistance was countered with deliberate attempts to increase white fears and spur black demand.[75] Agents would go door to door warning white residents of the impending "invasion" and offer to purchase or rent homes on generous terms. They often selected ostentatiously lower-class blacks to be the first settlers in the neighborhood in order to heighten fears and encourage panic; at times, these "settlers" were actually confederates of the realtor. In neighborhoods of family homes, a realtor might divide up the first black-occupied house into small units, which were intentionally rented to poor southern arrivals who were desperate for housing and willing to pay high rents for cramped rooms of low quality. While white panic was spreading, the realtors would advertise widely within the black community, pointing out the availability of good housing in a newly opened neighborhood, thereby augmenting black demand.

Given the intensity of black demand and the depths of white prejudice, the entry of a relatively small number of black settlers would quickly surpass the threshold of white tolerance and set off a round of racial turnover.[76] No white renters or home buyers would enter the area under the cloud of a black invasion, and as the rate of white departures accelerated, each departing white family would be replaced with one or more black families. As the threat of violence subsided and whites gave up defending the neighborhood, black demand soared and agents reaped substantial profits, because the new entrants were willing to pay prices much higher than those previously paid by whites.

In neighborhoods of single-family homes, the initial black entrants tended to be middle- and upper-class families seeking to escape the deplorable conditions of the ghetto.[77] Like other middle-class people, they sought more agreeable surroundings, higher-quality schools, lower crime rates, bigger houses, larger properties, and a "better class of people." Because white banks did not make loans to black applicants, realtors were able to augment their profits by acting as bankers as well as sales agents; and given the racially segmented credit market, they were able to charge interest rates and demand down payments well above those paid by whites.[78]

The attempts of black middle-class families to escape the ghetto were continually undermined, however, by real estate agents seeking quick profits. Often they sold homes to black families who needed quality housing but were in no position to pay for it. As both seller and lender, the agent would collect a cash advance and several months of mortgage payments before the buyer defaulted; then the family was evicted and the house was resold to another family under similar terms. In this way, agents could "sell" a home several times in the course of a year, generating extra profits. Frequently agents bought homes in single-family neighborhoods, subdivided them into rooming houses, and then leased the resulting "kitchenette" apartments at high rents to poor families.[79]

The prevalence of these quick-profit schemes meant that the ghetto constantly followed the black middle class as it sought to escape from the poverty, blight, and misery of the black slum. Following resegregation, neighborhoods fell into progressive neglect and disrepair as owners were shuffled in and out of homes, which sat vacant between sales. Nor could owners who were paying rents and mortgages beyond their means afford repairs and routine maintenance. In addition, the illegal subdivision of single-family homes brought the very poor into what were originally middle-class areas. Complaints to city inspectors by black homeowners usually went unheard, because real estate agents were typically careful to pay off local officials; many were only too happy to turn a blind eye to problems in the black community if there was money to be made.

During the 1920s and 1930s, therefore, black ghettos expanded behind a leading edge of middle-class pioneers who were subsequently swamped by an influx of poor families, which caused the progressive deterioration of the neighborhood. As the decline accelerated, affluent families were prompted to seek new quarters in adjacent white neighborhoods, beginning a new round of neighborhood transition and decay. This process, when repeated across neighborhoods, yielded a distinct class gradient in the ghetto, with the poorest families being concentrated toward the center in the worst, most crowded, and least desirable housing, and the middle and upper classes progressively increasing their share of the population as one moved from the core toward the periphery of the ghetto.[80]

As the black ghetto became more dense and spatially concentrated, a struggle for power, influence, and ideological control emerged within the black community between the old elite and the "New Negroes" of the 1920s and 1930s.[81] The latter were politicians and, to a lesser extent, business owners who benefited from the spatial concentration of black demand within a racially segmented market. In ideological terms, the struggle was symbolized by the debate between the adherents of W. E. B. Du Bois and the followers of Booker T. Washington. The former argued that blacks should fight white injustice and demand their rightful share of the fruits of American society; the latter advocated accommodating white racism while building an independent black economic base.

The rise of the ghetto, more than anything else, brought about the eclipse of the old elite of integrationist blacks who dominated African American affairs in northern cities before 1910. These professionals and tradespeople who catered to white clients and aspired to full membership in American society were supplanted by a class of politicians and entrepreneurs whose source of power and wealth lay in the black community itself. Rather than being caterers, barbers, doctors, and lawyers who served a white or racially mixed clientele, the new elite were politicians and business owners with a self-interested stake in the ghetto. With their ascendancy, the ideal of an integrated society and the fight against racial segregation went into a long remission.[82]

These "New Negroes" included real estate tycoons, such as Chicago's Jesse Binga and New York's Philip A. Payton, men who specialized in opening up new areas for black settlement and made millions in the process.[83] Publishing newspapers for a black audience brought wealth and influence to Robert S. Abbott, who built the *Chicago Defender* into the most important black newspaper in the country, and Dr. P. M. H. Savory, who published the *Amsterdam News* from the 1920s until his death in the 1965.[84] With the concentration of black population, moreover, came the concentration of black votes and buying power, and a new generation of politicians and business owners came to the fore—people such as Oscar DePriest, who became Chicago's first black alderman and the first African American elected to Congress from the north,[85] and New York's Madame C. J. Walker, who made a fortune with a line of black cosmetics and hair-straightening products.[86] The interests of these new economic and political leaders were tied to the ghetto and its concerns rather than to issues growing out of an attempt to pursue an integrated life within the mainstream of American society.

Meanwhile, in the south, conditions for urban blacks were considerably less tolerant than in the north. The Jim Crow system of race relations was in its heyday during the early years of the twentieth century, but its paternalistic system of race relations guaranteed the subordination of blacks and paradoxically lessened the need for a rigid system of housing segregation. Among older southern cities, in particular, the traditional grid pattern of white avenues and black alleys kept segregation levels relatively low. Although direct evidence on the degree of racial segregation in southern cities is limited, the few available studies suggest that it was less severe in the early twentieth century than in the emerging ghettos of the north.

In 1910, the three southern cities for which there is data in Table 2.1 had an average black-white dissimilarity score of only 38, 21 points lower than the average in the north. In Charleston the level was particularly low at about 17; and although this value appears to represent an increase since the nineteenth century, it is an artifact of the exclusion of slaves from the earlier computation. When they are included in the 1860 calculation, the index falls to 11.5.[87] Of the three cities shown in 1910, moreover, none displays an index in the range generally accepted as high.

Southern whites were not completely immune to threats posed by black urbanization. After 1910 black populations also began to rise in southern cities, for essentially the same reasons as in the north, and whites similarly became alarmed at the influx of black migrants. In the context of Jim Crow, however, the reaction of southern whites never reached the extremes of panic and fear experienced in the north. Rather, given the tradition of legally enforced segregation in other spheres, southern whites turned to the law to promote greater separation between the races in housing.

The movement toward legally enforced residential segregation began in 1910, when Baltimore's city council passed an ordinance establishing separate white and black neighborhoods in the city. Additional laws to establish legal segregation in housing were passed in Virginia between 1911 and 1913, when Ashland, Norfolk, Portsmouth, Richmond, and Roanoke all adopted ordinances emulating Baltimore's. By 1913, the movement had spread southward to Winston-Salem and Greenville, North Carolina, and it reached Atlanta, Georgia, in the same year. By 1916, Louisville, St. Louis, Oklahoma City, and New Orleans all had passed laws establishing separate black and white districts in their cities.[88] As the movement gathered steam, some northern cities began to consider the possibility of adopting similar ordinances to resolve their racial difficulties.[89]

In 1916, however, the National Association for the Advancement of Colored People filed suit in federal court to block the implementation of Louisville's segregation law, and one year later the U.S. Supreme Court declared it unconstitutional.[90] The movement toward legally sanctioned housing segregation ended, and thereafter racial segregation in southern cities was accomplished by the same means as in the north: through violence, collective antiblack action, racially restrictive covenants, and discriminatory real estate practices. Segregation, nonetheless, continued to develop at a slower pace than in northern cities owing to the slower pace of industrialization, the unique spatial organization of southern cities, and the greater social control of blacks afforded by Jim Crow.

The 1940 black-white segregation indices in Table 2.1 conceal the lower segregation in the south because they rely on block rather than ward data. Although the average score of 81 is eight points lower than in the north, it is still quite high. The use of blocks rather than wards interacts with a classic white avenue/black alley settlement pattern to produce a misleading picture of segregation in the south. When ward tabulations are used, the level of segregation in Charleston falls from 60 to 27 (compared with a ward-level index of only 17 in 1910) while that in Jacksonville drops from 94 to 47 (up from 39 thirty years before).[91] Although the walls of the ghetto were rising in the south by 1940, they had not yet reached the height of those in the north, particularly in the older cities.

Shoring the Bulwarks of Segregation, 1940–1970

The outlines and form of the modern black ghetto were in place in most northern cities by the outbreak of World War II. Events unleashed by the war would not change the frontiers of black settlement so much as fill in the gaps. Once World War II was over, a great boom ushered in a new economic order that again dramatically transformed the social and spatial organization of cities, creating sprawling decentralized metropolises where compact settlements once stood. This new urban political economy mixed the public and private sectors to an unprecedented degree, and the distinguishing feature of racial segregation in the postwar era is the direct role that government played not only in maintaining the color line but in strengthening the walls of the ghetto.

By 1930 the perimeters of black settlement were well established in most cities and the level of black-white residential dissimilarity had reached a stable and very high level. Blacks were nearly as unevenly distributed in American cities as they would ever be, but as late as 1930 a significant number of whites still lived within the circumscribed areas that had been ceded to black settlement.[92] The Great Depression and World War II eliminated this residual white population and made northern ghettos the homogeneously black communities they are today.

The advent of the Depression brought widespread unemployment to blacks in the north. But if northern economic conditions were bad, they were worse in the south, and given the self-perpetuating dynamic inherent in mass migration, the movement from south to north continued: from 1930 to 1940, some 400,000 black migrants left the south for northern cities.[93] When they arrived, they faced unusually bleak residential circumstances, for the Great Depression had virtually ended new residential construction after 1929. Although housing construction began to pick up by 1940, the entry of the United States into World War II once again brought homebuilding to a halt. During the 1930s and 1940s, therefore, black migrants entered an urban environment with an essentially fixed and very limited supply of housing.

At first, the newcomers took the place of whites departing from racially changing neighborhoods located near the fringe of the ghetto. Once these neighborhoods had become all black, however, further ghetto expansion proved to be difficult because, given the housing shortage, there was nowhere for whites on the other side of the color line to go. As whites in adjacent neighborhoods stood firm and blocked entry, the expansion of the ghetto slowed to a crawl, and new black arrivals were accommodated by subdividing housing within the ghetto's boundaries. Apartments were carved out of bedrooms, closets, garages, basements, and sheds. As population densities within the ghetto rose, black spatial isolation increased.[94]

U.S. entry into the war brought full mobilization and a shortage of factory workers in the north. In response to the new demand for labor, black migration from south to north soared during the 1940s. The new migrants arrived in cities plagued by intense housing shortages and vacancy rates under 1%, even in white areas. Population densities within the ghetto increased to new, often incredible heights, a phenomenon that Otis and Beverly Duncan appropriately labeled "piling up."[95] This stage in the process of ghetto formation increased black isolation to new extremes, and from this time forward African Americans in large northern cities were effectively removed—socially and spatially—from the rest of American society.

World War II brought recovery from the economic malaise of the Great Depression, but four years of full employment combined with wartime consumer shortages produced a large surplus of savings and a tremendous pent-up demand for housing. Additional capital for home ownership was soon made available through new loan programs at the Federal Housing Administration and the Veterans Administration. The mix of surplus capital and frustrated demand ignited an unparalleled postwar boom in residential home construction.

As home construction skyrocketed during the late 1940s and 1950s, men and women began to marry and have babies at remarkable rates. After postponing marriage and childbearing during the hard times of the Depression and through the disruptions of war, American couples sought to make up for lost time: the baby boom was on. The growing families of the 1950s sought large houses on spacious lots in areas with good schools and plenty of room for supervised play, conditions that were most easily met by constructing new homes on inexpensive land located outside of central cities. The suburbanization of America proceeded at a rapid pace and the white middle class deserted inner cities in massive numbers. Only one-third of U.S. metropolitan residents were suburban residents in 1940, but by 1970 suburbanites constituted a majority within metropolitan America.

In making this transition from urban to suburban life, middle-class whites demanded and got massive federal investments in highway construction that permitted rapid movement to and from central cities by car. The surging demand for automobiles accelerated economic growth and contributed to the emergence of a new, decentralized spatial order. Whereas early industrialism was based on steam power, rail transportation, and rudimentary communications (e.g., the telegraph and surface mail), the new political economy grew up around electric power, automotive transport, and advanced telecommunications.

Industrial-era technology had encouraged spatial concentration in human activities. Factories were built compactly to conserve mechanical power and agglomerated to use common steam plants; rail lines moved large numbers of people along fixed routes to a single point, and crude communications put a premium on face-to-face interaction. In the new post-industrial order, however, the substitution of electricity for steam power eliminated the impetus for centralized manufacturing districts, and a growing reliance on truck transport made congested cities undesirable as centers of manufacturing and shipping. Widespread commuting by automobile extended residential development in all directions around the central city, not just along fixed rail lines. As workers and factories took advantage of the new technologies and moved to the suburbs, retail activities followed.[96]

This period of rapid economic growth and growing spatial deconcentration was accompanied by relatively low levels of immigration; and with the expansion of educational opportunities and the rise in service employment, the children of earlier immigrants increasingly left the ranks of manual workers. Employers once again turned to black migrants from the rural south to fill the demand for labor in manufacturing, heavy industry, and low-wage services. Within the south, a wave of mechanization and capital investment spread through agriculture, which put a definitive end to the sharecropping system and constricted the demand for rural labor.[97] As in earlier times, the coincidence of push and pull factors led to extensive black out-migration, with the net flow totaling 1.5 million during the 1950s and 1.4 million during the 1960s.[98]

Despite this rapid transformation of American cities, however, one feature of urban geography remained unchanged: the black ghetto. The institutional practices and private behaviors that had combined to maintain the color line before the war remained to support it afterward, with one significant change. Although whites were still highly resistant to racial integration in housing, withdrawal to the suburbs provided a more attractive alternative to the defense of threatened neighborhoods and led to a prevalence of flight over fight among whites in racially changing areas.[99] The combination of rapid white suburbanization and extensive black in-migration led to an unprecedented increase in the physical size of the ghetto during the 1950s and 1960s.[100]

In the postwar years, therefore, the percentage of blacks within northern cities shifted rapidly upward. Between 1950 and 1970, the percentage of blacks more than doubled in most large northern cities, going from 14% to 33% in Chicago, from 16% to 38% in Cleveland, from 16% to 44% in Detroit, and from 18% to 34% in Philadelphia. In the space of two decades Gary, Newark, and Washington were transformed from predominantly white to predominantly black cities; Gary was 53% black by 1970, and Newark and Washington were 54% and 71% black, respectively.[101]

What is striking about these transformations is how effectively the color line was maintained despite the massive population shifts. The white strategy of ghetto containment and tactical retreat before an advancing color line, institutionalized during the 1920s, was continued after 1945; the only change was the rate at which the leading edge of the ghetto advanced. In a few short years, the population of vast areas of Chicago's south and west sides became virtually all black, as occurred on Cleveland's east side, Philadelphia's north and west sides, and in most of central city Newark, Detroit, Baltimore, and Washington, D.C. All the while, however, the residential segregation of blacks was maintained.[102]

In cities receiving large numbers of black migrants, racial turnover was so regular and so pervasive that most neighborhoods could be classified by their stage in the transition process: all white, invasion, succession, consolidation, or all black. In six northern cities studied by Karl and Alma Taeuber, 90% of all neighborhoods inhabited by blacks in 1960 were either all black or clearly moving in that direction, a pattern that prevailed through 1970.[103]

The persistence of segregation despite the massive redistribution of whites and blacks is confirmed by Table 2.3, which presents indices of residential dissimilarity calculated at the block level for thirty U.S. cities from 1940 through 1970. These measures show that racial segregation became a permanent structural feature of the spatial organization of American cities in the years after World War II. In the three decades after 1940, black-white segregation remained high and virtually constant, averaging over 85 at all times in all regions. Segregation levels in the north peaked in 1950, and then edged slightly downward by 1970, whereas southern cities peaked somewhat later, in 1960. Only one city, San Francisco, experienced a significant long-term decline in the level of racial segregation. By 1970, at least 70% of blacks would have had to move to achieve an even residential configuration in most cities, and in many places the figure was closer to 90%.

Such consistently high levels of segregation imply that blacks and whites occupied separate and wholly distinct neighborhoods at each point between 1940 and 1970. Given the fact that northern cities received about 4.5 million black migrants during the period, the only possible outcome was a substantial increase in degree of black spatial isolation. Although no studies have computed decade-by-decade isolation indices for U.S. cities, census data allow us to carry out this task for 1970. Table 2.4 presents our results for thirty cities, along with Lieberson's 1930 isolation indices, which indicate long-term trends.

Among northern cities, the average level of black spatial isolation more than doubled between 1930 and 1970, going from 32% to nearly 74%. Whereas a typical northern black resident was likely to live in a neighborhood dominated by whites in 1930 (only Chicago and Cleveland were

Table 2.3 Block-level indices of nonwhite-white segregation for thirty cities, 1940–1970

	Segregation indices by year			
	1940	1950	1960	1970
Northern cities				
Boston	86.3	86.5	83.9	79.9
Buffalo	87.9	89.5	86.5	84.2
Chicago	95.0	92.1	92.6	88.8
Cincinnati	90.6	91.2	89.0	83.1
Cleveland	92.0	91.5	91.3	89.0
Columbus	87.1	88.9	85.3	84.1
Detroit	89.9	88.8	84.5	80.9
Gary	88.3	93.8	92.8	82.9
Indianapolis	90.4	91.4	91.6	88.3
Kansas City	88.0	91.3	90.8	88.0
Los Angeles	84.2	84.6	81.8	78.4
Milwaukee	92.9	91.6	88.1	83.7
Newark	77.4	76.9	71.6	74.9
New York	86.8	87.3	79.3	73.0
Philadelphia	88.0	89.0	87.1	83.2
Pittsburgh	82.0	84.0	84.6	83.9
St. Louis	92.6	92.9	90.5	89.3
San Francisco	82.9	79.8	69.3	55.5
Average	87.0	88.4	85.6	81.7
Southern cities				
Atlanta	87.4	91.5	93.6	91.5
Baltimore	90.1	91.3	89.6	88.3
Birmingham	86.4	88.7	92.8	91.5
Dallas	80.2	88.4	94.6	92.7
Greensboro	93.1	93.5	93.3	91.4
Houston	84.5	91.5	93.7	90.0
Memphis	79.9	86.4	92.0	91.8
Miami	97.9	97.8	97.9	89.4
New Orleans	81.0	84.9	86.3	83.1
Norfolk	96.0	95.0	94.6	90.8
Tampa	90.2	92.5	94.5	90.7
Washington	81.0	80.1	79.7	77.7
Average	87.3	90.1	91.9	89.1

Source: Annemette Sørensen, Karl E. Taeuber, and Lesslie J. Hollingsworth, Jr., "Indexes of Racial Residential Segregation for 109 Cities in the United States, 1940 to 1970," *Sociological Focus* 8 (1975):128–30.

Table 2.4 Indices of black isolation within neighborhoods of thirty cities, 1930–1970

Northern cities			Southern cities	
City	1930	1970	City	1970
Boston	19.2	66.1	Atlanta	88.0
Buffalo	24.2	75.2	Baltimore	84.8
Chicago	70.4	89.2	Birmingham	57.9
Cincinnati	44.6	63.9	Dallas	82.0
Cleveland	51.0	86.6	Greensboro	62.0
			Houston	72.1
Columbus	—	65.2		
Detroit	31.2	77.1	Memphis	82.9
Gary	—	83.2	Miami	81.5
Indianapolis	26.1	65.5	New Orleans	75.6
Kansas City	31.6	75.6	Norfolk	79.8
			Tampa	62.3
Los Angeles	25.6	73.9	Washington	88.1
Milwaukee	16.4	74.5		
New York	41.8	60.2	Average	76.4
Newark	22.8	78.3		
Philadelphia	27.3	75.6		
Pittsburgh	26.8	70.8		
St. Louis	46.6	85.1		
San Francisco	1.7	56.1		
Average	31.7	73.5		

Sources: Indices for 1930 are computed from ward-level data and come from Stanley Lieberson, *A Piece of the Pie: Blacks and White Immigrants since 1880* (Berkeley: University of California Press, 1980), pp. 266, 288. Indices for 1970 are computed from tract-level data and were calculated by the authors using U.S. Bureau of the Census, *Census of Population and Housing 1970, Fourth Court Summary Tapes, File A* (Washington, D.C.: U.S. Bureau of the Census, 1970).

exceptions), by 1970 the situation had completely reversed. Now blacks in *all* northern cities were more likely to live with other African Americans than with whites, and in four cities the average black person lived in a neighborhood that was over 80% black (in Chicago, Cleveland, Gary, and St. Louis). Unless they worked in the larger mainstream economy, blacks in these cities were very unlikely to have any contact with whites.

Although we lack an earlier reference point to discern long-term trends in the south, black isolation was clearly an accomplished fact in southern cities by 1970 as well. The average level of black isolation within cities of the south was slightly higher than in the north (76% versus 74%), and the index exceeded 80% in six cases (Atlanta, Baltimore, Dallas, Memphis, Miami, and Washington, D.C.). In all cities, blacks were very unlikely to share a neighborhood with members of other racial groups. Indeed, the *lowest* isolation index was 58% (in Birmingham), so that blacks throughout the south tended to live in residential areas where the vast majority of residents were black. Patterns for 1970, therefore, represent a complete reversal of conditions during the late nineteenth century, when residential contact between southern blacks and whites was the rule.

Throughout the United States—in both southern and northern cities—the ghetto had become an enduring, permanent feature of the residential structure of black community life by 1940, and over the next thirty years the spatial isolation of African Americans only increased. The highest isolation index ever recorded for any ethnic group in any American city was 56% (for Milwaukee's Italians in 1910), but by 1970 the *lowest* level of spatial isolation observed for blacks anywhere, north or south, was 56% (in San Francisco).[104]

The universal emergence of the black ghetto in American cities after 1940 rests on a foundation of long-standing white racial prejudice. Although attitudes cannot be studied directly before 1940, after this date opinion polls are available to confirm the depth of white prejudice against blacks in the area of housing. In 1942, for example, 84% of white Americans polled answered "yes" to the question "Do you think there should be separate sections in towns and cities for Negroes to live in?";[105] and in 1962, 61% of white respondents agreed that "white people have a right to keep blacks out of their neighborhoods if they want to, and blacks should respect that right."[106] It was not until 1970 that even a bare majority of white respondents (53%) disagreed with the latter statement.[107]

Throughout the period from 1940 to 1970, in other words, there was widespread support among whites for racial discrimination in housing and for the systematic exclusion of blacks from white neighborhoods. As a result, whites continued to resist any attempt at black entry through acts of harassment and violence, and once entry was achieved, the neighborhood was avoided by subsequent white homeseekers, thereby guaranteeing racial turnover and resegregation.[108] The only difference from earlier times was that the racial turnover was quicker and the ghetto's physical expansion more rapid.

The institutionalization of discrimination within the real estate industry likewise continued in the postwar era. Although racially restrictive covenants were declared unenforceable by the U.S. Supreme Court in 1948, a comprehensive study of real estate policies in the 1950s by Rose Helper revealed a pervasive pattern of discrimination against blacks in most American cities.[109] In her survey of real estate agents in Chicago, she found that 80% of realtors refused to sell blacks property in white neighborhoods, and 68% refused to rent them such property. Moreover, among those agents who did sell or rent to blacks, half said they would do so only under restrictive conditions, such as when a significant number of blacks had already entered the area.[110] Another survey of Chicago's real estate agents carried out by Harvey Molotch in the mid-1960s found that only 29% of agents were willing to rent to blacks unconditionally (regardless of local market conditions or racial composition), and half of these open-minded agents were black.[111]

Helper presented similar findings from studies of housing discrimination in other cities during the 1950s.[112] One study carried out in suburban New York identified forty-six separate techniques used by white realtors to exclude blacks from neighborhoods, and Helper identified twenty-six different methods in her Chicago survey; most could be grouped in one of two basic categories: 56% used a flat refusal and 24% employed some kind of subterfuge (e.g., saying a unit was sold when it was not).[113] When handling properties in black areas, 22% said they were more careful screening black applicants than whites, 14% said they required security deposits of blacks but not whites, and 25% said they charged higher rents to blacks.[114]

In their personal views, the realtors studied by Helper appeared to share the prejudices of their white clients. Some 59% of her respondents rejected racial integration in principle,[115] and 84% espoused an ideological stance that supported the exclusion of blacks from white neighborhoods.[116] Some 65% said they believed that the entry of blacks was bad for neighborhoods;[117] and among realtors who were members of Chicago's Real Estate Board, support for the exclusion of blacks was even stronger: 91% held views consistent with an exclusionary ideology.[118]

In her interviews with realtors, Helper also uncovered considerable evidence of discrimination by banks and savings institutions in denying loans to black homeseekers. Among realtors offering information on the issue, 62% felt that few or very few banks were willing to make loans to blacks, and half of the agents confirmed that banks would not make loans to areas that were black, turning black, or threatened with the possibility of black entry.[119]

There is, in summary, considerable evidence pointing to the persistence of prejudice against blacks in the postwar period, and to the widespread translation of this sentiment into systematic, institutionalized racial discrimination within urban housing markets. These private beliefs and actions, however, were not the only forces shoring the walls of ghetto between 1940 and 1970. What was new about the postwar era was the extent to which the federal government became involved in perpetuating racial segregation.

Beginning in the 1930s, the federal government launched a series of programs designed to increase employment in the construction industry and make home ownership widely available to the American public. The Home Owners' Loan Corporation (HOLC) was the first of these programs, and it served as a model for later efforts. Passed in the depression year of 1933, it provided funds for refinancing urban mortgages in danger of default and granted low-interest loans to former owners who had lost their homes through foreclosure to enable them to regain their properties. The HOLC was the first government-sponsored program to introduce, on a mass scale, the use of long-term, self-amortizing mortgages with uniform payments.[120]

Unfortunately for blacks, the HOLC also initiated and institutionalized the practice of "redlining."[121] This discriminatory practice grew out of a ratings system HOLC developed to evaluate the risks associated with loans made to specific urban neighborhoods. Four categories of neighborhood quality were established, and lowest was coded with the color red; it and the next-lowest category virtually never received HOLC loans. The vast majority of mortgages went to the top two categories, the highest of which included areas that were "new, homogenous, and in demand in good times and bad" (to HOLC this meant areas inhabited by "American business and professional men"); the second category consisted of areas that had reached their peak, but were still desirable and could be expected to remain stable.[122]

The HOLC's rating procedures thus systematically undervalued older central city neighborhoods that were racially or ethnically mixed. Jewish areas, for example, were generally placed in category two if their economic status was high enough, but if they were working class or located near a black settlement they would fall into the third category because they were "within such a low price or rent range as to attract an undesirable element."[123] Black areas were invariably rated as fourth grade and "redlined." As Kenneth Jackson points out, the HOLC did not invent these standards of racial worth in real estate—they were already well established by the 1920s—it bureaucratized them and applied them on an exceptional scale.[124] It lent the power, prestige, and support of the federal government to the systematic practice of racial discrimination in housing.

According to Jackson, HOLC underwriters were far more concerned about the location and movement of blacks than about any other demographic trend. He cites a confidential 1941 HOLC survey of real estate prospects in the St. Louis area that repeatedly mentions "the rapidly increasing Negro population" and the consequent "problem in the maintenance of real estate values." Every neighborhood analysis in the report includes maps of the density of black settlement. Black neighborhoods are always coded red; and even those with small black percentages were usually rated as "hazardous" and placed in the lowest category.[125]

Through this discriminatory ratings system, HOLC mortgage funds were invariably channeled away from established black areas and were usually redirected away from neighborhoods that looked as though they *might* contain blacks in the future. But funds distributed through the HOLC program itself were modest, and the major role that the agency played lay in serving as a model for other credit institutions, both private and public.

During the 1930s and 1940s, private banks relied heavily on the HOLC system to make their own loan decisions, and the agency's "Residential Security Maps" were widely circulated throughout the lending industry.[126] Banks adopted the HOLC's procedures (and prejudices) in constructing their own maps and ratings, thereby institutionalizing and disseminating the practice of redlining. Thus HOLC not only channeled federal funds away from black neighborhoods but was also responsible for a much larger and more significant disinvestment in black areas by private institutions.

By far the greatest effect of the HOLC rating system, however, came from its influence on the underwriting practices of the Federal Housing Administration (FHA) and the Veterans Administration (VA) during the 1940s and 1950s. The FHA loan program was created by the National Housing Act in 1937, and the VA program was authorized by the Servicemen's Readjustment Act of 1944.[127] These loan programs together completely reshaped the residential housing market of the United States and pumped millions of dollars into the housing industry during the postwar era. Loans made by the FHA and the VA were a major impetus behind the rapid suburbanization of the United States after 1945.

The FHA program operated by guaranteeing the value of collateral for loans made by private banks. Before this program, mortgages generally were granted for no more than two-thirds of the appraised value of a home, so buyers needed to acquire at least 33% of the value of a property in order to make a down payment; frequently banks required half the assessed value of a home before making a loan. The FHA program, in contrast, guaranteed over 90% of the value of collateral so that down payments of 10% became the norm. The FHA also extended the repayment period to twenty-five or thirty years, resulting in low monthly payments, and insisted that all loans be fully amortized.[128] The greater security afforded by FHA guarantees virtually eliminated the risk to banks, which lowered the interest rates they charged borrowers. When the VA program was established, it followed practices established by the earlier FHA program.[129]

As the cost and ease of purchasing a house dropped, home ownership became a mass phenomenon for the first time in American history. Between 1934 and 1969 the percentage of families living in owner-occupied dwellings increased from 44% to 63%; and during the 1940s and 1950s, the marriage of FHA financing and new construction techniques made it cheaper to buy new suburban homes than to rent comparable older dwellings in the central city.[130] As a result, the FHA and VA contributed significantly to the decline of the inner city by encouraging the selective out-migration of middle-class whites to the suburbs.

The bias in favor of the suburbs was evident in FHA practices and regulations, which favored the construction of single-family homes but discouraged the building of multi-family units. In addition, FHA loans for the remodeling of existing structures were small and had a short amortization period, making it easier and cheaper for a family to purchase a new home than to renovate an older one.[131] But the most important factor encouraging white suburbanization and reinforcing the segregation of blacks was the FHA requirement for an "unbiased," professional appraisal of insured properties, which naturally included a rating of the neighborhood.

In rating the home, the FHA established minimum standards for lot size, setbacks, and separation from existing structures that essentially eliminated from eligibility many inner-city dwellings, notably row houses and attached dwellings.[132] In evaluating neighborhoods, the agency followed the HOLC's earlier lead in racial matters; it too manifested an obsessive concern with the presence of what the 1939 FHA *Underwriting Manual* called "inharmonious racial or nationality groups." According to the manual, "if a neighborhood is to retain stability, it is necessary that properties shall continue to be occupied by the same social and racial classes."[133]

Thus, in the late 1940s, the FHA recommended the use and application of racially restrictive covenants as a means of ensuring the security of neighborhoods, and it did not change this recommendation until 1950, two years after covenants were declared unenforceable and contrary to public policy by the Supreme Court.[134] Like the HOLC, the FHA compiled maps and charts showing the location and movement of black families, and it frequently drew updated versions of the HOLC Residential Security Maps to determine the suitability of neighborhoods for FHA loans.[135]

As a result of these policies, the vast majority of FHA and VA mortgages went to white middle-class suburbs, and very few were awarded to black neighborhoods in central cities. It is difficult to determine the full extent of the resulting disinvestment in black neighborhoods, however, because the FHA did not publish loan statistics below the county level, which is curious given the agency's obsessive concern with neighborhood data prior to making the loans.[136] Kenneth Jackson has partially overcome this limitation by focusing on cases in which cities and counties are coterminous.

St. Louis County, for example, is a suburban area that surrounds the City of St. Louis, which has the status of a county in Missouri. From 1934 to 1960, the former received five times as many FHA mortgages as did the latter, and nearly six times as much loan money; per capita mortgage spending was 6.3 times greater. Jackson observed similar differentials in the dispersal of FHA mortgages between Washington, D.C., and its suburbs. Most startling was the case of New York City and its suburbs. Per capita FHA lending in Nassau County, New York (i.e., suburban Long Island) was eleven times that in Kings County (Brooklyn) and sixty times that in Bronx County (the Bronx).[137]

As the new post-industrial urban order developed, the disinvestment in central cities at the expense of suburbs increasingly meant the disinvestment in blacks as opposed to whites. Sometimes FHA procedures rendered whole cities ineligible for FHA-guaranteed loans simply because of a minority presence, thereby accelerating their decline. In 1966, for example, the FHA had no mortgages in either Paterson or Camden, New Jersey, both older cities where the non-Hispanic white population was declining during the 1950s (and actually became a minority in the 1970s).[138] Given the importance of the FHA in the residential housing market, such blanket redlining sent strong signals to private lending institutions, which followed suit and avoided making loans within the affected areas. The lack of loan capital flowing into minority areas made it impossible for owners to sell their homes, leading to steep declines in property values and a pattern of disrepair, deterioration, vacancy, and abandonment.[139]

Thus, by the late 1950s, many cities were locked into a spiral of decline that was directly encouraged and largely supported by federal housing policies. As poor blacks from the south entered cities in large numbers, middle-class whites fled to the suburbs to escape them and to insulate themselves from the social problems that accompanied the rising tide of poor.[140] As the growing demand for city services—and particularly social services—drove up the cost of local government, politicians were forced to raise taxes, which further accelerated the flight of the white middle class, creating additional pressures for tax increases, and so on.

Nevertheless, most cities were not completely stripped of their middle and upper classes. Whites associated with a variety of elite institutions—universities, hospitals, libraries, foundations, businesses—were often tied physically to the city by large capital investments, spatially immobile facilities, and long-standing traditions. Faced with a steady decline in the physical stock of the city and the progressive encroachment of the black ghetto, these powerful interests turned to the federal government for relief.

They received it from Congress in the form of the housing acts of 1949 and 1954, which provided federal funds to local authorities to acquire slum properties, assemble them into large parcels, clear them of existing structures, and prepare them for "redevelopment." But in order to qualify for federal funding, local redevelopment authorities had to guarantee that an adequate supply of replacement housing would be made available to displaced families at rents within their means. To satisfy the latter provision, local planning agencies turned to public housing.[141]

During the 1950s and 1960s, local elites manipulated housing and urban renewal legislation to carry out widespread slum clearance in growing black neighborhoods that threatened white business districts and elite institutions. Public housing was pressed into service to house black families displaced by the razing of neighborhoods undergoing renewal. Although liberal planners often tried to locate the projects away from ghetto areas, white politicians and citizens mobilized to block the construction of projects within their neighborhoods; white city councils and mayors usually obtained the right of veto over any proposed project site.[142] As a result, projects were typically built on cleared land within or adjacent to existing black neighborhoods.[143] In order to save money, maximize patronage jobs, and house within the ghetto as many blacks as possible, local authorities constructed multi-unit projects of extremely high density.

The razing of neighborhoods near threatened areas did check the spread of "urban blight," and "saved" many areas, but black critics complained that "urban renewal" simply meant "Negro removal," and the evidence largely bears them out.[144] As black neighborhoods adjacent to threatened white areas were torn down and converted to other uses, thereby blocking the expansion of the ghetto in that direction, public housing for displaced residents had to be constructed elsewhere. Because for political reasons projects could only be built in ghetto areas, other black neighborhoods were razed and high-density units constructed there to accommodate the residents of both neighborhoods.

In the end, urban renewal almost always destroyed more housing than it replaced.[145] Many poor blacks were permanently displaced into other crowded ghetto neighborhoods, which contributed to their instability and further decline. Moreover, delays between the time when neighborhoods were torn down and new projects were erected displaced many others into the ghetto on a temporary basis. Thus urban renewal programs frequently only shifted the problems of blight, crime, and instability from areas adjacent to elite white neighborhoods to locations deeper inside the black ghetto.

Established black neighborhoods, however, could not absorb all the families displaced by urban renewal and public housing construction, and some were forced to seek entry within working-class white neighborhoods located at points along the ghetto's periphery. An important secondary effect of urban renewal was to accelerate racial turnover, expand the ghetto, and shift the threat of ghetto expansion from elite white districts to working-class white neighborhoods.[146]

By 1970, after two decades of urban renewal, public housing projects in most large cities had become black reservations, highly segregated from the rest of society and characterized by extreme social isolation.[147] The replacement of low-density slums with high-density towers of poor families also reduced the class diversity of the ghetto and brought about a geographic concentration of poverty that was previously unimaginable.[148] This new segregation of blacks—in economic as well as social terms—was the direct result of an unprecedented collaboration between local and national government.

This unholy marriage came about when private actions to maintain the color line were overwhelmed by the massive population shifts of the 1950s and 1960s. The degree of racial segregation in public housing is directly and unambiguously linked to the differential growth of black and white urban populations in the postwar era: blacks are now most segregated in public housing precisely in the urban areas where their numbers were growing most rapidly compared with whites during the 1960s.[149] Public housing, in the words of the historian Arnold Hirsch, represents a new, federally sponsored "second ghetto," one "solidly institutionalized and frozen in concrete," where "government took an active hand not merely in reinforcing prevailing patterns of segregation, but in lending them a permanence never seen before."[150]

Epilogue: The Riots and Their Aftermath

By the late 1960s, virtually all American cities with significant black populations had come to house large ghettos characterized by extreme segregation and spatial isolation. Whereas before 1940 no racial or ethnic group in American history had ever experienced an isolation index above 60%, by 1970 this level was normal for blacks in large American cities. By the end of the 1960s, in other words, the average black city dweller lived in a neighborhood where the vast majority of his or her neighbors were also black.

Not only was the segregation of European ethnic groups lower, it was also temporary. Whereas Europeans' isolation indices began to drop shortly after 1920, the spatial isolation characteristic of blacks had become a permanent feature of the residential structure of large American cities by 1940. This profound segregation reversed nineteenth-century patterns, where neighborhoods were racially integrated and the social worlds of blacks and whites overlapped. Under the residential configurations prevailing in 1970, meaningful contact between blacks and whites outside the work force would be extremely unlikely.

These conditions came about because of decisions taken by whites to deny blacks access to urban housing markets and to exclude them from white neighborhoods. Throughout the postwar era, whites displayed a high degree of prejudice against black neighbors, and this sentiment was repeatedly expressed in violence directed at blacks who attempted to leave the ghetto. Restrictive covenants and deed restrictions were employed by neighborhood "improvement" associations to exclude blacks from housing outside the ghetto, boycotts were organized to punish merchants or agents who sold to blacks, and social pressure was applied to realtors, property owners, and public officials who did not adhere to the principle of racial exclusion. Discrimination in the real estate industry was institutionalized from 1920 onward.

After 1940, the federal government was drawn into the defense of the residential color line. Federally sponsored mortgage programs systematically channeled funds away from minority neighborhoods, bringing about a wholesale disinvestment in black communities during the 1950s and 1960s. Meanwhile, local officials, using funds from the U.S. Department of Housing and Urban Development, carried out systematic slum clearance in ghetto neighborhoods adjacent to threatened white districts and then built large blocks of high-density public housing in other black neighborhoods to contain black families displaced by this "renewal." The result was a new, more permanent, federally sponsored "second ghetto" in which blacks were isolated by class as well as by race.

The economic deprivation, social isolation, and psychological alienation produced by decades of segregation bore bitter fruit in a series of violent urban riots during the 1960s. The violence began in Birmingham, Alabama, in the summer of 1963, but the real bellwether was the Los Angeles riot of August 1965, which did $35 million worth of damage and left 4,000 injured and 34 dead.[151] After sporadic violence in Chicago and Cleveland during the summer of 1966, a convulsive wave of mob violence erupted during July and August of 1967, when black ghettos in sixty U.S. cities exploded in a cataclysm of frustration and rage.[152] The violence was particularly destructive in Detroit, Newark, and Milwaukee; Chicago's inferno followed Martin Luther King's assassination in April of 1968.[153]

Unlike the communal race riots of early 1900s, these disturbances arose from within the black community itself and were "commodity riots," directed at property rather than people.[154] Outside of confrontations with police and guardsmen, there was little black-on-white or white-on-black violence. Attacks were confined largely to the ghetto and were directed at white property, institutions, or authority symbols. Looting became the characteristic act of the disturbances. White people were not singled out for assault, and black rioters did not attempt to leave the ghetto. The participants did not express a racial hatred of whites per se, but an anger with the conditions of racial oppression and economic deprivation that had been allowed to fester in the ghetto for sixty years.[155]

In the wake of the violence and destruction, President Johnson appointed a national commission of elected officials and public figures chaired by Governor Otto Kerner of Illinois. The Kerner Commission issued its report in March 1968 and firmly concluded that the riots stemmed from the persistence of racial discrimination and a historical legacy of disadvantages in employment, education, and welfare; but one additional factor was clearly identified by the commissioners as underlying all other social and economic problems: segregation.[156]

A point "fundamental to the Commission's recommendations" was that "federal housing programs must be given a new thrust aimed at overcoming the prevailing pattern of racial segregation. If this is not done, those programs will continue to concentrate the most impoverished and dependent segments of the population into central-city ghettos where there is already a critical gap between the needs of the population and the public resources to deal with them."[157] To accomplish this aim, the commission recommended that the federal government "enact a comprehensive and enforceable open housing law to cover the sale or rental of all housing," and that it "reorient federal housing programs to place more low and moderate income housing outside of ghetto areas."[158]

Within months of the commission's report, the nation seemed to be moving decisively toward the implementation of these recommendations. In April 1968 the Fair Housing Act was passed by Congress and signed into law by the President; it banned discrimination in the sale or rental of housing. The following year a federal judge in Chicago ruled favorably on a major lawsuit alleging discrimination in public housing and ordered the Chicago Housing Authority to take remedial action.[159] Given these new tools in the fight against residential segregation, observers looked forward to the dismantling of the ghetto during the 1970s and to a reversal of historical trends toward segregation.

3

The Persistence of the Ghetto

When Martin Luther King, Jr., decided to take the southern movement north into Chicago, some thought he was pressing his luck.

From the television documentary "Eyes on the Prize"

As the 1970s dawned, the possibilities for rapid desegregation seemed bright: not only had the courts acted decisively to stop the systematic placement of public housing in black neighborhoods, but a new civil rights act banned discrimination in the rental and sale of housing.[1] Earlier legislation had already prohibited racial discrimination in other areas of American life, and whites expressed new support for the principle of open housing.[2]

Demographic trends in the early 1970s also seemed to favor residential integration. By the beginning of the decade blacks had begun to join the exodus of families from central cities to suburbs, and the pace of white suburbanization slowed.[3] At the same time, the migration of blacks from south to north decelerated and reversed, and for the first time since the Civil War, the south experienced a net in-migration of blacks. Between 1970 and 1980, the northeast and midwest together *lost* some 342,000 black migrants while the south *gained* 209,000 black entrants.[4] The drying up of this traditional south-to-north migration stream eliminated a key supply-side factor that had contributed to ghetto formation and white racial hostility for a hundred years.

Additional impetus for integration came from the steady improvement in black socioeconomic well-being. Although people, jobs, and housing continued to gravitate to suburban areas, cities still contained a large base of manufacturing and heavy industry during the early 1970s, which provided blacks with a strong foundation for economic and social mobility. Until the recession of 1973, black income levels were rising and levels of racial discrimination were falling.[5] In 1973 the rate of black poverty reached its lowest level in U.S. history.[6]

If the coincidence of rising economic status and growing civil rights incited hopes for desegregation, these sanguine expectations were dashed by decade's end. Despite what whites said on opinion polls and despite the provisions of the Fair Housing Act, segregation continued; and in contrast to the steady improvement in black socioeconomic status through 1973, the decade ended in record unemployment, inflation, falling wages, increasing income inequality, and rising rates of black poverty.[7] Not only did the ghetto fail to disappear; in many ways its problems multiplied. As segregation persisted, black isolation deepened, and the social and economic problems that had long plagued African American communities worsened. During the 1970s, the ghetto gave birth to the underclass.

Trends in Racial Segregation, 1970–1980

The 1970 U.S. Census made computerized data on American neighborhoods widely available for the first time, and the continuation of this practice in 1980 corrects several weaknesses of prior research. Computerized data files permit an analysis of racial segregation using constant neighborhood units, fixed metropolitan boundaries, and comparable definitions of racial groups. To a greater extent than was possible before, trends in the residential structure of urban black communities can now be measured accurately, without the confounding influence of changing geographic definitions.

Given the extensive suburbanization that occurred between 1945 and 1970, it is no longer appropriate to measure segregation within cities alone. By 1970, racial segregation in U.S. urban areas was characterized a largely black central city surrounded by predominantly white suburbs, or as one soul tune described it, a "chocolate city with vanilla suburbs."[8] For this reason, we assess segregation not within specific cities but across entire metropolitan regions, or more specifically, within "Standard Metropolitan Statistical Areas." These areas, used by the U.S. Bureau of the Census, are made up of a "central city" with at least 50,000 inhabitants, plus surrounding counties that have a high degree of social and economic integration with it.[9]

Rather than presenting results for all metropolitan areas in the United

States, however, we focus on those with the thirty largest black populations, thereby keeping the presentation of data within manageable limits. Although focusing on the largest black communities maximizes the conditions for segregation, it nonetheless depicts the circumstances under which most African Americans live. Over half of all blacks in the United States, and 60% of black urban dwellers, live in the thirty metropolitan areas described here. Moreover, because our findings are drawn from a larger series of articles examining segregation in sixty metropolitan areas, our actual base of generalization is much larger.[10]

The measurement of racial segregation requires the selection of a spatial unit to represent a "neighborhood," and the areal unit we have chosen is the census tract. Tracts are intermediate in size between wards and blocks, and range in population from about 3,000 to 8,000 inhabitants, averaging around 4,000 persons.[11] In contrast, blocks typically contain fewer than 1,000 residents and ward populations range upwards of 10,000 persons. Tracts were chosen because more information is published for them than for any other small geographic unit. Block-level tabulations are regularly suppressed by the Census Bureau to protect the privacy of respondents, and only limited information is released for wards, because they are political entities rather than statistical units. Among urban specialists, tracts are generally accepted as a reasonably accurate approximation of the concept of a "neighborhood."[12]

Definitions of metropolitan areas and tracts are not immutable, of course; through population growth and suburbanization, metropolitan boundaries expand and tract borders shift. Whenever we study trends in segregation, therefore, we adjust for changes in territorial definitions. The effect of urban growth is controlled by carrying 1970 metropolitan area definitions over into 1980, and we have systematically gone through all census tracts to create a common 1970–1980 tract grid.[13] Only when the analysis focuses on patterns for 1980 alone do we use 1980 metropolitan definitions.

The rapid growth of the Hispanic population during the 1970s requires another adjustment of census data. Hispanics may be of any race, but most are classified as white. As the number of Latinos in an area increases, therefore, larger shares of "whites" are classified as Hispanic, especially in places such as Los Angeles and Miami. In order to avoid confounding differences in segregation with differences in the ethnic composition of whites (and to a lesser extent blacks), we have removed all Hispanics from the general white and black populations. This action is especially important when considering trends in segregation, because the Census Bureau changed its racial coding procedures for Hispanics between 1970 and 1980, thereby producing artificial changes in the size of the white population.[14] Although we use the terms "white" and "black" throughout this chapter, readers should remember that these populations have been adjusted by removing white and black Hispanics. Thus we measure segregation between non-Hispanic whites and non-Hispanic blacks.

The indices in Table 3.1 testify to the persistence of the racial segregation during the 1970s. The two left-hand columns present indices of black-white dissimilarity for 1970 and 1980. This measure of segregation gives the percentage of all blacks who would have to move to achieve an even, or "integrated," residential configuration—one where each census tract replicates the racial composition of the metropolitan area as a whole.[15] Among northern areas, this index averaged over 80% in both 1970 and 1980, and it declined by only 4 points over the decade. This stability provides little evidence for the dismantling of the ghetto during the 1970s.

Among the oldest and largest northern ghettos—places where the riots of the 1960s were most severe—there was virtually no sign of progress in residential integration. In Boston, Chicago, Cleveland, Detroit, Gary, Philadelphia, Pittsburgh, and St. Louis, the decline in the segregation index was 4 points or less, and in two metropolitan areas (New York and Newark) segregation actually *increased* over the decade. Although a few places experienced sizable declines in segregation—notably Columbus, Los Angeles, and San Francisco—the prevailing trend was one of stability in the residential structure of the ghetto. The larger declines in these metropolitan areas are generally attributable to unusual instability in housing patterns caused by a combination of gentrification, immigration, and rapid housing construction rather than to an ongoing process of neighborhood racial integration.[16] As of 1980, no northern area displayed a dissimilarity index under 70%, which indicates a level of segregation well above the highest ever recorded for European ethnic groups.[17]

During the 1970s, southern metropolitan areas followed the traditional pattern of lower segregation compared with the north. In older southern cities, this outcome reflects the persistence of the Jim Crow pattern of black-inhabited alleys interspersed between white-inhabited avenues.[18] During the late Jim Crow period, moreover, white developers created black suburbs on the urban fringe in order to reinforce housing segrega-

Table 3.1 Trends in black segregation and isolation in thirty metropolitan areas with largest black populations, 1970–1980

Metropolitan area	Black-white segregation		Black isolation	
	1970	1980	1970	1980
Northern areas				
Boston	81.2	77.6	56.7	55.1
Buffalo	87.0	79.4	71.2	63.5
Chicago	91.9	87.8	85.5	82.8
Cincinnati	76.8	72.3	59.1	54.3
Cleveland	90.8	87.5	81.9	80.4
Columbus	81.8	71.4	63.5	57.5
Detroit	88.4	86.7	75.9	77.3
Gary–Hammond–E. Chicago	91.4	90.6	80.4	77.3
Indianapolis	81.7	76.2	64.5	62.3
Kansas City	87.4	78.9	74.2	69.0
Los Angeles–Long Beach	91.0	81.1	70.3	60.4
Milwaukee	90.5	83.9	73.9	69.5
New York	81.0	82.0	58.8	62.7
Newark	81.4	81.6	67.0	69.2
Philadelphia	79.5	78.8	68.2	69.6
Pittsburgh	75.0	72.7	53.5	54.1
St. Louis	84.7	81.3	76.5	72.9
San Francisco–Oakland	80.1	71.7	56.0	51.1
Average	84.5	80.1	68.7	66.1
Southern areas				
Atlanta	82.1	78.5	78.0	74.8
Baltimore	81.9	74.7	77.2	72.3
Birmingham	37.8	40.8	45.1	50.2
Dallas–Ft. Worth	86.9	77.1	76.0	64.0
Greensboro–Winston Salem	65.4	56.0	56.1	50.1
Houston	78.1	69.5	66.4	59.3
Memphis	75.9	71.6	78.0	75.9
Miami	85.1	77.8	75.2	64.2
New Orleans	73.1	68.3	71.3	68.8
Norfolk–Virginia Beach	75.7	63.1	73.5	62.8
Tampa–St. Petersburg	79.9	72.6	58.0	51.5
Washington, D.C.	81.1	70.1	77.2	68.0
Average	75.3	68.3	69.3	63.5

Source: Douglas S. Massey and Nancy A. Denton, "Trends in the Residential Segregation of Blacks, Hispanics, and Asians: 1970–1989," *American Sociological Review* 52 (1987):807–813, 815–16.

tion;[19] and in some metropolitan areas, suburbanization involved the expansion of white residential areas into territory inhabited by rural blacks.[20] As a result of these distinctive southern traits, segregation levels tend to be lower than in the north, particularly when measured at the tract level (it is considerably higher when measured at the block level—compare the 1970 columns of Tables 2.3 and 3.1).

Despite this propensity for lower segregation among southern metropolitan areas, ten of the twelve have 1980 segregation indices within the high range. In general, the larger, the more modern, and the more economically developed the metropolitan area, the higher the level of black-white segregation. The separation of the races is particularly severe in Atlanta, Baltimore, Dallas, Memphis, Miami, Tampa, and Washington, D.C., all of which had segregation indices over 70% in 1980. Although sizable declines were registered in rapidly growing areas such as Dallas, Houston, and Washington, the changes in most areas were modest. Moderate levels of segregation in Birmingham, Alabama, and Greensboro, North Carolina, stem from ecological features unique to urban areas in the south.

The two right-hand columns of Table 3.1 show 1970–1980 trends in the spatial isolation of blacks. These indices state the percentage of blacks living in the tract of the average African American; they measure the extent to which blacks live only among other blacks and gauge the potential for interracial contact within neighborhoods.[21] Isolation indices capture the experience of segregation from the viewpoint of the average black person. Their maximum value is 100%, which occurs when all black people live in all-black neighborhoods, thereby providing no opportunity for residential contact with whites.

When blacks are desegregated (i.e., evenly distributed among tracts), the index reaches its minimum value: the percentage of blacks in the metropolitan area. Thus the index depends on the racial composition of the urban area as well as on the geographic distribution of blacks. When the percentage of blacks is very small, even a relatively segregated (i.e., uneven) settlement pattern can yield a high degree of neighborhood contact with whites; but when blacks are a large share of the population, the chances for contact with whites tend to be low even when segregation is moderate.

The isolation indices reveal the full extent of black racial seclusion within U.S. metropolitan areas, both northern and southern. The average value changed little over the decade and remained close to 66% in both regions; and in 1980 no metropolitan area displayed an isolation index under 50%. Despite the legal banning of discrimination and the apparent easing of white racial hostility, blacks and whites were still very unlikely to share a neighborhood within most metropolitan areas. In many cases, the degree of black spatial isolation was extreme.

An index of 75%, for example, indicates a very profound degree of isolation in society that is roughly 20 points above the highest level ever recorded for any European ethnic group. As of 1980, blacks in four northern metropolitan areas (Chicago, Cleveland, Detroit, and Gary) and two southern areas (Atlanta and Memphis) equaled or exceeded this extreme level of racial isolation, and an additional eight metropolitan areas had isolation indices in the 65% to 75% range. African Americans in such cities are very unlikely to have significant social contact with whites unless they work within the larger white economy.

There are, however, several metropolitan areas where the isolation index falls close to 50%. As described earlier, such relatively low values may reflect the fact that blacks are not highly segregated, or they may simply mean that blacks comprise a small share of the population. Among northern cities, low levels of racial isolation generally stem from small black percentages rather than any clear trend toward integration. Boston, Cincinnati, Pittsburgh, and San Francisco, for example, all have isolation indices under 55%, yet all had black population percentages of 12% or lower and all had segregation indices above 70% in 1980.

In the south, lower indices in Birmingham and Tampa reflect the distinctive ecological organization of southern cities more than a decisive shift toward integration. Although Birmingham's segregation index is low, its value actually *increased* over the decade; and despite its decline, Tampa's black-white dissimilarity index remained well above 70% throughout the decade. Only Greensboro, North Carolina, displayed a consistent trend toward integration: its segregation score fell from 65% to 56%, and its isolation index was 50% (despite a relatively high black population percentage of 20%).

In sum, among the thirty largest black urban settlements in the United States, only one relatively unusual southern metropolis shows a pattern interpretable as a clear trend toward integration. In most areas, especially those in the north, the 1970s witnessed stable residential configurations that maintained a high degree of physical separation between the races and a high degree of spatial isolation among blacks. Although San Francisco displayed a noticeable decline in segregation, its index stayed high throughout the decade, and other evidence suggests that this apparent decline reflects a process of white-black displacement through gentrification rather than a true move toward integration.[22]

The high level of segregation experienced by blacks today is not only unprecedented compared with the experience of European ethnic groups; it is also unique compared with the experience of other large minority groups, such as Hispanics and Asians. When one considers the thirty metropolitan areas with the largest Hispanic populations, for example, Hispanic-white dissimilarity averaged only 49% in 1980, with a mean isolation index of 43% (compared with figures of 75% and 65% for blacks). Among the thirty largest Asian settlements, moreover, the average level of dissimilarity from whites was only 34%, and the isolation index was even lower at 23%. In fact, within most metropolitan areas, Hispanics and Asians are more likely to share a neighborhood with whites than with another member of their own group.[23]

The contrast between blacks, Hispanics, and Asians is well illustrated by the case of San Francisco, where each group makes up about 11% of the metropolitan population. In 1980, black isolation stood at 51%, compared with 19% for Hispanics and 23% for Asians, and the black segregation index of 72% was substantially higher than the Hispanic and Asian indices of 40% and 44%, respectively.[24] This contrast occurs within a region where black-white segregation had actually fallen in recent years. Thus, even under relatively favorable conditions, blacks are twice as isolated as Hispanics and Asians and about 60% more segregated.

Suburbanization and Segregation

The most salient feature of postwar segregation is the concentration of blacks in central cities and whites in suburbs. Although observers were initially optimistic about the prospects for integration when black suburbanization began in the early 1970s, relatively few blacks attained suburban residence during the decade in comparison with whites (see Table 3.2). Whereas an average of 71% of northern whites lived in suburbs by 1980, the figure for blacks was only 23%. Although rates of black suburbanization were higher in the south, the contrast was equally stark: only 34% of blacks in southern areas lived in suburbs in 1980, compared with 65% of whites. The classic pattern of a black core surround by a white ring persisted throughout the 1970s.

Blacks were extremely unlikely to live in the suburbs of Gary, India-

Table 3.2 Trends in black and white suburbanization in thirty metropolitan areas with largest black populations, 1970–1980

Metropolitan area	Whites		Blacks	
	1970	1980	1970	1980
Northern areas				
Boston	81.0	84.5	16.7	20.8
Buffalo	70.7	77.3	12.7	16.6
Chicago	62.2	72.8	10.0	15.8
Cincinnati	70.0	75.6	16.7	24.5
Cleveland	73.8	80.1	13.0	27.2
Columbus	52.0	63.0	7.8	18.9
Detroit	77.3	87.8	13.1	15.1
Gary–Hammond–E. Chicago	62.3	75.1	11.8	9.9
Indianapolis	36.4	43.4	2.2	1.8
Kansas City	50.9	60.2	2.1	4.8
Los Angeles–Long Beach	57.0	56.5	31.4	42.1
Milwaukee	53.3	62.1	0.8	2.4
New York	26.9	31.4	7.1	8.2
Newark	80.3	81.3	39.8	52.0
Philadelphia	67.6	73.5	21.4	26.7
Pittsburgh	81.5	84.7	38.0	42.6
St. Louis	81.7	87.2	32.7	49.3
San Francisco–Oakland	73.0	77.8	32.1	36.8
Average	64.3	70.8	17.2	23.1
Southern areas				
Atlanta	79.3	89.4	27.2	44.7
Baltimore	68.9	77.9	12.6	21.3
Birmingham	75.7	81.9	73.5	72.0
Dallas–Ft. Worth	53.5	64.3	12.6	15.3
Greensboro–Winston Salem	42.4	46.9	14.2	15.9
Houston	44.8	58.5	13.3	16.9
Memphis	20.6	19.0	19.1	27.4
Miami	85.9	90.8	57.9	68.4
New Orleans	55.6	69.6	17.7	20.6
Norfolk–Virginia Beach	24.3	27.3	24.0	32.0
Tampa–St. Petersburg	50.7	62.2	20.7	24.5
Washington, D.C.	90.5	91.7	22.7	46.2
Average	57.7	65.0	26.3	33.8

Source: Douglas S. Massey and Nancy A. Denton, "Suburbanization and Segregation in U.S. Metropolitan Areas," *American Journal of Sociology* 94 (1988):598–600.

napolis, Kansas City, Milwaukee, and New York, all of which had black suburbanization rates under 10%. Although Los Angeles, Newark, Pittsburgh, and St. Louis had relatively higher rates of black suburbanization (above 40%), in no case did the black rate approach that of whites. The metropolitan area where black suburbanization most closely approximated the white rate was Los Angeles, but the figure of 42% for blacks was still 15 percentage points lower than the white rate of 57%.

Relatively high levels black suburbanization in some metropolitan areas can be deceiving, however, because many black "suburbs" are simply poor, declining cities that happen to be located outside the city limits. Camden, New Jersey, for example, accounts for a sizable portion of Philadelphia's suburban black population, and East St. Louis, Illinois, likewise represents a large share of St. Louis's suburban blacks; but neither "suburb" fits the ideal of suburban life. In 1980, 32% of Camden's families fell below the federal poverty line, and in East St. Louis the figure was 39%. Poverty was more extensive and social dislocations more severe than in their corresponding central cities (where the poverty rate was only 17%).

As these examples show, black suburbanization often does not eliminate black-white disparities in residential quality. Indeed, suburbs that accept black residents tend to be older areas of relatively low socioeconomic status and high population density.[25] They are typically located adjacent to or near the central city and are relatively unattractive to white renters and home buyers.[26] Often they are older manufacturing suburbs characterized by a weak tax base, poor municipal services, and a high level of debt; they also tend to spend a large share of their revenues on social services.[27] In many ways, black suburbs replicate the problems of the inner city.

The figures on suburbanization in southern metropolitan areas again illustrate the distinctive nature of this region. Unlike in the north, blacks in the south have always lived outside of central cities; indeed, the vast majority of all African Americans once lived in the rural south. As urbanization proceeded during the twentieth century, and as outlying counties were progressively absorbed into larger metropolitan regions, rural blacks frequently were transformed into "suburbanites" without moving anywhere. There is also a long tradition of black suburban development in the south, going back to before the Civil War, when freedmen and "living out" slaves gravitated to the periphery to avoid white oversight.[28] This tradition was reinforced during the Jim Crow era by the development of black suburbs in order to strengthen racial segregation in housing.[29]

For all of these reasons, rates of black suburbanization in the south are generally higher than those in the north, and at times they can reach very high levels. In Birmingham, for example, over 70% of blacks lived outside the central city in 1980, and in Miami the figure was 68%. No metropolitan area in the south displayed a black suburbanization rate under 16% (compared with seven areas in the north) and by 1980 four areas displayed black suburban percentages of 40% or more. The overall black suburbanization rate of 34% in 1980 was 11 points higher than the northern figure of 23%.

Despite this advantage compared with northern blacks, however, rates of southern black suburbanization still lag behind those of whites—by a factor of nearly two to one on average. The contrast between black and white suburbanization was especially pronounced in larger industrial cities such as Atlanta, Baltimore, and Dallas. By far the largest increase in black suburban representation occurred in Washington, D.C. Between 1970 and 1980, the percentage of blacks living in Washington's suburbs doubled, going from 23% to 46%, but still lagged far behind the white figure of 92%.

In spite of blacks' increasing entry into suburbs, however, studies done in the 1970s and earlier suggest that suburban residence does not necessarily bring integration for blacks; rather, racial segregation persists in suburbs as well as in central cities.[30] Often black "suburbanization" only involves the expansion of an urban ghetto across a city line and does not reflect a larger process of racial integration.[31] As in central cities, once suburbs acquire a visible black presence, they tend to attract more blacks than whites, which leads to rapid racial turnover and the emergence of a suburban black enclave.[32] During the 1960s and 1970s, several black suburbs formed in this fashion, including areas such as Chillum, Suitland, and Hillcrest Heights in Prince Georges County, Maryland, just outside of Washington, D.C.[33]

The data in Table 3.3 suggest that this basic pattern of segregated black suburbs persisted through 1980, especially in the north, where there was no black settlement outside of cities prior to the suburban expansion. Among northern metropolitan areas, the average level of black-white segregation drops about 7 points going from central cities to suburbs (see the two left-hand columns), but this apparent effect of suburbanization testifies more to the extreme segregation of cities than to the low segrega-

Table 3.3 Degree of black segregation and isolation in central cities and suburbs of thirty metropolitan areas with largest black populations, 1980

Metropolitan area	Black-white segregation		Black isolation		% Black in suburbs
	Cities	Suburbs	Cities	Suburbs	
Northern areas					
Boston	78.9	54.1	66.8	10.3	1.5%
Buffalo	76.3	63.1	70.8	26.6	2.1
Chicago	90.6	75.4	89.9	45.4	5.5
Cincinnati	63.3	63.9	63.4	26.3	4.3
Cleveland	88.2	80.9	89.2	56.9	7.0
Columbus	69.8	62.1	62.9	33.2	3.8
Detroit	63.8	83.6	80.5	59.3	4.2
Gary–Hammond–E. Chicago	76.1	91.2	79.7	56.3	3.2
Indianapolis	70.7	69.4	63.3	4.2	0.6
Kansas City	75.8	46.8	72.3	4.3	1.2
Los Angeles–Long Beach	83.0	78.9	64.2	55.1	9.5
Milwaukee	76.8	63.4	71.1	2.6	0.5
New York	82.6	70.4	64.5	42.2	7.3
Newark	84.7	77.7	79.8	59.5	14.9
Philadelphia	83.5	65.0	81.1	38.1	7.7
Pittsburgh	76.5	63.7	71.8	30.3	4.0
St. Louis	83.7	75.7	86.7	58.7	10.5
San Francisco–Oakland	68.1	66.8	57.5	39.9	6.3
Average	77.4	69.6	73.1	36.1	5.2
Southern areas					
Atlanta	79.5	68.1	88.7	53.1	14.6
Baltimore	78.5	54.5	84.6	26.5	8.5
Birmingham	52.3	41.9	61.7	45.0	25.4
Dallas–Ft. Worth	77.6	55.7	71.8	24.3	3.9
Greensboro–Winston Salem	46.8	51.0	55.3	21.9	7.6
Houston	73.0	53.2	67.6	18.3	6.4
Memphis	75.1	56.7	77.6	65.1	41.2
Miami	77.5	75.4	75.9	58.8	14.7
New Orleans	61.8	58.5	75.7	42.0	12.4
Norfolk–Virginia Beach	68.1	48.6	68.1	50.8	32.6
Tampa–St. Petersburg	75.3	60.4	59.2	27.0	3.9
Washington, D.C.	75.6	55.4	88.3	43.7	16.5
Average	70.1	56.6	72.9	39.7	15.6

Source: Douglas S. Massey and Nancy A. Denton, "Suburbanization and Segregation in U.S. Metropolitan Areas," *American Journal of Sociology* 94 (1988):602–604, 610–12.

tion of suburbs. The average level of segregation in northern cities was 77% in 1980, compared with a figure of 70% in suburbs—both well within the range usually considered high.

Chicago remains the nation's most segregated central city with a dissimilarity index of 91%, followed by Cleveland, Newark, St. Louis, Philadelphia, Los Angeles, and New York. In all of these cities, at least 80% of blacks would have had to move to achieve a desegregated residential pattern; and all but two of the eighteen northern cities have indices in excess of 70%. Although levels of racial segregation are somewhat lower in suburban areas, only two cases display indices within the moderate range: Pittsburgh, with a suburban index of 54%; and Kansas City, with a suburban score of 47% (in the latter metropolitan area, however, only 5% of blacks live in suburbs). In five cases, suburban segregation equaled or exceeded that in central cities; and in suburban Gary, segregation reached an extreme equaled only in the city of Chicago. For blacks in the north, suburbanization during the 1970s generally brought not integration but, rather, a slightly less extreme form of segregation.

Owing to the special character of southern metropolitan development, however, racial segregation in suburbs of the south was less pronounced than in the north; but it was nonetheless very high in central cities. Eight of the twelve southern cities had segregation scores above 70% in 1980, and all except Birmingham and Greensboro were in the high range (above 60%). In contrast, nine of the twelve suburban areas had moderate levels of segregation (ranging from 42% to 59%), with especially modest values in Birmingham (42%) and Norfolk (49%). The average percentage of suburban blacks who would have to move to achieve an even residential configuration was 57%. Again, these modest levels of segregation reflect the distinctive nature of southern urban areas.

The third and fourth columns of Table 3.3 present isolation indices for blacks in central cities and suburbs. Because geographic isolation is affected by the relative number of blacks as well as by their spatial configuration, the fifth column shows the percentage of blacks in each suburban area. Because blacks make up an extremely small percentage of most suburbs, we expect a low degree of spatial isolation within them, other things equal.

Within central cities, however, black percentages tend to be high and the isolation indices show the by now familiar pattern of intense black isolation. In both regions, the average black isolation index in central cities was 73%, and values above 85% occurred in Atlanta, Baltimore,

Chicago, Cleveland, St. Louis, and Washington, D.C. Such intense levels of geographic isolation can only be achieved by distributing a large black population in an extremely uneven way. Meaningful contact with whites outside of the workplace is very unlikely in such places, an interpretation that acquires special poignancy when once considers that in 1982, 36% of black men in central cities were either unemployed or marginally attached to the labor force; and the figure was 54% for black men aged 18 to 29.[34]

In several northern suburbs, in contrast, the level of black spatial isolation is actually quite low, at times dramatically lower than in the central city. These exceptionally low levels of suburban isolation almost always occur in metropolitan areas where few blacks inhabit suburbs or where suburbs have very few blacks, and usually both. Although Boston, Indianapolis, Kansas City, and Milwaukee all display isolation indices under 10%, for example, blacks in these areas always make up less than 2% of the suburban population; and in all cases except Boston, fewer than 10% of blacks live in suburbs.

In fact, within most northern areas, black isolation in suburbs is remarkably high given the very small proportion of blacks they contain. In the suburbs of Chicago, Cleveland, Detroit, Gary, and Los Angeles, for example, the black isolation index exceeds 45%, even though blacks never exceed 10% of the total suburban population. In Newark and St. Louis, the isolation indices approach 60%, a high degree of isolation achieved by distributing their relatively large black populations very unevenly. In most northern suburbs, black isolation indices exceed their theoretical minimums by factors of four to ten.

Black isolation is generally greater in suburban areas of the south, owing to the larger representation of blacks within southern suburbs. Isolation indices are particularly high in Atlanta (53%), Memphis (65%), Miami (59%), and Norfolk (51%); and relatively high levels are also found in Birmingham (45%), New Orleans (42%), and Washington, D.C. (44%). In other metropolitan areas, however, isolation levels are more moderate.

In summary, during the 1970s, black-white segregation was maintained at high levels in most U.S. metropolitan areas, yielding high levels of racial isolation that were particularly intense within central cities. The characteristic pattern of black cities surrounded by white suburbs persisted, although distinctive ecological traits kept black segregation lower in some southern areas. Black suburbanization had begun in most metropolitan areas by 1980, but black entry into suburbs typically did not bring integration. On the contrary, suburban blacks experienced considerable segregation and isolation, both of which tended to be quite high in suburbs where blacks were represented in large numbers.

Hypersegregation

As forceful as the foregoing assessment of racial segregation is, it understates the magnitude of black segregation in U.S. metropolitan areas, for recent research has shown that segregation is not simply a matter of uneven settlement patterns and racial isolation within specific neighborhoods; it also matters where black neighborhoods are located.[35] Dissimilarity and isolation indices reveal nothing about the spatial arrangement of black community areas, which may be distributed over the urban landscape in a variety of ways.

In fact, segregation—or the general tendency for blacks and whites to live apart—may be conceptualized in terms of five distinct dimensions of geographic variation. The first two have already been discussed: blacks may be distributed so that they are overrepresented in some areas and underrepresented in others, leading to different degrees of *unevenness;* they may also be distributed so that their racial *isolation* is ensured by virtue of rarely sharing a neighborhood with whites. In addition, however, black neighborhoods may be tightly *clustered* to form one large contiguous enclave or scattered about in checkerboard fashion; they may be *concentrated* within a very small area or settled sparsely throughout the urban environment. Finally, they may be spatially *centralized* around the urban core or spread out along the periphery.

These five dimensions together define geographic traits that social scientists think of when they consider segregation. A high score on any single dimension is serious because it removes blacks from full participation in urban society and limits their access to its benefits. As segregation accumulates across multiple dimensions, however, its effects intensify. The indices of unevenness and isolation we have discussed so far cannot capture this multidimensional layering of segregation and, therefore, understate its real severity in American society. Not only are blacks more segregated than other groups on any single dimension of segregation, but they are also more segregated on all dimensions simultaneously; and in an important subset of U.S. metropolitan areas, they are very highly segregated on at least four of the five dimensions at once, a pattern we call hypersegregation.[36]

We consider the nature and prevalence of hypersegregation in U.S. metropolitan areas by presenting indicators for the five dimensions of segregation in 1980 (see Table 3.4). The first two columns repeat the indicators of unevenness and isolation included in Table 3.1. The third column contains an index of residential clustering developed by Michael White,[37] which measures the tendency for black areas to adhere together within one large agglomeration, rather than being scattered about the metropolitan area. It ranges from 0 to 100 and attains its maximum value when all blacks live together in one homogeneous black enclave; its minimum occurs when black settlement areas are interspersed in checkerboard fashion.[38]

The fourth column contains an index of centralization originally developed by Otis Dudley Duncan.[39] It assesses the extent to which blacks are spatially distributed close to, or far away from, the central business district. Residence near this district has long been associated with a relatively high level of crime, social disorder, and economic marginality.[40] The index varies between plus and minus 100, with positive values indicating a tendency for blacks to reside close to the city center and negative values signifying a tendency to live in outlying areas. A score of zero means that blacks have a uniform distribution throughout the metropolitan area. The index gives the proportion of blacks who would have to change census tracts to achieve a uniform distribution around the central business district.[41]

The index for the last dimension of segregation, concentration, is shown in the fifth column. It also varies between plus and minus 100, and was developed to measure the relative amount of physical space occupied by blacks within the metropolitan environment.[42] A score of zero is achieved when blacks and whites are equally concentrated within urban space and a score of −100 means that the concentration of whites exceeds that of blacks. The maximum value of 100 is achieved when blacks occupy the smallest neighborhoods possible within a metropolitan setting and whites occupy the largest possible neighborhoods.

In order to assess the prevalence of hypersegregation among U.S. metropolitan areas, we adopted an arbitrary set of cutpoints to determine what constitutes "high" segregation on each dimension. For simplicity, we consider any index that exceeds a value of 60 to be high. Metropolitan areas that display high segregation on at least four of the five dimensions are considered to be hypersegregated and are highlighted in boldface.[43]

According to these criteria, blacks in sixteen metropolitan areas were hypersegregated in 1980: Atlanta, Baltimore, Buffalo, Chicago, Cleve-

Table 3.4 Five dimensions of black segregation in thirty metropolitan areas with largest black populations (hypersegregated areas in boldface), 1980

	Dimension of segregation				
Metropolitan area	Unevenness	Isolation	Clustering	Centralization	Concentration
Northern areas					
Boston	77.6	55.1	49.1	87.1	79.9
Buffalo	**79.4**	**63.5**	**44.3**	**88.4**	**88.2**
Chicago	**87.8**	**82.8**	**79.3**	**87.2**	**88.7**
Cincinnati	72.3	54.3	15.8	88.3	66.9
Cleveland	**87.5**	**80.4**	**74.3**	**89.8**	**92.7**
Columbus	71.4	57.5	32.1	93.3	85.4
Detroit	**86.7**	**77.3**	**84.6**	**92.4**	**84.2**
Gary–Hammond–E. Chicago	**90.6**	**77.3**	**56.1**	**88.7**	**86.9**
Indianapolis	**76.2**	**62.3**	**41.1**	**94.2**	**80.4**
Kansas City	**78.9**	**69.0**	**46.1**	**92.1**	**85.7**
Los Angeles–Long Beach	**81.1**	**60.4**	**76.5**	**85.9**	**69.5**
Milwaukee	**83.9**	**69.5**	**68.9**	**95.1**	**94.4**
New York	**81.6**	**62.7**	**46.8**	**79.5**	**89.2**
Newark	**82.0**	**69.2**	**75.5**	**85.9**	**91.9**
Philadelphia	**78.8**	**69.6**	**67.3**	**85.5**	**75.7**
Pittsburgh	72.7	54.1	27.2	81.2	82.1
St. Louis	**81.3**	**72.9**	**26.4**	**93.1**	**89.3**
San Francisco–Oakland	71.7	51.1	28.2	83.6	68.7
Average	80.1	66.1	52.2	88.4	83.3
Southern areas					
Atlanta	**78.5**	**74.8**	**39.8**	**82.7**	**68.6**
Baltimore	**74.7**	**72.3**	**62.2**	**85.7**	**76.3**
Birmingham	40.8	50.2	5.9	83.0	77.5
Dallas–Ft. Worth	**77.1**	**64.0**	**33.4**	**74.9**	**69.3**
Greensboro–Winston Salem	56.0	50.1	5.3	60.1	61.3
Houston	69.5	59.3	23.8	84.0	56.9
Memphis	71.6	75.9	44.0	81.7	55.0
Miami	77.8	64.2	34.4	46.3	56.5
New Orleans	68.3	68.8	32.7	90.6	58.4
Norfolk–Virginia Beach	63.1	62.8	19.9	71.2	55.9
Tampa–St. Petersburg	72.6	51.5	24.6	58.1	49.3
Washington, D.C.	70.0	68.0	45.0	85.0	44.1
Average	68.3	63.5	30.9	75.3	60.8
"Hypersegregation" cutpoint	60+	60+	60+	60+	60+

Source: Douglas S. Massey and Nancy A. Denton, "Hypersegregation in U.S. Metropolitan Areas: Black and Hispanic Segregation along Five Dimensions," *Demography* 26 (1989):378–79.

land, Dallas, Detroit, Gary, Indianapolis, Kansas City, Los Angeles, Milwaukee, New York, Newark, Philadelphia, and St. Louis. The average level of unevenness in these metropolitan areas was 82, the average isolation index was 71, and the mean clustering index was 58; the centralization and concentration indices averaged 88 and 83, respectively. These sixteen metropolitan areas are among the most important in the country, containing six of the ten largest metropolitan areas in the United States. Together they house 35% of the nation's black population, and 41% of all blacks living in urban areas.

Thus one-third of all African Americans in the United States live under conditions of intense racial segregation. They are unambiguously among the nation's most spatially isolated and geographically secluded people, suffering extreme segregation across multiple dimensions simultaneously. Black Americans in these metropolitan areas live within large, contiguous settlements of densely inhabited neighborhoods that are packed tightly around the urban core. In plain terms, they live in ghettos.

Typical inhabitants of one of these ghettos are not only unlikely to come into contact with whites within the particular neighborhood where they live; even if they traveled to the adjacent neighborhood they would still be unlikely to see a white face; and if they went to the next neighborhood beyond that, no whites would be there either. People growing up in such an environment have little direct experience with the culture, norms, and behaviors of the rest of American society and few social contacts with members other racial groups. Ironically, within a large, diverse, and highly mobile post-industrial society such as the United States, blacks living in the heart of the ghetto are among the most isolated people on earth.

No other group in the contemporary United States comes close to this level of isolation within urban society. U.S. Hispanics, for example, are also poor and disadvantaged; yet in no metropolitan area are they hypersegregated. Indeed, Hispanics are never highly segregated on more than three dimensions simultaneously, and in forty-five of the sixty metropolitan areas we examined, they were highly segregated on only one dimension (typically centralization). Moreover, the large Hispanic community in Miami (the third largest in the country) is not highly segregated on any dimension at all. Despite their immigrant origins, Spanish language, and high poverty rates, Hispanics are considerably more integrated in U.S. society than are blacks.[44]

The measurement of multiple dimensions of segregation also highlights the ecological differences between northern and southern cities. Only three of the twelve southern metropolitan areas are hypersegregated, whereas twelve of the eighteen northern areas exhibit this pattern. In general, blacks in the south are less geographically concentrated, less confined to areas near the urban core, and scattered more widely around the metropolitan area. Thus even though black isolation within southern *neighborhoods* may be high, these neighborhoods are much less likely to form part of a large black *enclave*. In the south, the social worlds of blacks and whites continue to overlap, particularly in older, smaller, and less developed areas.

The Reproduction of the Ghetto

As described in Chapter 2, large black ghettos were created in American cities during the first half of the twentieth century by a distinct process of neighborhood transition. Whites, in essence, adopted a strategy of tactical retreat before an advancing color line.

The availability of computerized data allowed us to match 1970 and 1980 census tracts, thereby permitting us to determine whether this pattern of tactical retreat continued through the 1970s. Before the availability of computerized data, investigators were only able to examine patterns of racial transition within the neighborhoods of a handful of cities, and suburban areas were typically excluded.[45] Given the data at our disposal, however, we have been able to examine racial turnover in more than 20,000 census tracts located in central cities and suburbs of 60 metropolitan areas.[46]

Our results may be summarized by presenting estimated probabilities of white population loss and black population gain within different kinds of city and suburban neighborhoods (see Table 3.5). These figures reveal the population dynamics of neighborhoods located near to and far away from established black areas (those tracts that were greater than 50% black in 1980) and among neighborhoods that contained many and few black residents. These estimates control for the effects of black, Hispanic, and Asian population growth in the metropolitan area, as well as the age of the area's housing stock, the tightness of its housing market, its regional location, and its ethnic composition. We also control for each neighborhood's location relative to established Hispanic areas. The probabilities we have computed, therefore, are fairly "pure" indicators of the likelihood of black gain and white loss within different kinds of neighborhoods.

Table 3.5 Estimated probability of white loss and black gain within different kinds of urban neighborhoods, 1970–1980

Location and percentage black	Distance from nearest black neighborhood			
	Under 5 miles	5–10 miles	10–25 miles	25+ miles
Probability of White Loss				
City neighborhoods				
0%–5% black	.85	.61	.36	.29
10%–20% black	.89	.69	.44	.36
30%–40% black	.92	.77	.54	.46
Suburban neighborhoods				
0%–5% black	.74	.42	.21	.16
10%–20% black	.80	.50	.28	.22
30%–40% black	.86	.61	.37	.30
Probability of Black Gain				
City neighborhoods				
0%–5% black	.56	.56	.53	.41
10%–20% black	.62	.62	.60	.48
30%–40% black	.58	.58	.56	.44
Suburban neighborhoods				
0%–5% black	.50	.50	.47	.36
10%–20% black	.56	.56	.54	.42
30%–40% black	.52	.62	.50	.38

Source: Computed from equations presented in Table 4 of Nancy A. Denton and Douglas S. Massey, "Patterns of Neighborhood Transition in a Multiethnic World," *Demography* 28 (1991):56. Equations control for the presence or absence of other groups in the neighborhood, distance to nearest Hispanic area, ethnic composition of the metropolitan area, rates of white and minority population growth, job creation rate, home inflation rate, age of housing, and region. Blacks are assumed to be the only group present and all other control variables are evaluated at their means.

The characteristic postwar pattern of ghetto formation involved two sets of actions on the part of whites: discrimination against blacks to keep them from entering all neighborhoods except those near the ghetto border and the avoidance of those neighborhoods threatened with racial turnover. The estimates in Table 3.5 suggest that housing discrimination may have moderated somewhat, but that white avoidance of neighborhoods near ghettos continues unabated.

Evidence that discrimination has been reduced comes from the probabilities of black population gain. If old patterns of discrimination had continued, we would expect high probabilities of black gain in neighborhoods near established black areas and very small probabilities of black gain in others. In fact, the likelihood of black population increase was relatively high throughout the metropolitan environment, generally exceeding .50 in tracts up to 25 miles away from the nearest black area. The likelihood of black gain was also not particularly sensitive to whether the tract contained many or few black residents, or whether it was located in a central city or suburb. Only outlying areas more than twenty-five miles distant from the ghetto displayed relatively low probabilities of black gain. We found the same results when we examined the *pace* of black population gain in different neighborhoods.[47]

The probabilities of white loss, however, suggest that whites still avoid areas that are threatened by significant black settlement. Although results we have published elsewhere suggest that the mere presence of blacks no longer incites flight by whites,[48] the estimates in Table 3.5 reveal that whites are nonetheless highly cognizant of an area's location relative to the ghetto and are highly sensitive to the relative number of blacks that a neighborhood contains. Among neighborhoods located within five miles of an established black area, white population loss is extremely likely, and it becomes virtually certain as the percentage of blacks increases; this pattern holds for suburbs as well as for central cities.

The probability that a central city tract located within five miles of a black neighborhood would lose white residents between 1970 and 1980 was .85 when its black percentage was 0%–5% black; and it rose to .92 when the black percentage reached 30%–40%. The respective probabilities for suburban areas were .74 and .86. Only at distances beyond ten miles did the likelihood of white population loss fall below .50, and it reached truly low levels only at twenty-five miles from the closest black area. Yet even at these great distances from black settlements, whites were still sensitive to the percentage of blacks. In suburban areas twenty-five miles from the closest black neighborhood, the probability of white population loss increased from .16 in neighborhoods that were 0%–5% black to .30 in areas that were 30%–40% black. This basic pattern is replicated when we examine the pace of white population loss rather than its incidence.[49]

Thus the demographic mechanisms that led to the perpetuation of the ghetto in the 1950s and 1960s have remained largely intact through the 1970s. Whites continue to avoid neighborhoods located anywhere near established black areas, and they are highly sensitive to the number of black residents. Even though black population gains are now relatively likely within neighborhoods distant from the ghetto, this fact does not mean that discrimination against blacks has disappeared. Indeed, the probability of population gain for blacks remains significantly below that of whites in most neighborhoods and the rate of black population increase outside the ghetto is still quite low, suggesting that racial discrimination has persisted.[50]

The Never-Ending Story

Despite the optimism of the early 1970s, a comprehensive look at trends and patterns of racial segregation within large metropolitan areas in the ensuing decade provides little evidence that the residential color line has diminished in importance. Although segregation in southern cities and suburbs was at times moderate compared with levels in the north, this pattern predated 1970 and cannot be attributed to changes in federal housing policies, shifts in white attitudes, or reductions in racial discrimination. In the south, as in the north, there is little evidence of substantial change in the status quo of segregation.

On the contrary, among those metropolitan areas where a large share of African Americans live, segregation persists at extremely high levels that far surpass the experience of other racial or ethnic minorities. In sixteen metropolitan areas that house one-third of the nation's black population, racial separation is so intense that it can only be described as hypersegregation. Blacks in hypersegregated cities are unlikely to have any direct contact with the larger society unless they work outside of the ghetto; but according to recent data, up to 50% of young black men are at best weakly attached to the labor force.

Levels of segregation are particularly extreme in inner cities. Indeed, the systematic segregation and isolation of African Americans is in large measure realized by a spatial structure that concentrates blacks in central cities and whites in suburbs, a pattern that continued through the 1970s. But even the attainment of a suburban residence does not bring integration for most people of African origin. Except for a few areas where blacks are found in very small numbers, segregation and spatial isolation are maintained at high levels in suburbs as well as central cities.

It appears, therefore, that the black ghetto has remained a distinctive feature of the spatial organization of American cities. Whites continue to avoid neighborhoods located near the periphery of established black areas, and display considerable reluctance to enter neighborhoods containing black residents. Although the mere presence of blacks no longer guarantees automatic racial turnover and small numbers of blacks are now dispersed outside of ghetto areas, the probability of white loss still increases steadily as the percentage of blacks rises and as distance to the ghetto falls. The basic demographic mechanisms that originally created the ghetto still appear to operate with remarkable efficiency in perpetuating it.

The ghetto has endured despite the legal banning of discrimination in housing and the significant shift in white attitudes toward accepting the principle of open housing. It has survived the emergence of an increasingly large black middle class with the means to integrate, and it has persisted despite a series of court decisions forbidding the use of public housing to promote racial segregation.

4

The Continuing Causes of Segregation

Residential segregation has proved to be the most resistant to change of all realms—perhaps because it is so critical to racial change in general.

Thomas Pettigrew, 1966
review of **Negroes in Cities**
by Karl and Alma Taeuber

The spatial isolation of black Americans was achieved by a conjunction of racist attitudes, private behaviors, and institutional practices that disenfranchised blacks from urban housing markets and led to the creation of the ghetto.[1] Discrimination in employment exacerbated black poverty and limited the economic potential for integration, and black residential mobility was systematically blocked by pervasive discrimination and white avoidance of neighborhoods containing blacks. The walls of the ghetto were buttressed after 1950 by government programs that promoted slum clearance and relocated displaced ghetto residents into multi-story, high-density housing projects.

In theory, this self-reinforcing cycle of prejudice, discrimination, and segregation was broken during the 1960s by a growing rejection of racist sentiments by whites and a series of court decisions and federal laws that banned discrimination in public life. The Civil Rights Act of 1964 outlawed racial discrimination in employment, the Fair Housing Act of 1968 banned discrimination in housing, and the *Gautreaux* and *Shannon* court decisions prohibited public authorities from placing housing projects exclusively in black neighborhoods. Despite these changes, however, the nation's largest black communities remained as segregated as ever in 1980. Indeed, many urban areas displayed a pattern of intense racial isolation that could only be described as hypersegregation.

Although the racial climate of the United States improved outwardly during the 1970s, racism still restricted the residential freedom of black Americans; it just did so in less blatant ways. In the aftermath of the civil rights revolution, few whites voiced openly racist sentiments; realtors no longer refused outright to rent or sell to blacks; and few local governments went on record to oppose public housing projects because they would contain blacks. This lack of overt racism, however, did not mean that prejudice and discrimination had ended; although racist attitudes and behaviors went underground, they did not disappear. Despite whites' endorsement of racial equality in principle, prejudice against blacks continued in subtle ways; in spite of the provisions of the Fair Housing Act, real estate agents continued to practice surreptitious but widespread discrimination; and rather than conform to court decrees, local authorities stopped building projects.

Race versus Class: An Unequal Contest

Before exploring the continuing causes of segregation, we assess the extent to which the geographic separation of blacks and whites may be attributed to economic differences between the two groups. In the market-driven, status-conscious society of United States, affluent families live in different neighborhoods than poor families, and to the extent that blacks are poor and whites are affluent, the two groups will tend to be physically separated from one another. Is what appears to be racial segregation actually segregation on the basis of social class?

Economic arguments can be invoked to explain why levels of black-white segregation changed so little during the 1970s. After decades of steady improvement, black economic progress stalled in 1973, bringing about a rise in black poverty and an increase in income inequality.[2] As the black income distribution bifurcated, middle-class families experienced downward mobility and fewer households possessed the socioeconomic resources necessary to sustain residential mobility and, hence, integration. If the economic progress of the 1950s and 1960s had been sustained into the 1970s, segregation levels might have fallen more significantly. William Clark estimates that 30%–70% of racial segregation is attributable to economic factors, which, together with urban structure and neighborhood preferences, "bear much of the explanatory weight for present residential patterns."[3]

Arguments about whether racial segregation stems from white racism or from economic disadvantages are part of a larger debate on the relative importance of race and class in American society. Some observers hold that black social and economic problems now stem from the unusually disadvantaged class position of African Americans; they argue that black poverty has become divorced from race per se and is now perpetuated by a complex set of factors, such as joblessness, poor schooling, and family instability, that follow from the transformation of cities from manufacturing to service centers.[4] Other investigators place greater emphasis on racism; they argue that because white prejudice and discrimination have persisted in a variety of forms, both overt and subtle, skin color remains a powerful basis of stratification in the United States.[5]

Since the mid-1970s, the race-class debate has gone on without definitive resolution with respect to a variety of socioeconomic outcomes: employment, wealth, family stability, education, crime. But when one considers residential segregation, the argument is easily and forcefully settled: race clearly predominates. Indeed, race predominates to such an extent that speculations about what would have happened if black economic progress had continued become moot. Even if black incomes had continued to rise through the 1970s, segregation would not have declined: no matter how much blacks earned they remained spatially separated from whites. In 1980, as in the past, money did not buy entry into white neighborhoods of American cities.

The dominance of race over class is illustrated by Table 4.1, which presents black-white dissimilarity indices for three income groups within the thirty largest black communities of the United States. These data show the degree of residential segregation that blacks experience as their family income rises from under $2,500 per year to more than $50,000 per year. Although we computed segregation indices for all income categories between these two extremes, in the interest of brevity we only show one middle category ($25,000–$27,500). Little is added by including other income groups, because black segregation does not vary by affluence.[6]

Among northern metropolitan areas, for example, blacks, no matter what their income, remain very highly segregated from whites. As of 1980, black families earning under $2,500 per year experienced an average segregation index of 86, whereas those earning more than $50,000 had an average score of 83; blacks in the middle category displayed a score of 81. This pattern of constant, high segregation was replicated in virtually all northern urban areas. In Chicago, for example, the poorest blacks displayed an index of 91; the most affluent blacks had an index

Table 4.1 Segregation by income in thirty metropolitan areas with the largest black populations, 1980

Metropolitan area	Income category		
	Under $2,500	$25,000–$27,500	$50,000+
Northern areas			
Boston	85.1	83.9	89.1
Buffalo	85.2	80.0	90.0
Chicago	91.1	85.8	86.3
Cincinnati	81.7	70.9	74.2
Cleveland	91.6	87.1	86.4
Columbus	80.3	74.6	83.4
Detroit	88.6	85.0	86.4
Gary–Hammond–E. Chicago	90.6	89.5	90.9
Indianapolis	80.8	76.6	80.0
Kansas City	86.1	79.3	84.2
Los Angeles–Long Beach	85.4	79.8	78.9
Milwaukee	91.3	87.9	86.3
New York	86.2	81.2	78.6
Newark	85.8	79.0	77.5
Philadelphia	84.9	78.6	81.9
Pittsburgh	82.1	80.6	87.9
St. Louis	87.3	78.4	83.2
San Francisco–Oakland	79.9	73.7	72.1
Average	85.8	80.7	83.2
Southern areas			
Atlanta	82.2	77.3	78.2
Baltimore	82.4	72.3	76.8
Birmingham	46.1	40.8	45.2
Dallas–Ft. Worth	83.1	74.7	82.4
Greensboro–Winston Salem	63.2	55.1	70.8
Houston	73.8	65.5	72.7
Memphis	73.8	66.8	69.8
Miami	81.6	78.4	76.5
New Orleans	75.8	63.1	77.8
Norfolk–Virginia Beach	70.1	63.3	72.4
Tampa–St. Petersburg	81.8	76.0	85.7
Washington, D.C.	79.2	67.0	65.4
Average	74.4	66.7	72.8

Source: Nancy A. Denton and Douglas S. Massey, "Residential Segregation of Blacks, Hispanics, and Asians by Socioeconomic Status and Generation," *Social Science Quarterly* 69 (1988):811.

of 86. In New York, the respective figures were 86 and 79; and in Los Angeles they were 85 and 79. In no northern metropolitan area did blacks earning more than $50,000 per year display a segregation index lower than 72.

Although southern areas generally evinced lower levels of racial segregation, the basic pattern by income was the same: rising economic status had little or no effect on the level of segregation that blacks experienced. On average, segregation moved from 74 in the lowest income category to 73 in the highest, with a value of 67 in between. Segregation was particularly high and resistant to change in Atlanta, Baltimore, Dallas, Miami, and Tampa; but even in southern cities with relatively low levels of segregation, there was little evidence of a meaningful differential by income: the poorest blacks in Birmingham, Alabama, displayed a segregation index of 46, whereas the most affluent black families had a segregation index of 45.

One possible explanation for this pattern of constant segregation irrespective of income is that affluent blacks are not well informed about the cost and availability of housing opportunities in white neighborhoods. Reynolds Farley examined this possibility using special data collected in the University of Michigan's Detroit Area Survey. He found that blacks were quite knowledgeable about housing costs throughout the metropolitan area, even in distant white suburbs, and were well aware that they could afford to live outside the ghetto.[7] Whatever was keeping affluent blacks out of white areas, it was not ignorance.

The uniqueness of this pattern of invariant high segregation is starkly revealed when blacks are compared with Hispanics or Asians. In the Los Angeles metropolitan area, for example, the segregation index for Hispanics earning under $2,500 in 1979 was 64, and it declined to a moderate value of 50 among those earning $50,000 or more. In the largest Latino barrio in the United States, therefore, the *poorest* Hispanics were less segregated than the *most affluent* blacks (whose score was 79). Similarly, in the San Francisco–Oakland metropolitan area, which contains the largest concentration of Asians in the United States, the Asian-white segregation index fell from 64 in the lowest income category to 52 in the highest (compared with respective black-white indices of 86 and 79). These contrasts were repeated in cities throughout the United States: Hispanic and Asian segregation generally begins at a relatively modest level among the poor and falls steadily as income rises.[8]

Similar patterns are observed when segregation is examined by education and occupation. No matter how socioeconomic status is measured, therefore, black segregation remains universally high while that of Hispanics and Asians falls progressively as status rises. Only blacks experience a pattern of constant, high segregation that is impervious to socioeconomic influences. The persistence of racial segregation in American cities, therefore, is a matter of race and not class. The residential segregation of African Americans cannot be attributed in any meaningful way to the socioeconomic disadvantages they experience, however serious these may be.[9]

Attitudes in Black and White

Even if the segregation of African Americans cannot be linked to black socioeconomic disadvantages, it does not necessarily follow that current residential patterns are involuntary. It is conceivable, for example, that high levels of segregation reflect black preferences for racial separation, and that these desires for residential homogeneity are merely expressed through urban housing markets. If most black people prefer to live in neighborhoods that are largely black, then high levels of racial segregation may correspond to black desires for self-segregation and not discrimination or prejudice.[10]

This line of reasoning does not square with survey evidence, however. The vast majority of black Americans express strong support for the ideal of integration, and when asked on national surveys whether they favor "desegregation, strict segregation, or something in-between" they generally answer "desegregation" in large numbers. Although support for the "in-between" option rose during the 1970s, an average of 68% favored desegregation across the decade.[11] Moreover, 98% of black respondents have consistently agreed that "black people have a right to live wherever they can afford to," and in 1978 71% said they would be willing to vote for a community-wide law to ban racial discrimination in housing.[12]

In both principle and action, therefore, blacks strongly favor the desegregation of American society. They endorse the ideal of integration, they unanimously state that people should be able to move wherever they want to regardless of skin color, and they support the passage of laws to enforce these principles. But the endorsement of abstract principles and laws does not really get at the kinds of neighborhoods that blacks actually prefer to live in, or the degree of neighborhood integration they find attractive and comfortable. The most widely cited source of information on this issue is the Detroit Area Survey.

Respondents to the survey were shown drawings of hypothetical neighborhoods with homes colored in either black or white. The percentage of black homes was systematically varied and respondents were asked how they felt about different racial compositions. Blacks expressed a strong preference for racial parity in neighborhoods: 63% chose a neighborhood that was half-black and half-white as most desirable, and 20% selected this option as their second choice (see Table 4.2). Virtually all blacks (99%) said they would be willing to live in such a neighborhood. At the same time, blacks appeared to resist strongly complete segregation: nearly a third would not be willing to move into a neighborhood that was all black, and 62% would be unwilling to enter an area that was all white. Nearly 90% ranked all-white neighborhoods as their fourth or fifth preference, and 62% placed all-black neighborhoods into one of these rankings.

Among racially mixed neighborhoods, blacks seem to prefer those with a relatively higher black percentage, other things equal. Thus the second choice of most blacks (55%) was a neighborhood that was 70% black, and only 17% selected an area where whites clearly predominated; neighborhoods that were 15% black were generally chosen as the third most desirable neighborhood. Even though blacks prefer a racial mixture of 50% black or higher, however, they are comfortable with almost any

Table 4.2 Neighborhood preferences of black respondents to Detroit Area Survey, 1976

	Preference ranking					
Neighborhood composition	First choice	Second choice	Third choice	Fourth choice	Last choice	Percentage willing to enter such a neighborhood
All black	12%	5%	21%	35%	27%	69%
70% black	14	55	18	10	2	99
50% black	63	20	14	2	1	99
15% black	8	17	40	32	3	95
All white	2	3	7	21	66	38
Total	100%	100%	100%	100%	100%	

Sources: Reynolds Farley, Suzanne Bianchi, and Diane Colasanto, "Barriers to the Racial Integration of Neighborhoods: The Detroit Case," *Annals of the American Academy of Political and Social Science* 441 (1979):104; Reynolds Farley, Howard Schuman, Suzanne Bianchi, Diane Colasanto, and Shirley Hatchett, " 'Chocolate City, Vanilla Suburbs': Will the Trend toward Racially Separate Communities Continue?" *Social Science Research* 7 (1978):330.

level of integration: 95% would be willing to live in any neighborhood with a black percentage lying between 15% and 70%.

These expressed preferences for integrated living coincide with comments made by black respondents to survey interviewers, which suggest that blacks not only favor integration but are motivated by an ideological commitment to racial harmony: "When you have different kinds of people around, children understand better"; "I'd rather live in a neighborhood that is mixed—don't have any trouble, no hostility"; "It might make it better to get along with white people."[13] Thus black support for residential desegregation comes not simply from a desire to achieve the social and economic benefits associated with residence in a white neighborhood, which are very real, but from a real commitment to the ideal of racial integration.

Despite this ideological stance, however, blacks express considerable reluctance about entering all-white neighborhoods. On the Detroit Area Survey, for example, 66% listed this racial mixture as their last choice, and only 38% were willing to move into such an area. This apprehension does not reflect a rejection of whites or white neighborhoods per se, but stems from fears of white hostility, rejection, or even worse. Among blacks who said they would not consider moving into a white area, 34% thought that white neighbors would be unfriendly and make them feel unwelcome, 37% said they would be made to feel uncomfortable, and 17% expressed a fear of violence.[14] Moreover, four-fifths of black respondents rejected the view that moving into a white neighborhood constituted a desertion of the black community.[15]

Although the level of antiblack violence has declined since the 1920s, black apprehensions about entering white neighborhoods are by no means unfounded. Some 213 racial "hate crimes" were reported in Chicago during 1990, about half directed at blacks. These crimes included 57 incidents of battery, 18 cases of vandalism, and 28 reports of threats or racial harassment. As in the past, these incidents occurred mainly along the color line: of 1,129 hate crimes reported in Chicago during 1985–1990, half were located in ten community areas undergoing racial change.[16] The Los Angeles Commission on Human Relations reported 167 racially motivated hate crimes during 1989, representing an increase of 78% over the prior year. About 60% of the crimes were directed against blacks and about 70% occurred at the victim's residence. The specific complaints included 54 instances of racist graffiti or literature, 53 assaults, 34 acts of vandalism, 19 threats, 6 cross-burnings, and one case of arson.[17]

Blacks moving into white neighborhoods in other cities encounter similar treatment. In Philadelphia, for example, an interracial couple made national headlines in 1985 when it moved into a white working-class neighborhood and was met by an angry mob and fire bombs.[18] When Otis and Alva Debnam became the first blacks to buy a home in an Irish neighborhood of Boston, they experienced a sustained campaign of racial intimidation, violence, and vandalism that culminated in a pitched battle with white youths on the eve of the nation's bicentennial in 1976.[19] In New York City, an Italian American told the sociologist Jonathan Rieder about the treatment he and his friends gave to Puerto Rican and black families who invaded their turf: "we got them out of Canarsie. We ran into the house and kicked the shit out of every one of them."[20]

This evidence suggests that the high degree of segregation blacks experience in urban America is not voluntary. By large majorities, blacks support the ideal of integration and express a preference for integrated living, and 95% are willing to live in neighborhoods that are anywhere between 15% and 70% black. Those who express a reluctance to enter all-white areas do so because of realistic fears of violence and harassment. If it were solely up to them, blacks would live primarily in racially mixed neighborhoods and levels of racial segregation would be markedly lower than they presently are.

The issue is not solely up to blacks to decide, however, because their preferences interact with those of whites to produce the residential outcomes we actually observe. Even though blacks may prefer neighborhoods with a 50–50 racial mixture, desegregation will not occur if most whites find this level of racial contact unacceptable. The smaller the percentage of blacks that whites are willing to tolerate, the less likely integration becomes.

On the surface, whites seem to share this ideological commitment to open housing. According to one national survey, the percentage of whites who agree that "black people have a right to live wherever they can afford to" rose from 76% in 1970 to 88% in 1978.[21] The percentage of whites on another national survey who disagreed with the statement that "white people have a right to keep blacks out of their neighborhoods if they want to" increased from 53% in 1970 to 67% in 1980.[22] By 1978, only 5% of whites called for the strict segregation of American society.[23]

Clearly, by the end of the 1970s most whites had come to acknowledge the legitimacy of integration as a social goal and supported open housing as a basic principle. This ideological stance logically implies an acceptance of residential desegregation, because, given black preferences, an open housing market will yield substantial racial mixing within neighborhoods. But surveys also reveal inconsistencies in white attitudes. Although whites may accept open housing in principle, they remain uncomfortable about its implications in practice and are reluctant to support legislation to implement it. Moreover, negative stereotypes about black neighbors remain firmly entrenched in white psyches.

Unlike blacks, whites are more committed to open housing and residential integration in principle than in practice. Although 88% of whites in 1978 agreed that blacks have a right to live wherever they want to, only 40% in 1980 were willing to vote for a community-wide law stating that "a homeowner cannot refuse to sell to someone because of their race or skin color."[24] That is, as recently as 1980, 60% of whites would have voted against a fair housing law, even though one had been on the federal books for a dozen years.

Although whites may support fair housing in the abstract, their willingness to act on this ideal generally declines as the number of blacks increases. Whereas 86% of whites in 1978 said they would not move if "a black person came to live next door," only 46% stated they would not move if "black people came to live in large numbers."[25] Only 28% of whites in 1978 were willing to live in a neighborhood whose population was half black.[26]

Again, however, these questions about broad ideals and abstract principles do not really get at how whites feel about living with blacks, or how comfortable they are with different racial mixtures. When they are asked detailed questions about specific neighborhood racial compositions, it becomes very clear that whites still harbor substantial prejudice against blacks as potential neighbors, and that their tolerance for racial mixing is really quite limited.

We may summarize white neighborhood preferences using data from the Detroit Area Survey (see Table 4.3). As with blacks, whites were asked how they felt about hypothetical neighborhoods that contained black and white homes in different proportions. In their responses, whites indicated they were still quite uncomfortable with the prospect of black neighbors in practice, despite their endorsement of open housing in principle. Roughly a fourth of whites said they would feel uncomfortable in a neighborhood where 8% of the residents were black, and about the same percentage would be unwilling to enter such an area. When the black percentage reached 21%, half of all whites said they would be unwilling to enter, 42% would feel uncomfortable, and 24% would seek

Table 4.3 Neighborhood preferences of white respondents to Detroit Area Survey, 1976

Neighborhood composition	Percentage who would feel uncomfortable in neighborhood	Percentage who would try to move out of neighborhood	Percentage unwilling to move into neighborhood
8% black	24%	7%	27%
21% black	42	24	50
36% black	57	41	73
57% black	72	64	84

Source: Reynolds Farley, Howard Schuman, Suzanne Bianchi, Diane Colasanto, and Shirley Hatchett, " 'Chocolate City, Vanilla Suburbs': Will the Trend toward Racially Separate Communities Continue?" *Social Science Research* 7 (1978):335.

to leave. Once a neighborhood reached about one-third black, the limits of racial tolerance were reached for the majority of whites: 73% would be unwilling to enter, 57% would feel uncomfortable, and 41% would try to leave. At the 50–50 threshold, a neighborhood became unacceptable to all but a small minority of whites: 84% said they would not wish to enter a neighborhood that was 57% black, 64% would try to leave, and 72% would feel uncomfortable.

Whereas 63% of blacks picked a 50–50 racial mixture as the most desirable, the great majority of whites would not be willing to enter such a neighborhood and most would try to leave. Although blacks and whites may share a common commitment to "integration" in principle, this word connotes very different things to people in the two racial groups. For blacks, integration means racial mixing in the range of 15% to 70% black, with 50% being most desirable; for whites, it signifies much smaller black percentages.

This fundamental disparity between blacks and whites has been confirmed by surveys conducted in Milwaukee, Omaha, Cincinnati, Kansas City, and Los Angeles, all of which show that blacks strongly prefer a 50–50 mixture and that whites have little tolerance for racial mixtures beyond 20% black.[27] When the New York newspaper *Newsday* asked whites and blacks on suburban Long Island what "integration" meant to them, 64% of black respondents chose a neighborhood composition that was 40% black or higher, whereas 52% of whites selected a mixture that was 40% black or lower.[28] On a nationwide survey carried out by

Lou Harris in 1988, 69% of blacks said the races were better off living next to each other "in the long run," but only 53% of whites shared this sentiment.[29]

White apprehensions about racial mixing are associated with the belief that having black neighbors undermines property values and reduces neighborhood safety. According to the *Newsday* poll, 58% of Long Island's whites believe that property values fall once blacks enter a neighborhood[30] (in fact, evidence suggests the opposite, at least during the transition process[31]). Likewise, among whites in Detroit who said they would leave if blacks moved into their neighborhoods, 40% believed that property values would decrease after black entry, and 17% believed that the crime rate would rise.[32]

Given that a home is widely viewed as a symbol of a person's worth,[33] these views imply that whites perceive blacks to be a direct threat to their social status.[34] This interpretation is underscored by a 1985 study of white voters commissioned by the Michigan state Democratic Party. After carrying out a series of focus-group interviews in blue-collar suburbs of Detroit, the study concluded that working-class whites "express a profound distaste for blacks, a sentiment that pervades almost everything they think about government and politics . . . Blacks constitute the explanation for their vulnerability and for almost everything that has gone wrong in their lives; not being black is what constitutes being middle class; not living with blacks is what makes a neighborhood a decent place to live."[35]

The belief that blacks have deleterious effects on neighborhoods is consistent with a broader set of pejorative racial stereotypes. Among whites surveyed in the San Francisco area in 1973, for example, 41% believed that blacks were less likely to take care of their homes than whites; 24% said that blacks were more likely to cheat or steal; and 14% said that blacks were more prone to commit sex crimes.[36] Similar results were uncovered in the Detroit Area Survey: 70% of whites believed that blacks were less likely to take good care of their house and yard; 59% believed that blacks were prone to violence; 50% felt that blacks were not as quiet as whites; and nearly half believed that blacks were less moral than whites.[37]

When respondents in these samples were queried about the racial beliefs of others, moreover, they saw their fellow citizens as even more racially prejudiced than themselves (or at least more prejudiced than they acknowledged themselves to be). Whereas 56% of whites in Detroit said they would be willing to sell their house to a black family even if their neighbors objected, only 31% thought their neighbors would do the same.[38] Of whites in the San Francisco area, 70% said that "most Americans" believed blacks were likely to cheat or steal, and 60% said they thought that most Americans believed blacks were prone to commit sex crimes.[39]

These pejorative racial stereotypes are not local aberrations of San Francisco or Detroit; they are consistent with findings from recent national surveys. When Tom Smith of the University of Chicago's National Opinion Research Center asked respondents to compare blacks and other ethnic groups on a variety of personal traits in 1990, he found that 62% of nonblack respondents thought that blacks were lazier than other groups, 56% felt they were more prone to violence, 53% saw them as less intelligent, and 78% thought they were less self-supporting and more likely to live off welfare.[40] A 1988 survey by Lou Harris asked whites to evaluate blacks more directly, and 36% stated that blacks have less ambition than whites, 17% said they were less intelligent, 21% thought they were more likely to commit crimes, and 26% felt blacks were unable to get equal work at equal pay because they lacked a work ethic.[41]

Although overt expressions of racism are now publicly unacceptable, when questioned more specifically most white Americans still admit to holding a host of antiblack stereotypes. They continue to believe that blacks do not keep up their homes and are more prone to violence, and these negative images lead directly to fears that black neighbors lower property values and increase crime rates. These beliefs promote white resistance to black entry and avoidance of residential areas that contain black residents. Whites also display considerable aversion to the intimate contacts that inevitably grow out of residential proximity: 70% of whites in a 1978 national survey rejected interracial marriage on principle.[42] Perhaps for this reason, the negative view that whites have of black neighbors holds up even when one controls for neighborhood location, crime rate, upkeep, and cleanliness.[43]

The contrasting attitudes of blacks and whites create a huge disparity in the demand for housing in racially mixed neighborhoods. Given the harassment that historically has followed their entry into white areas, blacks express considerable reluctance at being the first to cross the color line. Once one or two black families have entered a neighborhood, however, black demand grows rapidly given the high value placed on integrated housing. This demand escalates as the black percentage rises toward 50%, the most preferred neighborhood configuration; beyond this point, black demand stabilizes until the neighborhood reaches 70% black, after which demand falls off.

The pattern of white demand for housing in racially mixed areas follows precisely the opposite trajectory. Demand is strong for homes in all-white areas, but once one or two black families enter a neighborhood, white demand begins to falter as some white families leave and others refuse to move in. The acceleration in residential turnover coincides with the expansion of black demand, making it very likely that outgoing white households will be replaced disproportionately with black families. As the black percentage goes up, white demand drops ever more steeply as black demand rises at an increasing rate. By the time black demand peaks at the 50% mark, practically no whites are willing to enter and the majority (64%) are trying to leave. It is no surprise, therefore, that most black households relocate within areas that are at least 50% black, whereas most white families move into neighborhoods that are overwhelmingly white.[44] As in the past, segregation is created by a process of racial turnover fueled by the persistence of significant antiblack prejudice.

Discrimination with a Smile

The foregoing model of racial change was essentially proposed two decades ago by Thomas Schelling.[45] He sought to show how rather small differences in racial tolerances between blacks and whites can lead to a high degree of residential segregation. According to the Schelling model, integration is an unstable outcome, because whites prefer somewhat lower minority proportions in neighborhoods than do blacks—even though whites might accept *some* black neighbors—and because racial preferences differ from person to person. As a result, when a black family moves into a formerly all-white neighborhood, at least one white family's tolerance threshold is exceeded, causing it to leave. Given strong black preferences for integrated housing, this departing white family is likely to be replaced by a black family, pushing the black percentage higher and thereby exceeding some other family's tolerance limit, causing it to leave and be replaced by another black family, which violates yet another white family's preferences, causing it to exit, and so on.

According to Schelling, therefore, black-white differences in racial preferences and interpersonal variability in racial attitudes build a self-perpetuating dynamic into neighborhood change that leads to rapid racial turnover and inevitable resegregation. By itself, however, the Schelling model is incomplete. Although it accurately captures the dynamic effects of prejudice, it accepts as a given the existence of racial discrimination. Black entry leads to neighborhood racial turnover not simply because of the interaction of white and black preferences but because the model implicitly assumes a racially segmented housing market maintained by discrimination.

Whites can only avoid co-residence with blacks if mechanisms exist to keep blacks out of most white neighborhoods. They can only flee a neighborhood where blacks have entered if there are other all-white areas to go to, and this escape will only be successful if blacks are unlikely to follow. Some method must exist, therefore, to limit black entry to a few neighborhoods and to preserve racial homogeneity in the rest. Although white prejudice is a necessary precondition for the perpetuation of segregation, it is insufficient to maintain the residential color line; active discrimination against blacks must occur also.

One mechanism that traditionally has been used to defend the color line is violence, as discussed in Chapter 2. Public opinion data make it plain that African Americans are still apprehensive about integration because of the violence they expect to follow. Although racial intimidation has declined in frequency and intensity, it still operates to sustain the walls of the ghetto. As a method of social control, however, violence has its drawbacks, and over time whites have shifted tactics to adopt less overt and more socially acceptable ways of defending the color line.

The most important of these mechanisms is racial discrimination. Evidence suggests that discriminatory behavior was widespread among realtors at least until 1968, when the Fair Housing Act was passed.[46] After this date, outright refusals to rent or sell to blacks became rare, given that overt discrimination could lead to lawsuits and prosecution under the Fair Housing Law. Realtors were no longer free to reject black clients as they walked through the door.

The absence of overt discrimination does not mean that exclusionary practices have ended, however; rather, the character of discrimination has changed. Black homeseekers now face a more subtle process of exclusion. Rather than encountering "white only" signs, they face a covert series of barriers. Instead of being greeted with the derisive rejection "no niggers allowed," they are met by a realtor with a smiling face who, through a series of ruses, lies, and deceptions, makes it hard for them to learn about, inspect, rent, or purchase homes in white neighborhoods.

Black clients who inquire about an advertised unit may be told that it has just been sold or rented; they may be shown only the advertised unit and told that no others are available; they may be shown only houses in black or racially mixed areas and led systematically away from white neighborhoods; they may be quoted a higher rent or selling price than whites; they may be told that the selling agents are too busy and to come back later; their phone number may be taken but a return call never made; they may be shown units but offered no assistance in arranging financing; or they may be treated brusquely and discourteously in hopes that they will leave.[47]

Although each individual act of discrimination may be small and subtle, together they have a powerful cumulative effect in lowering the probability of black entry into white neighborhoods. Because the discrimination is latent, however, it is usually unobservable, even to the person experiencing it. One never knows for sure. It may be true, for example, that the agent has no additional units to show the client right then, or that all agents are indeed busy. The only way to confirm whether or not discrimination has occurred is to compare the treatment of black and white clients who have similar social and economic characteristics. If white clients receive systematically more favorable treatment, then we conclude that discrimination has taken place.

Differences in the treatment of white and black homeseekers are determined by means of a housing audit. Teams of white and black auditors are paired and sent to randomly selected realtors to pose as clients seeking a home or apartment. The auditors are trained to present comparable housing needs and family characteristics, and to express similar tastes; they are assigned equivalent social and economic traits by the investigator. Typically the order of presentation is varied so that half the time the black auditor goes first, and the other half of the time the white auditor leads off. A sufficient span of time is left between encounters to prevent realtors from growing suspicious and linking the two cases. After each encounter, the auditors fill out a detailed report of their experiences and the results are tabulated and compared to determine the nature and level of discrimination.[48]

Local fair housing organizations began to carry out audit studies toward the end of the 1960s, and these efforts quickly revealed that discrimination against blacks continued despite the Fair Housing Law. A 1969 audit of realty companies in St. Louis, for example, documented a pattern and practice of discrimination that was sufficient to force four realtors to sign a consent decree with the U.S. Department of Justice wherein they agreed to change their behavior. A 1971 audit study carried out in Palo Alto, California, found that blacks were treated in a discriminatory fashion by 50% of the area's apartment complexes; and a 1972 audit of apartments in suburban Baltimore uncovered discrimination in more than 45% of the cases.[49]

Systematic housing discrimination apparently continued into the 1980s. A series of audits carried out in the Chicago metropolitan area, for example, confirmed that realtors still employed a variety of exclusionary tactics to keep blacks out of white neighborhoods. In one 1983 study, suburban realtors showed homes to 67% of white auditors but to only 47% of black auditors.[50] Another study done in 1985 revealed that whites were offered financial information at nearly twice the rate of blacks.[51] One developer working near Chicago's South Side black community refused to deal with blacks at all: blacks were *always* told that no properties were available, even though 80% of whites were shown real estate.[52] In the same 1988 study, realtors told 92% of whites that apartments were available but gave this information to only 46% of blacks.

Given its unusual history of racial animosity, Chicago might be dismissed as an extreme case, but audit studies of other metropolitan areas reveal similar patterns of racial discrimination. According to John Yinger's review of audit studies carried out in metropolitan Boston and Denver during the early 1980s, black homeseekers had between a 38% and a 59% chance of receiving unfavorable treatment compared with whites on any given real estate transaction.[53] Through various lies and deceptions, blacks were informed of only 65 units for every 100 presented to whites, and they inspected fewer than 54 for every 100 shown to whites.

In 1987 George Galster wrote to more than two hundred local fair housing organizations and obtained written reports of seventy-one different audit studies carried out during the 1980s: twenty-one in the home sales market and fifty in the rental market.[54] Despite differences in measures and methods, he concluded that "racial discrimination continues to be a dominant feature of metropolitan housing markets in the 1980s."[55] Using a very conservative measure of bias, he found that blacks averaged a 20% chance of experiencing discrimination in the sales market and a 50% chance in the rental market.

Studies have also examined the prevalence of "steering" by real estate agents in different urban areas. Racial steering occurs when white and black clients are guided to neighborhoods that differ systematically with respect to social and economic characteristics, especially racial composition. A study carried out in Cleveland during the early 1970s found that 70% of companies engaged in some form of racial steering;[56] and an examination of realtors in metropolitan Detroit during the mid-1970s revealed that, compared to whites, blacks were shown homes in less-expensive areas that were located closer to black population centers.[57]

Galster studied six real estate firms located in Cincinnati and Memphis and found that racial steering occurred in roughly 50% of the transactions sampled during the mid-1980s. As in the Detroit study, homes shown to blacks tended to be in racially mixed areas and were more likely to be adjacent to neighborhoods with a high percentage of black residents. White auditors were rarely shown homes in integrated neighborhoods unless they specifically requested them, and even after the request was honored, they continued to be guided primarily to homes in white areas. Sales agents also made numerous positive comments about white neighborhoods to white clients but said little to black home buyers.[58] In a broader review of thirty-six different local audit studies, Galster discovered that such selective commentary by agents is probably more common than overt steering.[59]

These local studies, however suggestive, do not provide a comprehensive assessment of housing discrimination in contemporary American cities. The only entity capable of undertaking this task is the federal government, and the first such effort was mounted by the U.S. Department of Housing and Urban Development (HUD) in 1977. The study covered forty metropolitan areas chosen to represent those areas with central cities that were at least 11% black. The study confirmed the results of earlier local housing audits and demonstrated that discrimination was not confined to a few isolated cases. Nationwide, whites were favored on 48% of transactions in the sales market and on 39% of those in the rental market.[60]

The HUD audit was large enough to develop measures of racial discrimination for a variety of different metropolitan areas. Among the thirty metropolitan areas discussed in Chapter 3, twelve were audited by HUD and the results are summarized in Table 4.4. Our index of discrimination is the percentage of real estate transactions in which whites were clearly favored.[61] Corresponding to overall patterns of segregation, discrimination appears to be more severe in the north than in the south. On average, whites in northern urban areas received more favorable treatment from

Table 4.4 Probability of encountering racial discrimination in selected U.S. metropolitan housing markets, 1977

	Percentage of encounters where whites are favored		Number of audits	
Metropolitan area	Rental units	Sales units	Rental units	Sales units
Northern areas				
Boston	46%	43%	119	78
Cincinnati	48	65	29	48
Columbus	52	63	29	40
Detroit	67	64	30	51
Indianapolis	64	54	28	50
Los Angeles	63	42	30	50
Milwaukee	32	53	108	80
New York	45	50	29	50
Average	52	54	50	56
Southern areas				
Atlanta	45	42	110	73
Dallas	40	41	114	80
Louisville	40	46	30	39
Tampa–St. Petersburg	53	34	30	44
Average	45	41	71	59

Source: Ronald Wienk, Cliff Reid, John Simonson, and Fred Eggers, *Measuring Racial Discrimination in American Housing Markets: The Housing Market Practices Survey* (Washington, D.C.: U.S. Department of Housing and Urban Development, 1979), pp. ES-21, ES-23.

Note: White favoritism defined to occur when white auditor receives favorable treatment on at least one of the following items and black auditors receive favorable treatment on none: housing availability, courtesy to client, terms and conditions of sale or rental, information requested of client, information supplied to client.

realtors in 52% of rental transactions and in 54% of sales transactions, whereas in southern cities the figures were 45% and 41%, respectively.[62] Blacks experienced an especially high degree of bias in the rental markets of Detroit, Indianapolis, and Los Angeles and in the sales markets of Cincinnati, Columbus, and Detroit. Blacks in these areas had at least a 60% chance of receiving unfavorable treatment on any given real estate transaction.

After a long hiatus, the 1977 HUD audit survey was replicated in 1988. Twenty audit sites were randomly selected from among metropolitan areas having a central city population exceeding 100,000 and a black percentage of more than 12%. Real estate ads in major metropolitan newspapers were randomly sampled and realtors were approached by auditors who inquired about the availability of the advertised unit; they also asked about other units that might be on the market. The Housing Discrimination Study (HDS) covered both the rental and the sales markets, and the auditors were given incomes and family characteristics appropriate to the housing unit advertised.[63]

The typical advertised unit was located in a white, middle to upper-class area, as were most of the real estate offices; few homes were in black or racially mixed neighborhoods. Even after controlling for the social and economic composition of its neighborhood, race was a strong predictor of whether or not a unit was advertised in the newspaper.[64] George Galster and his colleagues found a similar bias in the real estate ads of one large company in Milwaukee from 1981 to 1984.[65] Compared with homes in white areas, those in racially mixed or black areas were much less likely to be advertised, much more likely to be represented by one-line ads when they appeared, and much less likely to be favorably described. Real estate companies, it appears, do a poor job advertising and marketing homes in racially mixed neighborhoods, thereby restricting white demand for integrated housing and promoting segregation.

The HDS provides little evidence that discrimination against blacks has declined since the first nationwide assessment in 1977.[66] Indeed, results suggest that the earlier HUD study understated both the incidence and the severity of housing discrimination in American cities. This understatement occurred because the earlier methodology rested on several false assumptions about the effect of random errors in housing audits, and because the earlier analyses failed to control for the opportunity to discriminate.[67]

John Yinger analyzed the 1988 HDS audit data and applied statistical techniques that corrected for these methodological defects. Although the sample size of the HDS audit was not large enough to generate measures for specific metropolitan areas, the national estimates he derived proved to be much higher than those reported in earlier studies. According to his findings, housing was systematically made more available to whites in 45% of the transactions in the rental market and in 34% of those in the sales market. Whites also received more favorable credit assistance in 46% of sales encounters, and were offered more favorable terms in 17% of rental transactions.[68]

When housing availability and financial assistance were considered together, the likelihood of discrimination rose to 53% in both the rental and sales markets.[69] The sales audits also assessed the frequency of racial steering—or the systematic guiding of black clients to black or mixed neighborhoods and whites to white neighborhoods—and when this form of discrimination was considered as well, the likelihood that a black client would experience discrimination in the sales market rose to 60%.[70] Because these figures refer to the odds on any single visit to a realtor, over a series of visits they cumulate to extremely high probabilities—well over 90% in three visits. In the course of even the briefest search for housing, therefore, blacks are almost certain to encounter discrimination.

In addition to measuring the incidence of discrimination (i.e., the percentage of encounters where discrimination occurs), the HDS study also measured its severity (the number of units made available to whites but not to blacks). Table 4.5 summarizes Yinger's estimates of severity with respect to the availability of housing.[71] Because real estate agents were sampled through newspaper ads, the table presents estimates separately for advertised units and other housing units. These estimates control directly for the opportunity to discriminate, because if an agent truly has

Table 4.5 Severity of discrimination with respect to housing availability in U.S. metropolitan housing markets, 1988

	Probability that an additional unit was presented to white but not to black auditor			
	Rental units		Sales units	
Kind of discrimination	Advertised unit	Other units	Advertised unit	Other units
Inspected units	65%	62%	66%	76%
Recommended units	91	90	89	80
Total available units	64	75	88	76

Source: John Yinger, *Housing Discrimination Study: Incidence of Discrimination and Variation in Discriminatory Behavior* (Washington, D.C.: U.S. Department of Housing and Urban Development, Office of Policy Development and Research, 1991), Tables 42 and 44.

no additional units to offer clients, then blacks and whites *must* be treated equally no matter what the agent's proclivity for discrimination. Only if a realtor has additional units to show will he or she be in a position to discriminate against blacks by inviting them to see fewer units than whites, a consideration that needs to be taken into account in estimating the severity of discrimination.

The severity of housing discrimination is such that blacks are systematically shown, recommended, and invited to inspect many fewer homes than comparably qualified whites. As a result, their access to urban housing is substantially reduced. Among advertised rental units, the likelihood that an additional unit was shown to whites but not to blacks was 65%, and the probability that an additional unit was recommended to whites but not to blacks was 91%. The HDS auditors encountered equally severe bias in the marketing of nonadvertised units: the likelihood that an additional unit was inspected by whites only was 62%, whereas the probability that whites alone were invited to see another unit was 90%. Comparable results were found in urban sales markets, where the severity of discrimination varied from 66% to 89%. Thus, no matter what index one considers, between 60% and 90% of the housing units made available to whites were not brought to the attention of blacks. Yinger's estimates suggest that when realtors have a chance to discriminate, they usually do.

The 1988 HDS audit found equally severe discrimination in the provision of credit assistance to home buyers. Out of every 100 additional opportunities that agents took to discuss a fixed-rate mortgage, 89 of the discussions were with whites alone, and out of 100 times that adjustable rate loans were brought up, in 91 of the cases blacks were excluded from the discussion.[72] Blacks not only see fewer homes and get fewer recommendations, therefore, they also have more difficulty arranging financing.

Although racial steering proved not to be as widespread or severe as other forms of discrimination, the HDS did find that blacks are guided to areas that are less affluent and less predominantly white than those where white home buyers are taken. The study developed a composite index to assess the prevalence of steering with respect to three neighborhood attributes: racial composition, per capita income, and median home values. Steering was defined to occur if, compared with white auditors, blacks were shown homes in areas that had more minorities, lower home values, or lower median incomes. Defined in this way, systematic steering occurred in about one of every three encounters beyond the advertised unit.[73]

These rigorous nationwide findings only confirm what blacks have been saying for years: that housing discrimination has continued despite the 1968 Fair Housing Act. In one national survey carried out in 1977, 74% of blacks said they perceived discrimination in housing.[74] When queried in 1990 by *Newsday* about housing conditions on suburban Long Island, one-fifth of black respondents said they had experienced discrimination while trying to rent an apartment, and 21% said they had encountered bias while trying to buy a house.[75] Nearly a quarter of blacks interviewed in a 1989 *USA Today* poll said they had encountered prejudice while seeking housing, and the number rose to 36% among blacks with incomes over $50,000 (the group most likely to attempt integration).[76] Nearly two-thirds of blacks responding to a 1988 Lou Harris poll thought they fared less well with respect to housing than other groups with the same income and education.[77] Given the subtlety of housing bias today, moreover, these figures most likely underrepresent the extent of discrimination these respondents actually experienced.

The black ghetto, however, was maintained not only by the discriminatory actions of real estate agents but also by the racially biased practices of financial institutions. As described in Chapter 2, various federal banking agencies, contributed to the institutionalization of racial discrimination by rating anyplace in or near a black neighborhood as not worthy of credit. Areas containing minorities were systematically cut off from mortgage monies and home improvement loans.[78]

Government-produced rating maps continue not only to influence the provision of federally insured loans but to serve as important guides for private lending decisions.[79] In their survey of banking practices in Boston during the mid-1970s, for example, Harriet Taggart and Kevin Smith several times stumbled on FHA maps in bank offices that delineated minority neighborhoods in certain cities as "high risk areas" with "adverse environmental factors" and "questionable economic viability."[80] As late as 1970, examiners from the Federal Home Loan Bank Board routinely red-lined postal zipcode areas in which the percentage of blacks was rising.[81]

Until quite recently, it was difficult to measure precisely the extent of the disinvestment in black, inner-city neighborhoods; neither the government nor private lending institutions published information on the number and size of loans made to different areas of cities. Only one study, that of Karen Orren, was able to document conclusively the withdrawal of funds from black neighborhoods, and it covered a rather specialized segment of the credit industry.

Orren obtained information on mortgages held by life insurance companies in different census tracts of Cook County, Illinois, between 1935 and 1966. Her analysis revealed that black neighborhoods were completely cut off from life insurance mortgage funds until 1955, and after that date only token investments were made.[82] As the number of minority tracts increased through black in-migration, moreover, larger and larger shares of the city were marked for disinvestment. The percentage of city tracts that received *no* mortgage money rose from 23% in 1945–1954 to 30% in 1955–1964, and finally reached 67% during 1965–1966.[83] By the mid-1960s, life insurance companies had virtually written off the city and shifted their lending portfolios to the suburbs. This decision was taken primarily on racial grounds. As one company executive put it: "There is one big fear—that the city of Chicago will be controlled by minorities."[84]

The ability to detect and measure racial bias in home lending was improved in 1975 when Congress passed, over the protests of the banking industry, the Home Mortgage Disclosure Act, which requires depository institutions to identify the number and size of the loans they make to specific neighborhoods. Since then researchers have carried out detailed studies of mortgage lending practices. Most of these analyses use statistical models to predict the number and size of loans made within different census tracts based on their geographic location, social traits, and economic characteristics. If racial composition remains a significant predictor after these characteristics are held constant, investigators suspect that some form of racial discrimination is at work.

Despite the diverse array of characteristics that have been controlled in different studies, one result consistently emerges: black and racially mixed neighborhoods receive less private credit, fewer federally insured loans, fewer home improvement loans, and less total mortgage money than socioeconomically comparable white neighborhoods.[85] A study in Boston, for example, found that the ratio of loans to potentially mortgageable housing units was significantly lower in black areas, even after taking into account neighborhood characteristics such as median income, wealth, housing value, and local development activity. After these factors were controlled, a 24% gap in lending rates remained between black and white areas.[86] Another study in Boston compared the amount of money deposited in neighborhood savings institutions with the amount of money reinvested in the neighborhood through mortgages and found a substantial exportation of funds from the city to the suburbs; the level of disinvestment was especially pronounced in minority neighborhoods.[87]

Many early studies of home lending were criticized for not adequately adjusting for differences in housing demand between white and black neighborhoods.[88] When studies have attempted to control directly for demand conditions, however, they have still uncovered a systematic bias against black and racially mixed neighborhoods.[89] Richard Hula, for example, used a series of economic indicators to derive the distribution of loans that should have occurred through the market in Dallas County, Texas. He then compared this market distribution with the observed distribution of loans and found that white suburban neighborhoods were characterized by a relative surplus of mortgage capital whereas black and inner-city areas experienced a sizeable deficit. Moreover, the shortfall tended to increase as the percentage of blacks grew; and those areas that received the most mortgage money were those where the percentage of blacks was *declining*.[90]

As Hula's study of Dallas suggests, the degree of disinvestment depends partly on the relative number of blacks involved. In their study of FHA lending patterns in Milwaukee between 1983 and 1984, Gregory Squires and William Velez found that city loan activity followed a U-shaped pattern as the black percentage changed.[91] Loan activity was high in all-white neighborhoods, fell to a minimum at around 55% black, and then increased somewhat. Other studies report similar a pattern: recently integrated tracts with modest black populations experience the greatest underinvestment compared with areas that are either predominantly white or predominantly black.[92] Banks appear to be most apprehensive about the instability associated with neighborhood change. Faced with initial black in-migration, banks reduce credit; but once a stable black neighborhood has been achieved, credit is increased to a level closer to market demand (although never to the same level as in white neighborhoods).

The failure to support recently integrated neighborhoods with credit, therefore, institutionally restricts white demand for racially mixed neighborhoods and builds resegregation structurally into urban housing markets. Not only does a neighborhood's racial composition affect the *amount* of mortgage money loaned, however, it also determines the *kind* of credit it receives. Anne Shlay found that conventional home mortgages flowed mainly to suburbs and gentrified parts of the city of Chicago during 1980 to 1983, while minority neighborhoods in the inner city depended on FHA financing, a pattern that has been observed by other investigators as well.[93] Shlay also showed that FHA loans did not compensate for the shortfall in conventional mortgages, and that black neighborhoods received significantly less investment as a result. This systematic disinvestment in black neighborhoods was not related to the age of housing, but was clearly attributable to racial composition.

Given the widespread attention paid to the effect of neighborhood composition on lending rates, there are surprisingly few examinations of discrimination against blacks as individuals. One study by Harold Black and Robert Schweitzer examined mortgage loan applications to a "large commercial bank" in a "large metropolitan area" during the first six months of 1978. After controlling for various social, economic, and neighborhood characteristics, they found that whites received systematically lower interest rates and longer repayment periods.[94]

In 1989, reporters working for the *Atlanta Constitution* carried out what is perhaps the largest single study of racial discrimination in home lending ever conducted in the United States.[95] Using data obtained through the Freedom of Information Act, they systematically examined 10 million applications to savings and loan associations between 1983 and 1988. They found that blacks were substantially disadvantaged in the loan application process compared with other groups. The overall rejection rate was 11% for whites but 24% for blacks; and in three of the five years examined, high-income blacks were rejected more often than low-income whites in thirty-five metropolitan areas. Although long-term trends in rejection rates could be charted only within seventeen metropolitan areas, the racial differential was widening in thirteen areas, including Atlanta, Baltimore, Buffalo, Chicago, Cleveland, Memphis, Tampa, and Washington, D.C.

Similarly, the *New York Times* reported in 1991 that unpublished data from the Federal Reserve showed dramatic racial disparities in loan-rejection rates that could not be explained by income.[96] The Manufacturers Hanover Trust Company of New York, for example, rejected 43% of its mortgage applications from high-income blacks, but only 18% from high-income whites. Similarly, NCNB Bank of Texas rejected 36% of its middle-income black applicants in Houston but only 13% of middle-income whites; and the rejection rate for blacks seeking mortgages from the Bank of America in San Francisco was 39% for blacks, but 26% for whites.

These results confirm statements made by black respondents to social survey interviewers. According to Louis Pol and his colleagues, a significantly higher percentage of blacks than whites say they expect to encounter discrimination in the home lending market. This anticipated discrimination, in turn, plays an important role in lowering the probability that an individual black family will own a home.[97] Seeing the cards so obviously stacked against them, many otherwise qualified African Americans simply abandon their quest to purchase a home without really trying.

The Continuing Significance of Race

Putting together the trends in segregation discussed in Chapter 3 with the evidence on prejudice and discrimination reviewed here leads to three conclusions. First, residential segregation continues unabated in the nation's largest metropolitan black communities, and this spatial isolation cannot be attributed to class. Second, although whites now accept open housing in principle, they have not yet come to terms with its implications in practice. Whites still harbor strong antiblack sentiments and they are unwilling to tolerate more than a small percentage of blacks in their neighborhoods. Third, discrimination against blacks is widespread and continues at very high levels in urban housing markets.

Although these conclusions may provide a damning indictment of theoretically "color-blind" markets, they do not conclusively prove that prejudice and discrimination cause segregation. The persistence of prejudice, discrimination, and segregation in American cities strongly suggests a possible causal connection, but a mere coincidence of trends does not necessarily link racist attitudes and behaviors to segregation. We have shown only that three conceptually related conditions persist across time, not that they are causally connected.

Fortunately, several studies have been carried out to document and quantify the link between discrimination, prejudice, and segregation. Using data from the 1977 HUD audit study, George Galster related cross-metropolitan variation in housing discrimination to the degree of racial segregation in different urban areas.[98] He confirmed the empirical link between discrimination and segregation, and he also discovered that segregation itself has important feedback effects on socioeconomic status.[99] Not only does discrimination lead to segregation, but segregation, by restricting economic opportunities for blacks, produces interracial economic disparities that incite further discrimination and more segregation.

Galster has also shown that white prejudice and discrimination are connected to patterns of racial change within neighborhoods. In a detailed study of census tracts in the Cleveland area, he found that neighborhoods that were all white or racially changing evinced much higher rates of discrimination than areas that were stably integrated or predominantly black.[100] The pace of racial change was also strongly predicted by the percentage of whites who agreed with the statement that "white people have a right to keep blacks out of their neighborhoods." Areas with a high degree of racist sentiment experienced systematic white population loss after only a few blacks had entered, and the speed of transition accelerated rapidly after the population became only 3% black. Tracts where whites expressed a low degree of racist sentiment, however, showed little tendency for white flight up to a population composition of around 40% black.[101]

These studies confirm a strong link between levels of prejudice and discrimination and the degree of segregation and spatial isolation that blacks experience. The accumulated information on the persistence of prejudice, the continuation of discrimination, and their close connection to racial segregation underscore the continued salience of race in American society and suggest that race remains the dominant organizing principle of U.S. urban housing markets. When it comes to determining where, and with whom, Americans live, race overwhelms all other considerations.

This conclusion, however, may appear to be challenged by certain trends in segregation we have not fully explored here. By focusing on the largest black communities in the United States, does our analysis overstate the persistence of racial segregation? By concentrating on large, older industrial areas in the northeast and midwest, we fail to mention a substantial and marked decline in black segregation that occurred in some small and mid-sized metropolitan areas in the south and west. In fact, the level of black-white segregation fell by more than 10 points in twenty-two of the sixty largest metropolitan areas between 1970 and 1980.[102] Consistent with this finding, Barrett Lee and his colleagues report that, by the 1980s, racial turnover was relatively unlikely in the neighborhoods of smaller southern and western cities.[103]

Such large and widespread declines in segregation are unprecedented in urban America, and they led Reynolds Farley to conclude that they are "indicative of declining racism."[104] Scott McKinney has similarly concluded that "the decade of the 1970s witnessed substantial progress in integrating residential neighborhoods in metropolitan areas."[105] We believe, however, that rather than indicating significant racial progress, these declines in segregation paradoxically confirm the persisting significance of race in the United States. Instead of indicating an end to prejudice, they more accurately reveal the new character that prejudice has assumed.

As we discussed earlier, although large majorities of whites agree that people should be free to live wherever they want to regardless of skin color, most would not vote for a community law to implement this principle, and most would not want to live in a neighborhood where more than a small percentage of the families were black. This ambivalent attitude implies entirely different behaviors and outcomes in urban areas with large and small black populations.[106]

If whites accept integration in principle but remain fearful of living with blacks in practice, then blacks are more likely to be tolerated as neighbors when they constitute a small share of the population than when they are a relatively large proportion. When the number of blacks is small, an open housing market yields neighborhood racial compositions that are within the limits of white tolerance, and fears of resegregation are muted by the small number of potential black in-migrants. In a city with a large black population, however, an open market generates neighborhood racial compositions that are unacceptable to the vast majority of whites, and fears of resegregation are strong because the number of blacks seeking entry is potentially very large.

As the proportion of blacks in an urban area rises, therefore, progressively higher levels of racial segregation must be imposed in order to keep the probability of white-black contact within levels that are tolerable to whites.[107] In urban areas where racial composition is such that open housing can be implemented without threatening white preferences for limited contact with blacks, desegregation should occur; but in areas where relatively large numbers of blacks imply a high degree of black-white mixing under an open market, racial segregation will be maintained.[108]

This is precisely what happened in American metropolitan areas during the 1970s. Virtually all of the areas that experienced sharp declines in segregation had small black percentages, so that in spite of rapid desegregation, the probability of white-black contact within neighborhoods did not increase noticeably. In Tucson, for example, the level of black-white segregation fell by 24 points between 1970 and 1980 (from 71 to 47), but because the percentage of blacks in the metropolitan area was so small (under 3%), the probability of white-black contact rose only from .017 to .021.[109] Despite the massive desegregation of Tucson's black community, in other words, the percentage of blacks in the neighborhood of the average white resident moved only from 1.7% to 2.1%.

In U.S. metropolitan areas, the likelihood of white-black contact rarely exceeds 5% no matter what the trends in segregation have been. Douglas Massey and Andrew Gross have derived a formula that computes the degree of segregation that is required to keep neighborhood racial mixtures at 5% black or less.[110] Their formula depends primarily on the relative number of blacks in the metropolitan area: when the black percentage is low, little or no segregation needs to be applied to keep white-black contact within limits tolerable to most whites; but as the black percentage increases, progressively higher levels of segregation must be enforced to keep neighborhood racial compositions within these bounds.

According to their calculations, essentially no residential segregation needed to be imposed on blacks to keep the likelihood of white-black contact under 5% in areas such as Denver, Seattle, Tucson, and Phoenix, where large declines did take place, but levels of 85 or above were required in Chicago, Cleveland, Detroit, Philadelphia, and New York, precisely those areas where little change occurred. In statistical terms, the hypothetical level of segregation required to keep white-black contact low strongly predicted whether or not a decline, in fact, occurred, and the extent of the decline was strongly correlated with the size of the shift.[111] Desegregation only occurred in those metropolitan areas where the number of blacks was relatively small and where an open housing market would not lead to significant racial mixing within neighborhoods.

The persisting significance of race can be demonstrated in one final way: by considering patterns of segregation among Caribbean Hispanics. In the United States, this group consists mainly of Puerto Ricans and Cubans, but also includes Dominicans, Panamanians, and others. Caribbean Hispanics are distinguished from native whites by their use of the Spanish language, their common Spanish colonial heritage, their Latin Catholicism, and their remarkable racial diversity. Owing to a unique history of slavery and miscegenation quite distinct from that in the United States, Hispanics originating in the Caribbean region display a wide variety of racial characteristics and identities: some consider themselves black, others call themselves white, and large numbers identify themselves as something in-between black and white, a mixture of European and African origins.[112]

This racial diversity creates a natural experiment that allows us to examine the effects of race on segregation while holding ethnicity constant. Caribbean Hispanics of all races entered the United States under similar conditions and have the same cultural background, class composition, and family characteristics. Indeed, dark-skinned and light-skinned Hispanics are frequently members of the same family; what differentiates them is race and the way that it is treated in U.S. housing markets. If black and racially mixed Hispanics prove to be more segregated than white Hispanics, this fact cannot easily be attributed to different preferences or tastes. Rather, the segregation of African-origin Hispanics provides strong proof of the crucial role of race in determining residential outcomes.

We compiled segregation indices for Hispanics in ten metropolitan areas where Latinos of Caribbean origin predominate (see Table 4.6). Hispanic-white dissimilarity indices are calculated for three different Hispanic racial groups: those who said they were white, those who said they were black, and those who identified themselves as something in-between. From these figures, it is apparent that race is a powerful determinant of segregation, even among an otherwise homogeneous ethnic

Table 4.6 Indices of segregation of Hispanics in three racial groups from whites in ten metropolitan areas, 1980

Metropolitan area	White Hispanics	Mixed-race Hispanics	Black Hispanics
Boston	44.8	79.0	85.1
Chicago	57.0	74.0	85.2
Jersey City	49.0	54.3	68.1
Los Angeles	53.2	64.0	77.0
Miami	51.9	66.2	71.5
Nassau-Suffolk	31.7	63.2	79.4
New York	56.7	76.8	81.1
Newark	61.8	78.1	84.2
Paterson	67.4	80.0	83.8
Philadelphia	45.7	83.4	84.4
Average	51.9	71.9	80.0

Source: Nancy A. Denton and Douglas S. Massey, "Racial Identity among Caribbean Hispanics: The Effect of Double Minority Status on Residential Segregation," *American Sociological Review* 54 (1980):803.

group. The average level of segregation increases steadily as one moves from white Hispanics, with an index of 52, to mixed-race Hispanics, with an index of 72, to black Hispanics, whose index of 80 is comparable to that observed for black Americans.

The New York metropolitan area houses the largest single concentration of Caribbeans in the United States. Here white Hispanics are moderately segregated from whites at 57, whereas those who are black or racially mixed are highly segregated at 81 and 77, respectively. Similar patterns are replicated in all of the other metropolitan areas, a contrast that persists even when adjustments are made for socioeconomic differences between the racial categories.[113] And John Yinger has shown, using 1988 HDS audit data, that dark-skinned Hispanics are significantly more likely to encounter discriminatory treatment in metropolitan housing markets than are those with light skin, a finding that has been replicated in at least one local study.[114]

When it comes to housing and residential patterns, therefore, race is the dominant organizing principle. No matter what their ethnic origin, economic status, social background, or personal characteristics, African Americans continue to be denied full access to U.S. housing markets. Through a series of exclusionary tactics, realtors limit the likelihood of black entry into white neighborhoods and channel black demand for housing into areas that are within or near existing ghettos. White prejudice is such that when black entry into a neighborhood is achieved, that area becomes unattractive to further white settlement and whites begin departing at an accelerated pace. This segmentation of black and white housing demand is encouraged by pervasive discrimination in the allocation of mortgages and home improvement loans, which systematically channel money away from integrated areas. The end result is that blacks remain the most spatially isolated population in U.S. history.

5

The Creation of Underclass Communities

The pathologies of the ghetto community perpetuate themselves through cumulative ugliness, deterioration, and isolation and strengthen the Negro's sense of worthlessness.

Kenneth B. Clark

The mass migration of blacks from the rural south to the industrial north during the early twentieth century radically transformed urban black life.[1] In the space of a few years, a small, dispersed, and integrated community became a large, compact, and highly segregated ghetto. Before the great migration, northern blacks were led by an elite of professionals, artisans, and service workers who catered to whites and maintained close ties to the white upper class; afterward the black community was dominated by an elite of business owners and politicians whose economic base lay in the black community itself and who were indifferent to the larger white world.

The ghettoization of black America seemed to resolve, for a time, the simmering debate between the adherents of W. E. B. Du Bois and Booker T. Washington. The rise of a large, segregated black community in the north seemed to offer the fulfillment of Washington's dreams. The ghetto constituted a city within a city that supported a parallel economy of black-owned banks, real estate companies, newspapers, shops, stores, theaters, nightclubs, and factories.[2] The emergence of the ghetto also gave rise to a vibrant culture, symbolized by the "Harlem Renaissance" and its "New Negroes," who glorified the popular culture of southern blacks.[3]

Despite jeremiads from members of the old, northern-born black elite about hardening racism, worsening slums, and the economic fragility of the ghetto, the mood of black America was decidedly upbeat in the late 1920s. With their urbanization, African Americans seemed on the verge of a revolution that would ensure their independence from white society. To be sure, discrimination and prejudice had to be protested, especially in employment, but the prevailing attitude toward residential segregation was decidedly ambivalent. Although segregation may have been rooted in prejudice and discrimination, it also concentrated black demand, thereby supporting black businesses, just as it clustered black voters to enable the election of black politicians. As the sociologist E. Franklin Frazier noted, black migration and the segregation it engendered created a new African American elite with a vested interest in the ghetto and its perpetuation.[4]

As quickly as the promise of economic and political power arose, however, it collapsed. The Great Depression of the 1930s ravaged the black communities of the north and quickly wiped out the gains of prior decades. As consumer demand fell and factories closed, black workers were the first to be fired.[5] As income in the ghettos dropped, black businesses withered and the renaissance came to an abrupt halt. Within a few months of Black Thursday in 1929, Jesse Binga's State Bank, the pride of south Chicago, had collapsed, and John Nail's Harlem realty company declared bankruptcy.[6] Among intellectuals, W. E. B. Du Bois lost his home and life insurance, and the poet and publisher Countee Cullen wrote his former wife to explain that owing to the drop in his newspaper's circulation, he could no longer meet his alimony payments.[7] If segregation concentrated the growth in black demand during the 1920s, it also amplified the constriction of that demand during the 1930s, ensuring that the fall of black capitalism would be as steep as its rise.

Although the Great Depression hurt all Americans, conditions were far worse in the northern black ghettos than anywhere else. To illustrate the misery created in black Chicago by the Great Depression, St. Clair Drake and Horace Cayton in 1945 published a map of community areas showing the percentage of families on relief in 1934. The higher the percentage, the darker the neighborhood was colored.[8] The swath of dark colors depicted on the map clearly traces the contours of Chicago's black ghetto. The only three areas with relief percentages over 50%—Douglas, Oakland, and Grand Boulevard—were all located in Chicago's "black belt," and four other established black neighborhoods—the Near West Side, the Near South Side, Armor Square, and Washington Park—had relief percentages between 30% and 50%. No other neighborhood—whether

Mexican, Polish, Jewish, or Italian—approached the level of spatially concentrated hardship prevalent in the ghetto. In effect, all of the deprivation and dependency created by the Depression was taken by segregation and confined to a narrow segment of the urban geography defined by the color line.

Fifty years later William Julius Wilson, again pondering the plight of blacks in the wake of widespread economic upheavals, published another map showing the proportion of families below the federal poverty line in Chicago's community areas.[9] The map is strikingly similar to the map of families on relief published earlier by Drake and Cayton (rates of relief and poverty are highly correlated). Of the three areas with relief rates over 50% in 1934, two—Oakland and Grand Boulevard—had poverty rates over 50% in 1980, and the third, Douglas, had a poverty rate of 43%.[10] Of the four neighborhoods with 1934 relief rates between 30% and 50%, three had poverty rates in this range in 1980. Only Armor Square's rate of 23% was under this mark, but by 1980 its black percentage had shrunk to 25%, and within the black portion of the neighborhood the poverty rate stood at 45%.[11] The only community areas Wilson added to Drake and Cayton's map of concentrated deprivation were those incorporated into the ghetto after 1930: Garfield Park, North Lawndale, Woodlawn, Englewood, and Riverdale, all of which had poverty rates between 30% and 50% in 1980. As during the Great Depression, no other ethnic or racial group experienced such a high degree of spatially concentrated deprivation during the economic upheavals of the 1970s.

Drake and Cayton's map notwithstanding, Wilson saw the concentration of black poverty in 1980 as something new and attributed it to a new alignment of economic and demographic forces. According to Wilson, the expansion of civil rights generated new opportunities for middle- and working-class blacks, who moved out of the ghetto in large numbers, leaving behind an isolated and truly disadvantaged black community lacking the institutions, resources, and values necessary for success in modern society. These people became mired in poverty because the decline of manufacturing, the suburbanization of employment, and the rise of the low-wage service sector eliminated high-paying jobs for unskilled men. As a result, the pool of black males able to support a family shrank, female-headed families proliferated, and persistent poverty became a way of life in poor black communities.[12]

As we have seen, however, the geographic concentration of black poverty is not new: poverty was just as concentrated in the ghetto of the

1930s as in the black underclass communities of the 1970s. Nor are the causes of poverty concentration unique to the post–civil rights era. Black poverty was very highly concentrated during the Depression years, when there were no civil rights laws and when blacks experienced considerably less freedom of movement. What the black communities of the 1930s and the 1970s share is a high degree of segregation from the rest of society and a great deal of hardship stemming from larger economic upheavals.

Geographically concentrated poverty is built into the experience of urban blacks by racial segregation. Segregation, not middle-class out-migration, is the key factor responsible for the creation and perpetuation of communities characterized by persistent and spatially concentrated poverty.[13] Concentrated poverty is created by a pernicious interaction between a group's overall rate of poverty and its degree of segregation in society.[14] When a highly segregated group experiences a high or rising rate of poverty, geographically concentrated poverty is the inevitable result, and from this geographic concentration of poverty follow a variety of other deleterious conditions.[15]

In a racially segregated city, any increase in black poverty created by an economic downturn is necessarily confined to a small number of geographically isolated and racially homogeneous neighborhoods. During times of recession, therefore, viable and economically stable black neighborhoods are rapidly transformed into areas of intense socioeconomic deprivation. Joblessness, welfare dependency, and single parenthood become the norm, and crime and disorder are inextricably woven into the fabric of daily life. The coincidence of rising poverty and high levels of segregation guarantees that blacks will be exposed to a social and economic environment that is far harsher than anything experienced by any other racial or ethnic group.

How Segregation Concentrates Poverty

Scientists customarily demonstrate the effect of one variable on another by carrying out an experiment in which all factors under investigation are held constant except one, the presumed causal factor, which the investigator systematically manipulates to observe its effect on some outcome of interest. Social scientists, unfortunately, cannot readily conduct experiments in the social world. They cannot randomly assign blacks to live in segregated and integrated urban areas, and then observe differences in the degree of poverty concentration. They can, however, carry out the equivalent of a laboratory exercise by defining a set of hypothetical cities, giving them constant characteristics that correspond to those in the real world, and then assigning a different level of racial segregation to each city. If segregation acts to concentrate poverty spatially, then we should observe higher levels of poverty concentration as segregation rises.

Such a hypothetical experiment, or simulation, is carried out in Figure 5.1, which depicts four ideal cities, each of which contains the same number of neighborhoods, the same total population size, the same racial composition, and the same black and white poverty rates. Each city contains 96,000 whites and 32,000 blacks (for a black percentage of 25%) and all neighborhoods have 8,000 residents (slightly larger than the typical census tract), yielding a total city population of 128,000 inhabitants spread evenly across sixteen neighborhoods. Blacks are assumed to be poorer, on average, than whites, so they have a poverty rate of 20% compared with 10% for whites (that is, 20% of blacks live in families with incomes below the federal poverty line, but only 10% of whites do). This differential accurately reflects the situation in many U.S. metropolitan areas as of 1970. In Chicago, for example, the black poverty rate in 1970 was 20% while the white rate was 6%; in Los Angeles the rates were 22% (black) and 9% (white); and in New York the rates were 21% (black) and 9% (white).[16]

The only thing that differs among the four hypothetical cities is the level of racial segregation imposed on blacks. City 1 illustrates the condition of no segregation, where blacks and whites are evenly distributed throughout the city and each neighborhood has exactly 2,000 whites and 6,000 blacks. In this case, each neighborhood replicates the racial composition of the city as a whole, so each person lives in an area that is 25% black and 75% white. Blacks and whites experience the same neighborhood poverty rate, 12.5%, which is an average of their separate group rates. (The black rate of 20% implies that 400 of the 2,000 blacks are poor, and the white rate of 10% implies that 600 of the 6,000 whites fall into this category; together they constitute a total poverty population of 1,000 people, which, divided by the neighborhood size of 8,000, yields a rate of 12.5%.) With no residential segregation, therefore, blacks and whites experience the same concentration of poverty within neighborhoods.

City 2 shows what happens to the level of black poverty concentration

Figure 5.1 Effect of racial segregation on the concentration of poverty within neighborhoods of four hypothetical cities (B = blacks; W = whites)

CITY 1: NO RACIAL SEGREGATION

B = 2,000 W = 6,000 1	B = 2,000 W = 6,000 2	B = 2,000 W = 6,000 3	B = 2,000 W = 6,000 4
B = 2,000 W = 6,000 5	B = 2,000 W = 6,000 6	B = 2,000 W = 6,000 7	B = 2,000 W = 6,000 8
B = 2,000 W = 6,000 9	B = 2,000 W = 6,000 10	B = 2,000 W = 6,000 11	B = 2,000 W = 6,000 12
B = 2,000 W = 6,000 13	B = 2,000 W = 6,000 14	B = 2,000 W = 6,000 15	B = 2,000 W = 6,000 16

Black-White Segregation Score:	0.0%
Neighborhood Poverty Rate	
Average Black Family:	12.5%
Average White Family:	12.5%

CITY 2: LOW RACIAL SEGREGATION

B = 0 W = 8,000 1	B = 0 W = 8,000 2	B = 0 W = 8,000 3	B = 0 W = 8,000 4
B = 2,666 W = 5,334 5	B = 2,666 W = 5,334 6	B = 2,666 W = 5,334 7	B = 2,666 W = 5,334 8
B = 2,666 W = 5,334 9	B = 2,666 W = 5,334 10	B = 2,666 W = 5,334 11	B = 2,666 W = 5,334 12
B = 2,666 W = 5,334 13	B = 2,666 W = 5,334 14	B = 2,666 W = 5,334 15	B = 2,666 W = 5,334 16

Black-White Segregation Score:	33.3%
Neighborhood Poverty Rate	
Average Black Family:	13.3%
Average White Family:	12.2%

CITY 3: HIGH RACIAL SEGREGATION

B = 0 W = 8,000 1	B = 0 W = 8,000 2	B = 0 W = 8,000 3	B = 0 W = 8,000 4
B = 0 W = 8,000 5	B = 0 W = 8,000 6	B = 0 W = 8,000 7	B = 0 W = 8,000 8
B = 4,000 W = 4,000 9	B = 4,000 W = 4,000 10	B = 4,000 W = 4,000 11	B = 4,000 W = 4,000 12
B = 4,000 W = 4,000 13	B = 4,000 W = 4,000 14	B = 4,000 W = 4,000 15	B = 4,000 W = 4,000 16

Black-White Segregation Score: 66.7%
Neighborhood Poverty Rate
Average Black Family: 15.0%
Average White Family: 11.7%

CITY 4: COMPLETE RACIAL SEGREGATION

B = 0 W = 8,000 1	B = 0 W = 8,000 2	B = 0 W = 8,000 3	B = 0 W = 8,000 4
B = 0 W = 8,000 5	B = 0 W = 8,000 6	B = 0 W = 8,000 7	B = 0 W = 8,000 8
B = 0 W = 8,000 9	B = 0 W = 8,000 10	B = 0 W = 8,000 11	B = 0 W = 8,000 12
B = 8,000 W = 0 13	B = 8,000 W = 0 14	B = 8,000 W = 0 15	B = 8,000 W = 0 16

Black-White Segregation Score: 100.0%
Neighborhood Poverty Rate
Average Black Family: 20.0%
Average White Family: 10.0%

when blacks are excluded from some neighborhoods. In this hypothetical city, blacks are barred from the four northernmost neighborhoods and the remaining areas are surrounded by a thick border setting them off from the rest of the city. For ease of expression, we call neighborhoods that exclude blacks "white areas" and those that accept blacks "black areas," even though the latter contain some white residents. Within their respective areas, we assume that the races are evenly distributed, so that each black area contains 2,666 blacks and 5,334 whites, and each white area has 8,000 whites and no blacks. This configuration yields a dissimilarity index of 33.3, corresponding roughly to a low degree of segregation.

The imposition of even this low level of segregation creates an immediate deterioration in the neighborhood environment experienced by blacks. Applying their respective poverty rates to the numbers of blacks and whites in each black area yields a total of 533 poor blacks (20% × 2,666) and 533 poor whites (10% × 5,334) for a total neighborhood poverty rate of 13.3% (1,066/8,000). But whereas all blacks experience this higher poverty rate (compared with a rate of 12.5% in an integrated city), only two-thirds of whites do so. The one-third of whites (32,000 people) who live in all-white neighborhoods experience the lower white poverty rate of 10%, yielding an average neighborhood poverty rate of only 12.2% for whites as a whole.

By imposing racial segregation, therefore, some whites are better off and all blacks are worse off. One-third of whites are able to isolate themselves from higher rates of black poverty and to insulate themselves from the social problems associated with income deprivation (e.g., crime, housing abandonment, unstable families, poor schools, etc.). Through racial segregation, the average residential environment of whites improves while the average neighborhood environment of blacks deteriorates.

As Cities 3 and 4 show, the higher the degree of segregation, the higher the level of poverty concentration experienced by blacks and the lower the exposure to poverty experienced by whites. In City 3, a relatively high degree of segregation is imposed on blacks by reducing the number of black areas to eight out of sixteen. In this city, blacks are excluded from all neighborhoods to the north of a line running through the center of town, yielding a segregation index of 66.7. In City 4, complete segregation is imposed by confining blacks to four all-black neighborhoods on the south side of the city, yielding a segregation index of 100.

As we move from City 2 through City 3 to City 4, the discrepancy between the neighborhood poverty rates experienced by blacks and whites grows. With a high level of segregation (City 3), the neighborhood poverty rate of blacks reaches 15% (each black neighborhood is half black and half white, so the average rate falls midway between the rates for the two groups). At the same time, the average poverty rate experienced by whites falls to 11.7%, as two-thirds of whites are now insulated from the higher rates of black poverty and experience the lower white rate of 10%. When segregation becomes total, of course, all whites experience the white poverty rate of 10% and all blacks experience the black poverty rate of 20%, and their respective poverty concentrations reach their maximum divergence.

Thus, if we begin with a poor minority group whose poverty rate is twice that of the majority (a situation common for blacks in American cities) and impose successively higher levels of segregation on blacks, then *with no other changes,* the degree to which minority members experience geographically concentrated poverty increases steadily from a level at parity with whites to a level twice that of whites. As segregation rises, in other words, the neighborhood environment of whites steadily improves while that experienced by blacks progressively deteriorates; and this outcome is achieved without the movement of any nonpoor blacks out of the ghetto.

This result, however, assumes no segregation by social class; poor blacks and poor whites are evenly distributed throughout black and white neighborhoods. In reality, of course, there are rich and poor neighborhoods as well as black and white ones. We therefore repeated our simulation under the more realistic assumption of social class segregation. For each of the four hypothetical cities shown in Figure 5.1, we created a "right" and a "wrong" side of the tracks by drawing a line running north-south through the center of town. We then excluded poor people from neighborhoods east of this class line, yielding a poor versus nonpoor dissimilarity index of 62.5 for blacks and 55.5 for whites. These values lie toward the upper end of the continuum of class segregation, but are within established ranges.[17]

We will not work through the class-based simulation here, but its principal results are easily summarized: whether or not one assumes segregation between the rich and the poor, racial segregation acts to concentrate poor blacks in a small number of neighborhoods, raising the poverty rate to which they are exposed and lowering the corresponding rate for whites.[18] By itself, racial segregation concentrates poverty in *black* neighborhoods, but the addition of class segregation concentrates poverty primarily in *poor black* neighborhoods. By adding class segregation to the simulation exercise, we exacerbate the degree of poverty concentration that is imposed on poor blacks because of racial segregation.

This point is illustrated in the first column of Table 5.1, which presents

Table 5.1 Poverty concentration experienced by poor blacks and poor whites under different conditions of poverty and racial segregation

	Percentage poor in neighborhood of average poor family		
Level of racial segregation	Black poverty rate of 20%	Black poverty rate of 30%	Change
Poor Whites			
with no class segregation			
No racial segregation	12.5%	15.0%	2.5%
Low racial segregation	12.2	14.4	2.2
High racial segregation	11.7	13.3	1.6
Complete racial segregation	10.0	10.0	0.0
with class segregation			
No racial segregation	25.0	30.0	5.0
Low racial segregation	25.0	30.0	5.0
High racial segregation	25.0	30.0	5.0
Complete racial segregation	20.0	20.0	0.0
Poor Blacks			
with no class segregation			
No racial segregation	12.5	15.0	2.5
Low racial segregation	13.3	16.7	3.4
High racial segregation	15.0	20.0	5.0
Complete racial segregation	20.0	30.0	10.0
with class segregation			
No racial segregation	25.0	30.0	5.0
Low racial segregation	28.3	35.0	6.7
High racial segregation	35.0	45.0	10.0
Complete racial segregation	40.0	60.0	20.0

Source: Douglas S. Massey, "American Apartheid: Segregation and the Making of the Underclass," *American Journal of Sociology* 96 (1990):338–39.

the principal results from these simulations. As we saw earlier, without class segregation the poverty rate in the neighborhood of the average poor black family grew from 12.5% with complete racial integration to 20% under complete racial segregation. When class segregation is also assumed, the degree of poverty concentration among blacks is doubled, going from 25% to 40% as racial segregation increases from minimum to maximum (see column 1). This doubling occurs because, in a class-segregated city, poverty is confined not simply to black neighborhoods but to poor black neighborhoods (those that lie west of the class barrier we placed through the center of town). Although racial and class segregation act independently to concentrate poverty, their simultaneous occurrence yields a more marked deterioration in the neighborhood environment experienced by poor blacks.

As before, however, racial segregation improves the social environment to which poor whites are exposed. Without class segregation, the poverty rate in the neighborhood of the average poor white family dropped from 12.5% to 10% as racial segregation went from minimum to maximum, but with class segregation poverty concentration falls from 25% to 20% (see column 1). In essence, although class segregation concentrates poverty among whites as well as among blacks, the imposition of racial segregation insulates poor whites from the higher rates of black poverty and keeps white poverty concentration at a markedly lower level.

The effect of class segregation, therefore, is to heighten and reinforce the poverty-concentrating effects of racial segregation, but it does not change the basic conclusion: racial segregation concentrates poverty, and it does so without anyone having to move anywhere. With or without class segregation, residential segregation between blacks and whites builds concentrated poverty into the residential structure of the black community and guarantees that poor blacks experience a markedly less advantaged social environment than do poor whites.

Economic Dislocation in a Segregated City

The 1930s and the 1970s were both decades of severe economic hardship for urban blacks. During the 1930s, as already described, the Great Depression brought a wave of factory closings, bankruptcies, bank failures, and very high rates of unemployment in the black community.[19] During the 1970s, successive recessions, bursts of inflation, and increased foreign competition eliminated many high-paying jobs in manufacturing, lowered wages, and decreased the real value of welfare payments. These dislocations took a heavy toll on the distribution of black income, especially among families in the industrial cities of the northeast and midwest.[20] As a result of the downward shift in black incomes, poverty rates increased substantially in both decades.

If racial segregation concentrates poverty in space, it also focuses and amplifies any *change* in the economic situation of blacks. In a segregated environment, any economic shock that causes a downward shift in the distribution of black income will not only bring about an increase in the poverty rate for the group as a whole; it will also cause an increase in the geographic concentration of poverty. This geographic intensification of poverty occurs because the additional poverty created by the shock is spread unevenly around the metropolitan area. In a racially segregated city, any increase in black poverty is confined to a small number of black neighborhoods; and the greater the segregation, the smaller the number of neighborhoods absorbing the shock and the more severe the resulting concentration of poverty. If neighborhoods are also segregated by class, not only is the additional poverty restricted to black neighborhoods, it is confined primarily to *poor* black neighborhoods.

Given the extreme segregation characteristic of Chicago in the 1930s, therefore, the only possible outcome of the Great Depression was a geographic concentration of black families on relief, as observed by Drake and Cayton. Similarly, the only possible effect of the economic restructuring of the 1970s, given Chicago's persisting racial segregation, was the concentration of poverty observed by Wilson. During both periods, poor blacks increasingly inhabited poor places.

The underlying cause of this concentration of black poverty was the same in both decades: an economic downturn drove up the rate of black poverty, which because of racial segregation was translated directly into spatially concentrated poverty. Out-migration by middle- and working-class blacks may have occurred during the 1970s (although evidence on this point is unclear[21]) and this movement could have exacerbated the concentration of poverty in black neighborhoods, but Wilson's map of concentrated poverty would have resulted with or without black out-migration because segregation builds concentrated poverty into the residential structure of the black community.

This fact can be demonstrated by using the hypothetical cities described earlier to simulate the effect of an increase in the rate of black poverty—from 20% to 30%—holding the white rate constant, a pattern of change that parallels quite closely what happened in many American cities during the 1970s.[22] The results of this exercise are summarized in Table 5.1, which shows levels of poverty concentration for blacks and whites before and after the assumed shift in black poverty rates, given various levels of racial segregation.

If there were no class segregation, and if blacks were completely integrated with whites, a sharp rise in the black poverty rate would be harmful to the well-being of the group as a whole, but it would not greatly alter the neighborhood environment in which blacks live. The average rate of neighborhood poverty to which blacks are exposed would increase from 12.5% to 15%, an absolute increment of only 2.5 percentage points. It is doubtful whether an increase of this size would be particularly noticeable to people living in the neighborhood; and because blacks and whites occupy the same neighborhoods, this relatively small increment in poverty concentration would be experienced equally by both groups.

As racial segregation rises, however, the increase in black poverty is confined to an increasingly smaller number of black neighborhoods, and the change in the neighborhood environment becomes more dramatic for blacks and less noticeable for whites. With a low level of segregation, the degree of black poverty concentration increases from 13.3% before the shift to 16.7% afterward (an increment of 3.4 percentage points, or 26%). In contrast, the extent of poverty concentration for whites goes from 12.2 to 14.4 (a change of only 2.2 points, or 18%).

Under conditions of high segregation, the difference between blacks and whites increases. Black poverty concentration grows by 5 points (or 33%) as a result of the overall increase in black poverty, reaching an absolute level of 20%. In contrast, white poverty concentration increases by only 1.6 points (or 14%), reaching an absolute level of only 13.3%. When the two groups are completely segregated, of course, *all* of the increase in black poverty is absorbed by black neighborhoods, so their poverty concentration increases to 30%, whereas white poverty concentration remains constant at 10%, one-third of the black level.

Thus with complete racial segregation (and note that the city of Chicago had a black-white segregation index of 91 in 1980), the degree of poverty concentration among blacks can reach alarming proportions following a downward shift in the distribution of black income, as occurred in many cities during the 1970s. This transformation in the residential environment of blacks occurs solely through an interaction between the distributional structure of income and the residential structure of segregation, and not as a result of middle-class blacks fleeing poor blacks.

In a city segregated by class as well as by race, any increase in black poverty is absorbed not simply by black neighborhoods but by *poor* black neighborhoods. In essence, the imposition of segregation by class as well as by race takes a bad situation and makes it worse. Before the shift in black incomes, poverty rates in the typical poor black neighborhood ranged from 25% in a city with no racial segregation to 40% in a city with complete racial segregation. After the shift in poverty rates, the economic situation in poor black neighborhoods deteriorates appreciably at all segregation levels, but the deterioration is disastrous at higher levels. With a black-white dissimilarity index of 66.7, the neighborhood poverty rate of the average poor black family goes from 35% to 45% as a result of the shift in black incomes, an increase of 10 points (or 29%); and with complete segregation, the neighborhood poverty rate for poor blacks climbs to 60%, up from 40% before the shift (an increase of 50%).

Under conditions of complete racial segregation, therefore, a 50% rise in the black poverty rate translates directly into a 50% increase in the spatial concentration of poverty within poor black neighborhoods. In a racially segregated city, such a downward shift in the black income distribution *necessarily* causes poor blacks to live in an environment where the vast majority of their neighbors are also poor. The *same change* in the absence of racial segregation would yield only a 20% increase in the poverty concentration of poor blacks, and would leave them in neighborhoods where the vast majority are not poor.

As segregation rises, in other words, the disparity between the neighborhood conditions experienced by whites and blacks widens markedly. With no racial segregation, of course, poor whites and poor blacks suffer the consequences of sagging black incomes equally, even if the city is quite divided by social class. Both groups experience a 20% increase in neighborhood poverty and end up living in neighborhoods where three of every ten persons are poor. As segregation rises, however, poor whites are increasingly insulated from the consequences of falling black incomes. As one moves from complete integration to complete segregation under conditions of high black poverty, the poverty rate prevailing in poor white neighborhoods *falls* from 30% to 20% while that in poor black neighborhoods *rises* from 30% to 60%.

The net effect of racial segregation is to expose whites and blacks to very different socioeconomic environments and to leave the economic base of urban black communities uniquely vulnerable to any downturn in the group's economic fortunes. When the poverty rate of a segregated group rises, its members suffer a systematic deterioration in their neighborhood environment with or without middle-class out-migration.

Table 5.2 confirms this line of theoretical reasoning by presenting indices of black and white poverty concentration computed for hypersegregated metropolitan areas in 1970 and 1980. Our index of concentrated poverty is the percentage of poor families in the neighborhood of the average poor family.[23] If our theory is correct, we expect high and rising concentrations of poverty among blacks and much lower and more stable poverty concentrations among whites during the decade, because in all of these cities, segregation levels were very high, black poverty rates rose, and white poverty rates stayed fairly constant. In New York, for example, the black poverty rate increased from 21% to 30%, the white rate remained fixed at 10%, and the area's segregation index of about 82 didn't

Table 5.2 The geographic concentration of poverty among blacks and whites in hypersegregated cities

	Percentage poor in neighborhood of average poor black family			Percentage poor in neighborhood of average poor white family		
	1970	1980	Change	1970	1980	Change
Atlanta	31.7%	37.1%	5.4%	12.4%	12.5%	0.1%
Baltimore	30.4	34.6	4.3	11.4	13.9	2.5
Buffalo	27.0	36.0	9.2	11.8	14.4	2.6
Chicago	25.6	36.7	11.1	8.6	10.3	1.7
Cleveland	31.0	38.0	7.0	10.5	12.8	2.3
Dallas–Ft. Worth	30.0	31.2	1.2	13.2	11.7	−1.5
Detroit	22.5	31.5	9.0	10.1	12.4	2.3
Gary–Hammond–E. Chicago	23.7	28.4	4.7	8.8	9.6	0.6
Indianapolis	22.3	27.0	4.6	11.1	13.7	2.7
Kansas City	25.4	28.5	3.1	12.6	12.1	−0.6
Los Angeles–Long Beach	26.7	29.3	2.6	12.1	13.7	1.6
Milwaukee	30.0	33.2	3.2	10.4	11.7	1.3
New York	25.9	37.6	11.7	13.8	17.7	3.9
Newark	23.4	34.1	10.8	10.1	12.3	2.2
Philadelphia	26.0	34.7	8.7	10.8	13.8	3.0
St. Louis	30.7	33.7	2.4	12.2	11.9	−0.3
Average	27.0	33.2	6.2	11.2	12.8	1.6

Source: Douglas S. Massey and Mitchell L. Eggers, "The Ecology of Inequality: Minorities and the Concentration of Poverty, 1970–1980," *American Journal of Sociology* 95 (1990):1175–77.

change—essentially the conditions we assumed in our simulation exercise.

As the indices of Table 5.2 show, blacks experienced systematically greater concentrations of poverty than whites. In 1970, for example, the average level of black poverty concentration, 27%, was nearly three times the white level of 11%; and over the ensuing decade this disparity grew, with the average black concentration index rising to 33%, an increase of 6 percentage points, while the index for whites increased only modestly to 13%, a change of only 2 points. The increase in black poverty concentration was especially marked in Chicago, New York, Newark, Buffalo, and Philadelphia. By the end of the decade, the typical poor black family in these hypersegregated metropolitan areas lived in a neighborhood where at least a third of the families were poor. In contrast, poor white families in these areas generally lived in neighborhoods where the poverty rate was 15% or less.

In statistical terms, levels and trends in poverty concentration during the 1970s correlate strongly with the product of the index of black-white segregation and the rate of black poverty, suggesting a powerful interaction between the two factors.[24] An interaction means that the effect of rising poverty on poverty concentration depends crucially on the level of racial segregation at which the increase in poverty occurs. Black poverty concentration increased most dramatically in metropolitan areas where a sharp increase in black poverty was paired with a high and unchanging level of racial segregation. By 1980 poverty concentration was greatest in urban areas where blacks were both highly segregated and very poor, and was lowest in areas where they were neither poor nor segregated. Segregation was thus the key conditioning factor responsible for the transformation of urban black communities observed by William Julius Wilson during the 1970s. In the absence of racial segregation, the same downward economic trends would not have produced such dramatic changes in the concentration of poverty.

The Creation of Underclass Communities

Poverty, of course, is not a neutral social factor. Associated with it are a variety of other social ills such as family instability, welfare dependency, crime, housing abandonment, and low educational achievement. To the extent that these factors are associated with poverty, any structural process that concentrates poverty will concentrate them as well. Segregation, interacting with high or rising poverty rates, guarantees that blacks will face a harsh and uniquely disadvantaged social environment, no matter what their personal characteristics.

Segregation, moreover, is crucial to understanding why a self-perpetuating spiral of neighborhood decline is built into urban black communities. The socioeconomic health of black neighborhoods is fragile and easily jolted into a pattern of decay because of a subtle interaction between individual and collective behavior that comes into play whenever independent actors make decisions that affect the welfare of the community. This interaction occurs because a neighborhood's socioeconomic status is, to a large extent, determined by the decisions and behaviors of its inhabitants. Each individual decision affects the social and economic context within which subsequent decisions are made, creating a powerful feedback loop between individual and collective behavior.[25]

Consider, for example, the case of a working-class neighborhood that has just made the transition from white to black. The homes and apartments are well maintained and there is no abandoned housing or physical dilapidation. But suppose the new black residents have somewhat lower incomes than the former white occupants. Black renters can afford less rent and some black owners are less able to make investments in upkeep. As a result, a few owners and landlords decide to spend less money on the maintenance of their properties. Soon their buildings begin to show signs of disinvestment in the form of physical disrepair: peeling paint, rotting gutters, unkept yards, crumbling porches, and so on.

The presence of dilapidated dwellings changes the context within which other landlords and homeowners make their decisions on whether or not to invest. Studies suggest that property owners are extremely sensitive to small signs of physical deterioration.[26] The presence of even a small number of dilapidated buildings is taken as a signal that the neighborhood is going "downhill." To the extent that property owners perceive a decline as possible or likely, they have little incentive to invest in upkeep and improvement on their own buildings, because money put into neighborhoods that are declining is unlikely to be recouped in the form of higher rents or greater home equity.

As a result of the initial disinvestment by a few owners, therefore, others are led to cut back on the money they invest. With every additional property owner who decides not to invest, it becomes increasingly likely that others will reach similar decisions, even if they are otherwise disposed to maintain their buildings. At some point, a threshold is crossed, beyond which the pattern becomes self-reinforcing and irreversible.[27]

Racial segregation makes neighborhoods where blacks live particularly vulnerable to this sort of disinvestment and decay. Poor blacks are more likely than the poor of any other group to be trapped in neighborhoods caught in the grip of such downward spirals, because segregation acts to concentrate poverty and all things associated with it. Increasing the poverty rate of a segregated group concentrates not only poverty but housing dilapidation and abandonment.

In essence, segregation and rising poverty interact to deliver an exogenous shock to black neighborhoods that pushes them beyond the point where physical decay and disinvestment become self-perpetuating. The potential strength of this shock has been demonstrated in a series of simulation exercises that are summarized in Table 5.3. Again using the hypothetical class-segregated cities we described earlier, we ask what would happen to black neighborhoods if black poverty rates rose under different conditions of segregation.[28] At different segregation levels, of course, the shift in black poverty rates yields different concentrations of poverty, and using empirical correlations between neighborhood poverty levels and various indicators of community well-being, we predict the neighborhood environment created by a particular combination of segregation and poverty. In carrying out the simulations, we consider the general case of a class-segregated city and document the effect of a shift in black poverty rates from 20% to 30%.

Consider the degree of housing abandonment likely to result from an increase in black poverty under different conditions of segregation. In the absence of racial segregation, the poverty rate in neighborhoods where poor blacks live increases from 25% to 30% as a result of the assumed shift in black poverty rates from 20% to 30% (as was shown in Table 5.1). Given the empirical relationship between a tract's poverty rate and its percentage of boarded-up dwellings, this shift in neighborhood poverty is predicted to increase the incidence of boarded-up structures from 1.2% before the shift to 1.5% afterward.

Although these figures are quite small, a review carried out by the U.S. Department of Housing and Urban Development shows that the threshold of neighborhood stability occurs at remarkably low percentages of boarded-up buildings.[29] Once a few structures become abandoned, the process of decay quickly becomes cumulative and "spreads from older, dilapidated sections to areas with sound housing that would be well worth the cost of maintenance and renovation if neighborhood condi-

Table 5.3 Simulated effects of a shift in the black poverty rate on neighborhood conditions experienced by poor blacks, assuming different levels of racial segregation

Neighborhood condition and level of racial segregation	Effect of shift in black poverty rate		
	Poverty rate of 20%	Poverty rate of 30%	Change
Percentage of houses boarded up			
No racial segregation	1.2	1.5	0.3
Complete racial segregation	2.3	3.3	1.0
Median household income			
No racial segregation	$13,020	$11,235	$1,785
Complete racial segregation	$8,160	$4,523	$3,637
Major crime rate (per 1,000 people)			
No racial segregation	57.8	61.8	4.0
Complete racial segregation	68.3	84.2	15.9
Percentage of families on welfare			
No racial segregation	21.1	24.6	3.5
Complete racial segregation	36.1	51.0	14.9
Percentage of female-headed families			
No racial segregation	19.2	22.2	3.0
Complete racial segregation	33.5	45.5	12.0
Percentage of high school students scoring below 15th percentile			
No racial segregation	32.6	35.3	2.7
Complete racial segregation	47.1	57.8	10.7

Source: Douglas S. Massey, "American Apartheid: Segregation and the Making of the Underclass," *American Journal of Sociology* 96 (1990):343, 348–49.

Note: Simulation results assume residential structures depicted in Figure 5.1 with class segregation between poor and nonpoor families added; test referred to in last panel is the California Achievement Test.

tions were more stable."[30] The study concludes that a "tipping point" is reached once 3%–6% of a neighborhood's dwellings are abandoned, "the point at which investment psychology becomes so depressed that reversal of the abandonment process is impossible without major external intervention."[31]

In the absence of racial segregation, therefore, an exogenous economic shock that causes black poverty rates to rise does not concentrate housing abandonment enough to reach this tipping point. Under conditions of complete segregation, however, the same increase in black poverty brings a substantial increase in the concentration of boarded-up dwellings, from 2.3% to 3.3%, putting the level of abandonment within the range of neighborhood instability. In a segregated city, any exogenous economic shock that raises the black poverty rate is likely to push black neighborhoods across the tipping point to begin the process of disinvestment and abandonment. The same shock delivered to blacks in an integrated city would leave all neighborhoods stable and economically healthy.

The empirical correlation upon which this simulation rests was estimated using data from sixty metropolitan areas, many of which only recently attained metropolitan rank and therefore have new housing stocks where the incidence of boarded-up dwellings is near zero. The simulation has also been carried out based on correlations estimated from the city of Philadelphia, where abandonment is considerably more common.[32] Under conditions of complete racial segregation, this alternate simulation predicts that the percentage of boarded up dwellings will reach 10% after the shift in black incomes, well in excess of the threshold of stability.

Once a process of housing abandonment has taken root in one part of a community, moreover, it tends to spread outward into otherwise stable and healthy neighborhoods through a process of diffusion. One of the principal mechanisms by which abandonment spreads laterally is through fire.[33] The presence of abandoned and boarded-up buildings is strongly associated with arson and a high incidence of residential fires.[34] Once a few buildings have burned, neighborhoods no longer attract stable households and become a magnet for other social problems, such as rats, litter, drugs, crime, and delinquency.[35]

The lateral spread of decay occurs because fires in abandoned buildings inevitably spread to adjacent structures that are inhabited, which displaces poor families from their dwellings and causes them to seek shelter in surrounding neighborhoods. The influx of destitute and socially disorganized fire refugees into these neighborhoods increases their housing densities, levels of homelessness, and dilapidation, setting off new cycles of disinvestment and decline.[36] Roderick Wallace has called this process "urban desertification," denoting a sequence of events whereby entire neighborhoods become depopulated and devoid of stable social institutions.[37] By concentrating abandonment, segregation promotes this desertification and builds it into the residential structure of black communities.

This process of neighborhood decay also occurs through the loss or withdrawal of commercial institutions. According to Loic Wacquant and William Julius Wilson, Chicago's West Side ghetto lost 75% of its business establishments between 1960 and 1970, and by the 1980s its North Lawndale neighborhood included "48 state lottery agents, 50 currency exchanges, and 99 licensed bars and liquor stores, but only one bank and one supermarket for a population of some 50,000."[38]

Segregation plays a key role in depriving poor black families of access to goods and services because it interacts with poverty to create neighborhood conditions that make it nearly impossible to sustain a viable retail sector. Just as it concentrates poverty during times of economic upheaval, segregation also concentrates the loss in income and consumer demand that accompany any economic downturn. As a result of racial segregation, therefore, poor blacks live in neighborhoods that typically contain only the barest rudiments of retail trade. They are left without goods and services that are routinely available to the poor of other groups.

A simulation again illustrates the potential of segregation to concentrate income loss and undermine black businesses. As before, we generate poverty concentrations from different combinations of segregation and black poverty rates, but this time we use the neighborhood poverty rates to predict median incomes in areas inhabited by poor blacks.[39] In a racially integrated city, a shift in the rate of black poverty from 20% to 30% increases the degree of poverty concentration experienced by poor blacks, and given the empirical association between a neighborhood's poverty rate and median income, this shift is predicted to lower the median neighborhood income for poor blacks from $13,020 before the shift to $11,235 afterward, yielding a loss of $1,785 (see Table 5.3).

Assuming there are roughly 3,000 households per neighborhood and that the median and mean income are about the same,[40] this drop in income implies a loss of about $5.4 million per neighborhood where poor blacks live (i.e., 3,000 × $1,785). Within these areas, therefore, retail profits will fall, services will be cut, and some businesses will fail, but the drop in income is not enough to bring about the wholesale elimination of goods and services to poor blacks. The demand density remains fairly high at $33.7 million ($11,235 × 3,000), and because poor whites and blacks share the same residential areas in an integrated city, they experience these reductions in retail goods and services equally and there is no basis for the formation of a racially distinctive underclass community.

Racial segregation dramatically alters the picture. When the black poverty rate rises in a totally segregated city, the drop in income and potential demand is confined to neighborhoods inhabited exclusively by blacks, and primarily by poor blacks, leaving the latter trapped in neighborhoods with insufficient income to sustain a viable retail sector. Under conditions of complete racial segregation, poor black neighborhoods face a precarious situation *before* the shift in black incomes, with a predicted median household income of only $8,160; but after the shift, the predicted median income plummets to $4,523, for a loss of $3,637 (see Table 5.3).

In a segregated city, therefore, neighborhoods inhabited by poor blacks have a weak potential demand of only $24.5 million before the assumed shift in black incomes ($8,160 x 3,000), compared with a figure of $39.1 million in an integrated city ($13,020 x 3,000), and are thus in a poor position to absorb an economic shock; but racial segregation intensifies the loss of income created by the general increase in black poverty and focuses it precisely upon these very fragile neighborhoods. After the shift in black poverty rates, the potential demand in poor black neighborhoods is almost halved to $13.6 million ($4,523 x 3,000), for a loss of $10.9 million, or 44%. A loss of this magnitude from an already small income base would rapidly cause the failure of most nonessential businesses and eliminate many services that depend on the ability of clients to pay.

The difference between poor blacks living in a neighborhood with a demand density of $39.1 million (in an integrated city with a black poverty rate of 20%) and poor blacks living in an area with a demand density of $13.6 million (a segregated city with a black poverty rate of 30%) is explained entirely by the interaction between segregation and the rate of black poverty. It is this pernicious interaction that explains the rapid demise of black businesses during the Great Depression and the absence of commercial institutions within inner city black neighborhoods today, for if segregation concentrates black demand to support black businesses during periods of black income growth (such as the 1920s and 1950s), it also concentrates falling demand to promote business failure during periods of rising poverty and joblessness (such as the 1930s and 1970s).

Thus, although we share William Julius Wilson's view that the structural transformation of the economy played a crucial role in creating the urban underclass during the 1970s,[41] we argue that what made it disproportionately a *black* underclass was racial segregation. The decline of manufacturing and the rise of a two-tiered service economy harmed many racial and ethnic groups, but only black Americans were highly segregated, so only among them was the resulting income loss confined to a small set of spatially contiguous and racially homogeneous neighborhoods. Rather than being spread evenly around the metropolitan environment, the drop in consumer demand was confined to a few neighborhoods inhabited exclusively by poor blacks. Black neighborhoods such as Chicago's North Lawndale therefore lost the normal range of goods and services and its business district became a wasteland of empty storefronts, burned-out buildings, and vacant lots.

In contrast, Mexican Americans in Chicago are considerably less segregated, and their core neighborhood of Little Village, immediately adjacent to North Lawndale, remained a beehive of commercial activity throughout the 1970s and 1980s despite the economic recession. The Little Village shopping district continues to house a variety of supermarkets, banks, restaurants, bakeries, travel agents, butchers, auto shops, hardware stores, and other retail outlets. The difference between North Lawndale and Little Village cannot be explained by the wave of factory closings that occurred on the city's West Side between 1950 and 1980,[42] because these economic shocks undermined the well-being of Mexican Americans as well as blacks and the two neighborhoods are separated by only a few hundred yards. Rather, the key difference between the Mexican and black communities in Chicago is the degree of segregation they experience.

In 1980 the average Mexican American in Chicago lived in a neighborhood that was 50% non-Hispanic white, but the average black lived in an area that was 90% black.[43] Even in Little Village itself about 25% of the population was non-Hispanic, compared with North Lawndale, which was only 2% nonblack.[44] Because of this disparity in the degree of segregation, the economic dislocations of the 1970s brought an acute withdrawal of income from North Lawndale, pushing it well beyond the threshold of stability into disinvestment, abandonment, and commercial decline; but the same economic troubles brought only a moderate concentration of poverty in Little Village, leaving it well shy of the tipping point.

Segregation also concentrates other social and physical problems associated with poverty. Research by Wesley Skogan and his associates shows that inhabitants of urban neighborhoods are quite sensitive to signs of social disorder such as street-corner drinking, catcalling, sexual harassment, graffiti, and littering. Although these behaviors are not dangerous or criminal in themselves, they violate norms that are widely shared—by both blacks and whites—about what constitutes a good and desirable neighborhood. Their presence is interpreted to signify a breakdown in social order and security, and if the disorders are allowed to persist, they promote psychological and physical withdrawal from the community.[45]

In the face of persistent neighborhood disorder, residents come to distrust their neighbors and to look upon them as threats rather than as sources of support or assistance. Residents modify their routines and increasingly stay indoors; they minimize their time on the streets and limit their contacts outside of close friends and family. This withdrawal only promotes further disorder by lowering the number of watchful neighbors in public places and by undermining the community's capacity for collective action. By provoking withdrawal, disorder weakens informal processes of social control that operate to maintain a neighborhood's stability.

If disorder is allowed to increase, it ultimately creates conditions that promote not only additional disorder but also crime, which likewise feeds on itself in self-perpetuating fashion.[46] Perceptions of crime and danger gleaned from friends and neighbors who have been victimized, or who have heard of victimizations, cause residents to increase their mistrust of neighbors and to withdraw from public participation in the community. These actions, in turn, sow the seeds for more crime by undermining public vigilance and sapping the neighborhood's capacity for collective action.

Skogan's research demonstrates that crime and social disorder are strongly predicted by the neighborhood poverty rate.[47] By concentrating poverty, therefore, segregation also concentrates these maladies. We simulated the degree to which segregation concentrates crime using the same methods as used earlier. We derived poverty concentrations expected from assumed levels of segregation and rates of poverty and used these to predict crime rates, given an empirical association between neighborhood poverty and crime.[48] Our simulations show that a black poverty rate of 20% in an integrated city yields a major crime rate of 58 per thousand in neighborhoods inhabited by poor blacks (see Table 5.3). Given the same black poverty rate in a segregated city, however, the predicted crime rate is 68 per thousand. Because of racial segregation, in other words, poor blacks experience a 17% greater chance of becoming victims of a major crime.

As in our earlier examples, segregation also concentrates any *increase* in crime that grows out of an increase in black poverty rates. In the absence of racial segregation, a shift in the black poverty rate from 20% to 30% is predicted to increase the neighborhood crime rate for poor blacks from 58 per thousand to 62 per thousand, an increase of only 4 points, or 7%. It is doubtful whether such a change would be particularly noticeable within neighborhoods; it would be unlikely, therefore, to lead to psychological or physical withdrawal from the community.

In a racially segregated city, however, the same shift in black poverty rates causes a substantial increase in crime within neighborhoods inhabited by poor blacks, increasing the crime rate from 68 per thousand to 84 per thousand, a 23% increase. Such an increase is very likely to be noticed by neighbors, either indirectly through informal conversations or directly through personal experience. Over five years, a crime rate of 84 per thousand carries a 46% chance of victimization, meaning that each resident would have roughly a 50–50 chance of experiencing crime directly.

Because it is so noticeable, this increase in the crime rate is quite likely to exceed the threshold of neighborhood stability. Under conditions of racial segregation, a simple increase in the rate of black poverty is likely to ignite a cycle of escalating crime and disorder in the residential environment of poor blacks. The same shift in an integrated city produces only a small, barely noticeable change in the crime rate that leaves all neighborhoods stable, safe, and relatively secure.

Segregation also affects the normative environment that poor blacks experience on a daily basis. Sociologists have long argued that social behavior is transmitted from generation to generation through role models. Children learn by imitating adult behavior, so the kinds of people who prevail in settings where children grow up strongly affect the kinds of behavior they later exhibit as adults.[49] To the extent that racial segregation concentrates certain deleterious behavior patterns in the residential environment of poor blacks, it can be expected to exert a profound effect on their social and economic behavior.

William Julius Wilson and others have argued forcefully that concentrated poverty, in removing poor blacks from job networks and limiting their exposure to people with stable histories of work and family formation, isolates them from the mainstream of American society.[50] Young blacks who grow up in areas of concentrated poverty are much less likely to learn how to get and keep a job or to advance in school; rather, they come to expect a life of joblessness, single parenthood, and welfare dependency.

Because welfare receipt, unwed childbearing, and marital disruption are strongly associated with poverty, they are concentrated by any structural process that geographically concentrates poverty. Segregation is deeply implicated in the creation of a social environment within which these conditions are not only common but normative. By concentrating single-parent families on welfare, segregation plays a crucial role in creating the social isolation that Wilson and others have linked to the perpetuation of disadvantage among poor blacks.

Our simulations again demonstrate the power of segregation to undermine the residential environment of poor blacks.[51] In a racially integrated city, a black poverty rate of 20% implies that poor blacks reside in a neighborhood where 21% of the families are on welfare and 19% have female heads (see Table 5.3). Raising the black poverty rate to 30% increases the prevalence of these conditions somewhat, but the social environment of poor blacks does not change markedly in the absence of racial segregation. The percentage of female-headed families increases to only 25% while the share on welfare goes to 22%. In an integrated city, therefore, typical rates of black poverty do not produce a social environment dominated by welfare dependency or single parenthood, and even a substantial increase in black poverty leaves this situation unaltered.

In a segregated city, in contrast, a 20% rate of poverty implies that poor blacks live in an environment where 36% of all families are on welfare and a third are female-headed; and increasing the rate of black poverty shifts these percentages upward to create an environment where single parenthood and welfare receipt are the rule, or close to it. With complete racial segregation and a black poverty rate of 30%, 51% of the families in the neighborhood of the typical poor black family are predicted to be on welfare and 46% are expected to be female-headed.

Because segregation concentrates any factor associated with poverty and focuses it upon segregated black neighborhoods, high black poverty rates are translated directly into social environments where welfare dependency and single parenthood are the prevailing categories of social and economic behavior. The same change in the absence of segregation would expose poor blacks to a social milieu in which the vast majority of families with children are self-supporting and have two parents present. Poor black children growing up in a segregated city, therefore, are much more likely to be exposed to adult role models of dependency and single parenthood than are white children. If children learn by imitation, segregation means that poor blacks are much more likely to end up in these states themselves.

Children, however, learn not only through imitating adults but also through their schooling. But because poverty is associated with poor educational performance segregation also concentrates educational disadvantage.[52] The organization of public schools around geographical catchment areas, in other words, reinforces and exacerbates the social isolation that segregation creates in neighborhoods. By concentrating low-achieving students in certain schools, segregation creates a social context within which poor performance is standard and low expectations predominate.

Our last simulation illustrates this point by predicting the school environment associated with different concentrations of poverty (see Table 5.3). Data from Philadelphia were used to estimate the correlation between a census tract's poverty rate and its percentage of high school students scoring below the 15th percentile on a standardized achievement test (the California Achievement Test, or CAT). As in our earlier simulations, this empirical association was used to predict the percentage of low-scoring students generated by different combinations of racial segregation and black poverty.

In the absence of racial segregation, a 20% black poverty rate yields a school environment where 33% of the students score below the 15th percentile on the CAT. Although this percentage clearly indicates a poor educational environment—and testifies to the low quality of public education in inner cities generally—it is nonetheless one where two-thirds of students achieve a modicum of academic performance. Increasing the black poverty rate to 30% drives the percentage of low-achieving students up by 2 points to 35%, not a particularly noticeable change.

As the level of racial segregation increases, however, educational disadvantage is concentrated along with poverty. Given complete segregation between blacks and whites and a 20% rate of black poverty, our simulation predicts that children will attend high schools where 47% of the students score below the 15th percentile on the CAT; and raising the rate of black poverty to 30% increases the percentage of low-scoring students to 58%. Segregation thus accounts for the difference between an educational environment where 65% of students score above the 15th percentile and one where 58% score below this cutoff. All other variables are held constant in the simulation, which suggests the great power of racial segregation to concentrate disadvantage on poor urban blacks.

The Linchpin of the Underclass

Despite the pivotal role played by segregation in creating underclass communities, recent theories of urban poverty have largely ignored it as an explanatory factor. During the 1980s a number of important and influential books sought to explain the persistent nature and growing concentration of poverty in American cities. Although there is substantial disagreement about what the urban underclass is and whether or not it is growing,[53] the term popularly connotes people who are mired in poverty and unable to escape it. As ambiguous as the definition of the underclass is, however, there is even less consensus about its causes. About the only thing common to prevailing theories of urban poverty is that none of them sees racial segregation as part of the problem.

In his 1980 book *The Black Underclass,* Douglas Glasgow argued that "racism is probably the most basic cause of the underclass condition."[54] In his view, the persistence of black inner city poverty stems from the systematic failure of American institutions—the schools, the courts, the welfare system, the economy, the government—to address the desperate needs of poor blacks. He argues that bureaucratic practices motivated by racism act to maintain blacks in poverty and perpetuate their underclass position, a position that is generally echoed in Alphonso Pinkney's later work, *The Myth of Black Progress.*[55]

Ken Auletta brought the hopelessness and despair of urban poverty to national attention and probably did more than any other author to popularize the notion of the underclass. In *The Underclass,* published in 1982, he constructed a vivid portrait of poor people enrolled in a job training course organized by a nonprofit organization to help "ex-convicts, ex-addicts, long-term welfare recipients, school dropouts, and delinquent youths—the core of the underclass."[56] Auletta was unremittingly pessimistic about the prospects for improving the lot of these people through social intervention. He stated that "neither the domestic Marshall Plan schemes favored by liberals nor President Reagan's supply-side nostrums will by themselves solve the problems of this hard to reach group."[57]

By the mid-1980s, the right-wing attack on the American welfare state was in full swing and conservatives had weighed into the underclass debate. In his 1984 book *Losing Ground,* Charles Murray argued that generous welfare benefits made it "profitable for the poor to behave in the short term in ways that were destructive in the long term."[58] According to Murray, federal antipoverty programs implemented during the 1960s—notably Aid to Families with Dependent Children—altered the incentives governing the behavior of poor men and women. Welfare reduced the desirability of marriage for poor women, increased the benefits of unwed childbearing, and lowered the attractiveness of low-wage labor for poor men. As a result, male joblessness increased, rates of single motherhood rose, and female-headed families proliferated. As Murray lamented, "we tried to provide more for the poor and produced more poor instead."[59]

Lawrence Mead followed up this broadside in 1986 by arguing that it was not the generosity of the welfare state that was the problem. Rather, it was too permissive. In *Beyond Entitlement,* he argued that the poor should not be entitled to benefits simply for being poor, but should be required to discharge certain obligations of citizenship such as working hard, finishing school, obeying the law, and supporting themselves to the extent possible.[60] In Mead's view, welfare undermined the independence, equality, and competence of recipients by not requiring anything in return for benefits received.

The liberal counterattack was joined in 1987 by William Julius Wilson, who argued that the urban poor were not persistently poor because of overly generous or permissive welfare systems or because of persisting institutional racism (he did, however, accept racism as a contributing cause). Rather, in *The Truly Disadvantaged,* Wilson argued that it was the growing social isolation of poor blacks that perpetuated their misery and restricted their prospects for advancement.[61] This isolation was created not by racial segregation but by the out-migration of working- and middle-class blacks from ghetto neighborhoods and by the structural transformation of the urban economy, which eliminated high-paying jobs for manual workers and created a two-tiered service sector that generated only low-paying jobs for those without a college education. Residential segregation is mentioned only as a historical legacy, not as an active process created by ongoing institutional arrangements and individual actions.

None of these theories successfully explains the salient facts of the underclass, however. No theorist adequately accounts for the remarkable overrepresentation of blacks within it, and no one has yet explained why Puerto Ricans, among all other groups, are the only other ones to display the high rates of poverty, family dissolution, unwed childbearing, and other social problems that are commonly associated with the underclass. Moreover, no theorist has explained why underclass communities are confined to a relatively small number of places, despite the widespread prevalence of poverty, economic restructuring, and white racism in American cities. In the vast research literature on the underclass, scholars may differ on many issues, but they appear to agree that the underclass, however it is defined, is largely black and Puerto Rican and confined primarily to older industrial cities, located mainly in the northeast and midwest.[62]

Although the theory of institutional racism explains why blacks are overrepresented in the underclass, it does not explain why the problems are more severe in some cities than others, or why the problems worsened during the 1970s when racism was arguably in decline and black civil rights were expanding, or why Puerto Ricans but not Mexican Americans display the constellation of social and economic problems associated with the underclass. Similarly, neoconservatives cannot explain why blacks and Puerto Ricans should be so uniquely affected by the deleterious effects of welfare, given that other equally poor groups—such as Mexican Americans—experience the same welfare system but not the same interlocking set of social and economic disorders. Nor does welfare explain why unwed childbearing and single parenthood proliferated during the 1970s, when the real value of benefits stagnated.[63] Finally, liberal arguments about the transformation of the urban economy do not explain why the social isolation of blacks increased so much, while that of other groups did not. Although other minority groups experienced growing poverty during the 1970s, poverty only become spatially concentrated among blacks and Puerto Ricans, and only in certain places.

To account for the latter anomaly, Wilson posits a new process of out-migration from the ghetto on the part of working- and middle-class blacks, made possible by the civil rights breakthroughs of the 1960s. Class-selective out-migration from poor black neighborhoods is not new, however; it has been documented in historical studies going back to the 1930s.[64] But then as now, the persistence of racial segregation in the housing market has meant that middle-class blacks are less able to isolate themselves from the poor than the middle classes of other groups. As a result, middle-class blacks live in much poorer neighborhoods than do middle-class whites, Hispanics, or Asians.

Although the degree of class segregation between rich and poor blacks increased slightly during the 1970s, it is still considerably *lower* than that observed among other racial and ethnic groups.[65] Moreover, as black education and income rise, the degree of segregation from whites does not drop, but persists at extremely high levels.[66] As a result, levels of black-white segregation hardly changed during the 1970s in the nation's largest urban areas, and in sixteen metropolitan areas blacks were so isolated as to be considered "hypersegrated."[67]

The point, however, is not that class-selective out-migration from poor black neighborhoods did not happen (it might have), but that the increasing social isolation uncovered by William Julius Wilson would have occurred no matter what trends in black out-migration occurred. Given prevailing trends in black poverty and racial segregation during the 1970s, the geographic concentration of black poverty was *inevitable.* Rising poverty and persistent segregation in American urban areas could have produced no other outcome but an increase in black poverty concentration. To the extent that middle-class blacks left poor ghetto areas, their departure exacerbated a geographic concentration of poverty that was already built structurally into the black community through its segregation from the rest of society.

Focusing on the migratory behavior of middle-class blacks also obscures the real cause of underclass communities and deflects attention instead to a mobility process that is normal and natural in U.S. society: the process of geographic mobility that accompanies socioeconomic achievement. Throughout U.S. history, the wealthy of all groups have sought to put distance between themselves and the poor. As their levels of education, income, and occupational statuses have risen, Jews, Italians, Poles, Mexicans, and Asians have all sought improved housing in better neighborhoods not dominated by their own ethnic group.[68] What distinguishes blacks from everyone else is that this process of normal spatial mobility occurs within a segregated housing market. As a result of racial segregation, middle-class blacks are less able to achieve a neighborhood commensurate with their socioeconomic status, and poor blacks are forced to live under conditions of unparalleled poverty.

Normally, as members of one ethnic group move out of a low-income area, poor members of another group move in to take their place; but because of racial segregation, no other group will move into a poor black neighborhood except other poor blacks, thereby driving up the concentration of poverty. According to Gramlich and Laren, the probability of entering a poor neighborhood was 9% for poor blacks, 2.5% for middle-class blacks, and 0.3% for upper-class blacks.[69] Although the growing concentration of black poverty may reflect patterns of black migration, therefore, it is the structural constraint of segregation that causes the concentration, not the migration itself; and given the constraint of segregation, it is probably class-selective in-migration that concentrates poverty as much as middle-class out-migration.

As we have argued, however, focusing on migration obscures the fact that segregation and high poverty interact to make geographically concentrated poverty inevitable, no matter what patterns of movement occur. Under conditions of high racial segregation, a rise in poverty necessarily leads to a concentration of poverty for the segregated group. Social class segregation amplifies this basic effect, but does not alter the fundamental conclusion that concentrated poverty is inevitable when high rates of poverty and intense racial segregation are combined.

The concentration of poverty, moreover, sets off a series of ancillary changes in the social and economic composition of neighborhoods. By concentrating poverty, segregation also concentrates other conditions that are associated with it. Deleterious conditions such as falling retail demand, increasing residential abandonment, rising crime, spreading disorder, increasing welfare dependency, growing family disruption, and rising educational failure are all concentrated simultaneously by raising the rate of poverty under a regime of high segregation. They can be produced at any time by a simple rise in black poverty under conditions prevailing in most large U.S. cities, and certainly in the sixteen hypersegregated metropolitan areas we have identified. They can be generated for any fixed level of class segregation, and they do not require the out-migration of middle-class blacks from the ghetto.

Racial segregation, therefore, is crucial to understanding and explaining America's urban underclass, and an appreciation of its role in concentrating poverty resolves several outstanding issues in the underclass debate. First, it explains why the urban underclass, however one defines it, is so disproportionately composed of blacks and Puerto Ricans. In the nation's largest urban areas, these groups are the only ones that have *simultaneously* experienced high levels of residential segregation and sharp increases in poverty. Black-white dissimilarity indices generally exceed 70, and in the largest urban areas they are usually above 80.[70] Puerto Ricans are the only Hispanic group whose segregation indices are routinely above 70.[71] During the 1970s, other groups, such as Mexican, Cuban, and Asian Americans, experienced lower levels of segregation, smaller increases in poverty, or both.[72] The high segregation of Puerto Ricans is attributable to the fact that a large plurality are of African origin; simply put, Puerto Ricans are more segregated because they are more African than other Hispanic groups.[73]

Understanding segregation's role in concentrating poverty also explains why underclass communities are confined primarily to the northeast and midwest, primarily within older metropolitan areas such as New York, Chicago, Philadelphia, and Baltimore.[74] During the 1970s, not only did these older industrial areas experience the sharpest economic reversals, they also exhibited the highest levels of racial segregation in the United States.[75] Industrial restructuring thus drove minority poverty rates upward most sharply in cities where blacks and Puerto Ricans were most segregated. In the New York metropolitan area, for example, the black poverty rate increased from 21% to 30% between 1970 and 1980 in a residential environment where the black-white dissimilarity remained fixed at about 82; and in the Chicago metropolitan area the black poverty rate rose from 20% to 28% with a black-white dissimilarity index of around 88.[76]

Explaining the origins of underclass communities in terms of an interaction between racial segregation and rising poverty is also consistent with research showing that upper-income blacks remain highly segregated from whites, that this pattern has not changed over time, and that the degree of class segregation among blacks is actually lower than that among other minority groups. Segregation, therefore, is crucial to understanding the geographic concentration of black poverty and the creation of underclass communities. As Thomas Pettigrew has argued, racial segregation is the "structural linchpin" of American race relations,[77] and despite its glaring absence from theories of urban poverty to this point, it should be a central focus of the underclass debate.

6

The Perpetuation of the Underclass

One notable difference appears between the immigrant and Negro populations. In the case of the former, there is the possibility of escape, with improvement in economic status in the second generation.

1931 report to President Herbert Hoover by the Committee on Negro Housing

If the black ghetto was deliberately constructed by whites through a series of private decisions and institutional practices, if racial discrimination persists at remarkably high levels in U.S. housing markets, if intensive residential segregation continues to be imposed on blacks by virtue of their skin color, and if segregation concentrates poverty to build a self-perpetuating spiral of decay into black neighborhoods, then a variety of deleterious consequences automatically follow for individual African Americans.[1] A racially segregated society cannot be a race-blind society; as long as U.S. cities remain segregated—indeed, hypersegregated—the United States cannot claim to have equalized opportunities for blacks and whites. In a segregated world, the deck is stacked against black socioeconomic progress, political empowerment, and full participation in the mainstream of American life.

In considering how individuals fare in the world, social scientists make a fundamental distinction between individual, family, and structural characteristics. To a great extent, of course, a person's success depends on individual traits such as motivation, intelligence, and especially, education. Other things equal, those who are more highly motivated, smarter, and better educated will be rewarded more highly in the labor market and will achieve greater socioeconomic success.[2]

Other things generally are not equal, however, because individual traits such as motivation and education are strongly affected by family background. Parents who are themselves educated, motivated, and economically successful tend to pass these traits on to their children. Children who enter the middle and upper classes through the accident of birth are more likely than other, equally intelligent children from other classes to acquire the schooling, motivation, and cultural knowledge required for socioeconomic success in contemporary society.[3] Other aspects of family background, moreover, such as wealth and social connections, open the doors of opportunity irrespective of education or motivation.[4]

Yet even when one adjusts for family background, other things are still not equal, because the structural organization of society also plays a profound role in shaping the life chances of individuals. Structural variables are elements of social and economic organization that lie beyond individual control, that are built into the way society is organized. Structural characteristics affect the fate of large numbers of people and families who share common locations in the social order.[5]

Among the most important structural variables are those that are geographically defined. Where one lives—especially, where one grows up—exerts a profound effect on one's life chances.[6] Identical individuals with similar family backgrounds and personal characteristics will lead very different lives and achieve different rates of socioeconomic success depending on where they reside. Because racial segregation confines blacks to a circumscribed and disadvantaged niche in the urban spatial order, it has profound consequences for individual and family well-being.

Social and Spatial Mobility

In a market society such as the United States, opportunities, resources, and benefits are not distributed evenly across the urban landscape. Rather, certain residential areas have more prestige, greater affluence, higher home values, better services, and safer streets than others. Marketing consultants have grown rich by taking advantage of this "clustering of America" to target specific groups of consumers for wealthy corporate clients.[7] The geographic differentiation of American cities by socioeconomic status does more than conveniently rank neighborhoods for the benefit of demographers, however; it also creates a crucial connection between social and spatial mobility.

As people get ahead, they not only move up the economic ladder, they move up the residential ladder as well.[8] As early as the 1920s, sociologists at the University of Chicago noted this close connection between social and spatial mobility, a link that has been verified many times since.[9] As socioeconomic status improves, families relocate to take advantage of opportunities and resources that are available in greater abundance elsewhere. By drawing on benefits acquired through residential mobility, aspiring parents not only consolidate their own class position but enhance their and their children's prospects for additional social mobility.[10]

In a very real way, therefore, barriers to spatial mobility are barriers to social mobility, and where one lives determines a variety of salient factors that affect individual well-being: the quality of schooling, the value of housing, exposure to crime, the quality of public services, and the character of children's peers. As a result, residential integration has been a crucial component in the broader process of socioeconomic advancement among immigrants and their children.[11] By moving to successively better neighborhoods, other racial and ethnic groups have gradually become integrated into American society. Although rates of spatial assimilation have varied, levels of segregation have fallen for each immigrant group as socioeconomic status and generations in the United States have increased.[12]

The residential integration of most ethnic groups has been achieved as a by-product of broader processes of socioeconomic attainment, not because group members sought to live among native whites per se. The desire for integration is only one of a larger set of motivations, and not necessarily the most important. Some minorities may even be antagonistic to the idea of integration, but for spatial assimilation to occur, they need only be willing to put up with integration in order to gain access to socioeconomic resources that are more abundant in areas in which white families predominate.

To the extent that white prejudice and discrimination restrict the residential mobility of blacks and confine them to areas with poor schools, low home values, inferior services, high crime, and low educational aspirations, segregation undermines their social and economic well-being. The persistence of racial segregation makes it difficult for aspiring black families to escape the concentrated poverty of the ghetto and puts them at a distinct disadvantage in the larger competition for education, jobs, wealth, and power. The central issue is not whether African Americans "prefer" to live near white people or whether integration is a desirable social goal, but how the restrictions on individual liberty implied by severe segregation undermine the social and economic well-being of individuals.

Extensive research demonstrates that blacks face strong barriers to spatial assimilation within American society. Compared with other minority groups, they are markedly less able to convert their socioeconomic attainments into residential contact with whites, and because of this fact they are unable to gain access to crucial resources and benefits that are distributed through housing markets.[13] Dollar for dollar, blacks are able to buy fewer neighborhood amenities with their income than other groups.

Among all groups in the United States, only Puerto Ricans share blacks' relative inability to assimilate spatially; but this disadvantage stems from the fact that many are of African origin.[14] Although white Puerto Ricans achieve rates of spatial assimilation that are comparable with those found among other ethnic groups, those of African or racially mixed origins experience markedly lower abilities to convert socioeconomic attainments into contact with whites.[15] Once race is controlled, the "paradox of Puerto Rican segregation" disappears.[16]

Given the close connection between social and spatial mobility, the persistence of racial barriers implies the systematic exclusion of blacks from benefits and resources that are distributed through housing markets. We illustrate the severity of this black disadvantage with data specially compiled for the city of Philadelphia in 1980 (see Table 6.1).[17] The data allow us to consider the socioeconomic character of neighborhoods that poor, middle-income, and affluent blacks and whites can be expected to inhabit, holding education and occupational status constant.[18]

In Philadelphia, poor blacks and poor whites both experience very bleak neighborhood environments; both groups live in areas where about 40% of the births are to unwed mothers, where median home values are under $30,000, and where nearly 40% of high school students score under the 15th percentile on a standardized achievement test. Families in such an environment would be unlikely to build wealth through home equity, and children growing up in such an environment would be exposed to a peer environment where unwed parenthood was common and where educational performance and aspirations were low.

As income rises, however, whites are able to escape this disadvantaged setting by relocating to a more advantaged setting. With a middle-class income ($20,000 1979 dollars), whites no longer reside in a neighborhood where unwed parenthood predominates (only 10% of births are to single mothers) and housing values are well above $30,000. At the same

Table 6.1 Characteristics of neighborhoods inhabited by blacks and whites at different income levels in Philadelphia, 1980

	Level of household income					
	Poor ($8,000)		Middle ($20,000)		Affluent ($32,000)	
	Whites	Blacks	Whites	Blacks	Whites	Blacks
Percentage of births to unwed mothers	40.7	37.6	10.3	25.8	1.9	16.7
Median value of homes (in thousands of 1980 dollars)	$19.4	$27.1	$38.0	$29.5	$56.6	$31.9
Percentage of students scoring below 15th percentile on CAT in local high school	39.3	35.5	16.5	26.6	5.7	19.2

Source: Douglas S. Massey, Gretchen A. Condran, and Nancy A. Denton, "The Effect of Residential Segregation on Black Social and Economic Well-Being," *Social Forces* 66 (1987):46–47, 50.

Note: Household income is in 1979 dollars.

time, school performance is markedly better: only 17% of students in the local high school score below the 15th percentile.

Once whites achieve affluence, moreover, negative residential conditions are left far behind. Affluent whites in Philadelphia (those with a 1979 income of $32,000) live in neighborhoods where only 2% of the births are to unwed mothers, where the median home value is $57,000, and where a mere 6% of high school students score below the 15th percentile on achievement tests. Upwardly mobile whites, in essence, capitalize on their higher incomes to buy their way into improved residential circumstances.

Blacks, in contrast, remain mired in disadvantage no matter what income they achieve. Middle-income blacks live in an area where more than a quarter of the births are to unwed mothers, where housing values languish below $30,000, and where 27% of all students in the local high school score below the 15th percentile. Even with affluence, blacks achieve neighborhood environments that compare unfavorably with those attained by whites. With an income of $32,000, a black family can expect to live in a neighborhood where 17% of all births are to unwed mothers, home values are barely over $30,000, and where a fifth of high school students score below the 15th percentile.

For blacks, in other words, high incomes do not buy entrée to residential circumstances that can serve as springboards for future socioeconomic mobility; in particular, blacks are unable to achieve a school environment conducive to later academic success. In Philadelphia, children from an affluent black family are likely to attend a public school where the percentage of low-achieving students is three times greater than the percentage in schools attended by affluent white children. Small wonder, then, that controlling for income in no way erases the large racial gap in SAT scores.[19] Because of segregation, the same income buys black and white families educational environments that are of vastly different quality.[20]

Given these limitations on the ability of black families to gain access to neighborhood resources, it is hardly surprising that government surveys reveal blacks to be less satisfied with their residential circumstances than socioeconomically equivalent whites.[21] This negative evaluation reflects an accurate appraisal of their circumstances rather than different values or ideals on the part of blacks.[22] Both races want the same things in homes and neighborhoods; blacks are just less able to achieve them. Compared with whites, blacks are less likely to be homeowners,[23] and the homes they do own are of poorer quality, in poorer neighborhoods, and of lower value.[24] Moreover, given the close connection between home equity and family wealth, the net worth of blacks is a small fraction of that of whites, even though their incomes have converged over the years.[25] Finally, blacks tend to occupy older, more crowded dwellings that are structurally inadequate compared to those inhabited by whites;[26] and because these racial differentials stem from segregation rather than income, adjusting for socioeconomic status does not erase them.[27]

The Politics of Segregation

Socioeconomic achievement is not only a matter of individual aspirations and effort, however; it is also a matter of collective action in the political arena. Generations of immigrants have entered American cities and struggled to acquire political power as a means to enhance individual mobility. Ultimately most were incorporated into the pluralist political structure of American cities. In return for support at the polls, ethnic groups were awarded a share of public services, city contracts, and municipal jobs in rough proportion to their share of the electorate. The receipt of these public resources, in turn, helped groups consolidate their class position and gave their members a secure economic base from which to advance further.[28]

The process of political incorporation that followed each immigrant wave grew out of shared political interests that were, to a large extent, geographically determined. Although neighborhoods may have been labeled "Polish," "Italian," or "Jewish," neighborhoods in which one ethnic group constituted a majority were rare, and most immigrants of European origin never lived in them. As a result, levels of ethnic segregation never reached the heights typical of black-white segregation today.[29]

This geographic diversification of ethnicity created a situation in which ethnic groups necessarily shared common political interests.[30] In distributing public works, municipal services, and patronage jobs to ethnic groups in return for their political support, resources were also allocated to specific neighborhoods, which typically contained a diverse array of ethnicities. Given the degree of ethnic mixing within neighborhoods, political patronage provided to one group yielded substantial benefits for others as well. Building a new subway stop in an "Italian" neighborhood, for example, also provided benefits to Jews, Poles, and Lithuanians who shared the area; and allocating municipal jobs to Poles not only benefited merchants in "Polish" communities but generated extra business for nearby shopkeepers who were Hungarian, Italian, or Czech.

At the same time, threats to curtail municipal services encouraged the formation of broad, interethnic coalitions built around common neighborhood interests. A plan to close a firehouse in a "Jewish" neighborhood, for example, brought protests not only from Jews but from Scandinavians, Italians, and Slovaks who shared the neighborhood and relied on its facilities. These other ethnics, moreover, were invariably connected to friends and relatives in other neighborhoods or to co-ethnic politicians from other districts who could assist them in applying political pressure to forestall the closure. In this way, residential integration structurally supported the formation of interethnic coalitions, providing a firm base for the emergence of pluralist political machines.

Residential integration also made it possible for ethnic groups to compete for political leadership throughout the city, no matter what their size.[31] Because no single group dominated numerically in most neighborhoods, politicians from a variety of backgrounds found the door open to make a bid for elective office. Moreover, representatives elected from ethnically diverse neighborhoods had to pay attention to all voters irrespective of ethnic affiliation. The geographic distribution of political power across ethnically heterogeneous districts spread political influence widely among groups and ensured that all were given a political voice.

The residential segregation of blacks, in contrast, provided no basis for pluralist politics because it precluded the emergence of common neighborhood interests; the geographic isolation of blacks instead forced nearly all issues to cleave along racial lines.[32] When a library, firehouse, police station, or school was built in a black neighborhood, other ethnic groups derived few, if any, benefits; and when important services were threatened with reduction or removal, blacks could find few coalition partners with whom to protest the cuts. Since no one except blacks lived in the ghetto, no other ethnic group had a self-interest in seeing them provided with public services or political patronage.

On the contrary, resources allocated to black neighborhoods detracted from the benefits going to white ethnic groups; and because patronage was the glue that held white political coalitions together, resources allocated to the ghetto automatically undermined the stability of the pluralist machine. As long as whites controlled city politics, their political interests lay in providing as few resources as possible to African Americans and as many as possible to white ethnic groups. Although blacks occasionally formed alliances with white reformers, the latter acted more from moral conviction than from self-interest. Because altruism is notoriously unreliable as a basis for political cooperation, interracial coalitions were unstable and of limited effectiveness in representing black interests.[33]

The historical confinement of blacks to the ghetto thus meant that blacks shared few political interests with whites. As a result, their incorporation into local political structures differed fundamentally from the pluralist model followed by other groups.[34] The geographic and political isolation of blacks meant that they had virtually no power when their numbers were small; only when their numbers increased enough to dominate one or more wards did they acquire any influence at all. But rather than entering the pluralist coalition as an equal partner, the black community was incorporated in a very different way: as a machine within a machine.[35]

The existence of solid black electoral districts, while undermining interracial coalition-building, did create the potential for bloc voting along racial lines. In a close citywide election, the delivery of a large number of black votes could be extremely useful to white politicians, and inevitably black political bosses arose to control and deliver this vote in return for political favors. Unlike whites, who exercised power through politicians of diverse ethnicities, blacks were typically represented by one boss, always black, who developed a symbiotic and dependent relationship with the larger white power structure.[36]

In return for black political support, white politicians granted black bosses such as Oscar DePriest or William Dawson of Chicago and Charles Anderson of Harlem a share of jobs and patronage that they could, in turn, distribute within the ghetto.[37] Although these bosses wielded considerable power and status within the black community, they occupied a very tenuous position in the larger white polity. On issues that threatened the white machine or its constituents, the black bosses could easily be outvoted. Thus patronage, services, and jobs were allocated to the ghetto only as long as black bosses controlled racial agitation and didn't threaten the color line, and the resources they received typically compared unfavorably to those provided to white politicians and their neighborhoods.[38]

As with black business owners and professionals, the pragmatic adaptation of black politicians to the realities of segregation gave them a vested interest in the ghetto and its perpetuation.[39] During the 1950s, for example, William Dawson joined with white ethnic politicians to oppose the construction of public housing projects in white neighborhoods, not because of an ideological objection to public housing per se, but because integration would antagonize his white political sponsors and take voters outside of wards that he controlled.[40]

The status quo of a powerful white machine and a separate but dependent black machine was built on shifting sand, however. It remained viable only as long as cities dominated state politics, patronage was plentiful, and blacks comprised a minority of the population. During the 1950s and 1960s, white suburbanization and black in-migration systematically undermined these foundations, and white machine politicians became progressively less able to accommodate black demands while simultaneously maintaining the color line. Given the declining political clout of cities, the erosion of their tax base, and the rising proportion of blacks in cities, municipal politics became a racially charged zero-sum game that pitted politically disenfranchised blacks against a faltering coalition of ethnic whites.[41]

In cities where blacks came to achieve an absolute majority—such as Baltimore, Newark, Gary, Detroit, Cleveland, and Washington, D.C.—the white political machine was destroyed as blacks assumed power and ended white patronage. In cities where the share of blacks peaked at around 40%—as in Chicago and Philadelphia—blacks were able to acquire power only by pulling liberal whites and disaffected Hispanics into a tenuous coalition, but given prevailing patterns of segregation these alliances were not politically stable. Chicago, for example, quickly reverted to white control in a way that succinctly illustrates the vulnerability of black politicians under conditions of racial segregation.

By the beginning of the 1980s, black in-migration to Chicago had stopped, white out-migration had leveled off, and the movement of Hispanics into the city was accelerating. As the share of blacks stalled at just above 40%, it became clear that they would not soon, if ever, comprise a majority of the Chicago's population. Latinos had become the swing voters and whoever pulled them into a coalition would rule the city. Mexican Americans and Puerto Ricans, however, had traditionally been ignored by the city's white machine politicians, and in frustration they joined with blacks in 1983 to elect the city's first black mayor, Harold Washington.[42]

But under black leadership the fruits of political power did not come fast enough to satisfy rising Latino expectations. Given the high degree of residential segregation between blacks and Hispanics, resources provided to black constituents had few spillover benefits for Mexican Americans or Puerto Ricans, and when Mayor Washington died early in his second term, they bolted from the black politicians to form a new coalition with the chastened and now politically receptive ethnic whites. Together Latinos and European whites constituted a working majority of voters who elected a new white mayor, Richard M. Daley, son of the city's last white political boss. Given their relative integration, moreover, white Europeans and Latinos found a stable basis for coalition politics based on geographically structured self-interest.

Chicago's Latinos now appear to be following the pluralist political model of earlier European immigrant groups; and because they are the only major group in the city whose numbers are growing, their political power and influence can only be expected to increase. As long as the working coalition between Latinos and European whites holds, blacks will be unable to win citywide power. The political isolation of blacks continues because of the structural limitations imposed on them by racial segregation, which guarantees that they have will few interests in common with other groups.

Even in cities where blacks have assumed political leadership by virtue of becoming a majority, the structural constraints of segregation still remain decisive. Indeed, the political isolation experienced by blacks in places such as Newark and Detroit is probably more severe than that experienced earlier in the century, when ghetto votes were at least useful to white politicians in citywide elections. Once blacks gained control of the central city and whites completed their withdrawal to the surrounding suburbs, virtually all structural supports for interracial cooperation ended.

In the suburbs surrounding places such as Newark and Detroit, white politicians are administratively and politically insulated from black voters in central cities, and they have no direct political interest in their welfare. Indeed, money that flows into black central cities generally means increased taxes and lower net incomes for suburban whites. Because suburbanites now form a majority of most state populations—and a majority of the national electorate—the "chocolate city–vanilla suburb" pattern of contemporary racial segregation gives white politicians a strong interest in limiting the flow of public resources to black-controlled cities.[43]

In an era of fiscal austerity and declining urban resources, therefore, the political isolation of blacks makes them extremely vulnerable to cutbacks in governmental services and public investments. If cuts must be made to balance strained city budgets, it makes political sense for white politicians to concentrate the cuts in black neighborhoods, where the political damage will be minimal; and if state budgets must be trimmed, it is in white legislators' interests to cut subventions to black-controlled central cities, which now represent a minority of most states' voters. The spatial and political isolation of blacks interacts with declining public resources to create a powerful dynamic for disinvestment in the black community.

The destructiveness of this dynamic has been forcefully illustrated by Rodrick and Deborah Wallace, who trace the direct and indirect results of a political decision in New York City to reduce the number of fire companies in black and Puerto Rican neighborhoods during the early 1970s.[44] Faced with a shortage of funds during the city's financial crisis, the Fire Department eliminated thirty-five fire companies between 1969 and 1976, twenty-seven of which were in poor minority areas located in the Bronx, Manhattan, and Brooklyn, areas where the risk of fire was, in fact, quite high. Confronted with the unpleasant task of cutting services, white politicians confined the reductions to segregated ghetto and barrio wards where the political damage could be contained. The geographic and political isolation of blacks and Puerto Ricans meant that their representatives were unable to prevent the cuts.

As soon as the closings were implemented, the number of residential fires increased dramatically. An epidemic of building fires occurred within black and Puerto Rican neighborhoods.[45] As housing was systematically destroyed, social networks were fractured and institutions collapsed; churches, block associations, youth programs, and political clubs vanished. The destruction of housing, networks, and social institutions, in turn, caused a massive flight of destitute families out of core minority areas.[46] Some affected areas lost 80% of their residents between 1970 and 1980, putting a severe strain on housing in adjacent neighborhoods, which had been stable until then. As families doubled up in response to the influx of fire refugees, overcrowding increased, which led to additional fires and the diffusion of the chaos into adjacent areas. Black ghettos and Puerto Rican barrios were hollowed out from their cores.

The overcrowded housing, collapsed institutions, and ruptured support networks overwhelmed municipal disease prevention efforts and swamped medical care facilities.[47] Within affected neighborhoods, infant mortality rates rose, as did the incidence of cirrhosis, gonorrhea, tuberculosis, and drug use.[48] The destruction of the social fabric of black and Puerto Rican neighborhoods led to an increase in the number of unsupervised young males, which contributed to a sharp increase in crime, followed by an increase in the rate of violent deaths among young men.[49] By 1990, this chain reaction of social and economic collapse had turned vast areas of the Bronx, Harlem, and Brooklyn into "urban deserts" bereft of normal community life.[50]

Despite the havoc that followed in the wake of New York's fire service reductions, the cuts were never rescinded. The only people affected were minority members who were politically marginalized by segregation and thereby prevented, structurally, from finding allies to oppose the service reductions. Although residential segregation paradoxically made it easier for blacks and Puerto Ricans to elect city councillors by creating homogeneous districts, it left those that were elected relatively weak, dependent, and unable to protect the interests of their constituents.

As a result of their residential segregation and resultant political isolation, therefore, black politicians in New York and elsewhere have been forced into a strategy of angrily demanding that whites give them more public resources. Given their geographic isolation, however, these appeals cannot be made on the basis of whites' self-interest, but must rely on appeals to altruism, guilt, or fear. Because altruism, guilt, and fear do not provide a good foundation for concerted political action, the downward spiral of black neighborhoods continues and black hostility and bitterness grow while white fears are progressively reinforced. Segregation creates a political impasse that deepens the chasm of race in American society.

Under the best of circumstances, segregation undermines the ability of blacks to advance their interests because it provides ethnic whites with no immediate self-interest in their welfare. The circumstances of U.S. race relations, however, can hardly be described as "best," for not only do whites have little self-interest in promoting black welfare, but a significant share must be assumed to be racially prejudiced and supportive of policies injurious to blacks. To the extent that racism exists, of course, the geographic and political isolation of the ghetto makes it easier for racists to act on their prejudices. In a segregated society, blacks become easy targets for racist actions and policies.

The Isolation of the Ghetto

The high degree of residential segregation imposed on blacks ensures their social and economic isolation from the rest of American society. As we have seen, in 1980 ten large U.S. cities had black isolation indices in excess of 80 (Atlanta, Baltimore, Chicago, Cleveland, Detroit, Gary, Newark, Philadelphia, St. Louis, and Washington, D.C.), meaning that the average black person in these cities lived in a neighborhood that was at least 80% black. Averages in excess of 80% occur when a few blacks live in integrated areas, and the vast majority reside in areas that are 100% black.[51]

Such high levels of racial isolation cannot be sustained without creating a profound alienation from American society and its institutions. Unless ghetto residents work outside of their neighborhoods, they are unlikely to come into contact with anyone else who is not also black, and if they live in an area of concentrated poverty, they are unlikely to interact with anyone who is not also *poor* and black. The structural constraints on social interaction imposed by segregation loom large when one considers that 36% of black men in central cities are either out of the labor force, unemployed, or underemployed, a figure that rises to 54% among black men aged 18 to 29.[52]

The role that segregation plays in undermining blacks' connection to the rest of society has been demonstrated by William Yancey and his colleagues at Temple University.[53] They undertook a representative survey of people in the Philadelphia urban area and asked them to describe the race and ethnicity of their friends and neighbors. Not surprisingly, blacks were far more concentrated residentially than any other group, even controlling for social and economic background. They were also very unlikely to report friendships with anyone else but blacks, and this remarkable racial homogeneity in their friendship networks was explained entirely by their residential concentration; it had nothing to do with group size, birthplace, socioeconomic status, or organizational membership. Unlike other groups, blacks were prevented from forming friendships outside their group because they were so residentially segregated: spatial isolation leads to social isolation.

The intense isolation imposed by segregation has been confirmed by an ethnographic study of blacks living in Chicago's poorest neighborhoods.[54] Drawing on detailed, in-depth interviews gathered in William Julius Wilson's Urban Family Life Survey, Sophie Pedder found that one theme consistently emerged in the narratives: poor blacks had extremely narrow geographic horizons. Many of her informants, who lived on Chicago's South Side, had never been into the Loop (the city's center), and a large number had never left the immediate confines of their neighborhood. A significant percentage only left the neighborhood after reaching adulthood. According to Pedder, this racial isolation "is at once both real, in that movement outside the neighborhood is limited, and psychological, in that residents feel cut off from the rest of the city."[55]

Thus residents of hypersegregated neighborhoods necessarily live within a very circumscribed and limited social world. They rarely travel outside of the black enclave, and most have few friends outside of the ghetto. This lack of connection to the rest of society carries profound costs, because personal contacts and friendship networks are among the most important means by which people get jobs. Relatively few job seekers attain employment by responding to ads or canvassing employers; most people find jobs through friends, relatives, or neighbors, and frequently they learn of jobs through acquaintances they know only casually.[56]

The social isolation imposed on blacks by virtue of their systematic residential segregation thus guarantees their economic isolation as well. Because blacks have weak links to white society, they are not connected to the jobs that white society provides. They are put at a clear disadvantage in the competition for employment, and especially for increasingly scarce jobs that pay well but require little formal skill or education.[57] This economic isolation, moreover, is cumulative and self-perpetuating: because blacks have few connections outside the ghetto, they are less likely to be employed in the mainstream economy, and this fact, in turn, reduces the number and range of their connections to other people and institutions, which further undermines their employment chances. Given the levels of residential segregation typically found in large American cities, therefore, the inevitable result is a dependent black community within which work experience is lacking and linkages to legitimate employment are weak.

The Language of Segregation

The depth of isolation in the ghetto is also evident in black speech patterns, which have evolved steadily away from Standard American English. Because of their intense social isolation, many ghetto residents have come to speak a language that is increasingly remote from that spoken by American whites. Black street speech, or more formally, Black English Vernacular, has its roots in the West Indian creole and Scots-Irish dialects of the eighteenth century.[58] As linguists have shown, it is by no means a "degenerate," or "illogical" version of Standard American English; rather, it constitutes a complex, rich, and expressive language in its own right, with a consistent grammar, pronunciation, and lexicon all its own.[59] It evolved independently from Standard American English because blacks were historically separated from whites by caste, class, and region; but among the most powerful influences on black speech has been the residential segregation that blacks have experienced since early in the century.[60]

For several decades, the linguist William Labov and his colleagues have systematically taped, transcribed, and analyzed black and white speech patterns in American cities.[61] In city after city they have found that whites "constitute a single speech community, defined by a single set of norms and a single, extraordinarily uniform structural base. Linguistic features pass freely across ethnic lines within the white community. But not across racial lines: black(s) . . . have nothing to do with these sound changes in process."[62] Divergent black and white speech patterns provide stark evidence of the structural limits to interracial communication that come with high levels of residential segregation.

Whereas white speech has become more regionally specialized over time, with linguistic patterns varying increasingly between metropolitan areas, Labov and his colleagues found precisely the opposite pattern for Black English: it has become progressively more uniform across urban areas. Over the past two decades, the Black English Vernaculars of Boston, Chicago, Detroit, New York, and Philadelphia have become increasingly similar in their grammatical structure and lexicon, reflecting urban blacks' common social and economic isolation within urban America.[63] Although black speech has become more uniform internally, however, as a dialect it has drifted farther and farther away from the form and structure of Standard American English. According to Labov's measurements, blacks and whites in the United States increasingly speak different tongues, with different grammatical rules, divergent pronunciations, and separate vocabularies.[64]

Labov has concluded that this separate linguistic evolution stems from the high degree of segregation imposed on blacks in U.S. urban areas, which confines them to isolated and self-contained linguistic communities. In a series of critical tests, he and Wendell Harris demonstrated that the less contact blacks have with whites, the greater their reliance on Black English Vernacular and the less their ability to speak Standard American English.[65] Blacks who live within the ghetto, in particular, display speech patterns that are quite remote from the dialect spoken by most white Americans. Because of segregation, the languages spoken by blacks and whites are moving toward mutual unintelligibility.

The recognition of Black English Vernacular's progressive evolution away from Standard American English in no way implies that it is inferior as a language; nor does the fact that whites may have a difficult time understanding Black English mean that it is flawed as medium of human communication. The linguistic drift of black English does, however, symbolize the breakdown of communication between the races, and suggests at least two additional barriers to black socioeconomic advancement.

U.S. schools rely almost exclusively on the standard dialect for instruction and exposition. Thus when children grow up speaking Black English Vernacular rather than Standard American English, their educational progress is seriously hampered. When ghetto children enter schools where texts and instructional materials all are written in Standard English, and where teachers speak primarily in this dialect, they experience a culture shock akin to that felt by immigrant children from non-English-speaking countries. Because the language they are being taught to read and write is not the same as the one they speak, their confidence and self-esteem are threatened, thereby undermining the entire learning process.[66] Unless special efforts are made to compensate for the wide discrepancy between the language of the classroom and the spoken language of everyday life, formal education is likely to be a frustrating and alienating experience for ghetto children.

Acquiring fluency in Standard English is difficult for black children whose entire social world is bounded by the ghetto and whose families have no familiarity with the mainstream dialect. Children learn language through frequent interaction with other speakers. Although they will be able to understand Standard English from exposure to television, radio, and other media, children growing up in the ghetto will not be able to speak it unless they have had the opportunity to use it actively to manipulate their social environment.[67] The passive consumption of mass media does not provide this sort of active learning experience. Without systematic reinforcement in other social contexts, ghetto dwellers are unlikely to learn to speak a style of English familiar to most whites.

The educational barriers facing ghetto children are exacerbated by teachers and school administrators who view Black English as "wrong," "bad," or "inferior," thereby stigmatizing black children and further undermining their motivation to learn.[68] In many school settings, Black English is pejoratively stereotyped and taken to indicate a lack of intelligence, an absence of motivation, or the presence of a learning disability. These perceptions lead to a lowering of expectations and to the systematic tracking of ghetto children into remedial courses, thereby making low achievement a self-fulfilling prophecy. Thus black educational progress is hampered not only because segregation concentrates poverty within ghetto schools but also because segregation confines blacks to an isolated linguistic community. Segregation ensures that black children will speak a nonstandard dialect of English that is not taught, spoken, or appreciated in the American school system.

The difficulties caused by a reliance on Black English do not stop at the classroom door. Facility with Standard English is required for many jobs in the larger economy, especially those that carry good prospects for socioeconomic advancement and income growth. To the extent that an exclusive reliance on Black English undermines employability, therefore, it constitutes a second barrier to socioeconomic achievement.[69]

The ability to speak, write, and communicate effectively in Standard English is essential for employment in most white-collar jobs. The ability to speak Standard English, at least, is also widely demanded by employers for clerical or service positions that bring jobholders into frequent contact with the general public, most of whom are white.[70] Employers make frequent use of language as a screening device for blue-collar jobs, even those that involve little or no interaction with the public. They assume that people who speak Black English carry a street culture that devalues behaviors and attitudes consistent with being a "good worker," such as regularity, punctuality, dependability, and respect for authority.[71]

The inability to communicate in Standard American English, therefore, presents serious obstacles to socioeconomic advancement. Black Americans who aspire to socioeconomic success generally must acquire a facility in Standard English as a precondition of advancement, even if they retain a fluency in black speech. Successful blacks who have grown up in the ghetto literally become bilingual, learning to switch back and forth between black and white dialects depending on the social context.[72]

This "code switching" involves not only a change of words but a shift between contrasting cultures and identities. Although some people acquire the ability to make this shift without difficulty, it causes real social and psychological problems for others. For someone raised in the segregated environment of the ghetto, adopting white linguistic conventions can seem like a betrayal of black culture, a phony attempt to deny the reality of one's "blackness." As a result, black people who regularly speak Standard American English often encounter strong disapproval from other blacks. Many well-educated blacks recall with some bitterness the ridicule and ostracism they suffered as children for the sin of "talking white."[73]

The Culture of Segregation

This struggle between "black" and "white" speech patterns is symptomatic of a larger conflict between "black" and "white" cultural identities that arises from residential segregation. In response to the harsh and isolated conditions of ghetto life, a segment of the urban black population has evolved a set of behaviors, attitudes, and values that are increasingly at variance with those held in the wider society. Although these adaptations represent rational accommodations to social and economic conditions within the ghetto, they are not widely accepted or understood outside of it, and in fact are negatively evaluated by most of American society.

Middle-class American culture generally idealizes the values of self-reliance, hard work, sobriety, and sacrifice, and adherence to these principles is widely believed to bring monetary reward and economic advancement in society.[74] Among men, adherence to these values means that employment and financial security should precede marriage, and among women they imply that childbearing should occur only after adequate means to support the raising of children have been secured, either through marriage or through employment. In the ideal world, everyone is hardworking, self-sufficient, and not a burden to fellow citizens.

In most white neighborhoods the vast majority of working age men are employed. Because jobs are available and poverty is relatively uncommon, most residents can reasonably expect to conform to ideal values most of the time. Men generally do find jobs before marrying and women have reason to believe that men will help support the children they father. Although these ideals may be violated with some frequency, there is enough conformity in most white neighborhoods for them to retain their force as guides for behavior; there are still enough people who exemplify the values to serve as role models for others. Those failures that do occur are taken to reflect individual flaws, and most whites derive a sense of self-esteem and prestige by conforming to the broader ideals of American society.

Ghetto blacks, however, face very different neighborhood conditions created by residential segregation. A large share live in a geographically isolated and racially homogeneous neighborhood where poverty is endemic, joblessness is rife, schools are poor, and even high school graduates are unlikely to speak Standard English with any facility. Employment opportunities are limited, and given the social isolation enforced by segregation, black men are not well connected to employers in the larger economy. As a result, young men coming of age in ghetto areas are relatively unlikely to find jobs capable of supporting a wife and children,[75] and black women, facing a dearth of potential husbands and an absence of educational institutions capable of preparing them for gainful employment, cannot realistically hope to conform to societal ideals of marriage and childbearing.[76]

The conditions of the ghetto, in short, make it exceedingly difficult to live up to broader societal values with respect to work, marriage, and family formation, and poor blacks are thus denied the opportunity to build self-esteem and to acquire prestige through channels valued in the wider society. As a result, an alternative status system has evolved within America's ghettos that is defined *in opposition to* the basic ideals and values of American society. It is a culture that explains and legitimizes the social and economic shortcomings of ghetto blacks, which are built into their lives by segregation rather than by personal failings. This culture of segregation attaches value and meaning to a way of life that the broader society would label as deviant and unworthy.[77]

The effects of segregation on black cultural identity were first noted by the psychologist Kenneth Clark in *Dark Ghetto:* "Because the larger society has clearly rejected [the black ghetto dweller], he rejects . . . the values, the aspirations, and techniques of that society. His conscious or unconscious argument is that he cannot hope to win meaningful self-esteem through the avenues ordinarily available to more privileged individuals, [which] have been blocked for him through inadequate education, through job discrimination, and through a system of social and political power which is not responsive to his needs."[78] As a psychological defense mechanism, therefore, ghetto dwellers evolve a cultural identity defined in opposition to the larger ideals of white society.

The anthropologists John Ogbu and Signithia Fordham, building on Clark's work, have shown that the formation of such oppositional identities is a common psychological adaptation whenever a powerless minority group is systematically subordinated by a dominant majority.[79] "Subordinate minorities like black Americans develop a sense of collective identity or sense of peoplehood in opposition to the social identity of white Americans because of the way white Americans treat them in economic, political, social, and psychological domains . . . The oppositional identity of the minority evolves because they perceive and experience the treatment by whites as collective and enduring oppression. They realize and believe that, regardless of their individual ability and training or education, and regardless of their place of origin . . . , they cannot expect to be treated like white Americans."[80]

As a protection against the persistent assaults to self-esteem that are inherent in ghetto life, black street culture has evolved to legitimate certain behaviors prevalent within the black community that would otherwise be held in contempt by white society. Black identity is thus constructed as a series of oppositions to conventional middle-class "white" attitudes and behavior. If whites speak Standard American English, succeed in school, work hard at routine jobs, marry, and support their children, then to be "black" requires one to speak Black English, do poorly in school, denigrate conventional employment, shun marriage, and raise children outside of marriage. To do otherwise would be to "act white."

By concentrating poor people prone to such oppositional identities in racially homogeneous settings, segregation creates the structural context for the maintenance and perpetuation of an ongoing oppositional culture, "which includes devices for protecting [black] identity and for maintaining boundaries between [blacks] and white Americans. [Blacks] regard certain forms of behavior and certain activities or events, symbols, and meanings as *not appropriate* for them because . . . [they] are characteristic of white Americans. At the same time, they emphasize other forms of behavior and other events, symbols, and meanings as more appropriate for them because they are *not* a part of white Americans' way of life."[81]

Ogbu and Fordham are educational specialists who have specifically documented the effect of oppositional black culture on educational achievement among black children. Their investigations show how bright, motivated, and intellectually curious ghetto children face tremendous pressure from their peers to avoid "acting white" in succeeding in school and achieving academic distinction.[82] The pressure for educational failure is most intense during the teenage years, when peer acceptance is so important and black young people live in fear of being labeled "Oreos," "Uncle Toms," or "Aunt Jemimahs" for speaking Standard English or doing well in school. If they actually achieve academic distinction, they risk being called a "brainiac," or worse, a "pervert brainiac" (someone who is not only smart but of questionable sexuality as well).[83]

Black children who do overcome the odds and achieve academic success in inner-city schools typically go to great lengths, and adopt ingenious strategies, to lessen the burden of "acting white." Some deliberately fail selected courses, others scale back their efforts and get B's or C's rather than the A's they are capable of, and still others become class clowns, seeking to deflect attention away from their scholarly achievements by acting so ridiculous that their peers no longer take them seriously.[84] Better to be called "crazy" or a "clown" than a "pervert brainiac."

The powerful effect of oppositional ghetto culture on black educational performance is suggested by the recent work of James Rosenbaum and his colleagues at Northwestern University.[85] Working in the Chicago area, they compared low-income black students from families assigned to scattered site housing in a white suburb (under the *Gautreaux* court decision) with comparable students from families assigned to public housing in Chicago's ghetto. Although the two groups were initially identical, once removed from ghetto high schools black students achieved higher grades, lower dropout rates, better academic preparation, and higher rates of college attendance compared with those who remained behind in ghetto institutions.

Another study by Robert Crain and Rita Mahard, who used a nationwide sample, found that northern blacks who attended racially mixed schools were more likely to enter and stay in college than those who went to all-black high schools.[86] Susan Mayer followed students who attended the tenth grade in poor and affluent high schools in 1980 and determined the likelihood of their dropping out before 1982. Controlling for family background, she discovered that students who went to affluent schools were considerably less likely to drop out than those who attended poor schools, and that girls in affluent schools were much less likely to have a child. Moreover, white students who attended predominantly black high schools were considerably more likely to drop out and have a child than those who attended predominantly white schools.[87]

All too often, whites observe the workings of black oppositional culture and conclude that African Americans suffer from some kind of "cultural defect," or that they are somehow "culturally disadvantaged." In doing so, they blame the victims of segregation rather than the social arrangements that created the oppositional culture in the first place.[88] It is not a self-perpetuating "culture of poverty"[89] that retards black educational progress but a structurally created and sustained "culture of segregation" that, however useful in adapting to the harsh realities of ghetto life, undermines socioeconomic progress in the wider society.

As Kenneth Clark pointed out in 1965, "the invisible walls of a segregated society are not only damaging but protective in a debilitating way. There is considerable psychological safety in the ghetto; there one lives among one's own and does not risk rejection among strangers. One first becomes aware of the psychological damage of such 'safety' when the walls of the ghetto are breached and the Negro ventures out into the repressive, frightening white world . . . Most Negroes take the first steps into an integrated society tentatively and torn with conflict. To be the first Negro who is offered a job in a company brings a sense of triumph but also the dread of failure."[90] More recently, Shelby Steele has written of the "integration shock" that envelops blacks who enter white society directly from the isolated world of the ghetto.[91]

The origins of black oppositional culture can be traced to the period before 1920, when black migration fomented a hardening of white racial attitudes and a systematic limiting of opportunities for African Americans on a variety of fronts.[92] Whereas urban blacks had zealously pursued education after the Civil War and were making great strides, the rise of Jim Crow in the south and de facto segregation in the north severed the links between hard work, education, sobriety, and their presumed rewards in society.[93] Although black elites continued to promote these values, the rise of the ghetto made them look increasingly pathetic and ridiculous to the mass of recent in-migrants: in the face of pervasive barriers to social and residential mobility, the moral admonitions of the elites seemed hollow and pointless.[94] If whites would not accept blacks on the basis of their individual accomplishments and if hard work and education went unrewarded, then why expend the effort? If one could never be accepted as white, it was just demeaning and humiliating to go through the motions of "acting white." Malcolm X summed up this attitude with his sardonic quip, "What do you call a Negro with a Ph.D.? A nigger."[95]

Unlike other groups, the force of oppositional culture is particularly powerful among African Americans because it is so strongly reinforced by residential segregation. By isolating blacks within racially homogeneous neighborhoods and concentrating poverty within them, segregation creates an environment where failure to meet the ideal standards of American society loses its stigma; indeed, individual shortcomings become normative and supported by the values of oppositional culture. As transgressions lose their stigma through repetition and institutionalization, individual behavior at variance with broader societal ideals becomes progressively more likely.[96]

The culture of segregation arises from the coincidence of racial isolation and high poverty, which inevitably occurs when a poor minority group is residentially segregated. By concentrating poverty, segregation simultaneously concentrates male joblessness, teenage motherhood, single parenthood, alcoholism, and drug abuse, thus creating an entirely black social world in which these oppositional states are normative. Given the racial isolation and concentrated poverty of the ghetto, it is hardly surprising that black street culture has drifted steadily away from middle-class American values.

The steady divergence of black street culture from the white mainstream is clearly visible in a series of participant observer studies of ghetto life conducted over the past thirty years. Studies carried out during the 1960s and 1970s—such as Elliot Liebow's *Tally's Corner*, Lee Rainwater's *Behind Ghetto Walls*, Ulf Hannerz's *Soulside*, and Elijah Anderson's *A Place on the Corner*—were remarkably consistent in reporting that ghetto dwellers, despite their poverty and oppression, essentially subscribed to the basic values of American society.[97] What set ghetto blacks apart from other Americans was not their lack of fealty to American ideals but their inability to accomplish them. Specifically, the pervasiveness of poverty, unemployment, and dependency in the ghetto made it nearly impossible for them to live up to ideals they in fact held, which in turn undermined their self-esteem and thus created a psychological need for gratification through other means.

The participant observer studies indicated that feelings of personal inadequacy led black men to reject the unskilled and poorly paid jobs open to them, to denigrate the kind of work these jobs represented, and to seek gratification through more accessible channels, such as sexual liaisons or intoxication. Women and men tended to begin sexual relations at a young age, and woman generally found themselves pregnant as teenagers. Childbirth was typically followed by marriage or some informal living arrangement, at least for a time; but eventually the woman's demands for financial support undermined her partner's self-esteem, and family responsibilities blocked his access to the alternate status system of the streets. Given the cross-cutting pressures of poverty, joblessness, low self-esteem, family demands, and the allure of the streets, most male-female relationships were short-lived and devolved sooner or later into female-headed families.

Once they had been through this cycle of romance, pregnancy, family formation, and dissolution, black men and women came to see romantic relationships as a mutually exploitative contest whose pleasures were temporary and whose stability could not be relied upon. At the same time, the pervasive poverty of the ghetto meant that families were constantly bombarded with energy-sapping demands for assistance and debilitating requests for financial aid from extended family, friends, and neighbors. Given the association of poverty with crime and violence, moreover, they were constantly at risk of criminal victimization, injury, or even death.

In this social world, ghetto dwellers acquired a tough, cynical attitude toward life, a deep suspicion of the motives of others, and a marked lack of trust in the goodwill or benevolent intentions of people and institutions. Growing up in the ghetto, blacks came to expect the worst of others and to experience little sense of control over their lives. They adapted to these feelings by confining relationships of trust to close kin, especially maternal relatives.

Underlying this bleak portrait of ghetto life painted by studies carried out during the 1960s and 1970s was a common thread. Early participant observers saw ghetto culture as rooted in the structural conditions of poverty, dependency, and joblessness, over which ghetto residents had little control, and all characterized ghetto culture as essentially oppositional. That is, the attitudes and behaviors of ghetto blacks were fundamentally defined in opposition to the ideals of white society. Underneath the jaded rejection of conventional mores, ghetto dwellers, at least in the first or second generations, still clung to the basic values of American society. Indeed, it was because they judged themselves so harshly by broader standards that the psychological need for an oppositional identity arose in the first place.

Over time, however, as intense racial isolation and acutely concentrated poverty have continued, ghetto attitudes, values, and ideals have become progressively less connected to those prevailing elsewhere in the United States. More and more, the culture of the ghetto has become an entity unto itself, remote from the rest of American society and its institutions, and drifting ever further afield. As conditions within the ghetto worsen, as the social environment grows more hostile, and as racial isolation deepens, the original connection of ghetto culture to the broader values of American society—even if only in opposition—has faded.

The new culture of the ghetto increasingly rejects the values of American society as a farce and a sham, and traits that were once clearly oppositional and therefore somehow *linked* to the rest of American society have become ends in themselves, esteemed in their own right and disconnected from their relationship to the surrounding "white" society. Under the combined pressure of isolation and poverty, black street culture has increasingly become an autonomous cultural system. Participant observer studies of ghetto life done in the 1980s have an even darker and more pessimistic tone than those carried out in earlier decades. The contrast is clearly illustrated by two studies conducted by the sociologist Elijah Anderson: one carried out in the ghetto of Chicago during the early 1970s and the other conducted in a poor black neighborhood of Philadelphia during the late 1980s.

In Anderson's first study, *A Place on the Corner*, basic American values such as hard work, honesty, diligence, respect for authority, and staying out of trouble were still very much in evidence in the thoughts and words of the poor black men gathered around the corner bar he studied.[98] Indeed, these values provided the basis for an alternative status system that arose to confer esteem when broader standards were not met, and to encourage young men to live up to ideals despite the long odds. As a result, Anderson's subjects—who would be considered of "no account" by conventional standards—acquire a certain nobility for their pursuit of dignity and honor in the face of adversity.

In contrast, the subjects of Anderson's latest study, *Streetwise*, scorn and ridicule conventional American ideals.[99] Symbolic of the disappearance of traditional values from the ghetto is the breakdown of the longstanding relationship between "old heads" and young boys. According to Anderson, "an old head was a man of stable means who was strongly committed to family life, to church, and, most important, to passing on his philosophy, developed through his own rewarding experience with work, to young boys he found worthy. He personified the work ethnic and equated it with value and high standards of morality; in his eyes a workingman was a good, decent individual."[100]

In the ghetto environment of earlier decades, the old head "acted as a kind of guidance counselor and moral cheerleader who preached anticrime and antitrouble messages to his charges," and "the young boy readily deferred to the old head's chronological age and worldly experience."[101] In contrast, today, "as the economic and social circumstances of the urban ghetto have changed, the traditional old head has been losing prestige and credibility as a role model . . . When gainful employment and its rewards are not forthcoming, boys easily conclude that the moral lessons of the old head concerning the work ethnic, punctuality, and honesty do not fit their own circumstances."[102]

In the past, black ghettos also used to contain numerous "female old heads," who served as "neighborhood mothers," correcting and admonishing children in the streets and instructing them in proper behavior.

They "were seen as mature and wise figures in the community, not only by women and girls, but also by many young men" because of their motherly love and concern for children.[103] According to Anderson, however, these role models also have increasingly disappeared, indicating "a breakdown in feelings of community. Residents . . . keep more to themselves now, [and] no longer involve themselves in their neighbors' lives as they did as recently as ten years ago."[104]

In place of traditional mores that assign value to steady work, family life, the church, and respect for others, a drug culture and its economy have arisen, with profound effects on community well-being. Anderson and others have studied and written on the appeal of the underground drug economy to young men and women from the ghetto.[105] According to Anderson, "the roles of drug pusher, pimp, and (illegal) hustler have become more and more attractive. Street-smart young people who operate this underground economy are apparently able to obtain big money more easily and glamorously than their elders, including traditional male and female old heads. Because they appear successful, they become role models for still younger people."[106]

The proliferation of the drug culture within the ghetto has exacerbated the problems caused by segregation and its concentration of poverty, adding a powerful impetus to the cycle of neighborhood decline.[107] Given the financial gain to be had from drugs, ghetto dealers establish aggressive marketing strategies to capture business from disillusioned young people who see little hope for improvement through work, education, or staying out of trouble. Because limited economic opportunities in the ghetto as well as drug use itself make it difficult for drug users to support themselves, the spread of drug use leads inevitably to the escalation of crime and violence. As a by-product of the new drug culture, the violent death rate has skyrocketed among black men, prostitution has spread among black women, and the number of drug-addicted babies has mushroomed.[108] The old social order of the ghetto has increasingly broken down and veered off on an independent path dramatically different from that prevailing in the rest of American society.

At the same time, relations between the sexes, which were already antagonistic and mutually exploitative in the ghetto world of the 1960s, had by the 1980s lost all connection to conventional family values. According to Anderson, by the late 1980s sexual relations in the ghetto had degenerated into a vicious, competitive contest in which young men and women exploited each other with diametrically opposed goals.[109] For young ghetto men, sex had become strictly a means of enhancing status among male peers and of experiencing pleasure at the expense of women. "To the young man the woman becomes, in the most profound sense, a sexual object. Her body and mind are the object of a sexual game, to be won for personal aggrandizement. Status goes to the winner, and sex is prized not as a testament of love but as testimony to control of another human being. Sex is the prize, and sexual conquests are a game whose goal is to make a fool of the young woman."[110]

In the ghetto of the 1960s, a pregnancy growing out of such casual sexual encounters was relatively likely to be followed by a marriage or some other housekeeping arrangement, however unstable or short-lived it might have been. By the late 1980s, however, this bow to conventional culture had been eliminated in black street culture. "In the social context of persistent poverty, [black men] have come to devalue the conventional marital relationship, viewing women as a burden and children as even more of one."[111] Even if a young man "admits paternity and 'does right' by the girl, his peer group likely will label him a chump, a square, or a fool."[112]

Ghetto women, for their part, seek gratification less through sex than through pregnancy and childbirth. They understand that their suitors' sweet words and well-honed "rap" are fabrications being told in order to extract sex from them, and despite a few romantic self-deceptions along the way, they realize that if they become pregnant the father is unlikely to support their child. Nonetheless, they look forward to getting pregnant, for in the contemporary ghetto "it is becoming socially acceptable for a young woman to have children out of wedlock—supported by a regular welfare check."[113]

These findings are corroborated by other ethnographic interviews gathered as part of William Julius Wilson's larger study of urban poverty in Chicago. When the sociologist Richard Taub examined the interview transcripts, he found that marriage had virtually disappeared as a meaningful category of thought and discourse among poor blacks.[114] Informants consistently stated that husband-wife relationships were neither important nor reliable as a basis for family life and childrearing, and they were deeply suspicious of the intentions of the opposite sex.

The disappearance of marriage as a social institution was underscored by field observations that Taub and his associates undertook in black and Mexican neighborhoods. Whereas a four-block shopping strip in one of Chicago's poor Mexican neighborhoods yielded fifteen shops that provided goods or services explicitly connected to marriage, a trip to a comparable black shopping area uncovered only two shops that even mentioned marriage, and not very prominently at that.[115]

Elijah Anderson argues that childbearing has become increasingly disconnected from marriage in the ghetto; black women now seek childbirth to signal their status as adults and to validate their worth and standing before their own peer group—namely, other young black women. A baby is a young girl's entry ticket into what Anderson calls "the baby club."[116] This "club" consists of young black mothers who gather in public places with their children to "lobby for compliments, smiles, and nods of approval and feel very good when they are forthcoming, since they signal affirmation and pride. On Sundays, the new little dresses and suits come out and the cutest babies are passed around, and this attention serves as a social measure of the person. The young mothers who form such baby clubs develop an ideology counter to that of more conventional society, one that not only approves of but enhances their position. In effect, they work to create value and status by inverting that of the girls who do not become pregnant. The teenage mother derives status from her baby; hence, her preoccupation with the impression that the baby makes and her willingness to spend inordinately large sums toward that end."[117]

According to Anderson, sex is thus a key component in the informal status system that has evolved in the street culture of America's urban ghettos. In the absence of gratification through the conventional avenues of work and family, young men and women have increasingly turned to one commodity that lies within their reach. Through sex, young men get pleasure and a feeling of self-esteem before their peers, whereas young women get a baby and a sense of belonging within the baby club. This relationship of mutual exploitation, however, has come at a price. It has further marginalized black men from black women and has escalated the war of the sexes to new heights, a fact that is clearly revealed in the music of black street culture—rap.

An unabashedly misogynist viewpoint is extolled by rap groups such as N.W.A. ("Niggers with Attitude"), whose song "A Bitch Iz a Bitch" depicts black women as scheming, vain, whining mercenaries whose goal is to deprive black men of their self-esteem, money, and possessions. In the view of N.W.A., women are good for little more than sex, and their incessant demands for attention, constant requests for money and support, and their ever-present threats to male pride can only be checked through violence, " . . . 'cause a bitch is a bitch."[118]

The female side of the issue is aired by the female rap group H.W.A. ("Hoes [Whores] with Attitude") in songs such as "A Trick Is a Trick," "Little Dick," and "1-900-BITCHES," which attack men as vain, superficial creatures who are incompetent in their love-making, ill equipped to satisfy, and prone to meaningless violence when their inflated pride is punctured. Their metaphor for the state of male-female relations in the ghetto is that of a whorehouse, where all women are whores and men are either tricks or pimps. The liner notes leave little doubt as to the group's message: "Everybody is a pimp of some kind and pimpin' is easy when you got a Hoe Wit Attitude."[119]

The war of words between black men and women has also been fought in the black press, exemplified in 1990 by the appearance of *The Blackman's Guide to Understanding the Blackwoman*, by Shaharazad Ali, which presents a vituperative attack on black women for their supposedly historical emasculation of black men. The book advocates the violent subjugation of women by black men, advising male readers that "there is never an excuse for ever hitting a Blackwoman anywhere but in the mouth. Because it is from that hole, in the lower part of her face, that all her rebellion culminates into words. Her unbridled tongue is a main reason she cannot get along with the Blackman . . . If she ignores the authority and superiority of the Blackman, there is a penalty. When she crosses this line and becomes viciously insulting it is time for the Blackman to soundly slap her in the mouth."[120] Ten black scholars answered to the attack in a pamphlet entitled *Confusion by Any Other Name*, hoping "to respond to the range of insulting myths, half-truths and generalized personal experiences by the author."[121]

From a sociological point of view, the specific content of these works is less important than what they illustrate about the state of relations between the sexes within the black community. After evolving for decades under conditions of intense social and economic isolation, black street culture has become increasingly divorced from basic American ideals of family, work, and respect for others. By confining large numbers of black people to an environment within which failure is endemic, negative role models abound, and adherence to conventional values is nearly impossible, segregation has helped to create a nihilistic and violent counterculture sharply at odds with the basic values and goals of a democratic society. As Kenneth Clark presciently noted in 1965, "the pathologies of the ghetto community perpetuate themselves through cumulative ugliness, deterioration, and isolation."[122]

The social environment created by segregation places a heavy burden on black parents aspiring to promote conventional attitudes and behavior in their children and increase the odds for their socioeconomic success. Although the problem is most acute for the poor, segregation confines all blacks to segregated neighborhoods regardless of social class, so working- and middle-class blacks also have a very difficult time insulating their children from the competing values and attitudes of the street. Compared with children of middle-class whites, children of middle-class blacks are much more likely to be exposed to poverty, drugs, teenage pregnancy, family disruption, and violence in the neighborhoods where they live.

As a result, it requires a great deal of concerted effort by committed parents, and no small amount of luck, to raise children successfully within the ghetto.[123] Given the burden of "acting white," the pressures to speak Black English, the social stigma attached to "brainiacs," the allure of drug taking, the quick money to be had from drug dealing, and the romantic sexuality of the streets, it is not surprising that black educational achievement has stagnated.

Although participant observer studies and rap lyrics illustrate the harsh realities of black street life, they do not "prove" the harmful effects of growing up in a ghetto. Hard evidence about segregation's ill effects requires statistical studies using nationally representative data. Linda Datcher estimates that moving a poor black male from his typical neighborhood (66% black with an average income of $8,500) to a typical white neighborhood (86% white with a mean income of $11,500) would raise his educational attainment by nearly a year.[124] Mary Corcoran and her colleagues found similar results when they considered the effect of moving a man from a typical black to a typical white neighborhood;[125] and Jonathan Crane shows that the dropout probability for black teenage males increases dramatically as the percentage of low-status workers in the neighborhood rises, going from about 8% in areas where three-quarters of the workers are in low-status occupations to nearly 35% when the percentage reaches 97%.[126]

Growing up in a poor neighborhood also undermines the odds of success in the labor market. Linda Datcher's statistical estimates suggest that growing up in a poor black area lowers a man's earnings by at least 27%.[127] Although Mary Corcoran and her colleagues put the percentage loss at about 18%,[128] both teams of researchers agree that black men suffer a loss in earning ability simply for the misfortune of having grown up in a ghetto.

Exposure to conditions typical of the ghetto also dramatically increases the odds of pregnancy and childbirth among teenagers. According to estimates by Jonathan Crane, the probability of a teenage birth increases dramatically as the percentage of low-status workers in the child's neighborhoods increases from 70% to 95%, ultimately reaching a likelihood of about 20%.[129] Similarly, Dennis Hogan and Evelyn Kitagawa found that living in a very poor neighborhood raised the monthly pregnancy rate among black adolescents by 20% and significantly lowered the age at which they became sexually active;[130] and Frank Furstenburg and his colleagues have shown that attending school in integrated rather than segregated classrooms substantially lowers the odds that fifteen- to sixteen-year-old black girls will experience sexual intercourse.[131]

The quantitative evidence thus suggests that any process that concentrates poverty within racially isolated neighborhoods will simultaneously increase the odds of socioeconomic failure within the segregated group. No matter what their personal traits or characteristics, people who grow up and live in environments of concentrated poverty and social isolation are more likely to become teenage mothers, drop out of school, achieve only low levels of education, and earn lower adult incomes.

One study has directly linked the socioeconomic disadvantages suffered by individual minority members to the degree of segregation they experience in society. Using individual, community, and metropolitan data from the fifty largest U.S. metropolitan areas in 1980, Douglas Massey, Andrew Gross, and Mitchell Eggers showed that group segregation and poverty rates interacted to concentrate poverty geographically within neighborhoods, and that exposure to neighborhood poverty subsequently increased the probability of male joblessness and single motherhood among group members. In this fashion, they linked the structural condition of segregation to individual behaviors widely associated with the underclass through the intervening factor of neighborhood poverty, holding individual background characteristics constant.[132]

Their results are summarized in Table 6.2, which traces what happens to levels of black poverty concentration, male joblessness, and single motherhood when the black poverty rate is systematically increased from 10% to 40% under conditions of no segregation and high segregation (where the latter condition is defined to occur with a black-white dissimilarity index of 90). In the absence of segregation, changing the overall rate of black poverty has a relatively modest effect on the neighborhood environment that blacks experience. By increasing the number of poor

Table 6.2 Predicted neighborhood poverty concentrations, probabilities of male joblessness, and likelihoods of single parenthood, assuming different group poverty rates and levels of segregation

Group's poverty rate and level of segregation	Predicted poverty concentration in neighborhood	Predicted probability that a young black man is jobless	Predicted probability that a young black woman heads a family
No residential segregation			
Poverty rate 10%	7.8%	35.8%	22.8%
Poverty rate 20%	10.2	39.9	28.0
Poverty rate 30%	13.3	39.9	28.0
Poverty rate 40%	17.2	39.9	28.0
High residential segregation			
Poverty rate 10%	10.2	39.9	28.0
Poverty rate 20%	17.2	39.9	28.0
Poverty rate 30%	27.5	43.0	31.6
Poverty rate 40%	40.9	53.3	40.6

Source: Douglas S. Massey, Andrew B. Gross, and Mitchell L. Eggers, "Segregation, the Concentration of Poverty, and the Life Chances of Individuals," *Social Science Research* 20 (1991):415.

Note: No segregation means black-white dissimilarity index equals 0 and high segregation means this index equals 90; predicted probabilities control for age, nativity, education, marital status, and English-language ability.

blacks, the degree of poverty within neighborhoods where blacks live rises somewhat, but under integrated conditions the additional poor families are scattered evenly throughout the urban area, so the level of poverty concentration does not increase much in any single neighborhood. Overall, it rises modestly from about 8% to 17% as a result of shifting the rate of black poverty from 10% to 40%.

Although the probabilities of male joblessness and single motherhood are sensitive to the rate of poverty that people experience in their neighborhoods, this modest change in the concentration of neighborhood poverty is not enough to affect these individual outcomes very much. The probability of male joblessness rises only from 36% to 40% as a result of the increased poverty concentration, and the likelihood of single motherhood goes from 23% to 28%. In the absence of racial segregation, therefore, even substantial increases in the overall rate of black poverty (from 10% to 40%) would not greatly affect the welfare of individual blacks, because the additional black poverty would not be concentrated but spread widely around the metropolitan area.

In a highly segregated urban area, in contrast, increasing the rate of black poverty causes a marked increase in the concentration of poverty within the neighborhoods where blacks live. As the overall rate of poverty increases from 10% to 40%, the poverty rate in black neighborhoods goes from 10% to 41%. The degree of poverty concentration increases so dramatically because all of the additional poverty must be absorbed by a small number of geographically isolated black neighborhoods. As we demonstrated in the last chapter, segregation and poverty interact to yield geographically concentrated poverty.

This sharp increase in neighborhood poverty has profound consequences for the well-being of individual blacks, even those who have not been pushed into poverty themselves, because segregation forces them to live in neighborhoods with many families who are poor. As a result of the increase in neighborhood poverty to which they are exposed, individual probabilities of joblessness and single motherhood rise substantially. As the overall black poverty rate rises from 10% to 40% and the amount of poverty concentrated within black neighborhoods experiences a comparable increase, the probability of joblessness among young black males rises from 40% to 53% and the likelihood of single motherhood increases from 28% to 41%.

Increasing the rate of poverty of a segregated group thus causes its neighborhood environment to deteriorate, which in turn causes individual probabilities of socioeconomic failure to rise. The same rise in poverty without segregation would hardly affect group members at all, because it would have marginal effects on the neighborhoods where they live. Segregation, in other words, is directly responsible for the creation of a harsh and uniquely disadvantaged black residential environment, making it quite likely that individual blacks themselves will fail, no matter what their socioeconomic characteristics or family background. Racial segregation is the institutional nexus that enables the transmission of poverty from person to person and generation to generation, and is therefore a primary structural factor behind the perpetuation of the urban underclass.

How to Build an Underclass

The foregoing analysis of segregation and its consequences constitutes a primer on how to construct an urban underclass. To begin, choose a minority group whose members are somehow identifiably different from the majority.

Once the group has been selected, the next step in creating an underclass is to confine its members to a small number of contiguous residential areas, and then to impose on them stringent barriers to residential mobility. These barriers are effectively created through discrimination buttressed by prejudice. Those who attempt to leave the enclave are systematically steered away from majority neighborhoods and back to minority or racially mixed areas. If they inquire about homes in other areas, they are treated brusquely and told none are available, and if they insist on seeing an advertised unit, little information is provided about it and no other units are shown. If these deceptions are overcome and a minority homebuyer succeeds in making an offer on a home in a majority neighborhood, the sales agent provides as little information as possible about the options for financing the sale and makes no effort to assist the customer in obtaining a mortgage. At the same time, the seller is discouraged from coming down in price to meet the offer that has been made.

If, despite these efforts, a minority family succeeds in having its offer to buy a majority home accepted, financial institutions take over the task of enforcing the barriers to residential mobility by attempting to deny the family's application for a mortgage, either on the basis of "objective" criteria such as the applicant's income, employment, or family history or because of more subjective concerns about neighborhood "quality" or "stability." Through whatever means, minority loan applications are rejected at a rate several times that of majority applications.

If the foregoing barriers are still somehow overcome and a minority family actually succeeds in moving into a majority neighborhood, then the fallback mechanisms of prejudice come into play. The minority family is systematically harassed by threatening phone calls, rocks thrown through windows, property vandalism, burning crosses, and if these crass measures are unacceptable, through more genteel mechanisms of social ostracism. If acts of prejudice do not succeed in dislodging the family, the ultimate weapon is the avoidance by majority members of the neighborhood. Those in the immediate area seek to leave as soon as they are able and no potential majority homebuyers are shown properties in the area. As a result, the neighborhood rapidly turns from a majority to a minority population.

Through the systematic application of these principles, areas where members of the minority manage to gain entry can be restricted in number and confined largely to locations adjacent to existing minority neighborhoods, thereby maintaining the residential structure of the ghetto. Moreover, prejudice and discrimination applied in the manner just discussed have the additional effect of undermining minority self-esteem, because they make it very clear that no matter how much money or education a minority person may have, he or she will never be accepted or treated as an equal by majority neighbors.

Once a group's segregation in society has been ensured, the next step in building an underclass is to drive up its rate of poverty. Segregation paradoxically facilitates this task, because policies that harm a highly segregated minority group and its neighborhoods will have few untoward side effects on other racial or ethnic groups. Geographic isolation translates into political isolation, making it difficult for segregated groups to form political coalitions with others to end policies inimical to their self-interests or to promote policies that might advance their welfare. Racial segregation thus makes it politically easy to limit the number of government jobs within the ghetto, to reduce its public services, to keep its schools understaffed and underfunded, to lower the transfer payments on which its poor depend, and to close its hospitals, clinics, employment offices, and other social support institutions.

With the political marginalization of minority members ensured by their segregation, the only thing required to set off a spiral of decay within the ghetto is a first-class economic disaster that removes the means of subsistence from a large share of the population. If the minority migrated to cities largely to take industrial jobs vacated by upwardly mobile majority immigrants, the inner-city manufacturing base provides a particularly opportune point at which to undercut the economic supports of the minority community, thereby bringing about the necessary increases in minority poverty.

Through a combination of corporate disinvestments in older plants and equipment, a decentralization of blue-collar employment from city to suburban areas, the relocation of manufacturing processes to nonmetropolitan areas, the transfer of production jobs to the sunbelt or overseas, and the setting of high real interest rates to produce an overvalued dollar and relatively expensive U.S. products, inner-city manufacturing industries can effectively be driven out of the urban economy. As manufacturing employment falls and employment suburbanizes, thousands of ghetto dwellers, primarily men with little formal education, will be displaced from jobs that pay them relatively high wages and sent into a two-tiered service economy that generates a larger number of menial, low-paying jobs but few high-paying positions for people without education or training.

These inner-city economic dislocations drive up the rate of minority poverty.[133] The additional deprivation created by the economic flux is concentrated geographically within isolated ghetto neighborhoods. As neighborhood poverty concentrations rise, income is withdrawn from minority neighborhoods, and the resulting increase in dilapidation and abandonment sets off physical decay that soon spreads to surrounding stable neighborhoods. If, owing to the constraints of fiscal austerity and the political isolation of these neighborhoods, fire service to ghetto areas is simultaneously reduced, then the process of neighborhood decay will be substantially accelerated. The increase in poverty concentration also brings a sharp constriction of demand density within the ghetto, leading to the collapse of its retail sector and the elimination of most nonessential goods and services.

The interaction of poverty and segregation acts to concentrate a variety of deleterious social and economic characteristics, creating an environment where male joblessness, female welfare dependency, crime, drug abuse, teenage childbearing, and single parenthood are common or even normative. The ghetto comes to house an abundance of negative role models who exemplify attitudes and behaviors detrimental to success in the emerging post-industrial service economy.

Given the lack of opportunity, pervasive poverty, and increasing hopelessness of life in the ghetto, a social-psychological dynamic is set in motion to produce a culture of segregation. Under the structural conditions of segregation, it is difficult for ghetto dwellers to build self-esteem by satisfying the values and ideals of the larger society or to acquire prestige through socially accepted paths. Precisely because the ghetto residents deem themselves failures by the broader standards of society, they evolve a parallel status system defined in opposition to the prevailing majority culture. As new generations are born into conditions of increasing deprivation and deepening racial isolation, however, the oppositional origins of the status system gradually recede and the culture of segregation becomes autonomous and independent.

A sure sign that the culture of segregation is well advanced occurs when the language of the segregated group diverges sharply from the standard dialect spoken in the wider society. Not only will the breakdown in intergroup communications enhance feelings of racial separation between the underclass and the rest of society, but the lack of facility in the standard dialect will undermine the minority group's prospects for success in education and employment.

The emergence of a culture of segregation also limits the number of minority families who aspire to leave the ghetto. As "minority" culture becomes more firmly established and deeply rooted, members of the minority who seek integration within the larger social and economic institutions of the society will come under increasing pressure from others to stop acting like a majority member. Those who succumb to this pressure, or who themselves promote self-segregation in language, culture, and housing, will be unlikely to meet with socioeconomic success in the larger society and will be limited to a life of persistent poverty and deprivation. Through prolonged exposure to life in racially isolated and intensely poor neighborhoods, this poverty will quite likely be passed to children in the next generation. When this point is reached, a well-functioning and efficient social structure for the creation and maintenance of an urban underclass will have been created.

7

The Failure of Public Policy

Congress made a promise in 1968 that the Fair Housing Act cannot keep.

Robert G. Schwemm,
former chief trial counsel,
Leadership Council for Metropolitan Open Communities, Chicago

Policymakers have not squarely faced residential segregation as a social issue.[1] Although segregation is the social condition that makes black poverty not only likely but self-perpetuating and permanent, the ghetto continues to exist because white America has not had the political will or desire to dismantle it. Although the nation advanced to the brink of taking dramatic action against racial segregation in 1968, ultimately it retreated, and for the next two decades federal policies all but ensured the ghetto's perpetuation. Fair housing amendments implemented in 1989 provided a glimmer of hope for the future, but unless they are accompanied by more fundamental political changes, they too will fail.

As earlier chapters have shown, the black ghetto was constructed by institutionalized discrimination in the real estate and banking industries, supported by widespread acts of private prejudice and discrimination. Rather than combating these forces of segregation, however, during most of the postwar era federal policies actually abetted them. Discrimination in home lending originated in the Federal Housing Administration and its predecessor agencies. White suburbanization was subsidized by mortgage interest deductions and encouraged by FHA policies that denied credit to inner cities. White flight was enabled by massive federal investment in freeways, often constructed strategically to form barriers between black and white areas. Federal urban renewal programs and public housing projects were used by local governments, with federal acquiescence, to contain and isolate urban blacks.

Progress in dismantling these institutional bases of segregation has been slow and fitful. Executive orders to end racial bias in federally supported housing were ignored by a complacent and often hostile federal bureaucracy, and efforts to rid housing markets of bias were blocked repeatedly within Congress. When a fair housing act banning discrimination finally did pass Congress under unusual circumstances, it had its enforcement provisions systematically gutted as its price of enactment. The limited enforcement authority that Congress did grant under this act was interpreted narrowly by federal agencies, and the enforcement activities they did pursue were poorly funded and badly organized.

As a result of Congressional inaction, bureaucratic inertia, presidential disinterest, public ambivalence, and the active opposition of many vested interests, the fight against housing segregation has been foisted onto private citizens—typically the victims of discrimination themselves—who have turned to the courts for relief. The body of housing discrimination law that now exists, limited as it is, stems almost entirely from the efforts of individual citizens and fair housing organizations.

Such private efforts constitute a David and Goliath struggle, however, because the causes of segregation are systemic and institutional whereas the remedies available under federal law remain largely individual. Although private parties may occasionally find redress when they become victims of racial discrimination, the institutionalized practices that victimized them still continue.

The Struggle for Fair Housing

The long fight against the forces of racial segregation began early in the century, and fittingly, the first federal action came as a result of private litigation. Equally fittingly, given subsequent developments, the Supreme Court decision that barred the segregative force in question was completely ineffective in preventing the subsequent construction of the ghetto.

The case arose as a challenge to a 1914 Louisville city ordinance that prohibited blacks from residing in certain areas of the city designated as "white." Soon after the law's enactment, the president of the local branch of the NAACP, William Warley, arranged to buy a lot in Louisville's white zone from a white realtor, Charles Buchanan. In a prearranged scenario, Buchanan accepted Warley's offer, but Warley refused to make payment on the grounds that he would not be able to occupy the property because of Louisville's racial segregation law; Buchanan then sued Warley for breach of contract in order to initiate a civil test of the law.[2]

In a unanimous 1917 decision effectively ending the growing movement toward legal separation in American cities, the U.S. Supreme Court held that Louisville's segregation ordinance was unconstitutional.[3] But although *Buchanan v. Warley* deprived whites of the legal ability to enforce residential segregation, it did not bar private acts of discrimination in the housing market or restrict the ability of governments to act indirectly to foster segregation. The construction of the ghetto continued apace despite *Buchanan,* and levels of black-white segregation in U.S. cities rose steadily.

In the years after 1917, as rising racial bias became institutionalized within the real estate industry, the most open and flagrant method used to maintain the racial integrity of neighborhoods was the restrictive covenant, discussed in Chapter 2.[4] If this agreement was breached, any party to the covenant could call upon the courts for enforcement and sue the violator for damages.[5] The federal government took no action to block this practice, even though the 1866 Civil Rights Act clearly forbade it. Segregation's individual victims were instead forced to sue for redress in the courts. Legal challenges multiplied during the 1940s, and in 1943 a Chicago Municipal Court judge was the first to question the legality of covenants.[6] After further litigation, one challenge, *Shelly v. Kraemer,* finally worked its way through the judiciary to reach the U.S. Supreme Court in 1948. The high court declared restrictive covenants to be "unenforceable as law and contrary to public policy."[7]

Although this decision ended the real estate industry's reliance on restrictive covenants, it did not outlaw them per se or bar other forms of discrimination against black homeseekers.[8] Covenants continued to be used informally to organize resistance to black entry, and the FHA advocated their use until 1950.[9] The main effect of *Shelly* was to dispel the lingering clouds of doubt surrounding the titles of many homes already in black possession.[10]

With the elimination of these two overt institutional props for racial segregation, whites turned to other, less visible, means of shoring the ghetto's walls. In the private sector, as we have seen, realtors and bankers played leading roles in promoting segregation.[11] In the public sector, local governments took advantage of authority granted under urban renewal legislation to raze expanding black neighborhoods that threatened key white institutions and districts, and they used federal funds to construct massive public housing projects in order to contain displaced black residents.[12]

Throughout the 1950s civil rights groups lobbied Congress and the President to adopt regulations and legislation that would eliminate these discriminatory practices from public and private housing, but a solid bloc of southern Democrats effectively stymied all legislative efforts, and the Republican White House under President Dwight D. Eisenhower was interested neither in regulating markets nor in promoting racial equality. As the new decade approached, however, the civil rights movement gained momentum, especially after the Supreme Court's landmark *Brown v. Topeka* school desegregation decision in 1955.

During the 1960 presidential campaign, John F. Kennedy promised that, if elected, he would quickly sign an executive order to establish a fair housing policy in the executive branch.[13] After his election, however, this promise became bogged down in the politics of race. The fair housing order was only one of several items on the new President's civil rights agenda; he also sought to move a broader civil rights bill through Congress and to appoint Robert Weaver as the first black director of the U.S. Housing Agency, the predecessor to the U.S. Department of Housing and Urban Development. Kennedy's advisors warned that if he signed an order committing the executive branch to fair housing goals, he would lose the votes he needed in the Senate to pass the civil rights bill and to confirm Weaver's nomination.[14]

Kennedy therefore delayed action on fair housing for nearly two years, finally signing Executive Order 11063 on November 20, 1962, over the vociferous opposition of southern politicians within his own party. The order required federal agencies to "take all necessary and appropriate action to prevent discrimination" in federally supported housing[15] and represents the first explicit statement of a national policy against residential segregation.[16] The order applied to all property owned by the government or receiving federal assistance, and to all institutions handling housing loans insured by the U.S. government. Violators of the order were subject to cancellation of federal contracts and exclusion from other forms of federal assistance.[17]

Although Kennedy's order applied directly only to a minuscule fraction of the nation's housing stock (the U.S. government owns virtually no housing outside the military), indirectly it had a potentially wide-ranging effect. In theory it covered all public housing projects in the United States (nearly all received federal funds) and all properties bought using FHA or VA mortgages. Unfortunately, in practice, Executive Order 11063 turned out to be more symbolic than real. Federal housing officials were reluctant to make local authorities comply with the order, and the FHA was unwilling to apply 11063 to its own portfolio of loans.[18]

At nearly every level, the federal bureaucracy resisted a broad application of Kennedy's order. Administrators within the FHA, in particular, were closely tied to banking industry executives and shared many of their racial prejudices. Indeed, FHA officials had been instrumental in establishing the industry's discriminatory practices in the first place. It was not until 1980 that the U.S. Department of Housing and Urban Development finally issued the last regulations to implement the requirements of 11063.[19] Again it was left to segregation's individual victims to sue federal agencies to force them to comply with their own official policy.

On August 9, 1966, Dorothy Gautreaux and three other black tenants of the Chicago Housing Authority (CHA) filed a class action suit in federal court charging the CHA and the U.S. Department of Housing and Urban Development with discrimination in the location of federally assisted housing projects and in the assignment of tenants to projects, both clear violations of Executive Order 11063.[20] The plaintiffs alleged that most of the CHA's projects were all black by design and that these projects were deliberately and exclusively located within black neighborhoods; at the same time, blacks were prohibited from entering those few housing projects that had been constructed in white areas.[21]

In 1969, Judge Richard B. Austin, who initially seemed unsympathetic to the suit, found for the plaintiffs and ordered the Chicago Housing Authority to build the next seven hundred units in white areas and to ensure that 75% of all subsequent units were located outside the ghetto.[22] Rather than implement the order, however, the CHA brought public housing construction to an immediate halt.[23] In his decision, moreover, Judge Austin absolved HUD of complicity in the promotion of segregation in Chicago. This led the plaintiffs to file an appeal.[24] In September 1971, the U.S. Court of Appeals reversed Judge Austin's ruling and declared that HUD—that is, the U.S. government—was guilty of aiding and abetting racial segregation in the Chicago metropolitan area.

The reversal allowed the plaintiffs to seek relief on a metropolitan-wide basis. Rather than developing a desegregation plan for the city alone, HUD and the CHA would have to come up with one that incorporated the suburbs as well.[25] HUD Secretary Carla Hills chose to fight the decision and appealed to the U.S. Supreme Court. In a unanimous 1976 decision, however, the high court reaffirmed HUD's complicity in promoting segregation and declared that the entire metropolitan area was the relevant housing market for a remedy. It remanded the case back to district court to develop a metropolitan-wide desegregation plan.[26]

On June 17, 1981, Judge John P. Crowley finally approved an agreement between the plaintiffs, the CHA, and HUD to promote the desegregation of public housing in Chicago. The agreement left intact the intense segregation of existing public housing projects, but required the CHA to grant rent subsidy vouchers to 7,100 black families over the next ten years to enable them to leave the ghetto, at that point home to more than 1.2 million people.[27] Although a just remedy may finally have been achieved, the legal impact of the *Gautreaux* ruling was ultimately limited because it involved a relatively small number of families and applied only to the Chicago area. And justice came too late for Dorothy Gautreaux, who died more than a decade before the fifteen years of federal foot-dragging and obstructionism finally yielded a solution.[28]

When it became obvious in the late 1960s that the promise of Executive Order 11063 would remain unfulfilled, civil rights groups focused their efforts on Congress. They hoped to bring about the passage of a new law declaring racial discrimination in housing to be illegal and to force the government to desegregate federally supported housing. But among all areas of civil rights taken up during the 1960s, neighborhood segregation proved to be the most emotional and resistant to change.

Under the leadership of President Lyndon B. Johnson, Congress moved quickly on civil rights bills in other areas. In 1964, liberal Democrats and moderate Republicans succeeded in passing the Civil Rights Act, which prohibited discrimination in employment and in all organizations that received federal funds. This bill was followed in 1965 by the Voting Rights Act, through which the federal government became actively involved in enforcing the political enfranchisement of blacks. When the legislative agenda turned to housing, however, the momentum on civil rights stalled.

Fair housing legislation languished because many senators and representatives harbored strong sentiments against efforts to dismantle the ghetto. Indeed, Congress had specifically excluded programs of federal mortgage insurance from coverage under the 1964 Civil Rights Act, thereby allowing pervasive discrimination in the FHA and VA loan programs to continue.[29] Feelings against fair housing legislation ran particularly high among southern Democrats, and many liberal northern legislators feared the wrath of ethnic, blue-collar constituents who strongly opposed granting blacks equal access to housing. Conservative Republicans, apart from any racist feelings they might have had, objected to governmental interference in housing markets on ideological grounds.[30]

Given this solid wall of opposition, the prospects for fair housing legislation looked increasingly dim as the 1960s progressed. An omnibus civil rights bill containing fair housing provisions had passed the House in 1966, but under the threat of a southern filibuster the Senate refused to consider the measure. During 1967, the Senate Subcommittee on Housing and Urban Affairs held hearings on another housing bill, but it was never reported out of committee.[31] When President Johnson again renewed his call for fair housing legislation in January 1968, liberal senators were reluctant to introduce the bill given the certainty of strong opposition. Rather, as the focus of their civil rights efforts they substituted a rather mild bill (H.R. 2516) to protect civil rights workers from violence.

Just as the prospects for fair housing legislation seemed dead, however, a series of tactical blunders by conservatives and two gripping national events created a new momentum that culminated in the passage of the 1968 Fair Housing Act. The tactical blunder occurred when southern senators decided to launch an all-out attack on H.R. 2516, the civil rights workers' protection bill. This legislation was small in scope and insignificant in national impact, and its adoption would not have fundamentally altered race relations in the United States. But the southerners' instinctive desire to oppose all civil rights legislation gave liberal northerners little to lose by proposing a more far-reaching bill.[32]

After southern senators, led by Sam Ervin and Robert Byrd, succeeded in weakening the language of H.R. 2516 and blocking it with a filibuster, Senators Hart of Michigan, Mathias of Maryland, Clark of Pennsylvania, and Javits of New York caucused with staffers and civil rights lobbyists. Given that the milder bill was already locked up in a filibuster, they decided to go for broke and attach a fair housing amendment. On February 6, Senators Mondale of Minnesota and Brooke of Massachusetts introduced S. 1358, which amended H.R. 2516 to prohibit discrimination in the sale or rental of housing.[33]

The original Mondale-Brooke amendment banned discrimination in the sale or rental of virtually all of the nation's housing and authorized the Secretary of Housing and Urban Development to investigate allegations of discrimination, issue complaints against discriminators, hold hearings, and publish cease and desist orders. The Attorney General was empowered to prosecute real estate agents who engaged in a pattern and practice of discrimination, and individuals were permitted to file suit for significant damages and punitive awards, and to recover court costs and attorney's fees.[34]

Debate on the bill continued for ten days, and on February 16 Senate Majority Leader Mike Mansfield of Montana, seeking to avoid the expenditure of Senate time on what he felt to be a doomed piece of legislation, called for a vote to close off debate. Southern senators, seeking to prolong the debate until liberal Democrats would be forced to give up and move on to other business, opposed cloture.[35] The first cloture vote failed to achieve the required two-thirds majority, but it revealed a surprising amount of support for fair housing among moderate midwestern Republicans.[36]

Additional cloture motions were defeated on February 21 and 26, each time revealing better organization by Senate liberals and growing support among moderate Republicans. Sensing growing sentiment in favor of *some* fair housing legislation, Senator Everett Dirksen of Illinois offered a compromise amendment that reduced the bill's coverage to 80% of the nation's housing stock, mainly by excluding owner-occupied residences with four or fewer rental units. More important, his compromise markedly weakened the bill's enforcement provisions by eliminating HUD's authority to hold hearings, issue complaints, or publish cease and desist orders and by lowering the penalties for violations of the act. The compromise was adopted on February 28.[37]

At this point national events began to influence the tide of sentiment within Congress. The day after the Dirksen compromise was adopted by the Senate, the Kerner Commission released its controversial report on urban riots.[38] Identifying residential segregation as one of the leading causes of black poverty and racial tension, it called forcefully for national fair housing legislation. The ensuing maelstrom of publicity and debate greatly strengthened the growing consensus within Congress that something had to be done in the area of housing. After a last-minute flurry of amendments on the extent of coverage, cloture was finally voted on March 4. With the Dirksen compromise being adopted substantially intact, the final vote of 71 ayes and 20 nays occurred on March 11. All of the negative votes were cast by southern senators.[39]

The amended bill was then sent to the House of Representatives for concurrence; it had to be adopted without change or face the limbo of a House-Senate Conference Committee. Although the chairman of the House Judiciary Committee requested unanimous consent to the Senate bill, William Scott of North Carolina objected and it was referred to the Rules Committee, which deferred action until March 28, when it began to hear testimony from House members.[40] The hearings dragged on for more than a week, and rumors circulated that House Minority Leader Gerald R. Ford of Michigan planned to offer an amendment to allow discrimination in the sale of single-family homes upon the written request of homeowners, a position he had taken two years earlier.[41]

The bill's prospects looked bleak when the House adjourned on the afternoon of April 4, and liberal legislators feared that the bill would die in committee. A few hours after the House adjourned, however, Martin Luther King, Jr., was assassinated, and the mood of the nation changed radically. Over the weekend riots broke out in cities across the nation, and when the House reconvened on Monday, April 8, National Guard troops were positioned around the Capitol to safeguard it from the violence that had erupted in surrounding black neighborhoods.[42]

Twenty-one House Republicans immediately broke with Minority Leader Ford to urge passage of the Senate bill. Republicans on the Rules Committee remained steadfast in their opposition, however, and the legislation still appeared to be headed for an uncertain fate in House-Senate conference when, in a dramatic move, the Republican John Anderson of Illinois broke party ranks to provide the vote needed to send the bill to the House floor.[43] Anderson's switch was a brave and principled move, for his mail was running two to one against the bill and his own party leader was holding out to remand the bill to a conference committee.

With Anderson's switch, the pressures for a fair housing law became overwhelming. On April 9, the Rules Committee sent to the full House a resolution providing for agreement to the Senate amendments, and on April 10, with armed National Guardsmen still quartered in the basement of the Capitol, the motion passed 229 to 195.[44] On the next day, President Johnson signed the bill into law. The long struggle appeared to be over; the nation finally had a fair housing law and civil rights groups looked forward to using it.

Enforcing the Fair Housing Act

The 1968 Fair Housing Act committed the federal government to the goals of open housing. Within private housing markets, it expressly prohibited the kinds of discrimination that had evolved over the years to deny blacks equal access to housing: it made it unlawful to refuse to rent or sell a home to any person because of race; it prohibited racial discrimination in the terms and conditions of any rental or sale; it barred any and all discrimination in real estate advertising; it banned agents from making untrue statements about a dwelling's availability in order to deny a sale or rental to blacks; and it contained specific injunctions against blockbusting, prohibiting agents from making comments about the race of neighbors or those moving in in order to promote panic selling.[45]

The act exempted certain categories of housing from coverage, and upon adoption it applied only to 80% of the nation's housing stock. A Supreme Court decision adjudicated only two months after the bill's passage, however, extended the ban on discrimination to cover virtually all housing in the United States. In *Jones v. Mayer,* the Supreme Court held that the Reconstruction-era 1866 Civil Rights Act banned all racial discrimination, public and private, in the sale or rental of residential property.[46] By the end of 1968, therefore, racial discrimination was proscribed in virtually all real estate transactions.

Despite the declaration that discrimination was illegal in private housing markets, integration did not occur in the years after 1968. As we have seen, as of 1980, twelve years after the passage of the Fair Housing Act, the nation's urban black communities remained intensely isolated from the rest of society. This persistence of residential segregation followed directly from inherent weaknesses that were built into the act as part of Senator Dirksen's price of passage. Although the country had its fair housing law, it was intentionally designed so that it would not and could not work.

The problem with the Fair Housing Act lay not in its coverage or in the kinds of discrimination that it specifically banned but in its enforcement provisions. Although the act committed the federal government to fair housing goals at a symbolic level, the systematic removal of its enforcement mechanisms prior to passage meant that its lofty goals were virtually guaranteed to remain unrealized. In the words of the political scientist George Metcalf, "what Congress did was hatch a beautiful bird without wings to fly."[47] In February 1968 when the original legislation was introduced, the nation seemed to be on the verge of taking firm and forceful action to dismantle the ghetto, but by April, when the final bill passed, Congress had retreated to the politically more comfortable position of espousing principles that it knew could never be enforced.

In the original version of the Mondale-Brooke bill, the U.S. Department of Housing and Urban Development was granted substantial institutional powers to identify and root out discrimination in private housing markets, but these were eliminated wholesale by the Dirksen compromise.[48] Under Title VIII of the Fair Housing Act, HUD was authorized only to investigate complaints of housing discrimination made to the Secretary by "aggrieved persons"; it had thirty days to decide whether to pursue or dismiss the allegations, but if accepted, it was empowered only to engage in "conference, conciliation, and persuasion" to resolve the problem. Moreover, if the alleged violation occurred in a state where a "substantially equivalent" fair housing statute existed, HUD was not required to pursue the case at all—it was instructed to refer the complaint to state authorities.[49]

Even in those cases that HUD chose to pursue, the agency was given virtually no leverage to enforce a solution. If its investigations revealed that a victim had suffered blatant discrimination, HUD had no way to force compliance with the law, to grant a remedy, to assess damages, to prohibit the discriminatory practice from continuing, or to penalize the lawbreaker in any way. HUD could only refer the case to the Justice Department for possible prosecution, but according to the wording of Title VIII, the Attorney General was authorized to act only if there was evidence of "a pattern or practice" of discrimination or if the alleged discrimination raised an issue "of general public importance."[50] Needless to say, discrimination against an individual black person was hardly ever held to be a matter of general public importance.

These constraints on HUD's enforcement authority offered little satisfaction to victims of racial discrimination, and they provided an ineffective deterrent to would-be discriminators. According to former HUD Secretary Patricia R. Harris, the 1968 Fair Housing Act reduced HUD to "asking the discovered lawbreaker whether he wants to discuss the matter."[51] Investigations carried out during the 1970s revealed that only 20% to 30% of complaints filed with the Secretary ever reached formal mediation, and nearly half of the complaints that did so remained in noncompliance after conciliation efforts had terminated. Moreover, HUD made virtually no effort to follow up or to monitor compliance in the conciliation agreements it reached.[52]

For those offenders who remained recalcitrant to HUD conciliation, the probability of further action was very low. A study by the U.S. Commission on Civil Rights revealed that only 10% of the cases that HUD could not conciliate were referred to the Attorney General, and a very small percentage of these were ever pursued.[53] Despite this demonstrated record of ineffective action, however, complaints to HUD continued to grow during the 1970s and early 1980s, testifying to the persistence of discrimination and to the strong demand for federal action. Whereas 2,800 administrative complaints were filed with HUD in 1979, by 1982 the number had grown to 5,100, with the number fluctuating between 4,000 and 5,000 thereafter.[54]

The 1968 Fair Housing Act also promoted widespread regional variation in the degree of fair housing enforcement. Depending on the state in which the alleged violation occurred, enforcement was handled by a regional HUD office, a state or local office with stronger enforcement powers than HUD, or a poorly funded and badly managed agency with a "substantially equivalent" statute but little interest in enforcement.[55] Although HUD developed a "Fair Housing Assistance Plan" in 1980 to improve and standardize enforcement efforts by state and local authorities, one evaluation showed that only 35% of complaints led to some form of agreement, only half of those were settled in the complainant's favor, and again there was little effort to monitor compliance.[56]

During the 1970s and 1980s, therefore, discriminators had little to fear from HUD or the Justice Department, and people who believed they had suffered racial discrimination were forced to initiate legal proceedings on their own. Under Title VIII, "aggrieved persons" were specifically granted the right to file a civil suit in federal court to recover damages from a discriminator, a right that was established apart from any complaints filed with HUD.[57] This provision for individual litigation was the primary mechanism that Congress created to enforce the Fair Housing Act. According to the Supreme Court, "HUD has no power of enforcement,"[58] and the act's main enforcement mechanism "must be private suits in which the complainants act not only on their own behalf but also as private attorneys general in vindicating a policy that Congress considered to be of the highest priority."[59]

This enforcement strategy has proved to be inherently weak and ineffective, and it was undercut from the outset by other provisions of the Fair Housing Act. According to the stipulations of Title VIII, complainants were only entitled to sue for actual damages and a mere $1,000 in punitive awards. In addition, the act held plaintiffs specifically liable for all court costs and attorney's fees unless the court ruled they were financially unable to assume the burden. The latter provision stemmed from a late amendment introduced by Senator Robert Byrd of West Virginia, who sought to weaken further enforcement provisions that had already been hobbled by the Dirksen compromise.[60]

An additional flaw in the Fair Housing Act was its short statute of limitations, requiring that suits be filed within 180 days of the alleged violation, or 30 days from the end of HUD mediation.[61] Housing discrimination by 1968 had become a very subtle process, however. Victims often had to spend a great deal of time and effort to confirm that they had, in fact, been discriminated against, and to gather documentation necessary to support even a prima facie legal case. Typically victims had to secure the help of a fair housing organization, which would send out black and white testers to determine whether clients of different races were treated differently. If initial results confirmed the discrimination, the organization had to carry out enough tests to build a reliable and convincing case before filing the suit, which would tip off the discriminator and prompt a cover-up. In practice, it proved difficult to accomplish these activities within the 180-day time frame, a requirement that deterred many victims from pursuing legal action.

The fundamental weakness of the 1968 Fair Housing Act was its reliance on individual efforts to combat a social problem that was systemic and institutional in nature. The resulting contest was inherently unequal, so that enforcement efforts were intrinsically flawed and structurally condemned to ineffectiveness. For one thing, the act assumed that people knew when they had suffered discrimination, but after 1968 most discriminatory acts became clandestine and were not directly experienced by the individual. For another, even if people suspected they had been victimized, it was difficult to prove; and even when the discrimination could be documented, the act's reliance on individual lawsuits provided a piecemeal attack on a deeply ingrained, institutionalized process. In practice, therefore, the 1968 Fair Housing Act allowed a few victims to gain redress, but it permitted a larger system of institutionalized discrimination to remain in place.

As a result of the inherent weaknesses built into the Fair Housing

Act by the Dirksen compromise, therefore, the fight against residential segregation has been waged primarily in the federal courts by individual victims assisted by private fair housing groups. These private efforts have followed three basic strategies: they have used the courts to confirm that specific practices and behaviors are indeed illegal under the act; they have steadily expanded the kinds of people with standing to file suit as "aggrieved persons"; and they have attempted to increase the size of damages awarded under the act.

The courts have generally been sympathetic to victims of discrimination and have consistently interpreted the Fair Housing Act's proscriptions broadly. In *United States v. Mitchell,* the court in 1971 declared the practice of blockbusting to be illegal under the act, and in the following year the *Zuch v. Hussey* decision prohibited racial steering as well.[62] In the case of *Laufman v. Oakley Building and Loan,* adjudicated in 1976, the court outlawed the systematic denial of credit to a neighborhood because it contained black residents, and in 1977 the case of *Dunn v. The Midwestern Indemnity Company* extended the legal ban on "redlining" to cover the denial of homeowners' insurance to black areas.[63] In 1974 the court ruled in *United States v. The City of Black Jack* that plaintiffs need not prove discriminatory intent in suits filed under the Fair Housing Act, only "that the conduct of the defendant actually or predictably results in racial discrimination; in other words, that it has a discriminatory effect."[64]

Paralleling the gradual broadening of acts and behaviors prohibited under the Fair Housing Act, the federal courts have steadily expanded the list of people with standing to file suit under Title VIII. In *Trafficante v. Metropolitan Life Insurance Company,* the Supreme Court in 1972 granted standing to white tenants who claimed their landlord's discrimination deprived them of the benefits of integrated living, and in *Gladstone Realtors v. Village of Bellwood,* decided in 1979, standing was further expanded to all residents of a village who had suffered the adverse consequences of racial steering by a realtor.[65] In 1982 the Supreme Court decided in the case of *Havens v. Coleman* that testers used by a fair housing groups had standing to file suit under Title VIII. Writing for the majority, Justice William Brennan stated that testers "enjoy a legal right to truthful information about available housing," and that a tester who has received false information could be considered to be injured under the terms of the Fair Housing Act.[66]

In spite of the gradual strengthening of the legal foundations for open housing litigation, however, the ultimate deterrent effect of the 1968 Fair

Housing Act on discriminators proved to be minimal because of the low risk of being prosecuted. Because a plaintiff had to hire a lawyer, assume legal fees, pay court costs, and endure an emotionally taxing legal process, most victims of discrimination never bothered to file suit. Since 1968 only about four hundred fair housing cases have been decided,[67] compared with more than two million incidents of housing discrimination that are estimated to occur each year.[68] The probability of prosecution was thus minuscule under the 1968 act.

Yet even if a discriminator was so unlucky as to be prosecuted and convicted, he faced few serious consequences, because the damages granted to victims under the Fair Housing Act were small. The act explicitly limited punitive damages to $1,000, and although it stipulated no ceiling on actual damages, through 1980 only five plaintiffs had received awards in excess of $3,500.[69] A third avenue of litigation by fair housing advocates, therefore, has been to increase the size of awards, and to this end they have adopted a two-pronged strategy.

One tactic has been to request damages for the emotional stress and humiliation caused by housing discrimination, ambiguous injuries that often are generously recompensed by sympathetic judges and juries.[70] Although successful in some cases, however, awards for humiliation have rarely exceeded $20,000.[71] A second strategy has been to sue for damages under the 1866 Civil Rights Act, which carried no limit on punitive damages. In *Grayson v. Rotundi,* two black women who were denied an apartment on Long Island because of race filed a suit alleging violation of *both* the 1968 Fair Housing Act and the 1866 Civil Rights Act. Given the blatant nature of the discrimination and the unrepentant attitude of the defendants, a federal court awarded damages totaling $565,000 to the victims.[72]

During the 1970s and 1980s, however, such large awards remained the exception rather than the rule. Individual and institutional discriminators could persist in their behavior, knowing that the federal government was powerless to do anything about it, that the likelihood of individual prosecution was small, and that in the remote probability of a conviction, the financial penalties they faced were modest.

HUD's Affirmative Mandate

The Fair Housing Act not only banned discrimination in private housing markets but also called upon the Secretary of Housing and Urban Development to "administer the programs and activities relating to housing and urban development in a manner *affirmatively* to further the policies of this section [of the Act]" (emphasis added).[73] In other words, after 1968 HUD could not remain racially neutral in the administration of federal housing programs; in light of HUD's prior complicity in supporting segregation, Congress explicitly called upon it to administer its programs "affirmatively" to promote integration in federally supported housing.[74]

The sector over which HUD had the greatest control, of course, was the stock of federally subsidized housing. During the 1950s and 1960s, local governments had employed public housing as a key tool in their broader efforts to isolate and control growing urban black populations, a practice that had been tolerated, if not condoned, by HUD.[75] Although Executive Order 11063 theoretically ended this support of segregation, the order was never fully implemented. The 1968 act therefore sought nothing less than a complete reversal of HUD's long-standing policy of acquiescence to the use of public housing funds to foster residential segregation in American cities.

Despite its clear mandate for action, however, HUD's post-1968 record in promoting desegregation was weak. According to a 1979 report of the U.S. Commission on Civil Rights, "HUD has not been forceful in ensuring compliance with these requirements."[76] Indeed, three years after the Fair Housing Act, the judge in the *Gautreaux* case ruled that HUD was guilty of complicity in the segregation of blacks in Chicago and ordered the agency to implement a desegregation plan. Rather than obey the order, however, HUD appealed the case to the Supreme Court. When the high court finally and unequivocally ordered HUD to implement a desegregation plan in 1976, it took another five years before it did so.[77]

HUD was similarly obstructionist in the evolution of the *Black Jack* court case, adjudicated in 1974. The case began when a nonprofit developer sought to build federally subsidized apartments in an area outside the city of St. Louis. Fearing that the complex would be inhabited by blacks, local residents pressured HUD to quash the project's application for funding, and Secretary Carla Hills intervened to do so, violating HUD's affirmative mandate under the Fair Housing Act. Only feverish appeals and the threat of a public scandal succeeded in restoring the funding.[78]

In the case of *Shannon v. HUD,* residents of an urban renewal area of Philadelphia alleged that HUD had not fulfilled its affirmative mandate because it had not developed explicit procedures to consider the effect of a proposed project on the racial composition of the neighborhood.[79] HUD strenuously fought the suit, which demanded only that it comply with federal law, but the agency lost the case in 1970, when a federal judge ruled that HUD indeed had to weigh the effect of public housing projects on the racial balance of the neighborhoods where they were to be built.[80] HUD was ordered to develop an administrative procedure that took racial composition into account in selecting future sites for public housing.[81]

In response to the *Shannon* and *Gautreaux* rulings, President Richard M. Nixon in 1971 ordered HUD to promote equal housing opportunities, and the agency subsequently issued formal project selection criteria in 1972, four years after its affirmative mandate began. The degree of minority concentration was specified as one of eight factors to be considered in selecting neighborhoods for scattered-site housing projects. Each factor was assigned a rating of superior, adequate, or poor, and a "poor" rating with respect to minority concentration initially disqualified a location from further consideration.[82] These criteria were further refined in 1974 after passage of the Housing and Community Development Act, which consolidated scattered-site programs under the Section 8 rubric.[83]

In 1972, HUD also issued new regulations to require developers of federally assisted housing to make concrete efforts to market their units to black homeseekers outside of the ghetto.[84] The resulting "affirmative fair housing marketing plans" had to state the percentage of units the developer expected to be occupied by minority residents and the methods the developer planned to use to market them; but it was not until 1979 that HUD implemented any kind of program for monitoring compliance with these plans. For most developers, they were a meaningless bureaucratic exercise. The U.S. Commission on Civil Rights found that HUD reviewed only 1% of private developers and 3% of local housing authorities for compliance before 1979.[85] And only in 1980 did HUD issue regulations for fair housing advertising, which described the criteria by which developers and realtors were to be evaluated for compliance with the Fair Housing Act's ban on discriminatory advertising.[86]

Regulations implemented during the 1970s thus had a limited effect on public housing. The regulations did not apply to federally supported housing built before 1972, and so did nothing to ameliorate the high degree of segregation within the large stock of high-rise, multi-family projects built by local housing authorities during the 1950s and 1960s.[87] Faced with growing pressure to conform to the affirmative mandate of the Fair Housing Act, local housing authorities stopped constructing high-rise projects after 1970, a move that was supported philosophically by the Nixon Administration's shift toward market-oriented housing programs.[88] Even among rent voucher programs, however, integration efforts moved at a snail's pace.[89]

Consider black-white segregation scores and racial isolation indices computed for the stock of HUD-supported housing in selected metropolitan areas as of 1977 (see Table 7.1). (The year 1977 is the last for which racial data on public housing occupancy are available; in 1978 HUD suspended operation of its automated data system.) Overall indices of black-white segregation and racial isolation within metropolitan areas are presented for comparison.

The 1977 level of black-white segregation in public housing projects is very high and, with a few exceptions, closely parallels the degree of an

Table 7.1 Levels of black-white segregation and black racial isolation in federally supported housing: Selected metropolitan areas, 1977

	Black-white segregation		Black racial isolation	
	In metropolitan area as a whole	In public housing	In metropolitan area as a whole	In public housing
Baltimore	74.7	83.6	72.3	94.4
Boston	77.6	77.8	55.0	67.9
Chicago	87.8	90.7	82.8	94.6
Cleveland	87.5	58.5	80.4	64.5
Dallas–Ft. Worth	77.1	87.8	64.5	93.9
Detroit	86.7	67.6	77.3	90.6
Houston	69.5	51.8	59.3	66.4
Los Angeles	81.1	58.0	60.4	67.5
Milwaukee	83.9	65.5	69.5	73.9
Newark	81.6	75.8	69.2	82.7
New York	82.0	59.2	62.7	63.5
Philadelphia	78.8	82.4	69.6	88.3
San Francisco	71.7	68.0	51.1	77.2
St. Louis	81.3	88.4	72.9	94.4
Washington, D.C.	70.1	78.6	67.2	97.2
Average	79.4	72.9	67.6	81.1

Source: Adam Bickford and Douglas S. Massey, "Segregation in the Second Ghetto: Racial and Ethnic Segregation in American Public Housing, 1977," *Social Forces* 69 (1991):1024–25, 1028–29.

area's overall segregation. In several notable cases—Baltimore, Chicago, Dallas, Philadelphia, St. Louis, and Washington, D.C.—blacks are even more segregated in public housing than in the metropolitan area in general. Our segregation index states the percentage of blacks that would have to change projects to achieve an even distribution of races within a metropolitan area's public housing projects. Indices above 60 indicate a tendency toward all-black or all-white projects, with few developments containing members of both groups. Eleven of the fifteen metropolitan areas display black-white indices above this threshold.

When combined with a high percentage of blacks in public housing, such uneven racial distributions create conditions of intense racial isolation within projects. The indices in the right-hand columns of Table 7.1 measure the degree of isolation experienced by blacks within public housing. The index states the percentage of blacks in the average black person's housing project. In all cases save one, the extent of racial isolation exceeds that in metropolitan areas generally, and in six areas the index is over 90, meaning that most black residents of public housing live in projects that are virtually all black. As these figures confirm, the Fair Housing Act brought little progress toward integration in the sector of housing where HUD had the most direct control.

The 1968 act also directed HUD to advance fair housing goals in its mortgage insurance programs. Because the act did not explicitly authorize the Secretary to exempt programs from coverage, the courts concluded that Congress meant the act's affirmative mandate to apply to *all* of the agency's programs, including the popular FHA mortgage insurance programs.[90] As already described, HUD's administration of FHA loan programs prior to 1968 had contributed to the perpetuation of the ghetto. HUD Secretary George Romney acknowledged in testimony before Congress in 1970 that the FHA "generally withheld insurance from existing housing in central city areas," because it believed that neighborhoods "occupied largely by minority groups had an unfavorable economic future."[91] He added that this policy of redlining stemmed from "an unwritten but well-understood agreement between financial institutions and the FHA."[92]

Congress recognized that institutional racism within the FHA and its partners in the lending industry served to reinforce racial segregation, and even before it passed the Fair Housing Act it attempted to counter this abuse. In 1966, for example, Congress amended the National Housing Act explicitly to allow the FHA to insure mortgages in black neighborhoods where riots had occurred or were threatened;[93] and in 1968 Congress liberalized FHA loan policies through two sections of the Housing and Urban Development Act: Section 223(e) made FHA mortgage guarantees available to inner-city areas that did not meet the usual eligibility criteria, and Section 235 subsidized interest rates on home mortgages taken out by low-income families.[94]

Rather than using these programs to promote fair housing goals, however, the FHA administered them in a manner that promoted segregation. Specifically, the FHA cooperated with banks and realtors who used the new programs as oil for the well-worn machinery of blockbusting: Section 223(e) loans were used to finance the flight of whites from older inner cities, and Section 235 mortgages were given to poor blacks purchasing homes in the areas that whites were fleeing.[95] The programs were riddled with corruption and mismanagement, and a subsequent investigation by the U.S. Commission on Civil Rights found that brokers, developers, lenders, and the FHA all conspired to perpetuate the ghetto.[96] In particular, the commission found that FHA officials were well aware that segregation was occurring under the programs, but did nothing to stop it; indeed, HUD did not even collect data on the race of Section 235 buyers until 1971.[97]

Congressional dissatisfaction with the FHA's past performance led directly to its imposition of the Fair Housing Act's affirmative mandate. But a 1971 study by the U.S. Commission on Civil rights revealed that in St. Louis, 90% of black FHA homebuyers were located in racially changing neighborhoods (with the remaining 10% in all-black areas), whereas 60% of white buyers had moved from transitional neighborhoods where the blacks were arriving.[98] Likewise, a study conducted in Chicago during 1974 showed that 75% of all FHA purchases were by white buyers in white areas or by black buyers in black areas.[99] And a systematic review of HUD's policies carried out by Leonard Rubinowitz and Elizabeth Trosman in 1979, showed that "HUD has taken fewer steps toward [the affirmative action] goal with respect to the FHA single-family housing programs than it has in any other of its housing programs."[100] The lack of agency commitment left a large "administrative gap" between the affirmative duty imposed on HUD by Congress and the agency's actual policies and practices.[101]

Glimmers of Hope

Legislative initiatives to promote open housing did not end with the passage of the Fair Housing Act in 1968, of course. Throughout the

1970s, Congress continued to chip away at the institutionalized edifice of segregation through amendments to various bills. President Nixon's 1974 Housing and Community Development Act, for example, was specifically amended to require that communities prepare a detailed "housing assistance plan" before receiving federal block grants. Among other things, the HAP had to describe the housing needs of low-income families and include a statement of compliance with the Fair Housing Act.[102]

Congress saw HAPs as a means of prodding white suburban communities into accepting more poor minority families, but it also realized that segregation was strongly shaped by entrenched discrimination in the home lending industry. In 1974 it passed the Equal Credit Opportunity Act, which expressly prohibited discrimination in home lending and required banks to compile information on the race of clients it accepted and rejected for loans.[103]

Again, however, the federal bureaucracy dragged its feet in implementing these antidiscrimination policies. When the federal banking system still had not established a system for collecting racial data on home loan applicants by 1976, ten civil rights groups filed suit in federal court.[104] In settling the suit, three federal agencies—the Comptroller of the Currency, the Federal Deposit Insurance Corporation, and the Home Loan Bank Board—signed a court order and agreed to collect the necessary data, but the first two agencies suspended operations in 1981, when their court orders ran out. In the early 1990s, the Home Loan Bank Board is the only banking agency still under court order to gather information on the race of loan applicants. Recent analyses of this information have shown that blacks are still being rejected at rates several times those of whites.[105]

During the 1970s, Congress took two other steps to combat discrimination in the lending industry. In 1975 it passed the Home Mortgage Disclosure Act, which required banks to report which neighborhoods received mortgage and home-improvement loans.[106] This requirement greatly facilitated the prosecution of redlining cases under the Fair Housing Act, and research using these data has been extremely useful in showing that minority neighborhoods continue to be under-capitalized relative to economically comparable white neighborhoods.[107] In 1977 Congress passed the Community Reinvestment Act to strengthen its earlier antiredlining efforts. This law required banks to demonstrate that they were indeed providing credit to low-income areas that had historically been unable to secure capital.[108]

But despite these additions, fair housing efforts continued to be hampered during the 1970s and 1980s because of flaws inherent in the Fair Housing Act itself, which remained the primary vehicle for attacking racial segregation in American cities. During the 1980s the situation grew worse, for if the structure of the Fair Housing Act made it difficult for administrations genuinely committed to open housing to attack the problem of racial segregation, it allowed the Reagan counterrevolution even more latitude to preserve the status quo.

The conservative President's appointees were unremittingly hostile to civil rights, and they reversed many policies that HUD had earlier been pressured into adopting under the affirmative mandate of the Fair Housing Act. Typical of President Reagan's appointees was William Bradford Reynolds, the Assistant Attorney General for Civil Rights and the person to whom HUD referred its fair housing cases. In the case of *Havens v. Coleman,* he reversed the stance of earlier administrations and filed a Supreme Court brief arguing that fair housing testers should *not* be eligible to file suit under the Fair Housing Act.[109] Reynolds also steadfastly refused to change the Justice Department's test of discrimination from one of intent to one of effect, despite the Court's 1975 ruling in the *Black Jack* case.[110]

The number of cases prosecuted under the Fair Housing Act dropped precipitously under President Reagan. Between 1968 and 1978, the Justice Department prosecuted an average of thirty-two fair housing cases per year, although by the Carter Administration this figure had fallen to sixteen per year because of budgetary pressures.[111] During the first year of the Reagan Administration, in contrast, *not one* fair housing case was initiated, and in 1982 only two were filed.[112] This virtual abandonment of fair housing litigation occurred at a time when the number of complaints was rising; between 1979 and 1982 the number of discrimination complaints filed with HUD nearly doubled.[113] The number of fair housing filings rose to six in 1983, but it was not until the last year of Reagan's presidency that the total number filed equaled the yearly *average* of the Carter years.[114]

Moreover, the fair housing cases filed under President Reagan were not chosen to broaden and extend the jurisprudence of fair housing. Most of the cases were trivial and were unlikely to establish broad precedents, and those cases that were precedent-setting aimed primarily at undermining integration maintenance programs such as those in place at New York's Starrett City or Chicago's Atrium Village.[115] These programs had been implemented by well-meaning managers in order to create an integrated residential setting within an otherwise racially segmented and highly discriminatory housing market, and though arguably violating the letter of the Fair Housing Act, they were consistent with its spirit. More important, the prosecution of these cases had limited potential to open up housing opportunities for minorities.

The Reagan Administration also worked closely with the National Association of Realtors (NAR) to undermine HUD's already limited enforcement authority. A principal target was the Voluntary Affirmative Marketing Agreement, a pact between HUD and the NAR worked out under President Gerald R. Ford. The agreement established a nationwide network of housing resource boards to implement the Fair Housing Act with financial backing from HUD. Simply by joining one of these boards and promising to support fair housing, realtors received HUD approval for FHA mortgages and other federal funds.[116]

During the first year of the Reagan presidency, the agreement was modified substantially to move HUD away from affirmative administration of the Fair Housing Act. The new agreement relieved realtors of any responsibility for active enforcement of Title VIII provisions and it prohibited the use of testers by local housing resource boards, thereby limiting HUD's ability to detect housing discrimination. The agreement also made secret the list of real estate boards that had signed the agreement, so that local fair housing groups could no longer tell which realtors had agreed even to the minimal requirements of the new policy. Under Reagan, less than half of the nation's 1,500 local real estate boards signed Voluntary Affirmative Marketing Agreements.[117]

Realtors were not the only ones to attempt to roll back the tide of fair housing policy established during preceding administrations. Reagan's Office of Management and Budget attempted to use authority granted it under the Paperwork Reduction Act to restrict HUD's gathering of data on the race of participants in the various housing programs it administered. The sincerity of the Reagan Administration's desire for less paperwork in this area was doubtful, however, because except for eliminating boxes pertaining to race, sex, and ethnicity, the HUD forms were to be kept exactly the same. The proposed change was dropped only after five Republican and seven Democratic legislators sent a letter of protest to the administration.[118]

Over the course of the 1980s, Congress grew increasingly angry and disillusioned with President Reagan's civil rights record in general and his fair housing policy in particular. In the end, the Reagan counterrevolution went too far for its own good. Even moderate Republicans and conservative Democrats became fed up with the administration's obstructionist stance on civil rights, and ultimately Reagan's policies had the perverse effect of tipping the scales decisively toward the first significant strengthening of the Fair Housing Act. By 1988 even the National Association of Realtors and Vice President George Bush were working to pass amendments to the Fair Housing Act.[119]

The passage of the Fair Housing Amendments Act of 1988 was a long time coming. The inherent flaws of the 1968 act were extensively documented in Congressional hearings conducted in 1971 and 1972[120] and by exhaustive studies prepared by the U.S. Commission on Civil Rights in 1974 and 1979.[121] In 1978 a measure was introduced in the House to remedy the most obvious defects of the Fair Housing Act, but in committee hearings it encountered predictable opposition from the National Association of Realtors and conservative legislators.[122]

By 1980, however, enough support had gathered in the House to pass the amendments by a large margin. Among various actions, these amendments proposed increasing the limit on punitive damages, awarding attorney's fees to prevailing plaintiffs, and empowering HUD to initiate and adjudicate complaints against discriminators.[123] Although the bill cleared the House in mid-June, the Senate deferred action on the bill until after the November election; but with Reagan's landslide election and the Democrats' loss of the Senate, the measure's chances evaporated. Indeed, Orrin Hatch, the new chairman of the Senate Judiciary Committee, spoke of *rolling back* the provisions of the Fair Housing Act, not strengthening them.[124]

By 1987, however, the Democrats had regained control of the Senate and events favored a major push to strengthen the Fair Housing Act in spite of resistance from the Reagan Administration: the Iran-Contra scandal was in full bloom, stories of corruption and mismanagement at HUD were surfacing, the candidacy of the conservative Supreme Court nominee Robert Bork had gone down to defeat, and the Civil Rights Restoration Act had been passed to overcome an earlier ruling from the newly conservative Supreme Court. The Reagan counterrevolution appeared spent and the way finally seemed clear for comprehensive legislation on fair housing.[125]

The Fair Housing Amendments Act was introduced simultaneously in the House and the Senate in early 1987, and committee hearings promptly followed. The bill was reported out of the House Judiciary Committee on June 17, 1988, and passed the full House on June 29 by a vote of 376 to 23. The Senate took up the House bill on August 1, and after several minor amendments, it passed by a 94 to 3 vote on August 2. On August 8 the House voted its concurrence with the Senate version and on September 13 President Reagan, seeing the futility of a veto, signed the amendments into law.[126] The Fair Housing Amendments Act took effect on March 12, 1989, ending more than a decade of Congressional efforts to strengthen the Fair Housing Act.[127]

Robert Schwemm, a well-known scholar of housing law and a prominent civil rights litigator, has called the 1988 Fair Housing Amendments "the most important development in housing discrimination law in twenty years."[128] In one bold stroke, the amendments remedied the principal flaws of the 1968 act that had been so well documented in two decades of Congressional hearings, court cases, government reports, and academic treatises.

The 1988 amendments extended the time to file a housing discrimination complaint from 180 days to two years, allowed attorney's fees and court costs to be recovered by prevailing plaintiffs, created a streamlined process for trying cases before an administrative law judge, and empowered administrative judges to order full compensation for damages plus civil fines of up to $10,000 for a first violation, and $50,000 for a third offense.[129]

The amendments also increased the risks and costs facing would-be discriminators. In addition to raising the punitive awards to $10,000 for a first offense, the new legislation authorized the Attorney General to seek a penalty of $50,000 for a first conviction in "pattern and practice" cases and to assess a fine of $100,000 for subsequent violations. The new law also set a stringent time frame for HUD investigations and the resolution of complaints, and it shifted the burden away from "aggrieved persons" by allowing the Attorney General to seek monetary damages on individuals' behalf in order to "vindicate the public interest."[130]

A serious weakness of the original 1968 act was the strictures it placed on HUD's enforcement activities. Under the new amendments, in contrast, HUD Secretaries were empowered to initiate investigations on their own without waiting for private suits; they could also file complaints with the Attorney General, who was required to undertake prompt judicial action. More important, HUD was now *required* to try a case before an administrative law judge if it found reasonable cause to believe that discrimination had occurred, unless one of the parties elected to have the case heard in U.S. district court. The administrative law judges were empowered not only to award higher civil penalties, attorney's fees, and court costs but also to seek injunctive or other equitable relief.[131]

Finally, the 1988 amendments expanded the role of the Justice Department in fair housing enforcement. The Attorney General was empowered to act on behalf of a complainant when authorized by the HUD Secretary and was authorized to file a civil action for any breach of a conciliation agreement. In addition to seeking monetary damages and injunctive relief in order to vindicate the public interest, the Attorney General was now *required* to prosecute the cases of aggrieved persons whenever defendants elected to have their trial in a U.S. district court rather than before an administrative law judge.[132]

Although it is too early to know whether the 1988 amendments will be successful in overcoming the institutional mechanisms that have supported segregation in the past, preliminary indications suggest that the amendments have for the first time put real teeth into fair housing enforcement. The first housing discrimination case to be processed under the new administrative law system was settled in only six months and resulted in a fine of $75,000 against a discriminator in Georgia.[133] Damages in cases filed by private fair housing organizations have gone as high as $624,000 in a Toledo case, and conciliation agreements arranged by HUD since the law's enactment have brought in more than $2 million in settlements.[134] In the Chicago regional HUD office alone, fair housing complaints were up by 35% after the amendments' implementation.[135]

The amendments may have come too late, however. Conditions in the ghetto have deteriorated markedly since the 1968 Fair Housing Act was originally passed, and almost every problem defined by the Kerner Commission has become worse. At the same time, many deeply rooted, self-feeding processes of poverty and deprivation have taken root. It is not at all clear that the new amendments, as tough as they are, will succeed in overcoming the entrenched discriminatory processes that sustain the ghetto and perpetuate segregation.

If history is any guide, they will not. In the past each time that one discriminatory process has been suppressed after a long and bitter struggle (e.g., legal segregation or restrictive covenants), a new mechanism has arisen to take its place. The new amendments still lean heavily on the efforts of individuals, and success will be heavily determined by the institutional backing given to these "private attorneys general" by the President, the Justice Department, and HUD.

Blame Enough for All

Despite the promise of the 1988 Fair Housing Amendments, they cannot erase the past. For at least fifty years, from 1940 through 1990, African Americans were subject to a system of institutionalized housing discrimination. Each time that a legislative or judicial action was undertaken to ameliorate segregation, it was fought tenaciously by a powerful array of people who benefited from the status quo (realtors, bankers, politicians); these actors, in turn, relied on the broader indifference and hostility of most white Americans.

Even as conditions deteriorated rapidly in segregated neighborhoods after 1960, legislative efforts to promote open housing were blocked at every juncture, and when a fair housing law finally passed in the aftermath of urban riots and the King assassination, the bill that emerged was deliberately stripped of its enforcement provisions, yielding a Fair Housing Act that was structurally flawed and all but doomed to fail. As documentation of the act's inherent flaws accumulated, little was done to repair the situation. Until 1989, the institutionalized system of housing discrimination that perpetuated the ghetto as the enabling condition of black oppression was left intact.

Given the clear evidence of segregation's ill effects on American society, why wasn't something done about it? Why didn't political leaders and policymakers take forceful steps to dismantle the ghetto, especially after 1960, when violent riots and the unmistakable spread of social disorder within the black community made clear the price the nation was paying for the persistence of segregation? Why did the country tolerate, for two decades, a fair housing law that was so obviously defective? The simple answer to all of these questions, sadly, is that most people wanted blacks confined to ghettos and were content to work around the unpleasant social consequences.

Ultimate responsibility for the persistence of racial segregation rests with white America. On issues of race and residence, white America continues to be fundamentally hypocritical and self-deceiving. Whites believe that people should be able to live wherever they want to regardless of skin color, but in practice they think that people—at least black people—should want to live with members of their own race. As already noted, whereas 88% of white respondents to a national survey agreed that "black people have a right to live wherever they can afford to,"[136] only 43% of whites in one local survey would feel "comfortable" in a neighborhood that was one-third black.[137]

Given these contradictory beliefs, whites are content to espouse the principles of open housing, but are unwilling to take action to implement them. Although 57% of white respondents in 1977 felt that white people did not have a right to discriminate against black people, only 35% would vote for a law stating that a homeowner could not refuse to sell to someone because of his or her race or color.[138] The fundamental dilemma of white America is that though it truly believes that housing markets should be fair and open, it equally truly does not want to live with black people. Thus the 1968 Fair Housing Act perfectly reflects the unresolved contradiction between white America's principles and its racial preferences: the act allowed the nation to go on record in support of the ideal of open housing, but it made sure that this goal was in no danger of being realized.

Although white antipathy to the prospect of actually living with blacks is the ultimate cause of segregation's persistence, the proximate causes generally have more to do with the self-interested stake that certain individuals and organizations—both black and white—have in the ghetto's perpetuation. Real estate agents, of course, have long reaped profits along the boundary of the ghetto;[139] and within the broader housing market, realtors discriminate against blacks to avoid antagonizing white clients and possibly losing business. Because realtors believe their clients to be racially prejudiced, they are reluctant to incur the enmity of white communities by introducing "unwanted" elements into white neighborhoods.[140]

Less frequently mentioned, however, is the self-interested stake that black politicians and, to a lesser extent, black business owners have in the perpetuation of the ghetto. Segregation concentrates black dollars to produce a relatively closed market for black entrepreneurs who espouse an ideology of economic independence and self-help. More important, segregation concentrates black votes to create safe legislative seats for black politicians and a ready gallery for community activists. The price paid by the larger black community, however, is economic disinvestment by the wider society and permanent dependence brought about by political marginalization.

Segregation has persisted, in part, because black politicians and civil rights leaders have not pushed nearly as hard for better opportunities in the housing market as for improved opportunities in employment and education. It has been many years since civil rights leaders have organized marches in support of residential integration, demanded desegregation in the real estate industry, or supported efforts to disperse black housing demand outside the ghetto—most likely because it has not been in their interest to do so.

Indeed, black leaders have from time to time obstructed efforts to integrate urban America. When Robert Taylor, the black head of the Chicago Housing Authority, found himself locked in a bitter political struggle with the Chicago City Council to locate public housing projects outside of the ghetto, he received virtually no support from the head of the black political machine, Congressman William Dawson. "Taylor, an old ally of Dawson's, had violated two of Dawson's cardinal rules: he had come out for integration publicly . . . and he had tried to locate significant numbers of black voters outside the wards that Dawson controlled."[141]

This pattern of ambivalence on the part of black leaders persisted after the passage of the Fair Housing Act in 1968, when Chicago's Leadership Council for Metropolitan Open Communities attempted to organize a housing service to expand black residential opportunities outside the ghetto. In doing so they attempted to enlist the support of black community leaders, but to their surprise, they encountered considerable resistance: "some blacks felt that the Leadership Council was just a front organization for the white power structure whose scheme was to disperse blacks throughout the city and thus weaken the black community as a cohesive political force."[142]

The ambivalence of black political leaders about residential integration again surfaced in 1978 when the General Accounting Office issued a report critical of HUD's slow progress in affirmatively integrating the Section 8 subsidized housing program, as required under the Fair Housing Act. The GAO report recommended that HUD define how residential deconcentration related to the Section 8 program, that it issue guidelines on how to achieve the deconcentration objective, and that it develop measures to assess deconcentration efforts. In her response to the report, HUD Secretary Patricia Harris expressed concern over the GAO's apparent overemphasis of the deconcentration objective, arguing that it had to be balanced against other goals.[143]

One year later, HUD was pressured into issuing a "clarification" of its site selection standards by black members of Congress, who felt that application of the agency's existing site selection criteria would dilute recently acquired black political power. In response to this concern, HUD stated that under some circumstances Section 8 projects might well be constructed in predominantly black areas.[144] This concern was later formalized in the 1980 Housing and Community Development Act, which at the insistence of the black Congressional caucus contained the statement that "the Secretary of HUD shall not exclude from consideration . . . under federally assisted housing programs proposals for housing projects solely because the site proposed is located with an impacted (minority) area."[145]

If integration were actually to be achieved, of course, black representatives would lose safe seats and be forced to compete with politicians from other ethnic groups in building coalitions across a diversity of interests. During the 1960s and 1970s, this self-interested stake in residential segregation acquired ideological support from black radicals who espoused a doctrine of black power. According to a classic treatise on black power by Stokely Carmichael and Charles Hamilton, "'Integration' as a goal today speaks to the problem of blackness not only in an unrealistic way but also in a despicable way. It is based on complete acceptance of the fact that in order to have a decent house . . . black people must move into a white neighborhood . . . This reinforces, among both black and white, the idea that 'white' is automatically superior and 'black' is by definition inferior. For this reason, 'integration' is a subterfuge for the maintenance of white supremacy."[146]

The combination of ideology and self-interest yielded a powerful resistance to residential integration that few people—black or white—were willing to challenge. As a consequence, segregation disappeared from the lexicon of civil rights and dropped off of its public policy agenda for most of the 1970s and 1980s. Unwilling to confront the rising tide of black separatism, white liberals rallied to the cause of segregation with their own defense of the residential status quo. In their essay "The Case against Urban Desegregation," Frances Fox Piven and Richard A. Cloward argued that "judging from the history of those ethnic groups that have succeeded . . . , separatism is a precondition for eventual penetration of the ruling circles and the achievement of full economic integration."[147] An essay published in *Commentary* observed that black power required "the building and strengthening of indigenous social and political institutions from within the ghetto from which power can be drawn."[148]

Despite the rhetoric of black nationalists and their white sympathizers, segregation leaves blacks in a position of permanent political dependency and vulnerability to economic dislocation. The truth lies closer to the position taken by Kenneth B. Clark so many years ago: "A most cruel . . . consequence of enforced segregation is that its victims can be made to accommodate to their victimized status and under certain circumstances to state that it *is* their desire to be set apart, or to agree that subjugation is not really detrimental but beneficial. The fact remains that exclusion, rejection . . . are not voluntary states. Segregation is neither sought nor imposed by healthy . . . human beings."[149]

8

The Future of the Ghetto

The isolation of Negro from white communities is increasing rather than decreasing . . . Negro poverty is not white poverty. Many of its causes . . . are the same. But there are differences—deep, corrosive, obstinate differences—radiating painful roots into the community, the family, and the nature of the individual.

President Lyndon Johnson,
address to Howard University,
June 4, 1965

After persisting for more than fifty years, the black ghetto will not be dismantled by passing a few amendments to existing laws or by implementing a smattering of bureaucratic reforms.[1] The ghetto is part and parcel of modern American society; it was manufactured by whites earlier in the century to isolate and control growing urban black populations, and it is maintained today by a set of institutions, attitudes, and practices that are deeply embedded in the structure of American life. Indeed, as conditions in the ghetto have worsened and as poor blacks have adapted socially and culturally to this deteriorating environment, the ghetto has assumed even greater importance as an institutional tool for isolating the by-products of racial oppression: crime, drugs, violence, illiteracy, poverty, despair, and their growing social and economic costs.

For the walls of the ghetto to be breached at this point will require an unprecedented commitment by the public and a fundamental change in leadership at the highest levels. Residential segregation will only be eliminated from American society when federal authorities, backed by the American people, become directly involved in guaranteeing open housing markets and eliminating discrimination from public life. Rather than relying on private individuals to identify and prosecute those who break the law, the U.S. Department of Housing and Urban Development and the Office of the Attorney General must throw their full institutional weight into locating instances of housing discrimination and bringing those who violate the Fair Housing Act to justice; they must vigorously prosecute white racists who harass and intimidate blacks seeking to exercise their rights of residential freedom; and they must establish new bureaucratic mechanisms to counterbalance the forces that continue to sustain the residential color line.

Given the fact that black poverty is exacerbated, reinforced, and perpetuated by racial segregation, that black-white segregation has not moderated despite the federal policies tried so far, and that the social costs of segregation inevitably cannot be contained in the ghetto, we argue that the nation has no choice but to launch a bold new initiative to eradicate the ghetto and eliminate segregation from American life. To do otherwise is to condemn the United States and the American people to a future of economic stagnation, social fragmentation, and political paralysis.

Race, Class, and Public Policy

In the United States today, public policy discussions regarding the urban underclass frequently devolve into debates on the importance of race versus class. However one defines the underclass, it is clear that African Americans are overrepresented within in it. People who trace their ancestry to Africa are at greater risk than others of falling into poverty, remaining there for a long time, and residing in very poor neighborhoods. On almost any measure of social and economic well-being, blacks and Puerto Ricans come out near the bottom.

The complex of social and economic problems that beset people of African origin has led many observers to emphasize race over class in developing remedies for the urban underclass.[2] According to these theories, institutional racism is pervasive, denying blacks equal access to the resources and benefits of American society, notably in education and employment. Given this assessment, these observers urge the adoption of racial remedies to assist urban minorities; proposals include everything from special preference in education to affirmative action in employment.

Other observers emphasize class over race. The liberal variant of the class argument holds that blacks have been caught in a web of institutional and industrial change.[3] Like other migrants, they arrived in cities to take low-skilled jobs in manufacturing, but they had the bad fortune to become established in this sector just as rising energy costs, changing technologies, and increased foreign competition brought a wave of plant closings and layoffs. The service economy that arose to replace manufacturing industries generated high-paying jobs for those with education, but poorly paid jobs for those without it.

Just as this transformation was undermining the economic foundations of the black working class, the class theorists argue, the civil rights revolution opened up new opportunities for educated minorities. After the passage of the 1964 Civil Rights Act, well-educated blacks were recruited into positions of responsibility in government, academia, and business, and thus provided the basis for a new black middle class.[4] But civil rights laws could not provide high-paying jobs to poorly educated minorities when there were no jobs to give out. As a result, the class structure of the black community bifurcated into an affluent class whose fortunes were improving and a poverty class whose position was deteriorating.[5]

The conservative variant of the class argument focuses on the deleterious consequences of government policies intended to improve the economic position of the poor.[6] According to conservative reasoning, federal antipoverty programs implemented during the 1960s—notably the increases in Aid to Families with Dependent Children—altered the incentives governing the behavior of poor men and women. The accessibility and generosity of federal welfare programs reduced the attractiveness of marriage to poor women, increased the benefits of out-of-wedlock childbearing, and reduced the appeal of low-wage labor for poor men. As a result, female-headed families proliferated, rates of unwed childbearing rose, and male labor force participation rates fell. These trends drove poverty rates upward and created a population of persistently poor, welfare-dependent families.

Race- and class-based explanations for the underclass are frequently discussed as if they were mutually exclusive. Although liberal and conservative class theorists may differ with respect to the specific explanations they propose, both agree that white racism plays a minor role as a continuing cause of urban poverty; except for acknowledging the historical legacy of racism, their accounts are essentially race-neutral. Race theorists, in contrast, insist on the primacy of race in American society and emphasize its continuing role in perpetuating urban poverty; they view class-based explanations suspiciously, seeing them as self-serving ideologies that blame the victim.[7]

By presenting the case for segregation's present role as a central cause of urban poverty, we seek to end the specious opposition of race and class. The issue is not whether race *or* class perpetuates the urban underclass, but how race *and* class *interact* to undermine the social and economic well-being of black Americans. We argue that race operates powerfully through urban housing markets, and that racial segregation interacts with black class structure to produce a uniquely disadvantaged neighborhood environment for African Americans.

If the decline of manufacturing, the suburbanization of employment, and the proliferation of unskilled service jobs brought rising rates of poverty and income inequality to blacks, the negative consequences of these trends were exacerbated and magnified by segregation. Segregation concentrated the deprivation created during the 1970s and 1980s to yield intense levels of social and economic isolation. As poverty was concentrated, moreover, so were all social traits associated with it, producing a structural niche within which welfare dependency and joblessness could flourish and become normative. The expectations of the urban poor were changed not so much by generous AFDC payments as by the spatial concentration of welfare recipients, a condition that was structurally built into the black experience by segregation.

If our viewpoint is correct, then public policies must address both race and class issues if they are to be successful. Race-conscious steps need to be taken to dismantle the institutional apparatus of segregation, and class-specific policies must be implemented to improve the socioeconomic status of minorities. By themselves, programs targeted to low-income minorities will fail because they will be swamped by powerful environmental influences arising from the disastrous neighborhood conditions that blacks experience because of segregation. Likewise, efforts to reduce segregation will falter unless blacks acquire the socioeconomic resources that enable them to take full advantage of urban housing markets and the benefits they distribute.

Although we focus in this chapter on how to end racial segregation in American cities, the policies we advocate cannot be pursued to the exclusion of broader efforts to raise the class standing of urban minorities. Programs to dismantle the ghetto must be accompanied by vigorous efforts to end discrimination in other spheres of American life and by class-specific policies designed to raise educational levels, improve the quality of public schools, create employment, reduce crime, and strengthen the family. Only a simultaneous attack along all fronts has any hope of breaking the cycle of poverty that has become deeply rooted within the ghetto. Before discussing policies to end residential segregation, however, we take a quick look at preliminary data from the 1990 Census to see if there is any hint of progress toward integration under current policies.

Segregation in the 1980s

As this book was being completed, early data from the 1990 Census had just become available to update the segregation patterns we observed for the 1970s. Although a complete analysis of the 1990 data is beyond the scope of this brief section, a general sense of trends can be gleaned from Table 8.1, which presents indices of black-white residential dissimilarity computed for the thirty largest metropolitan black communities in 1970, 1980, and 1990. These indices give the relative percentage of blacks who would have to change their census tract (i.e., neighborhood) of residence in order to achieve an even, or desegregated, residential pattern.[8]

Little of the information presented in earlier chapters leads us to expect significant declines in black-white segregation during the 1980s, and segregation indices computed for northern metropolitan areas confirm our pessimistic expectations. In the north, the prevailing pattern during the 1980s was one of stasis: the average index changed by only 2.3 percentage points (compared with 4.4 points during the prior decade), and of the eighteen northern metropolitan areas shown, thirteen had 1990 indices within 3 points of their 1980 values (five were actually a little higher). Only Boston, Columbus, Kansas City, Los Angeles, and St. Louis displayed declines worth mentioning; but at the average rate of change they displayed, it would take northern areas another twenty-eight years just to reach the upper bound of the moderate range (about 60). At the average rate of change across all northern areas, this threshold would not be reached for another seventy-seven years. As of 1990, eight northern metropolitan areas (Buffalo, Chicago, Cleveland, Detroit, Gary, Milwaukee, New York, and Newark) had segregation indices above 80, indicating an extreme separation of the races.

Segregation trends in southern metropolitan areas are more complex. Although average segregation levels did not change much between 1980 and 1990 (the mean dropped by only 1.8 percentage points), this overall stability was achieved by counterbalancing several different trends. Modest but significant declines in segregation occurred in six of the twelve southern metropolitan areas, but these were offset by a 5-point increase

Table 8.1 Trends in black-white segregation in thirty metropolitan areas with largest black populations, 1970–1990

Metropolitan area	1970	1980	1990
Northern areas			
Boston	81.2	77.6	68.2
Buffalo	87.0	79.4	81.8
Chicago	91.9	87.8	85.8
Cincinnati	76.8	72.3	75.8
Cleveland	90.8	87.5	85.1
Columbus	81.8	71.4	67.3
Detroit	88.4	86.7	87.6
Gary–Hammond–E. Chicago	91.4	90.6	89.9
Indianapolis	81.7	76.2	74.3
Kansas City	87.4	78.9	72.6
Los Angeles–Long Beach	91.0	81.1	73.1
Milwaukee	90.5	83.9	82.8
New York	81.0	82.0	82.2
Newark	81.4	81.6	82.5
Philadelphia	79.5	78.8	77.2
Pittsburgh	75.0	72.7	71.0
St. Louis	84.7	81.3	77.0
San Francisco–Oakland	80.1	71.7	66.8
Average	84.5	80.1	77.8
Southern areas			
Atlanta	82.1	78.5	67.8
Baltimore	81.9	74.7	71.4
Birmingham	37.8	40.8	71.7
Dallas–Ft. Worth	86.9	77.1	63.1
Greensboro–Winston Salem	65.4	56.0	60.9
Houston	78.1	69.5	66.8
Memphis	75.9	71.6	69.3
Miami	85.1	77.8	71.8
New Orleans	73.1	68.3	68.8
Norfolk–Virginia Beach	75.7	63.1	50.3
Tampa–St. Petersburg	79.9	72.6	69.7
Washington, D.C.	81.1	70.1	66.1
Average	75.3	68.3	66.5

Sources: For 1970 and 1980: Douglas S. Massey and Nancy A. Denton, "Trends in the Residential Segregation of Blacks, Hispanics, and Asians: 1970–1980," *American Sociological Review* 52 (1987):815–16. For 1990: Roderick J. Harrison and Daniel H. Weinberg, "Racial and Ethnic Segregation in 1990," presented at the annual meetings of the Population Association of America, April 30–May 2, 1992, Denver, CO.

in Greensboro, and a very marked increase of 31 points in Birmingham, Alabama (where blacks were unusually integrated in earlier years). Segregation levels showed no significant change in Houston, Memphis, New Orleans, and Tampa (where the total change was under 3 points).

In general, southern metropolitan areas appear to be converging to a level of black-white segregation in the range of 65 to 70: with one exception, those areas with indices lying below this range in 1980 increased their segregation, whereas those with indices above it decreased; and those with segregation levels in that range stayed roughly constant. An average segregation index of 67 would put southern metropolitan areas about 10 points below their northern counterparts, yielding a north-south differential close to the historical average. This level of racial segregation remains well within the high range, and at the average level of change recorded during the 1980s it would take southern areas another thirty-six years to cross into the moderate range of segregation.

Thus there is little in recent data to suggest that processes of racial segregation have moderated much since 1980, particularly in the north, where segregation remains high and virtually constant. Among the thirty areas we examined, eighteen had indices above 70 in 1990, seventeen experienced no significant change over the prior decade, and twenty-nine displayed 1990 indices that could be described as high according to conventional criteria. Given that these thirty areas contain 60% of all urban blacks in the United States, we conclude that the ghetto remains very much a part of the urban black experience. Racial segregation still constitutes a fundamental cleavage in American society.

Past Integration Efforts: A Scorecard

During the 1970s and 1980s, the fight to end racial segregation was spearheaded by individuals and by private fair housing organizations. The National Committee Against Discrimination in Housing was founded in 1950 with a small coterie of local open housing groups, but after 1968 additional chapters were set up around the country to take advantage of new enforcement mechanisms created by the Fair Housing Act; presently the NCDH has seventy-five local affiliates.[9] These local chapters assist individuals in filing and pursuing fair housing suits: they supply low-cost legal advice to victims of discrimination; they organize testing efforts; they assist litigants in compiling evidence of discrimination; and they provide legal counsel to plaintiffs in trial proceedings.

Though hamstrung by weak enforcement provisions in the Fair Housing Act itself and hampered by limited financial resources, personnel shortages, and a lack of community support, these private organizations have established a variety of legal precedents to enable the more effective prosecution of housing discriminators. Over the years they have gradually expanded the list of parties with legal standing to file fair housing suits; they have firmly established the housing audit as an acceptable method for proving discrimination in court; and they have succeeded in declaring a variety of real estate practices illegal under the Fair Housing Act.[10]

Despite these successes, however, discrimination and segregation persist in urban America. The heroic efforts of individual victims, idealistic activists, and dedicated organizations are not enough to dismantle the institutional apparatus of segregation. Whereas the processes that perpetuate segregation are pervasive and institutionalized, fair housing enforcement has been individual, sporadic, and confined to a small number of isolated cases (since 1968, only about four hundred fair housing cases have been decided).[11] Rather than eliminating the systemic foundations of segregation, private efforts have only chipped away at its facade.

Although the 1988 amendments provide tougher penalties against those who violate the Fair Housing Act and make it easier to prosecute discriminators, the basic organization of enforcement still relies heavily on individuals. As long as the Fair Housing Act is enforced by these "private attorneys general" rather than by federal authorities, it is unlikely to be effective.

Proof of the inefficacy of individual enforcement comes from Chicago, which has led the nation in fair housing litigation. Since 1966, the Leadership Council for Metropolitan Open Communities has mounted an aggressive campaign against residential segregation in the Chicago metropolitan area.[12] It has established affirmative real estate marketing programs; it has filed numerous fair housing complaints against realtors and developers; it has repeatedly defeated discriminators in court; it has pioneered the use of testers to uncover those guilty of a "pattern and practice" of discrimination; and it has taken the lead in prosecuting HUD and the Chicago Housing Authority for promoting racial segregation in public housing.[13]

As a result of these efforts, litigation initiated in Chicago has produced some of the most important fair housing rulings of the past two decades, including such landmark cases as *Hills v. Gautreaux,* which confirmed

HUD's complicity in promoting public housing segregation;[14] *Metropolitan Housing Development Corporation v. Village of Arlington Heights,* which paved the way for an effects criterion in proving Title VIII violations;[15] *Gladstone Realtors v. Village of Bellwood,* which significantly expanded standing to file suit under the Fair Housing Act;[16] *Phillips v. Hunter,* which set a precedent for large punitive awards;[17] and *Williamson v. Hampton,* which helped to establish the legitimacy of testing as a method of proving discrimination in court.[18]

Probably no fair housing group in the country has been more energetic or successful in promoting equal housing opportunities than the Leadership Council for Metropolitan Open Communities and its allies; but despite its efforts, the Chicago metropolitan area remains one of the most segregated areas in the United States. In the twenty years since the passage of the Fair Housing Act, the level of black-white segregation has hardly changed; as of 1990 the index of black-white residential dissimilarity stood at 86, within 2 points of where it stood a decade earlier and within 5 points of its 1970 value. At the rate of change observed between 1980 and 1990, the level of racial segregation would not even reach 70 (still a very high level of segregation) until the year 2042.

Although Chicago's fair housing groups have pushed private fair housing enforcement to the legal limit, they have produced *essentially no change* in the degree of racial segregation within that urban area. If Chicago's vigorous fair housing efforts have been unable to bring about any significant movement toward residential desegregation, then private efforts in other metropolitan areas with large black populations are unlikely to succeed either.

Private enforcement of the Fair Housing Act is not the only weapon in the battle against housing segregation, however; integration maintenance programs have also been used.[19] These programs employ a variety of race-conscious techniques to maintain racially balanced populations within specific housing developments, apartment complexes, neighborhoods, or even entire communities. They are typically used in residential settings that lie near or adjacent to existing black areas and are likely to attract substantial black housing demand. White demand in such settings tends to be weak and sensitive to small changes in the relative number of blacks. In the absence of any intervention, white housing demand drops precipitously as black demand and the black percentage increase, leading to racial turnover and residential resegregation.

Integration maintenance programs intervene within targeted residential settings to forestall this process. The techniques of intervention vary depending on the setting, but all essentially work to maintain blacks as a minority. In apartment complexes and specific housing developments, such as New York's Starrett City or Chicago's Atrium Village, integration maintenance programs may involve the simple imposition of a racial quota.[20] The number of minority- and white-inhabited units is fixed, and separate waiting lists are created for each race. Given the disparity in white and black demand for integrated housing, the black list quickly grows to be several times longer than the white list. Most whites who seek housing in the complex are admitted rather quickly; blacks are forced to endure a long wait until a "black" unit is vacated.

When the targeted setting is an entire neighborhood or community, simple quotas cannot be employed and other methods must be used to maintain blacks as a minority. In order to prevent panic selling by whites, "For Sale" signs may be banned and special insurance schemes implemented to guarantee the value of white homes. Meanwhile, white housing demand is fostered by taking steps to improve the quality of schools and increase public security. At the same time, realtors are specially trained to engage in "reverse steering," whereby they deliberately encourage white homeseekers to consider units in integrated neighborhoods. Integration maintenance programs also engage in extensive public relations, including the preparation of attractive brochures, the placement of ads in magazines, recruiting white homeseekers at local universities, and working with employers and corporate relocation services to attract white residents.[21]

In contrast, little is done to make blacks aware of housing opportunities within the targeted area. Black racial concentrations within the community are carefully monitored, and special efforts are taken to avoid the development of black clusters. Landlords are often required to furnish monthly reports on the race of new tenants, and homeowners are asked to maintain logs of the race of potential buyers brought in by realtors. In contrast to whites, black homeseekers are steered away from black "clusters" toward homes in areas that are all white or that contain few black residents.[22]

Although integration maintenance programs are consistent with the spirit of residential desegregation, ultimately they operate by restricting black residential choice and violating the letter of the Fair Housing Act. They limit black housing options either directly, by applying quotas, or indirectly through a series of tactics designed to control the rate of black entry. As the geographers Robert Lake and Jessica Winslow point out, "ensconced in fair housing rhetoric, integration management relies on a highly restrictive interpretation of the goals and procedures of national fair housing policy. The maintenance of black minorities, rather than the guarantee of equal housing access, is the underlying objective of integration management programs."[23]

These violations leave fair housing advocates vulnerable to attack from interests opposed to the expansion of black civil rights. As noted in Chapter 7, for example, during the early 1980s the Reagan Administration filed lawsuits attacking integration maintenance schemes implemented at New York's Starrett City development and elsewhere.[24] Civil rights groups were forced into the awkward position of devoting scarce time and resources to defending housing practices of questionable legality.

The most serious flaw of integration maintenance schemes, however, is that they do nothing to change the larger system of housing discrimination in the United States: they deal with the symptoms rather than the causes of residential segregation. Integrated settings are at risk of turnover in the first place because a racially biased housing market discourages black entry in most other neighborhoods, thereby funneling black demand to a few isolated areas close to existing black communities. Rather than seeking to change this discriminatory system of housing allocation, integration management programs accept it and seek to preserve a few islands of integration within a larger sea of racial exclusivity. Inevitably, many deserving black families with high aspirations for residential mobility are kept out so that a few privileged whites and blacks can enjoy the benefits of an economically stable, integrated neighborhood.

Public housing programs provide a third avenue for the promotion of residential integration. But as the preceding chapters and other case studies and statistical analyses have shown, local housing authorities, with the tacit support of the federal government, used public housing as an institutional means of reinforcing racial segregation during the period of rapid black migration from 1945 to 1970.[25] When it became clear after 1970 that local authorities would eventually have to conform to the affirmative mandate of the Fair Housing Act and locate new projects outside the ghetto, they decided to forgo federal housing funds and stopped constructing projects.[26]

During the early 1970s, the Nixon and Ford administrations shifted federal housing priorities away from the construction of large, authority-owned projects to the funding of small, scattered-site units erected by private developers.[27] Yet even these low-density subsidized housing programs encountered spirited resistance by neighborhoods and communities, especially in suburban areas where racial barriers were buttressed by restrictive zoning ordinances designed to maintain class integrity.[28] Fair housing groups were constantly forced into court to compel local authorities to conform to federal housing laws.

The most notorious case of resistance to public housing desegregation occurred in Yonkers, New York.[29] In 1980, the NAACP filed suit on behalf of black residents to end the city's forty-year practice of systematic segregation in subsidized housing. After a long period of discovery and an exhaustive ninety-day trial, Federal Judge Leonard B. Sand found Yonkers officials guilty of intentional discrimination in the location of federally subsidized housing. In his 1986 decision, *NAACP v. Yonkers Board of Education et al.*, the judge cited specific illegal activities that local officials had used to promote racial segregation: they had employed different procedural rules to select housing sites in white and black neighborhoods; they had readily acquiesced to racially motivated opposition to public housing construction; they had systematically located subsidized housing in black areas; they had refused to seek all of the Section 8 housing certificates for which they qualified although there was a pressing need for low-income housing; and they had limited the use of Section 8 certificates they did acquire to the black quadrant of the city.[30]

The judge ordered the city of Yonkers to designate a set of sites outside of the ghetto for the construction of two hundred new subsidized housing units and to develop a long-term plan for the desegregation of subsidized housing. City officials refused to comply, however, and obstructed all remedial efforts.[31]

Although Judge Sand's settlement was confirmed by a federal appeals court in December 1987, the city still refused to obey the court order, and during the summer of 1988 Yonkers made headlines by incurring $800,000 in fines as a result of a contempt-of-court citation for failure to comply. As the fines mounted daily, city officials undertook a vitriolic and racially based media campaign against the judge, the federal courts, black residents of Yonkers, and the NAACP. It was not until September 1988—eight years after the original lawsuit was filed and two years after the initial court order—that the City Council, under financial duress, finally accepted a plan to build the two hundred units on eight sites scattered among white neighborhoods of Yonkers, an action that was unlikely to alter the racial composition of any neighborhood or significantly change the structure of segregation.[32]

Although other attempts to desegregate public housing have not achieved the notoriety of the Yonkers case, they have met with similar hostility and organized political resistance. Events surrounding the *Black Jack* case, involving a nonprofit developer who sought to build subsidized housing in an unincorporated area outside of St. Louis, lasted seven years from start to finish; and by the time of the settlement, financing for construction had fallen through and the contested apartments were never built.[33] The *Gautreaux* case, as we have seen, dragged on for fifteen years until the U.S. Supreme Court finally settled it.[34] A proposal in the early 1980s to build 105 units of subsidized housing in a white neighborhood of Houston met with heated protests and marches until the plan was finally shelved, and a proposal for an eighty-unit development later met with a similar fate.[35]

Partly because of the staunch legal and political resistance that public housing desegregation efforts inspire, they have not been successful in promoting the broader integration of urban America. Even if scattered-site programs could be smoothly desegregated, moreover, the potential effect on overall segregation levels is limited by the small number of units involved. Scattered-site units constitute only about one-third of all public housing units in the United States, which, in turn, represent only 2 percent of the nation's total housing stock;[36] and even if the desegregation of scattered-site units could be achieved, it would leave intact the intense segregation of large, authority-owned housing projects.[37]

Dismantling the Ghetto

Public policies to end racial segregation must attack racial discrimination in private housing markets, where 98% of all dwellings are allocated. In particular, they must interrupt the institutionalized process of neighborhood racial turnover, which is the ultimate mechanism by which the ghetto is reproduced and maintained. Racial turnover is built into the structure of urban housing markets through a combination of white prejudice and racial discrimination, which restrict black access to most white neighborhoods and systematically channel black housing demand to a few black or racially mixed areas.

The elimination of racial barriers in urban housing markets requires the direct institutional involvement of the federal government. To an unprecedented degree the U.S. Department of Housing and Urban Development, in particular, must fully commit itself to fair housing enforcement.

First, HUD must increase its financial assistance to local fair housing organizations to increase their ability to investigate and prosecute individual complaints of housing discrimination. Grants made to local agencies dedicated to fair housing enforcement will enable them to expand their efforts by hiring more legal staff, implementing more extensive testing programs, and making their services more widely available. In the early history of fair housing, many testers and legal assistants were funded by federal programs such as the Comprehensive Education and Training Act and the Office of Economic Opportunity.[38] The elimination of these programs by the Reagan Administration undercut the ability of local organizations to enforce fair housing law, and these cuts must be restored if racial discrimination is to be overcome.

But spirited individual prosecution, even when federally assisted, is not enough. As a second step, HUD must establish a permanent testing program capable of identifying realtors who engage in a pattern of discrimination. A special unit dedicated to the regular administration of large-scale housing audits should be created in HUD under the Assistant Secretary for Fair Housing and Equal Opportunity. Audits of randomly selected realtors should be conducted annually within metropolitan areas that have large black communities, and when evidence of systematic discrimination is uncovered, the department should compile additional evidence and turn it over to the Attorney General for vigorous prosecution.

Neither of these two proposals requires significant changes in fair housing law. Indeed, the 1988 Fair Housing Amendments, in making it easier to pursue discriminations and increasing the costs for those who are caught, make the 1990s a particularly opportune time to redouble enforcement efforts. The new law authorized a Fair Housing Initiatives Program at HUD to fund state and local governments and nonprofit corporations seeking to carry out programs to prevent or eliminate discriminatory housing practices.[39] The amendments empowered HUD to initiate investigations on its own, without a prior complaint of discrimination, clearing the way for a bureaucratically based testing program.[40]

Racial discrimination is a problem not only in real estate transactions, however, but also in the home loan industry, where blacks are rejected at rates considerably above those of whites.[41] Congress therefore has required financial institutions to compile detailed racial data on their lending practices. The 1974 Equal Credit Opportunity Act requires them to tabulate the race of clients they accept and reject for home loans;[42] the 1975 Home Mortgage Disclosure Act requires them to report which neighborhoods receive mortgage funds;[43] and the 1977 Community Reinvestment Act requires them to demonstrate that they have provided credit to areas that have been unable to secure capital in the past.[44]

But despite these requirements, little has been done with these data to monitor lender compliance with fair housing statutes. As a third policy initiative, a staff should be created under the Assistant Secretary for Fair Housing and Equal Opportunity to scrutinize lending data for unusually high rates of rejection among minority applicants and black neighborhoods. When the rejection rates cannot be explained statistically by social, demographic, economic, or other background factors, a systematic case study of the bank's lending practices should be initiated. If clear evidence of discrimination is uncovered, the case should be referred to the Attorney General for prosecution, and if not, an equal opportunity lending plan should be conciliated, implemented, and monitored.

Because HUD continues to play a large role in overseeing federally subsidized housing, a fourth policy initiative must be a more vigorous promotion of desegregation under the affirmative mandate of the Fair Housing Act. Given the reality of intense opposition to the construction of projects outside the ghetto, significant desegregation is unlikely to occur by building new projects. More promise has been shown through the use of subsidized rental vouchers that enable poor blacks to obtain units through the private market. In one evaluation of the remedy arising from the *Gautreaux* decision, blacks who moved into integrated settings through the use of rental vouchers experienced greater success in education and employment than did a comparable group who remained behind in the ghetto; and, significantly, participants did not encounter the kind of white hostility commonly experienced by project inhabitants.[45] Funding for housing certificate programs authorized under Section 8 of the 1974 Housing and Community Development Act should therefore be expanded, and programs modeled on the Gautreaux Demonstration Project should be more widely implemented.

Finally, effective enforcement of the Fair Housing Act requires prompt judicial action and timely relief. Since 1968, fair housing enforcement has been a long, drawn-out, expensive, and emotionally draining process for plaintiffs, even if they ultimately prevail. Congress recognized this problem in 1988 when it passed amendments to create an administrative process for adjudicating fair housing cases; but acting on a motion by Senator Orrin Hatch of Utah, Congress also granted defendants the right to request a trial in federal court.[46]

Most accused discriminators elect to have their cases heard in federal court, which slows down the judicial process considerably and defeats the new administrative hearing process. Because defendants are usually realtors or developers with significant financial resources, a long trial provides them with a decided advantage over plaintiffs, whose resources are generally more modest. In order to expedite fair housing judgments and grant more timely relief to victims of discrimination, Congress should amend the Fair Housing Act to require that initial trials be held before an administrative law judge and to provide access to federal courts only upon appeal.

Even if these five policy initiatives are successful in lowering racial barriers in urban housing markets, however, they are not likely to end racial segregation unless black demand is simultaneously allowed to spread more evenly around metropolitan housing markets. To a great extent, blacks are reluctant to enter white neighborhoods because they fear becoming victims of racial hate crimes.[47] These fears can only be allayed by vigorous and swift punishment of those who commit crimes against minority families seeking to integrate white neighborhoods.

Given the overriding importance of residential mobility to individual well-being, and in view of the great social and economic harm done to the nation by segregation, hate crimes directed against black in-migrants must be considered more severe than ordinary acts of vandalism or assault. Rather than being left to local authorities, they should be prosecuted at the federal level as violations of the victim's civil rights. Stiff financial penalties and jail terms should be imposed, not in recognition of the severity of the vandalism or violence itself, but in acknowledgment of the serious damage that segregation does to the nation's well-being.

Black housing demand is also geographically skewed by racial segregation within the real estate industry itself. Most real estate brokers depend on the cooperation of other agents for sales and referrals, a fact that is formalized through multiple listing services (MLS). These services provide extensive listings of properties for sale or rent throughout a metropolitan area, and when MLS transactions are completed, the commission is divided between the participating agents. But these listings typically cover only white suburbs and select city neighborhoods, and are available only to agents serving those areas; brokers serving black communities generally do not have access to these services. Moreover, access is typically controlled by local real estate boards, and in some instances suburban brokers who sell to blacks have been denied membership on the board and hence prevented from using multiple listing services.[48]

Under prevailing marketing practices in the real estate industry, therefore, homeseekers living in segregated black neighborhoods do not have full access to information about wider housing opportunities, and black housing searches are consequently much less efficient than those of whites. Frequently blacks are forced to rely on drives through neighborhoods in search of "For Sale" signs.[49] If black demand is ever to be expressed naturally and widely, realtors serving black clients must be given complete access to multiple listing services. Congress should adopt legislation removing monopoly control of multiple listing services from local realty boards; access to the service should be open to all agents willing to pay a standard membership fee, irrespective of their race or that of their clients.

HUD should also establish new programs, and expand existing programs, to train realtors in fair housing marketing procedures. Agents catering primarily to white clients should be instructed about advertising and marketing methods to ensure that blacks in segregated communities gain access to information about housing opportunities outside the ghetto; agents serving the black share of the market should be trained to market homes throughout the metropolitan area and should be instructed especially in how to use multiple listing services. HUD officials and local fair housing groups should carefully monitor whether realtors serving blacks are given access to the MLS.

Such programs should be implemented in concert with a strengthening of the Voluntary Affirmative Marketing Agreement.[50] In strengthening the terms of the agreement, the list of realtors that signed it should once again be made public, the use of testers should be encouraged, and the responsibilities of realtors to enforce the Fair Housing Act should be spelled out explicitly.

Although it is important for HUD to work with the National Association of Realtors and local real estate boards, efforts should also be made to monitor realtor compliance with Title VIII. Ultimately the Assistant Secretary for Fair Housing and Equal Opportunity at HUD must take a more active role in overseeing real estate advertising and marketing practices, two areas that have received insufficient federal attention in the past. Realtors in selected metropolitan areas should be sampled and their advertising and marketing practices regularly examined for conformity with federal fair housing regulations. HUD should play a larger role in ensuring that black homeseekers are not being systematically and deliberately overlooked by prevailing marketing practices.

The Case for National Action

For the most part, the policies we have recommended do not require major changes in legislation. What they require is political will. Given the will to end segregation, the necessary funds and legislative measures will follow. But political will is precisely what has been lacking over the past several decades, and resistance to desegregation continues to be strong. For each proposal that is advanced to move the fair housing agenda forward, there are other efforts to set it back.

At the time the 1988 Fair Housing Amendments were being debated, for example, Senator Orrin Hatch of Utah introduced a bill endorsed by the National Association of Realtors to limit the filing of fair housing suits to parties actually intending to rent or buy real estate (as opposed to testers, fair housing staff members, or others harmed by discriminatory practices), thereby attempting to undo twenty years of court decisions that had broadened the question of standing and made fair housing enforcement easier.[51] The Hatch bill also would have banned the hearing of fair housing cases before administrative law judges and relied instead on secret conciliation as the principal means of fair housing enforcement.[52]

After the Hatch bill was discarded in favor of legislation sponsored by Senators Kennedy and Specter, the Reagan Administration offered regulations implementing the amendments that could have banned a variety of affirmative marketing strategies used by fair housing organizations.[53] In addition, the National Association of Realtors attempted to limit funding for the Fair Housing Initiatives Program, which was intended to support local antidiscrimination efforts;[54] and in 1991, a House banking subcommittee quietly added a provision to pending legislation that would have exempted more than 85% of U.S. banks from the 1977 Community Reinvestment Act, which required financial institutions to meet the credit needs of low-income minority areas.[55] Later that year the Bush Administration proposed abolishing the U.S. Commission on Civil Rights,[56] which for years had kept pressure on HUD to improve fair housing enforcement.[57]

Although race has become embroiled in partisan politics during the 1980s and 1990s, residential desegregation is not intrinsically a cause of either the right or the left; it is neither liberal nor conservative, democrat nor republican. Rather it is a bipartisan agenda in the national interest. The ghetto must be dismantled because only by ending segregation will we eliminate the manifold social and economic problems that follow from its persistence.

For conservatives, the cause of desegregation turns on the issue of market access. We have marshaled extensive evidence to show that one particular group—black Americans—is systematically denied full access to a crucial market. Housing markets are central to individual social and economic well-being because they distribute much more than shelter; they also distribute a variety of resources that shape and largely determine one's life chances. Along with housing, residential markets also allocate schooling, peer groups, safety, jobs, insurance costs, public services, home equity, and, ultimately, wealth. By tolerating the persistent and systematic disenfranchisement of blacks from housing markets, we send a clear signal to one group that hard work, individual enterprise, sacrifice, and aspirations don't matter; what determines one's life chances is the color of one's skin.

For liberals, the issue is one of unfinished business, for residential segregation is the most important item remaining on the nation's civil rights agenda. In many areas of civil life, desegregation has occurred; in the south, Jim Crow is dead, and throughout the country blacks are accepted in unions, sports, entertainment, journalism, politics, government, administration, and academia. Many barriers have fallen, but still the residential color line remains—and from residential segregation follows a host of deadly social ills that continue to undercut and overwhelm the progress achieved in other areas.

Residential desegregation should be considered an effort of national unity; any other course of action is politically indefensible. For conservatives, turning away from the task means denying the importance of markets and individual enterprise; for liberals it means sweeping the last piece of unfinished civil rights business under the rug. Ultimately, however, residential desegregation requires a moral commitment and a bipartisan leadership that have been lacking among politicians for the past two decades. Without a willingness to lead and take risks on the part of elected officials, and without a will to change on the part of the American people, none of the legal changes and policy solutions we propose will succeed.

For America, the failure to end segregation will perpetuate a bitter dilemma that has long divided the nation. If segregation is permitted to continue, poverty will inevitably deepen and become more persistent within a large share of the black community, crime and drugs will become more firmly rooted, and social institutions will fragment further under the weight of deteriorating conditions. As racial inequality sharpens, white fears will grow, racial prejudices will be reinforced, and hostility toward blacks will increase, making the problems of racial justice and equal opportunity even more insoluble. Until we face up to the difficult task of dismantling the ghetto, the disastrous consequences of residential segregation will radiate outward to poison American society. Until we decide to end the long reign of American apartheid, we cannot hope to move forward as a people and a nation.

Notes

Index

Notes

1. The Missing Link

1. Epigraph from Edgar H. Brookes, *Apartheid: A Documentary Study of Modern South Africa* (London: Routledge and Kegan Paul, 1968), p. 142.
2. Gunnar Myrdal, *An American Dilemma*, vol. 1 (New York: Harper and Brothers, 1944), p. 618; see also Walter A. Jackson, *Gunnar Myrdal and America's Conscience* (Chapel Hill: University of North Carolina Press, 1990), pp. 88–271.
3. Kenneth B. Clark, *Dark Ghetto: Dilemmas of Social Power* (New York: Harper and Row, 1965), p. 11.
4. U.S. National Advisory Commission on Civil Disorders, *The Kerner Report* (New York: Pantheon Books, 1988), p. 1.
5. Ibid.
6. Ibid., p. 2.
7. Ibid., p. 22.
8. Ibid.
9. Ibid.
10. A few scholars attempted to keep the Kerner Commission's call for desegregation alive, but their voices have largely been unheeded in the ongoing debate. Thomas Pettigrew has continued to assert the central importance of residential segregation, calling it the "linchpin" of American race relations; see "Racial Change and Social Policy," *Annals of the American Academy of Political and Social Science* 441 (1979):114–31. Gary Orfield has repeatedly pointed out segregation's deleterious effects on black prospects for education, employment, and socioeconomic mobility; see "Separate Societies: Have the Kerner Warnings Come True?" in Fred R. Harris and Roger W. Wilkins, eds., *Quiet Riots: Race and Poverty in the United States* (New York: Pantheon Books, 1988), pp. 100–122; and "Ghettoization and Its Alternatives," in Paul E. Peterson, ed., *The New Urban Reality* (Washington, D.C.: Brookings Institution, 1985), pp. 161–96.
11. See Thomas B. Edsall and Mary D. Edsall, *Chain Reaction: The Impact of Race, Rights, and Taxes on American Politics* (New York: Norton, 1991).
12. For an informative history of the evolution of the concept of the underclass, see Michael B. Katz, *The Undeserving Poor: From the War on Poverty to the War on Welfare* (New York: Pantheon, 1989), pp. 185–235.

13. Oscar Lewis, *La Vida: A Puerto Rican Family in the Culture of Poverty—San Juan and New York* (New York: Random House, 1965); "The Culture of Poverty," *Scientific American* 215 (1966):19–25; "The Culture of Poverty," in Daniel P. Moynihan, ed., *On Understanding Poverty: Perspectives from the Social Sciences* (New York: Basic Books, 1968), pp. 187–220.
14. The complete text of this report is reprinted in Lee Rainwater and William L. Yancey, *The Moynihan Report and the Politics of Controversy* (Cambridge: MIT Press, 1967), pp. 39–125.
15. Edward C. Banfield, *The Unheavenly City* (Boston: Little, Brown, 1970).
16. William Ryan, *Blaming the Victim* (New York: Random House, 1971).
17. Carol Stack, *All Our Kin: Strategies of Survival in a Black Community* (New York: Harper and Row, 1974).
18. Douglas C. Glasgow, *The Black Underclass: Poverty, Unemployment, and Entrapment of Ghetto Youth* (New York: Vintage, 1981), p. 11; Alphonso Pinkney, *The Myth of Black Progress* (Cambridge: Cambridge University Press, 1984), pp. 78–80.
19. Charles Murray, *Losing Ground: American Social Policy, 1950–1980* (New York: Basic Books, 1984).
20. Lawrence M. Mead, *Beyond Entitlement: The Social Obligations of Citizenship* (New York: Free Press, 1986).
21. William Julius Wilson, *The Declining Significance of Race: Blacks and Changing American Institutions* (Chicago: University of Chicago Press, 1978).
22. William Julius Wilson, *The Truly Disadvantaged: The Inner City, the Underclass, and Public Policy* (Chicago: University of Chicago Press, 1987), pp. 1–108.
23. Ibid., pp. 49–62.
24. The subject indices of *Losing Ground* and *Beyond Entitlement* contain no references at all to residential segregation.
25. The subject index of *The Truly Disadvantaged* contains two references to pre-1960s Jim Crow segregation.
26. Again with the exception of Thomas Pettigrew and Gary Orfield.
27. We have published several studies documenting how the decline of manufacturing, the surburbanization of jobs, and the rise of low-wage service employment eliminated high-paying jobs for manual workers, drove up rates of black male unemployment, and reduced the attractiveness of marriage to black women, thereby contributing to a proliferation of female-headed families and persistent poverty. See Mitchell L. Eggers and Douglas S. Massey, "The Structural Determinants of Urban Poverty," *Social Science Research* 20 (1991):217–55; Mitchell L. Eggers and Douglas S. Massey, "A Longitudinal Analysis of Urban Poverty: Blacks in U.S. Metropolitan Areas between 1970 and 1980," *Social Science Research* 21 (1992):175–203.
28. The evidence on the extent of middle-class out-migration from ghetto areas is inconclusive. Because racial segregation does not decline with rising socioeconomic status, out-movement from poor black neighborhoods certainly has not been to white areas. When Kathryn P. Nelson measured rates of black out-migration from local "zones" within forty metropolitan areas, however, she found higher rates of out-movement for middle- and upper-class blacks compared with poor blacks; but her "zones" contained more than 100,000 inhabit-

ants, making them considerably larger than neighborhoods (see "Racial Segregation, Mobility, and Poverty Concentration," paper presented at the annual meetings of the Population Association of America, Washington, D.C., March 19–23, 1991). In contrast, Edward Gramlich and Deborah Laren found that poor and middle-class blacks displayed about the same likelihood of out-migration from poor census tracts (see "Geographic Mobility and Persistent Poverty," Department of Economics, University of Michigan, Ann Arbor, 1990).

29. See Eggers and Massey, "A Longitudinal Analysis of Urban Poverty."
30. See International Defense and Aid Fund for Southern Africa, *Apartheid: The Facts* (London: United Nations Centre against Apartheid,1983), pp. 15–26.
31. We are not the first to notice the striking parallel between the institutionalized system of racial segregation in U.S. cities and the organized, state-sponsored system of racial repression in South Africa. See John H. Denton, *Apartheid American Style* (Berkeley, Calif.: Diablo Press, 1967); James A. Kushner, "Apartheid in America: An Historical and Legal Analysis of Contemporary Racial Residential Segregation in the United States," *Howard Law Journal* 22 (1979):547–60.

2. The Construction of the Ghetto

1. Epigraph from W. E. B. Du Bois, "The Problem of the Twentieth Century Is the Problem of the Color Line," in Dan S. Green and Edwin D. Driver, eds., *W. E. B. Du Bois on Sociology and the Black Community* (Chicago: University of Chicago Press, 1978), p. 281.
2. Amos H. Hawley, *Urban Society: An Ecological Approach* (New York: Ronald, 1971), pp. 63–105; Gideon Sjoberg, *The Preindustrial City: Past and Present* (New York: Free Press), pp. 80–107; William L. Yancey, Eugene P. Ericksen, and Richard N. Juliani, "Emergent Ethnicity: A Review and Reformulation," *American Sociological Review* 41 (1976):391–403.
3. Theodore Hershberg, "Free Blacks in Antebellum Philadelphia: A Study of Ex-Slaves, Freeborn, and Socioeconomic Decline," in Theodore Hershberg, ed., *Philadelphia: Work, Space, Family, and Group Experience in the Nineteenth Century* (New York: Oxford University Press, 1981), pp. 368–91; Theodore Hershberg, Alan N. Burstein, Eugene P. Ericksen, Stephanie W. Greenberg, and William L. Yancey, "A Tale of Three Cities: Blacks, Immigrants, and Opportunity in Philadelphia, 1850–1880, 1930, 1970," in Hershberg, *Philadelphia*, pp. 461–91.
4. Our discussion summarizes case studies of ghetto formation from a variety of sources: Darrel E. Bigham, *We Ask Only a Fair Trial: A History of the Black Community of Evansville, Indiana* (Bloomington: Indiana University Press, 1987); Harold X. Connolly, *A Ghetto Grows in Brooklyn* (New York: New York University Press, 1977); Douglas H. Daniels, *Pioneer Urbanites: A Social and Cultural History of Black San Francisco* (Philadelphia: Temple University Press, 1980); Lawrence B. DeGraaf, "The City of Black Angels: Emergence of the Los Angeles Ghetto, 1890–1930," *Pacific Historical Review* 39 (1970):323–52; David A. Gerber, *Black Ohio and the Color Line: 1860–1915* (Urbana: University of Illinois Press, 1976); David M. Katzman, *Before the Ghetto: Black Detroit in the Nineteenth Century* (Urbana: University of Illinois Press, 1973); Kenneth L. Kusmer, *A Ghetto Takes*

Shape: Black Cleveland, 1870–1930 (Urbana: University of Illinois Press, 1976); Kenneth L. Kusmer, "The Origins and Development of Black Ghettos in the North: 1870–1930," paper presented at the Workshop on Social History, University of Chicago, 1976; Gilbert Osofsky, *Harlem: The Making of a Ghetto—Negro New York, 1890–1930* (New York: Harper and Row, 1968); Thomas L. Philpott, *The Slum and the Ghetto: Neighborhood Deterioration and Middle-Class Reform, Chicago, 1880–1930* (New York: Oxford University Press, 1978); Allan H. Spear, *Black Chicago: The Making of a Negro Ghetto, 1890–1920* (Chicago: University of Chicago Press, 1967); Henry Louis Taylor, "Spatial Organization and the Residential Experience: Black Cincinnati in 1850," *Social Science History* 10 (1986):45–69; Joe William Trotter, Jr., *Black Milwaukee: The Making of an Industrial Proletariat, 1915–1945* (Urbana: University of Illinois Press, 1985); Olivier Zunz, *The Changing Face of Inequality: Urbanization, Industrial Development, and Immigrants in Detroit, 1880–1920* (Chicago: University of Chicago Press, 1982).

5. John Kellogg, "Negro Urban Clusters in the Post-Bellum South," *Geographical Analysis* 67 (1977):310–21; Osofsky, *Harlem*, p. xvi; Spear, *Black Chicago*, p. 14; Henry L. Taylor, "The Use of Maps in the Study of the Black Ghetto-Formation Process: Cincinnati, 1802–1910," *Historical Methods* 17 (1984):44–58; Zunz, *The Changing Face of Inequality*, pp. 140–41.
6. Recent reviews of the literature on the measurement of segregation are provided by David R. James and Karl E. Taeuber, "Measures of Segregation," in Nancy Tuma, ed., *Sociological Methodology, 1985* (San Francisco: Jossey-Bass, 1985), pp. 1–32; Douglas S. Massey and Nancy A. Denton, "The Dimensions of Residential Segregation," *Social Forces* 67 (1988):281–315; Michael J. White, "Segregation and Diversity: Measures in Population Distribution," *Population Index* 52 (1986):198–221.
7. Nathan Kantrowitz, "Racial and Ethnic Segregation in Boston: 1830–1970," *Annals of the American Academy of Political and Social Science* 441 (1979):41–54.
8. Historical studies of ethnic segregation are reviewed in Douglas S. Massey, "Ethnic Residential Segregation: A Theoretical Synthesis and Empirical Review," *Sociology and Social Research* 69 (1985):315–50; see also Hershberg et al., "A Tale of Three Cities."
9. See Allen B. Ballard, *One More Day's Journey: The Story of a Family and a People* (New York: McGraw-Hill, 1984), pp. 26–38; Katzman, *Before the Ghetto*, pp. 81–84, 135–74; Kusmer, *A Ghetto Takes Shape*, pp. 98–101; Spear, *Black Chicago*, pp. 51–70; Trotter, *Black Milwaukee*, pp. 20–21.
10. Spear, *Black Chicago*, pp. 55–56.
11. Ibid., pp. 56–70.
12. Kusmer, *A Ghetto Takes Shape*, pp. 126–30.
13. Katzman, *Before the Ghetto*, pp. 135–37, 160–61.
14. Trotter, *Black Milwaukee*, pp. 20–21.
15. For a discussion of the isolation index, see Stanley Lieberson, "An Asymmetrical Approach to Segregation," in Ceri Peach, Vaughn Robinson, and Susan Smith, eds., *Ethnic Segregation in Cities* (London: Croom Helm, 1981), pp. 61–82; Massey and Denton, "The Dimensions of Segregation"; White, "Segregation and Diversity."

16. Stanley Lieberson, *A Piece of the Pie: Blacks and White Immigrants since 1880* (Berkeley: University of California Press, 1980), pp. 266–88.
17. Richard C. Wade, "Residential Segregation in the Ante-bellum South," in John H. Brace, Jr., August Meier, and Elliot Rudwick, eds., *The Rise of the Ghetto* (Belmont, Calif.: Wadsworth Publishing, 1971), pp. 10–14.
18. Slaves who were "living out" worked outside the slave-owner's household for wages and turned the proceeds over to their master after deducting an allowance for food and lodging; see Richard C. Wade, *Slavery in the Cities: The South, 1820–1860* (New York: Oxford University Press, 1964), pp. 275–77.
19. Ira Berlin, *Slaves without Masters: The Free Negro in the Antebellum South* (New York: Pantheon, 1974), pp. 250–65; John W. Blassingame, *Black New Orleans, 1860–1880* (Chicago: University of Chicago Press, 1973), pp. 16, 208; John Kellogg, "Negro Urban Clusters in the Postbellum South," *Geographical Review* 67 (1977):310–21; Karl E. Taeuber and Alma F. Taeuber, *Negroes in Cities: Residential Segregation and Neighborhood Change* (Chicago: Aldine Publishing, 1965), pp. 43–53; Wade, *Slavery in the Cities.*
20. The data come from Wade, "Residential Segregation," p. 11, and Taeuber and Taeuber, *Negroes in Cities*, p. 46.
21. C. Vann Woodward, *The Strange Career of Jim Crow*, 3rd ed. (New York: Oxford University Press, 1974).
22. N. J. Demerath and H. W. Gilmore, "The Ecology of Southern Cities," in Rupert B. Vance and N. J. Demerath, eds., *The Urban South* (Chapel Hill: University of North Carolina Press, 1954), pp. 120–25; Rudolf Heberle, "Social Consequences of Industrialization of Southern Cities," *Social Forces* 27 (1948):29–37.
23. Wade Clark Roof, Thomas L. Van Valey, and Daphne Spain, "Residential Segregation in Southern Cities: 1970," *Social Forces* 55 (1976):59–71; Leo F. Schnore and Philip C. Evenson, "Segregation in Southern Cities," *American Journal of Sociology* 72 (1966):58–67.
24. Brian J. L. Berry, *The Human Consequences of Urbanization* (New York: St. Martin's Press, 1973), pp. 1–26; Stephanie W. Greenberg, "Industrial Location and Ethnic Residential Patterns in an Industrializing City: Philadelphia, 1880," in Hershberg, *Philadelphia*, pp. 204–232; Hershberg et al., "A Tale of Three Cities"; Yancey et al., "Emergent Ethnicity."
25. Charlotte Erickson, *American Industry and the European Immigrant, 1860–1885* (Cambridge: Harvard University Press, 1957); J. M. Perry, *The Impact of Immigration on Three American Industries, 1865–1914* (New York: Arno Press, 1978).
26. John S. MacDonald and Leatrice D. MacDonald, "Chain Migration, Ethnic Neighborhood Formation, and Social Networks," in Charles Tilly, ed., *An Urban World* (Boston: Little, Brown, 1974), pp. 226–36; Ewa Morawska, "The Sociology and Historiography of Immigration," in Virginia Yans-McLaughlin, ed., *Immigration Reconsidered: History, Sociology, and Politics* (New York: Oxford University Press, 1990), pp. 187–240; Charles Tilly and C. H. Brown, "On Uprooting, Kinship, and the Auspices of Migration," *International Journal of Comparative Sociology* 8 (1967):139–64.
27. Sam Bass Warner, Jr., and Colin B. Burke, *Streetcar Suburbs: The Process of Growth in Boston* (Cambridge: Harvard University Press, 1962); Sam Bass Warner, Jr.,

The Private City: Philadelphia in Three Periods of Its Growth (Philadelphia: University of Pennsylvania Press, 1968); David Ward, *Cities and Immigrants: A Geography of Change in Nineteenth Century America* (New York: Oxford University Press, 1971).

28. See Stanley Lieberson, *Ethnic Patterns in American Cities* (New York: Free Press, 1963), pp. 44–158, 182–90; Massey, "Ethnic Residential Segregation."
29. Reynolds Farley and Walter R. Allen, *The Color Line and the Quality of Life in America* (New York: Russell Sage, 1987), p. 113.
30. Brinley Thomas, *Migration and Economic Growth: A Study of Great Britain and the Atlantic Economy* (Cambridge: Cambridge University Press, 1954); Dorothy S. Thomas, *Social and Economic Aspects of Swedish Population Movements: 1750–1933* (New York: Macmillan, 1947).
31. Thomas, *Migration and Economic Growth*, pp. 130–34.
32. Kusmer, *A Ghetto Takes Shape*, pp. 69–70; Osofsky, *Harlem*, p. 42; Spear, *Black Chicago*, pp. 36–40; Trotter, *Black Milwaukee*, pp. 56–57; Zunz, *The Changing Face of Inequality*, p. 373.
33. Ballard, *One More Day's Journey*, p. 231; James R. Grossman, *Land of Hope: Chicago, Black Southerners, and the Great Migration* (Chicago: University of Chicago Press, 1989), pp. 208–245; Kusmer, *A Ghetto Takes Shape*, pp. 197–99; Trotter, *Black Milwaukee*, pp. 3–33.
34. Grossman, *Land of Hope*, pp. 208–245.
35. Farley and Allen, *The Color Line*, p. 113.
36. Grossman, *Land of Hope*, pp. 38–65.
37. Ibid., pp. 13–15; Spear, *Black Chicago*, p. 132.
38. Farley and Allen, *The Color Line*, p. 113.
39. Grossman, *Land of Hope*, pp. 66–97; Spear, *Black Chicago*, pp. 135–38.
40. Kusmer, *A Ghetto Takes Shape*, p. 175; Osofsky, *Harlem*, p. 107.
41. Grossman, *Land of Hope*, pp. 246–58; Kusmer, *A Ghetto Takes Shape*, pp. 61–64; Lieberson, *A Piece of the Pie*, pp. 234–36; Spear, *Black Chicago*, pp. 203–205.
42. Katzman, *Before the Ghetto*, pp. 81–103; Kusmer, *A Ghetto Takes Shape*, pp. 35–52; Spear, *Black Chicago*, pp. 29–49; Trotter, *Black Milwaukee*, pp. 24–25.
43. Bigham, *We Ask Only a Fair Trial*, pp. 103–108; Chicago Commission on Race Relations, *The Negro in Chicago: A Study of Race Relations and a Race Riot* (Chicago: University of Chicago Press, 1922); Kusmer, *A Ghetto Takes Shape*, p. 54; Osofsky, *Harlem*, pp. 46–52; Elliot Rudwick, *Race Riot at East St. Louis: July 2, 1917* (Urbana: University of Illinois Press, 1964).
44. Ballard, *One More Day's Journey*, pp. 191–216; Bigham, *We Ask Only a Fair Trial*, pp. 108–119; DeGraaf, "City of Black Angels"; Gerber, *Black Ohio and the Color Line*, pp. 288–89; Grossman, *Land of Hope*, pp. 174–75; Kusmer, *A Ghetto Takes Shape*, pp. 35–52; Lieberson, *A Piece of the Pie*, pp. 253–91; Osofsky, *Harlem*, pp. 105–132, 189–91; Philpott, *The Slum and the Ghetto*, pp. 146–61; Spear, *Black Chicago*, pp. 11–27; Trotter, *Black Milwaukee*, pp. 66–74.
45. Taeuber and Taeuber, *Negroes in Cities*, pp. 39–41.
46. Thomas L. Van Valey and Wade Clark Roof, "Measuring Residential Segregation in American Cities: Problems of Intercity Comparison," *Urban Affairs Quarterly* 11 (1976):453–68.
47. Lieberson, *A Piece of the Pie*, p. 260.

48. Philpott, *The Slum and the Ghetto,* pp. 113–45.
49. Ibid., p. 136.
50. Ibid., p. 137.
51. Ibid., pp. 139–42.
52. Ibid., pp. 141–42.
53. Lieberson, *A Piece of the Pie,* p. 266.
54. Lieberson, *Ethnic Patterns in American Cities,* pp. 44–158, 182–90; Lieberson, *A Piece of the Pie,* pp. 270–84; Massey, "Ethnic Residential Segregation."
55. Ballard, *One More Day's Journey,* pp. 198–99; Bigham, *We Ask Only a Fair Trial,* pp. 109–113; Kusmer, *A Ghetto Takes Shape,* pp. 170–71; Philpott, *The Slum and the Ghetto,* pp. 154–56; Spear, *Black Chicago,* pp. 21–25; Zunz, *The Changing Face of Inequality,* pp. 393–98.
56. Bigham, *We Ask Only a Fair Trial,* pp. 103–108; Chicago Commission on Race Relations, *The Negro in Chicago;* Kusmer, *A Ghetto Takes Shape,* p. 54; Osofsky, *Harlem,* pp. 46–52; Rudwick, *Race Riot at East St. Louis;* Spear, *Black Chicago,* pp. 214–22.
57. St. Clair Drake and Horace R. Cayton, *Black Metropolis: A Study of Negro Life in a Northern City* (New York: Harcourt, Brace, 1945), pp. 62–64, 178–79; Kusmer, *A Ghetto Takes Shape,* pp. 167–71; Philpott, *The Slum and the Ghetto,* pp. 162–80; Spear, *Black Chicago,* pp. 211–14; Zunz, *The Changing Face of Inequality,* pp. 373–75.
58. Drake and Cayton, *Black Metropolis,* p. 178–79.
59. Spear, *Black Chicago,* pp. 177–78.
60. Kusmer, *A Ghetto Takes Shape,* pp. 168–70.
61. Zunz, *The Changing Face of Inequality,* pp. 324, 373–75.
62. See, for example, Julia Cass, "The Elmwood Incident," *Philadelphia Inquirer Magazine,* May 4, 1986; J. Anthony Lukas, *Common Ground: A Turbulent Decade in the Lives of Three American Families* (New York: Vintage, 1985), pp. 509–535; Jonathan Rieder, *Canarsie: The Jews and Italians of Brooklyn against Liberalism* (Cambridge: Harvard University Press, 1985), pp. 87–88, 198–202.
63. Philpott, *The Slum and the Ghetto,* pp. 147–48, 154–55; Spear, *Black Chicago,* pp. 20–24.
64. Connolly, *A Ghetto Grows in Brooklyn,* pp. 58–60; Osofsky, *Harlem,* pp. 107–109.
65. John F. Bauman, *Public Housing, Race, and Renewal: Urban Planning in Philadelphia, 1920–1974* (Philadelphia: Temple University Press, 1987), pp. 162–63; DeGraaf, "The City of Black Angels," pp. 336–37; Trotter, *Black Milwaukee,* p. 184.
66. Spear, *Black Chicago,* p. 155.
67. DeGraaf, "The City of Black Angels," pp. 336–37; Drake and Cayton, *Black Metropolis,* pp. 182–90; Kusmer, *A Ghetto Takes Shape,* pp. 46, 167; Osofsky, *Harlem,* pp. 106–110; Philpott, *The Slum and the Ghetto,* pp. 189–99; Trotter, *Black Milwaukee,* pp. 70–71, 182–83; Zunz, *The Changing Face of Inequality,* p. 374.
68. The case was *Shelly v. Kraemer;* see Brian J. L. Berry, *The Open Housing Question: Race and Housing in Chicago, 1966–1976* (Cambridge, Mass.: Ballinger, 1979). See also Kenneth T. Jackson, *Crabgrass Frontier: The Suburbanization of the United States* (New York: Oxford University Press, 1985), p. 208.

69. Philpott, *The Slum and the Ghetto,* pp. 189–93.
70. Rose Helper, *Racial Policies and Practices of Real Estate Brokers* (Minneapolis: University of Minnesota Press, 1969), p. 201.
71. Drake and Cayton, *Black Metropolis,* pp. 185, 206–207; Grossman, *Land of Hope,* p. 169; Harvey L. Molotch, *Managed Integration: Dilemmas of Doing Good in the City* (Berkeley: University of California Press, 1972), pp. 22–27; Osofsky, *Harlem,* pp. 110–13, 135–41; Philpott, *The Slum and the Ghetto,* p. 157; Trotter, *Black Milwaukee,* p. 70.
72. Helper, *Racial Policies and Practices,* p. 4.
73. Philpott, *The Slum and the Ghetto,* pp. 149–53, 163–64; Arnold R. Hirsch, *Making the Second Ghetto: Race and Housing in Chicago, 1940–1960* (Cambridge: Cambridge University Press, 1983), pp. 34–35.
74. Homer Hoyt, *The Structure and Growth of Residential Neighborhoods in American Cities* (Washington, D.C.: U.S. Government Printing Office, 1939).
75. Philpott, *The Slum and the Ghetto,* pp. 149–53; Zunz, *The Changing Face of Inequality,* p. 375.
76. For theoretical descriptions of neighborhood change, see Thomas C. Schelling, "Dynamic Models of Segregation," *Journal of Mathematical Sociology* 1 (1971):143–86; Richard L. Morrill, "The Negro Ghetto: Problems and Alternatives," *Geographical Review* 55 (1965):339–61. For early empirical examples, see Otis D. Duncan and Beverly Duncan, *The Negro Population of Chicago* (Chicago: University of Chicago Press, 1957), pp. 87–107; Drake and Cayton, *Black Metropolis,* pp. 189–90; Taeuber and Taeuber, *Negroes in Cities,* pp. 108–111.
77. Duncan and Duncan, *The Negro Population of Chicago,* pp. 237–52; Kusmer, *A Ghetto Takes Shape,* pp. 98–100; Philpott, *The Slum and the Ghetto,* pp. 148–49; Spear, *Black Chicago,* pp. 24–25; Taeuber and Taeuber, *Negroes in Cities,* pp. 154–73.
78. Helper, *Racial Policies and Practices,* pp. 172–82; Hirsch, *Making the Second Ghetto,* pp. 31–33.
79. Drake and Cayton, *Black Metropolis,* pp. 576–77, Spear, *Black Chicago,* p. 150.
80. Drake and Cayton, *Black Metropolis,* pp. 604–605; Duncan and Duncan, *The Negro Population of Chicago,* pp. 237–98; E. Franklin Frazier, "Negro Harlem: An Ecological Study," *American Journal of Sociology* 43 (1937):72–88.
81. Kusmer, *A Ghetto Takes Shape,* pp. 247–51, 270–73; Osofsky, *Harlem,* pp. 181–84; Spear, *Black Chicago,* pp. 193–200; Trotter, *Black Milwaukee,* pp. 102–109.
82. Discussions of the elite's vested interest in segregation may be found in Drake and Cayton, *Black Metropolis,* pp. 114–15, 201–202; E. Franklin Frazier, "Human, All Too Human: The Negro's Vested Interest in Segregation," in G. Franklin Edwards, ed., *E. Franklin Frazier on Race Relations* (Chicago: University of Chicago Press, 1968), pp. 283–91; Trotter, *Black Milwaukee,* pp. 184–85.
83. Drake and Cayton, *Black Metropolis,* pp. 465–68; Osofsky, *Harlem,* pp. 93–104; Spear, *Black Chicago,* pp. 74–75, 112–13.
84. Grossman, *Land of Hope,* pp. 74–75; Osofsky, *Harlem,* p. 133; Spear, *Black Chicago,* pp. 81–85, 114–15.
85. Spear, *Black Chicago,* pp. 78–79, 122–24.
86. Osofsky, *Harlem,* p. 34.

87. Computed from data published in Taeuber and Taeuber, *Negroes in Cities*, p. 46.
88. Roger L. Rice, "Residential Segregation by Law, 1910–1917," *Journal of Southern History* 47 (1968):179–99.
89. Drake and Cayton, *Black Metropolis*, pp. 69–70.
90. Rice, "Residential Segregation by Law."
91. Computed from data published in Taeuber and Taeuber, *Negroes in Cities*, pp. 45–53.
92. Kusmer, *A Ghetto Takes Shape*, pp. 171–73; Lieberson, *A Piece of the Pie*, p. 259; Trotter, *Black Milwaukee*, p. 67; Zunz, *The Changing Face of Inequality*, pp. 342–54.
93. Farley and Allen, *The Color Line*, p. 113.
94. Drake and Cayton, *Black Metropolis*, pp. 200–213; Duncan and Duncan, *The Negro Population of Chicago*, pp. 133–262; Lieberson, *A Piece of the Pie*, pp. 258–60; Osofsky, *Harlem*, pp. 138–43; Spear, *Black Chicago*, pp. 147–50; Trotter, *Black Milwaukee*, pp. 175–86.
95. Duncan and Duncan, *The Negro Population of Chicago*, pp. 142–55.
96. For an account of the metropolitanization of urban America, see Berry, *Human Consequences*, pp. 27–73; Hawley, *Urban Society*, pp. 145–240.
97. Neil Fligstein, *Going North: Migration of Blacks and Whites from the South, 1900–1950* (New York: Academic Press, 1981).
98. Farley and Allen, *The Color Line*, p. 113.
99. William H. Frey, "Central City White Flight: Racial and Nonracial Causes," *American Sociological Review* 44 (1979):425–48; William H. Frey, "Black In-Migration, White Flight, and the Changing Economic Base of the Central City," *American Journal of Sociology* 85 (1980):1396–1417.
100. See the maps reproduced in Drake and Cayton, *Black Metropolis*, p. 63; Duncan and Duncan, *The Negro Population of Chicago*, pp. 92–93; Taeuber and Taeuber, *Negroes in Cities*, pp. 256–75; Trotter, *Black Milwaukee*, pp. 22, 177.
101. U.S. Bureau of the Census, *Statistical Abstract of the United States* (Washington, D.C.: U.S. Government Printing Office, 1956); U.S. Bureau of the Census, *Statistical Abstract of the United States* (Washington, D.C.: U.S. Government Printing Office, 1966); U.S. Bureau of the Census, *Statistical Abstract of the United States* (Washington, D.C.: U.S. Government Printing Office, 1976).
102. Taeuber and Taeuber, *Negroes in Cities*, pp. 256–75.
103. Douglas S. Massey and Brendan P. Mullan, "Processes of Hispanic and Black Spatial Assimilation," *American Journal of Sociology* 89 (1984):836–73; Taeuber and Taeuber, *Negroes in Cities*, p. 109.
104. Lieberson, *A Piece of the Pie*, p. 266.
105. Gordon W. Allport, *The Nature of Prejudice* (Garden City, N.Y.: Doubleday Anchor, 1958), p. 74.
106. Howard Schuman, Charlotte Steeh, and Lawrence Bobo, *Racial Attitudes in America: Trends and Interpretations* (Cambridge: Harvard University Press, 1985), pp. 74–75.
107. Ibid.
108. Massey and Mullan, "Processes of Spatial Assimilation"; Taeuber and Taeuber, *Negroes in Cities*, p. 109; Hirsch, *Making the Second Ghetto*, pp. 1–99.
109. Helper, *Racial Policies and Practices*.

110. Ibid., p. 317.
111. Molotch, *Managed Integration,* p. 23.
112. Helper, *Racial Policies and Practices,* pp. 349–52.
113. Ibid., p. 321.
114. Ibid., p. 322.
115. Ibid., p. 331.
116. Ibid., p. 335.
117. Ibid., p. 329.
118. Ibid., p. 339.
119. Ibid., p. 337.
120. Jackson, *Crabgrass Frontier,* p. 196.
121. Ibid., p. 197.
122. Ibid.
123. Ibid., pp. 197–98.
124. Ibid., p. 199.
125. Ibid., pp. 199–201.
126. Ibid., p. 203.
127. Ibid.; R. Allen Hays, *The Federal Government and Urban Housing: Ideology and Change in Public Policy* (Albany: State University of New York Press, 1985).
128. Jackson, *Crabgrass Frontier,* p. 204.
129. Ibid.
130. Ibid., pp. 205–206.
131. Ibid., p. 206.
132. Ibid.
133. Ibid., p. 208.
134. Ibid.
135. Ibid., pp. 208–209.
136. Ibid., p. 209.
137. Ibid., p. 211.
138. Ibid., p. 213.
139. Ibid.
140. Frey, "Central City White Flight."
141. Ibid., pp. 219–30; Bauman, *Housing Race and Renewal,* pp. 79–117; Hirsch, *Making the Second Ghetto,* pp. 100–170.
142. Hirsch, *Making the Second Ghetto,* pp. 40–99, 171–214; Bauman, *Public Housing, Race, and Renewal,* pp. 160–69.
143. Bauman, *Public Housing, Race, and Renewal,* pp. 144–82; Hirsch, *Making the Second Ghetto,* pp. 212–58; Ira Goldstein and William L. Yancey, "Public Housing Projects, Blacks, and Public Policy: The Historical Ecology of Public Housing in Philadelphia," in John M. Goering, ed., *Housing Desegregation and Federal Policy* (Chapel Hill: University of North Carolina Press, 1986), pp. 262–89.
144. Hirsch, *Making the Second Ghetto,* pp. 170, 273–74.
145. Michael J. White, *Urban Renewal and the Residential Structure of the City* (Chicago: Community and Family Studies Center, 1980), pp. 149–209.
146. Hirsch, *Making the Second Ghetto,* pp. 130–31.
147. Bauman, *Public Housing, Race, and Urban Renewal,* pp. 144–82; Adam Bickford

and Douglas S. Massey, "Segregation in the Second Ghetto: Racial and Ethnic Segregation in U.S. Public Housing, 1977," *Social Forces* 69 (1991):1011–36; Hirsch, *Making the Second Ghetto*, pp. 262–89; Lee Rainwater, *Behind Ghetto Walls: Black Life in a Federal Slum* (Chicago: Aldine, 1970).

148. Douglas S. Massey and Shawn M. Kanaiaupuni, "Public Housing and the Concentration of Poverty," *Social Science Quarterly*, forthcoming.
149. Bickford and Massey, "Segregation in the Second Ghetto."
150. Hirsch, *Making the Second Ghetto*, pp. 252–54.
151. U.S. National Advisory Commission on Civil Disorders, *The Kerner Report* (New York: Pantheon Books, 1988), pp. 35–108; see also Helper, *Racial Policies and Practices*, pp. 12–13.
152. U.S. National Advisory Commission on Civil Disorders, *Kerner Report*, pp. 35–108.
153. Hirsch, *Making the Second Ghetto*, p. 1.
154. Morris Janowitz, "Patterns of Collective Racial Violence," in Hugh Davis Graham and Ted Robert Gurr, eds., *Violence in America: Historical and Comparative Perspectives* (New York: New American Library, 1969), pp. 412–44; August Meier and Elliot Rudwick, "Black Violence in the Twentieth Century: A Study in Rhetoric and Retaliation," ibid., pp. 399–412.
155. U.S. National Advisory Commission on Civil Disorders, *Kerner Report*, pp. 109–158.
156. Ibid., p. 2.
157. Ibid., p. 28.
158. Ibid.
159. Hays, *The Federal Government*, pp. 131–32; Hirsch, *Making the Second Ghetto*, pp. 265–68; Michael J. Vernarelli, "Where Should HUD Locate Assisted Housing?: The Evolution of Fair Housing Policy," in John M. Goering, ed., *Housing Desegregation and Federal Policy* (Chapel Hill: University of North Carolina Press, 1986), pp. 214–34.

3. The Persistence of the Ghetto

1. Epigraph from Henry Hampton and Steve Fayer, *Voices of Freedom: An Oral History of the Civil Rights Movement from the 1950s through the 1980s* (New York: Bantam Books, 1990), p. 297.
2. Howard Schuman, Charlotte Steeh, and Lawrence Bobo, *Racial Attitudes in America: Trends and Interpretations* (Cambridge: Harvard University Press, 1985), pp. 74–75.
3. Harold X. Connolly, "Black Movement into Suburbs: Suburbs Doubling Their Black Populations during the 1960s," *Urban Affairs Quarterly* 9 (1973):91–111; Reynolds Farley, "The Changing Distribution of Negroes within Metropolitan Areas: The Emergence of Black Suburbs," *American Journal of Sociology* 75 (1970):512–29; Avery Guest, "The Changing Racial Composition of the Suburbs: 1950–1970," *Urban Affairs Quarterly* 14 (1978):195–206.
4. Reynolds Farley and Walter R. Allen, *The Color Line and the Quality of Life in America* (New York: Russell Sage, 1987), p. 118.

5. Reynolds Farley, *Blacks and Whites: Narrowing the Gap?* (Cambridge: Harvard University Press, 1984), pp. 56–81; Farley and Allen, *The Color Line,* pp. 283–358.
6. Farley, *Blacks and Whites,* pp. 130–71; see also James P. Smith, "Poverty and the Family," in Gary D. Sandefur and Marta Tienda, eds., *Divided Opportunities: Minorities, Poverty, and Social Policy* (New York: Plenum Press, 1988), pp. 141–72.
7. Farley, *Blacks and Whites,* pp. 56–81, 130–71; Farley and Allen, *The Color Line,* pp. 283–358; Frank Levy, *Dollars and Dreams: The Changing American Income Distribution* (New York: Russell Sage, 1987); Douglas S. Massey and Mitchell L. Eggers, "The Ecology of Inequality: Minorities and the Concentration of Poverty, 1970–1980," *American Journal of Sociology* 95 (1990):1270–99.
8. Malbix/Ricks Music, "Chocolate City," BMI(1976), available on Casablanca Records NBLP 7014; cited in Reynolds Farley, Howard Schuman, Suzanne Bianchi, Diane Colasanto, and Shirley Hatchett, " 'Chocolate City, Vanilla Suburbs': Will the Trend toward Racially Separate Communities Continue?" *Social Science Research* 7 (1978):319–44.
9. U.S. Bureau of the Census, *Users' Guide, Part B: Glossary,* 1980 Census of Population and Housing, PHC80-R1-B (Washington, D.C.: U.S. Government Printing Office, 1982), p. 45.
10. The principal articles in the series are: Douglas S. Massey and Nancy A. Denton, "Trends in the Residential Segregation of Blacks, Hispanics, and Asians," *American Sociological Review* 52 (1987):802–825; Douglas S. Massey and Nancy A. Denton, "Suburbanization and Segregation in U.S. Metropolitan Areas," *American Journal of Sociology* 94 (1988):592–626; Nancy A. Denton and Douglas S. Massey, "Residential Segregation of Blacks, Hispanics, and Asians by Socioeconomic Status and Generation," *Social Science Quarterly* 69 (1988):797–817; Douglas S. Massey and Nancy A. Denton, "Residential Segregation of Mexicans, Puerto Ricans, and Cubans in U.S. Metropolitan Areas," *Sociology and Social Research* 73 (1989):73–83; Douglas S. Massey and Nancy A. Denton, "Hypersegregation in U.S. Metropolitan Areas: Black and Hispanic Segregation along Five Dimensions," *Demography* 26 (1989):373–93.
11. U.S. Bureau of the Census, *Users' Guide,* pp. 8–9.
12. See Michael J. White, *American Neighborhoods and Residential Differentiation* (New York: Russell Sage, 1987), pp. 18–20.
13. For details about our methods of achieving intercensal comparability, see Massey and Denton, "Trends in Residential Segregation."
14. U.S. Bureau of the Census, *Users' Guide,* pp. 37–39.
15. See David R. James and Karl E. Taeuber, "Measures of Segregation," in Nancy Tuma, ed., *Sociological Methodology 1985* (San Francisco: Jossey-Bass, 1985), pp. 1–32; Douglas S. Massey and Nancy A. Denton, "The Dimensions of Residential Segregation," *Social Forces* 67 (1988):281–315; Michael J. White, "Segregation and Diversity: Measures in Population Distribution," *Population Index* 52 (1986):198–221.
16. See Massey and Denton, "Trends in Residential Segregation"; Douglas S. Massey and Andrew B. Gross, "Explaining Trends in Residential Segregation, 1970–1980," *Urban Affairs Quarterly* 27 (1991):13–36; Kathryn P. Nelson, *Gentrification and Distressed Cities* (Madison: University of Wisconsin Press, 1988), pp. 113–52.

17. Stanley Lieberson, *A Piece of the Pie: Blacks and White Immigrants since 1880* (Berkeley: University of California, 1980), pp. 253–91.
18. N. J. Demerath and H. W. Gilmore, "The Ecology of Southern Cities," in Rupert B. Vance and N. J. Demerath, eds., *The Urban South* (Chapel Hill: University of North Carolina Press, 1954), pp. 120–25; Rudolf Beberle, "Social Consequences of Industrialization of Southern Cities," *Social Forces* 27 (1948):29–37.
19. Karl E. Taeuber and Alma F. Taeuber, *Negroes in Cities: Residential Segregation and Neighborhood Change* (Chicago: Aldine, 1965), pp. 5–7, 124–25, 186–94.
20. Farley, "The Changing Distribution of Negroes"; Harvey H. Marshall and John M. Stahura, "Determinants of Black Suburbanization: Regional and Suburban Size Category Patterns," *Sociological Quarterly* 20 (1979):237–53; Harvey M. Marshall and John M. Stahura, "Black and White Population Growth in American Suburbs: Transition or Parallel Development?" *Social Forces* 58 (1979):305–328; Leo Schnore, "Social Classes in Cities and Suburbs," in Amos H. Hawley and Vincent P. Rock, eds., *Segregation in Residential Areas* (Washington, D.C.: National Academy of Sciences, 1973), pp. 189–235; John M. Stahura, "Determinants of Change in the Distribution of Blacks across Suburbs," *Sociological Quarterly* 24 (1983):421–33; Taeuber and Taeuber, *Negroes in Cities*, pp. 102–114, 186–94.
21. For a discussion of isolation indices, see Stanley Lieberson, "An Asymmetrical Approach to Segregation," in Ceri Peach, Vaughn Robinson, and Susan Smith, eds., *Ethnic Segregation in Cities* (London: Croom Helm, 1981), pp. 61–82; Massey and Denton, "The Dimensions of Segregation"; and White, "Segregation and Diversity."
22. See Nelson, *Gentrification and Distressed Cities*, pp. 138–39; many of the areas she identifies as undergoing extensive gentrification within San Francisco are traditional areas of black settlement.
23. Massey and Denton, "Trends in Segregation."
24. Ibid.
25. Phillip L. Clay, "The Process of Black Suburbanization," *Urban Affairs Quarterly* 14 (1979):405–424; Farley, "The Changing Distribution of Negroes"; Guest, "The Changing Racial Composition of the Suburbs"; Robert W. Lake, *The New Suburbanites: Race and Housing in the Suburbs* (New Brunswick: Rutgers University Center for Urban Policy Research, 1981); John R. Logan and Mark Schneider, "Racial Segregation and Racial Change in American Suburbs: 1970–1980," *American Journal of Sociology* 89 (1984):874–88; John R. Logan and Linda B. Stearns, "Suburban Racial Segregation as a Non-Ecological Process," *Social Forces* 60 (1981):61–73; Leo Schnore, Carolyn Andre, and Harry Sharp, "Black Suburbanization: 1930–1970," in Barry Schwartz, ed., *The Changing Face of the Suburbs* (Chicago: University of Chicago Press, 1976), pp. 69–94.
26. Clay, "The Process of Black Suburbanization"; Guest, "The Changing Composition of the Suburbs"; Lake, *The New Suburbanites;* Larry Long and Diana DeAre, "The Suburbanization of Blacks," *American Demographics* 3 (1981):17–44; Logan and Schneider, "Racial Segregation and Racial Change."
27. Clay, "The Process of Black Suburbanization"; Farley, "The Changing Distribution of Negroes"; John R. Logan and Reid M. Golden, "Suburbs and Satellites: Two Decades of Change," *American Sociological Review* 51 (1986):430–37; Logan and Schneider, "Racial Segregation and Racial Change"; Gerald S. McDougall

and Harold Bunce, "Race, Moving Status, and Urban Services in Central Cities," *Social Science Research* 15 (1986):82–92; Gerald S. McDougall and Harold Bunce, "Urban Services and the Suburbanization of Blacks," *Social Science Quarterly* 67 (1986):596–603; Mark Schneider and John R. Logan, "Suburban Racial Segregation and Black Access to Local Public Resources," *Social Science Quarterly* 63 (1982):762–70; Mark Schneider and John R. Logan, "Suburban Municipalities: The Changing System of Intergovernmental Relations in the Mid-1970s," *Urban Affairs Quarterly* 21 (1985):87–105.

28. See Chapter 2, note 18; see also Richard C. Wade, *Slavery in the Cities: The South, 1820–1860* (New York: Oxford University Press, 1964), pp. 275–77.
29. Taeuber and Taeuber, *Negroes in Cities*, pp. 124–25, 186–94.
30. Albert I. Hermalin and Reynolds Farley, "The Potential for Residential Integration in Cities and Suburbs: Implications for the Busing Controversy," *American Sociological Review* 38 (1973):595–610; Douglas S. Massey, "Residential Segregation of Spanish Americans in United States Urbanized Areas," *Demography* 16 (1979):653–64.
31. Inspection of maps suggests the process of ghetto expansion across a city line has occurred in Chicago, Cleveland, Detroit, Philadelphia, and Washington, D.C., among others.
32. Guest, "The Changing Racial Composition of the Suburbs"; Logan and Stearns, "Suburban Racial Segregation"; Logan and Schneider, "Racial Segregation and Racial Change"; Sam Marullo, "Targets for Racial Invasion and Reinvasion: Housing Units where Racial Turnovers Occurred, 1974–1977," *Social Forces* 63 (1985):748–74; Schneider and Logan, "Suburban Racial Segregation"; Schnore, Andre, and Sharp, "Black Suburbanization"; Linda B. Stearns and John R. Logan, "The Racial Structuring of the Housing Market and Segregation in Suburban Areas," *Social Forces* 65 (1986):28–42.
33. See Farley, "The Changing Distribution of Negroes"; Guest, "The Changing Racial Composition of the Suburbs"; Kathryn P. Nelson, "Recent Suburbanization of Blacks: How Much, Who, Where," *American Planning Association Journal* 46 (1980):287–300; Long and DeAre, "The Suburbanization of Blacks."
34. Daniel T. Lichter, "Racial Differences in Underemployment in American Cities," *American Journal of Sociology* 93 (1988):771–92.
35. Massey and Denton, "Dimensions of Segregation"; Michael J. White, "The Measurement of Spatial Segregation," *American Journal of Sociology* 88 (1983): 1008–19.
36. Massey and Denton, "Hypersegregation in U.S. Metropolitan Areas."
37. White, "The Measurement of Spatial Segregation."
38. See also Massey and Denton, "Dimensions of Segregation"; Michael J. White, "Reply to Mitra," *American Journal of Sociology* 90 (1984):189–91; White, "Segregation and Diversity."
39. Otis Dudley Duncan, "The Measurement of Population Distribution," *Population Studies* 11 (1957):27–45.
40. See, for example, the classic work of Ernest W. Burgess, "The Growth of the City: An Introduction to a Research Project," in Robert E. Park and Ernest W. Burgess, *The City* (Chicago: University of Chicago Press, 1925), pp. 47–62.

41. For elaboration of the centralization index, see George C. Galster, "On the Measurement of Metropolitan Decentralization of Blacks and Whites," *Urban Studies* 21 (1984):465–70; Massey and Denton, "Dimensions of Segregation."
42. See Massey and Denton, "Dimensions of Segregation."
43. For the sake of parsimony we have simplified the criteria for defining hypersegregation compared with the criteria in our earlier article (see Massey and Denton, "Hypersegregation in U.S. Metropolitan Areas"); the simplification adds six additional metropolitan areas to the list of hypersegregated places and increases the percentage of U.S. blacks covered from 23% to 35%. We believe that the larger list more accurately reflects the true extent of extreme segregation among U.S. urban areas.
44. See Massey and Denton, "Hypersegregation in U.S. Metropolitan Areas."
45. See, for example, Otis Dudley Duncan and Beverly Duncan, *The Negro Population of Chicago* (Chicago: University of Chicago Press, 1957), pp. 87–107; Taeuber and Taeuber, *Negroes in Cities*, pp. 99–125.
46. Nancy A. Denton and Douglas S. Massey, "Patterns of Neighborhood Transition in a Multiethnic World," *Demography* 28 (1991): 41–64.
47. Ibid.
48. Ibid.
49. Ibid.
50. Ibid.

4. The Continuing Causes of Segregation

1. Epigraph from Thomas Petigrew, Book Review of *Negroes in Cities: Residential Segregation and Neighborhood Change*, *American Journal of Sociology* 82 (1966): 112–13.
2. Douglas S. Massey and Mitchell L. Eggers, "The Ecology of Inequality: Minorities and the Concentration of Poverty, 1970–1980," *American Journal of Sociology* 95 (1990):1153–89.
3. William A. V. Clark, "Residential Segregation in American Cities: A Review and Interpretation," *Population Research and Policy Review* 5 (1986):95–127.
4. The most forceful exposition of the argument is by William Julius Wilson, *The Declining Significance of Race: Blacks and Changing American Institutions* (Chicago: University of Chicago Press, 1978); see also William Julius Wilson, *The Truly Disadvantaged: The Inner City, the Underclass, and Public Policy* (Chicago: University of Chicago Press, 1987).
5. See Douglas S. Glasgow, *The Black Underclass: Poverty, Unemployment, and the Entrapment of Ghetto Youth* (New York: Vintage, 1980); Alphonso Pinkney, *The Myth of Black Progress* (Cambridge: Cambridge University Press, 1984); Bettylou Valentine, *Hustling and Other Hard Work* (New York: Macmillan, 1978); Charles V. Willie, "The Inclining Significance of Race," *Society* 15 (1978):10–15.
6. Nancy A. Denton and Douglas S. Massey, "Residential Segregation of Blacks, Hispanics, and Asians by Socioeconomic Status and Generation," *Social Science Quarterly* 69 (1988):797–818.
7. Reynolds Farley, "Can Blacks Afford to Live in White Residential Areas? A

Test of the Hypothesis That Subjective Economic Variables Account for Racial Residential Segregation," paper presented at the annual meetings of the Population Association of America, Philadelphia, April 1979.

8. Denton and Massey, "Residential Segregation by Socioeconomic Status and Generation"; Douglas S. Massey, "Effects of Socioeconomic Factors on the Residential Segregation of Blacks and Spanish Americans in United States Urbanized Areas," *American Sociological Review* 44 (1979):1015–22.
9. Socioeconomic variables have also been entered into multivariate regression equations in an effort to explain away intergroup differences in segregation, but the very high degree of black segregation persists even when education, income, and occupational status are controlled statistically; see Douglas S. Massey and Nancy A. Denton, "Trends in the Residential Segregation of Blacks, Hispanics, and Asians: 1970–1980," *American Sociological Review* 52 (1987):802–25; and Douglas S. Massey and Nancy A. Denton, "Suburbanization and Segregation in U.S. Metropolitan Areas," *American Journal of Sociology* 94 (1988):592–626.
10. See the arguments in Clark, "Residential Segregation in American Cities"; and Stanley Lieberson and Donna K. Carter, "A Model for Inferring the Voluntary and Involuntary Causes of Residential Segregation," *Demography* 19 (1982): 511–26.
11. Howard Schuman, Charlotte Steeh, and Lawrence Bobo, *Racial Attitudes in America: Trends and Interpretations* (Cambridge: Harvard University Press, 1985), pp. 144–45.
12. Lawrence Bobo, Howard Schuman, and Charlotte Steeh, "Changing Racial Attitudes toward Residential Integration," in John M. Goering, ed., *Housing Desegregation and Federal Policy* (Chapel Hill: University of North Carolina Press, 1986), pp. 152–69.
13. Reynolds Farley, Howard Schuman, Suzanne Bianchi, Diane Colasanto, and Shirley Hatchett, "'Chocolate City, Vanilla Suburbs': Will the Trend toward Racially Separate Communities Continue?" *Social Science Research* 7 (1978): 319–44.
14. Reynolds Farley, Suzanne Bianchi, and Diane Colasanto, "Barriers to the Racial Integration of Neighborhoods: The Detroit Case," *Annals of the American Academy of Political and Social Science* 441 (1979):97–113.
15. Ibid.
16. Chicago Commission on Human Relations, *1990 Hate Crime Report* (Chicago: City of Chicago Commission on Human Relations, 1991).
17. Los Angeles Commission on Human Relations, *Hate Crime in the 1980s: A Decade of Bigotry,* report to the Los Angeles County Board of Supervisors (Los Angeles: Los Angeles Commission on Human Relations, 1990).
18. Julia Cass, "The Elmwood Incident," *Philadelphia Inquirer Magazine,* Sunday, May 4, 1986.
19. J. Anthony Lukas, *Common Ground: A Turbulent Decade in the Lives of Three American Families* (New York: Vintage, 1985), pp. 509–535.
20. Jonathan Rieder, *Canarsie: The Jews and Italians of Brooklyn against Liberalism* (Cambridge: Harvard University Press, 1985), p. 201.
21. Schuman, Steeh, and Bobo, *Racial Attitudes in America,* pp. 74–75.

22. Ibid.
23. Ibid.
24. Ibid., pp. 88–89; see also Howard Schuman and Lawrence Bobo, "Survey-Based Experiments on White Racial Attitudes toward Residential Integration," *American Journal of Sociology* 2 (1988):273–99.
25. Schuman, Steeh, and Bobo, *Racial Attitudes in America*, pp. 106–107.
26. Ibid.; see also Clark, "Residential Segregation in American Cities," p. 109.
27. William A. V. Clark, "Residential Preferences and Neighborhood Racial Segregation: A Test of the Schelling Segregation Model," *Demography* 28 (1991):1–19.
28. "A World Apart: Segregation on Long Island," *Newsday*, Monday, September 24, 1990.
29. Louis Harris and Associates, *The Unfinished Agenda on Race in America* (New York: NAACP Legal Defense and Education Fund, 1989).
30. "A World Apart."
31. Brian J. L. Berry, "Ghetto Expansion and Single-Family Housing Prices: Chicago, 1968–1972," *Journal of Urban Economics* 3 (1976):397–423; Harvey L. Molotch, *Managed Integration: The Dilemmas of Doing Good in the City* (Berkeley: University of California Press, 1972), pp. 22–37.
32. Farley, Bianchi, and Colasanto, "Barriers to the Racial Integration of Neighborhoods," pp. 106–107.
33. Brian J. L. Berry, *The Human Consequences of Urbanization* (New York: St. Martin's, 1973), p. 50.
34. Brian J. L. Berry, Carole A. Goodwin, Robert W. Lake, and Katherine B. Smith, "Attitudes toward Integration: The Role of Status in Community Response to Racial Change," in Barry Schwartz, ed., *The Changing Face of the Suburbs* (Chicago: University of Chicago Press, 1976), pp. 221–64; Brian J. L. Berry, *The Open Housing Question: Race and Housing in Chicago, 1966–76* (Cambridge, Mass.: Ballinger, 1979), pp. 375–99.
35. Stanley B. Greenberg, *Report on Democratic Defection* (Washington, D.C.: Analysis Group, 1985), pp. 13–18, 28, cited in Thomas B. Edsall and Mary D. Edsall, *Chain Reaction: The Impact of Race, Rights, and Taxes on American Politics* (New York: Norton, 1991), p. 182.
36. Richard A. Apostle, Charles Y. Glock, Thomas Piazza, and Marijean Suelzle, *The Anatomy of Racial Attitudes* (Berkeley: University of California Press, 1983), pp. 120–21.
37. Farley, Bianchi, and Colasanto, "Barriers to the Racial Integration of Neighborhoods," pp. 106–107.
38. Ibid.
39. Apostle, Glock, Piazza, and Suelzle, *The Anatomy of Racial Attitudes*, p. 120.
40. Tom W. Smith, "Ethnic Images," *GSS Technical Report No. 19*, National Opinion Research Center, Chicago, January 1991.
41. Harris and Associates, *The Unfinished Agenda*.
42. Schuman, Steeh, and Bobo, *Racial Attitudes in America*, pp. 74–75.
43. Craig St. John and Nancy A. Bates, "Racial Composition and Neighborhood Evaluation," *Social Science Research* 19 (1990):47–61.
44. William A. V. Clark, "Residential Mobility and Neighborhood Change: Some

Implications for Racial Residential Segregation," *Urban Geography* 1 (1980):95–117; William A. V. Clark, "Racial Transition in Metropolitan Suburbs: Evidence from Atlanta," *Urban Geography* 3 (1988):269–82.

45. Thomas C. Schelling, "Dynamic Models of Segregation," *Journal of Mathematical Sociology* 1 (1971):143–86; and Thomas C. Schelling, *Micromotives and Macrobehavior* (New York: Norton, 1978), pp. 135–66.
46. See Rose Helper, *Racial Policies and Practices of Real Estate Brokers* (Minneapolis: University of Minnesota Press, 1969), pp. 277–304, 349–52; and Juliet Saltman, "Housing Discrimination: Policy Research, Methods, and Results," *Annals of the American Academy of Political and Social Science* 441 (1979):186–96.
47. Helper, *Racial Policies and Practices.*
48. See Urban Institute, *Housing Discrimination Study: Methodology and Data Documentation* (Washington, D.C.: U.S. Department of Housing and Urban Development, Office of Policy Development and Research, 1991); John Yinger, "Measuring Discrimination in Housing Availability," Final Research Report No. 2 to the U.S. Department of Housing and Urban Development (Washington, D.C.: Urban Institute, 1989); and John Yinger, "Measuring Racial Discrimination with Fair Housing Audits: Caught in the Act," *American Economic Review* 76 (1986): 991–93.
49. Saltman, "Housing Discrimination."
50. Hans Hintzen, *Report of an Audit of Real Estate Sales Practices of 15 Northwest Chicago Real Estate Sales Offices* (Chicago: Leadership Council for Metropolitan Open Communities, 1983); results are also reviewed in Douglas S. Massey, "Segregation and the Underclass in Chicago," in The Chicago Community Trust Human Relations Task Force, *A Report on Race, Ethnic, and Religious Tensions in Chicago* (Chicago: Chicago Community Trust, 1989), pp. 111–27.
51. Ann Schroeder, *Report on an Audit of Real Estate Sales Practices of Eight Northwest Suburban Offices* (Chicago: Leadership Council for Metropolitan Open Communities, 1985); see also Massey, "Segregation and the Underclass in Chicago."
52. Susan Bertram, *An Audit of the Real Estate Sales and Rental Markets of Selected Southern Suburbs* (Homewood, Ill.: South Suburban Housing Center, 1988); see also Massey, "Segregation and the Underclass in Chicago."
53. John Yinger, "The Racial Dimension of Urban Housing Markets in the 1980s," in Gary A. Tobin, ed., *Divided Neighborhoods: Changing Patterns of Racial Segregation* (Newbury Park, Calif.: Sage Publications, 1987), pp. 43–67; see also John Yinger, "Measuring Racial Discrimination with Fair Housing Audits."
54. George C. Galster, "Racial Discrimination in Housing Markets during the 1980s: A Review of the Audit Evidence," *Journal of Planning Education and Research* 9 (1990):165–75.
55. Ibid., p. 172.
56. Saltman, "Housing Discrimination."
57. Diana M. Pearce, "Gatekeepers and Homeseekers: Institutional Patterns in Racial Steering," *Social Problems* 26 (1979):325–42.
58. George C. Galster, "Racial Steering by Real Estate Agents: Mechanisms and Motives," *Review of Black Political Economy* 19 (1990):39–63.
59. George C. Galster, "Racial Steering in Urban Housing Markets: A Review of the Audit Evidence," *Review of Black Political Economy* 18 (1990):105–129.

60. Ronald Wienk, Cliff Reid, John Simonson, and Fred Eggers, *Measuring Racial Discrimination in American Housing Markets: The Housing Market Practices Survey* (Washington, D.C.: U.S. Department of Housing and Urban Development, 1979).
61. White favoritism was defined to occur when whites received favorable treatment on at least one of five items and blacks received favorable treatment on none. The five items included overall availability of housing, courtesy shown to client, terms and conditions of sale or rental, and amount of information supplied to the client.
62. In the past, housing researchers have reported "net discrimination scores" from the 1977 HUD survey. These scores were obtained by subtracting the percentage of cases in which blacks were favored from those in which whites were favored. Recent research has shown, however, that this procedure understates the real incidence of discrimination, for a variety of technical reasons. The figures reported in the table are gross discrimination scores, or the percentage of encounters in which whites were favored, which still tend to understate the amount of discrimination, but not as severely as net scores; this issue is explained in John Yinger, *Housing Discrimination Study: Incidence of Discrimination and Variations in Discriminatory Behavior* (Washington, D.C.: U.S. Department of Housing and Urban Development, Office of Policy Development and Research, 1991), pp. 6–12; and John Yinger, *Housing Discrimination Study: Incidence and Severity of Unfavorable Treatment* (Washington, D.C.: U.S. Department of Housing and Urban Development, Office of Policy Development and Research, 1991), pp. 14–20.
63. Urban Institute, *Housing Discrimination Study: Methodology and Data Documentation.*
64. Margery A. Turner, John G. Edwards, and Maris Mikelsons, *Housing Discrimination Study: Analyzing Racial and Ethnic Steering* (Washington, D.C.: U.S. Department of Housing and Urban Development, Office of Policy Development and Research, 1991); Maris Mikelsons and Margery A. Turner, *Housing Discrimination Study: Mapping Patterns of Steering for Five Metropolitan Areas* (Washington, D.C.: U.S. Department of Housing and Urban Development, Office of Policy Development and Research, 1991).
65. George C. Galster, Fred Freiberg, and Diane L. Houk, "Racial Differentials in Real Estate Advertising Practices: An Exploratory Case Study," *Journal of Urban Affairs* 9 (1987):199–215.
66. Results from the 1988 Housing and Discrimination Survey are summarized in four basic reports: Mikelsons and Turner, *Housing Discrimination Study: Mapping Patterns of Steering for Five Metropolitan Areas;* Turner, Edwards, and Mikelsons, *Housing Discrimination Study: Analyzing Racial and Ethnic Steering;* Yinger, *Housing Discrimination Study: Incidence and Severity of Unfavorable Treatment;* and Yinger, *Housing Discrimination Study: Incidence of Discrimination and Variations in Discriminatory Behavior.*
67. See Yinger, *Housing Discrimination Study: Incidence and Severity of Unfavorable Treatment;* Yinger, *Housing Discrimination Study: Incidence of Discrimination and Variations in Discriminatory Behavior.*
68. Yinger, *Housing Discrimination Study: Incidence of Discrimination and Variation in Discriminatory Behavior*, pp. 23–43.
69. Ibid.

70. Ibid.
71. Ibid., Tables 42 and 44.
72. Ibid., Table 46.
73. Turner, Edwards, and Mikelsons, *Housing Discrimination Study Analyzing Racial and Ethnic Steering*, p. 27, Table 7.
74. Garth Taylor, "Housing, Neighborhoods, and Race Relations: Recent Survey Evidence," *Annals of the American Academy of Political and Social Science* 441 (1979):26–39.
75. "*Newsday* Poll: Experiencing Discrimination," *Newsday*, Monday, September 17, 1990.
76. "Poll: No Immunity from Racism," *USA Today*, September 5, 1989.
77. Harris and Associates, *The Unfinished Agenda*.
78. Kenneth T. Jackson, *Crabgrass Frontier: The Suburbanization of the United States* (New York: Oxford University Press, 1985), pp. 195–218.
79. Ibid., p. 203.
80. Harriet Tee Taggart and Kevin W. Smith, "Redlining: An Assessment of the Evidence of Disinvestment in Metropolitan Boston," *Urban Affairs Quarterly* 17 (1981):91–107.
81. Jackson, *Crabgrass Frontier*, p. 203.
82. Karen Orren, *Corporate Power and Social Change: The Politics of the Life Insurance Industry* (Baltimore: Johns Hopkins University Press, 1982), p. 126.
83. Ibid., p. 115.
84. Ibid., p. 122.
85. Katharine L. Bradbury, Karl E. Case, and Constance R. Dunham, "Geographic Patterns of Mortgage Lending in Boston, 1982–1987," mimeo, Federal Reserve Bank, Boston, Massachusetts, 1989; Dennis Dingemans, "Redlining and Mortgage Lending in Sacramento," *Annals of the Association of American Geographers* 69 (1979):225–39; Mike Dorning, "Who Gets Home Mortgages Still an Issue of Black and White," *Chicago Tribune*, Sunday, December 2, 1990, p. A1; Peter Hutchinson, James R. Ostas, and J. David Reed, "A Survey Comparison of Redlining Influences in Urban Mortgage Lending Markets," *Journal of the American Real Estate and Urban Economics Association* 5 (1977):467–72; Kentucky Commission on Human Rights, "Few Home Mortgage Loans Approved in Louisville's Predominantly Black Neighborhoods," *Human Rights Report*, Frankfort, Kentucky, May 1989; Peter J. Leahy, "Are Racial Factors Important for the Allocation of Mortgage Money? A Quasi-Experimental Approach to an Aspect of Discrimination," *American Journal of Economics and Sociology* 44 (1985):185–97; D. Listokin and S. Case, *Mortgage Lending and Race* (New Brunswick, N.J.: Center for Urban Policy Research, Rutgers University, 1980); Louis G. Pol, Rebecca F. Guy, and Andrew J. Bush, "Discrimination in the Home Lending Market: A Macro Perspective," *Social Science Quarterly* 63 (1982):716–28; Gregory D. Squires, William Velez, and Karl E. Taueber, "Insurance Redlining, Agency Location, and the Process of Urban Disinvestment," *Urban Affairs Quarterly* 26 (1991):567–88.
86. Bradbury, Case, and Dunham, "Geographic Patterns of Mortgage Lending in Boston."

87. Taggart and Smith, "Redlining."
88. George Benston and Dan Horsky, "Redlining and the Demand for Mortgages in the Central City and Suburbs," *Journal of Bank Research* 10 (1979):72–87; James R. Ostas, "Reduced Form Coefficients, Structural Coefficients, and Mortgage Redlining," *Journal of the American Real Estate and Urban Economics Association* 13 (1984):81–92.
89. Richard D. Hula, "Public Needs and Private Investment: The Case of Home Credit," *Social Science Quarterly* 62 (1981):685–703; Richard C. Hula, "The Allocation of House Credit: Market vs. Non-Market Factors," *Journal of Urban Affairs* 6 (1982):151–65; Pol, Guy, and Bush, "Discrimination in the Home Lending Market"; Taggart and Smith, "Redlining."
90. Hula, "Public Needs and Private Investment"; Hula, "The Allocation of House Credit."
91. Gregory D. Squires and William Velez, "Neighborhood Racial Composition and Mortgage Lending: City and Suburban Differences," *Journal of Urban Affairs* 9 (1987):217–32.
92. Roger S. Ahlbrandt, "Exploratory Research on the Redlining Phenomenon," *Journal of the American Real Estate and Urban Economics Association* 5 (1977):473–81; Hula, "The Allocation of House Credit."
93. Anne B. Shlay, "Not in That Neighborhood: The Effects of Population and Housing on the Distribution of Mortgage Finance with the Chicago SMSA," *Social Science Research* 17 (1983):137–63; see also Hutchinson, Ostas, and Reed, "A Survey Comparison of Redlining Influences."
94. Harold A. Black and Robert L. Schweitzer, "A Canonical Analysis of Mortgage Lending Terms: Testing for Lending Discrimination at a Commercial Bank," *Urban Studies* 22 (1985):13–20.
95. Bill Dedman, "Blacks Denied S&L Loans Twice as Often as Whites," *Atlanta Journal and Constitution*, Sunday, January 22, 1989, p. A1.
96. Michael Quint, "Racial Disparity in Mortgages Shown in U.S. Data," *New York Times*, Thursday, November 14, 1991.
97. Louis Pol, Rebecca Guy, Randy Ryker, and William Chan, "Anticipated Discrimination in the Home Lending Market," *Housing and Society* 8 (1981):3–11; Pol, Guy, and Bush, "Discrimination in the Home Lending Market".
98. George C. Galster, "More than Skin Deep: The Effect of Housing Discrimination on the Extent and Pattern of Racial Residential Segregation in the United States," in John M. Goering, ed., *Housing Discrimination and Federal Policy* (Chapel Hill: University of North Carolina Press, 1986), pp. 119–38.
99. George C. Galster and W. Mark Keeney, "Race, Residence, Discrimination, and Economic Opportunity: Modeling the Nexus of Urban Racial Phenomena," *Urban Affairs Quarterly* 24 (1988):87–117.
100. George C. Galster, "The Ecology of Racial Discrimination in Housing: An Exploratory Model," *Urban Affairs Quarterly* 23 (1987):84–107.
101. George C. Galster, "White Flight from Racially Integrated Neighbourhoods in the 1970s: The Cleveland Experience," *Urban Studies* 27 (1990):385–99; George C. Galster, "Neighborhood Racial Change, Segregationist Sentiments, and Affirmative Marketing Policies," *Journal of Urban Economics* 27 (1990):344–61.

102. Massey and Denton, "Trends in Residential Segregation."
103. Barrett A. Lee, "Racially Mixed Neighborhoods during the 1970s: Change or Stability?" *Social Science Quarterly* 66 (1985):346–64; Barrett A. Lee, "Is Neighborhood Racial Succession Place-Specific?" *Demography* 28 (1991):21–40.
104. Reynolds Farley, "After the Starting Line: Blacks and Women in an Uphill Race," *Demography* 25 (1988):476–96.
105. Scott McKinney, "Change in Metropolitan Area Residential Integration, 1970–1980," *Population Research and Policy Review* 8 (1989):143–64.
106. Douglas S. Massey and Andrew B. Gross, "Explaining Trends in Residential Segregation, 1970–1980," *Urban Affairs Quarterly* 27 (1991):13–15.
107. Ibid.
108. Ibid.
109. Ibid.; see also Massey and Denton, "Trends in Segregation."
110. The formula is: $E(D_{.05}) = (q - .05)/(q - q^2)$, where $E(D_{.05})$ is the level of residential dissimilarity required to keep the probability of white-black contact $({}_{w}P^{*}_{b})$ at .05 or less and q is the proportion of blacks in the urban area; see Massey and Gross, "Explaining Trends in Residential Segregation."
111. Ibid.
112. Clara E. Rodriguez, "Racial Classification among Puerto Rican Men and Women in New York," *Hispanic Journal of Behavioral Sciences* 12 (1990):366–80; Nancy A. Denton and Douglas S. Massey, "Racial Identity among Caribbean Hispanics: The Effect of Double Minority Status on Residential Segregation," *American Sociological Review* 54 (1980):790–808.
113. Denton and Massey, "Racial Identity among Caribbean Hispanics."
114. Yinger, *Housing Discrimination Study: Incidence of Discrimination and Variations in Discriminatory Behavior,* Table 32; see also John Hakken, *Discrimination against Chicanos in the Dallas Rental Housing Market: An Experimental Extension of the Housing Market Practices Survey* (Washington, D.C: Office of Policy Development and Research, U.S. Department of Housing and Urban Development, 1979).

5. The Creation of Underclass Communities

1. Epigraph from Kenneth B. Clark, *Dark Ghetto: Dilemmas of Social Power* (New York: Harper and Row, 1965), p. 12.
2. St. Clair Drake and Horace R. Cayton, *Black Metropolis: A Study of Negro Life in a Northern City* (New York: Harcourt, Brace, 1945), pp. 379–754; Kenneth L. Kusmer, *A Ghetto Takes Shape: Black Cleveland, 1870–1930* (Urbana: University of Illinois Press, 1976), pp. 91–156, 190–194; Allan H. Spear, *Black Chicago: The Making of a Negro Ghetto, 1890–1920* (Chicago: University of Chicago Press, 1967), pp. 71–128, 181–200.
3. David Levering Lewis, *When Harlem Was in Vogue* (New York: Oxford University Press, 1981); Spear, *Black Chicago,* pp. 197–200; Kusmer, *A Ghetto Takes Shape,* pp. 235–74.
4. E. Franklin Frazier, "Human, All Too Human: The Negro's Vested Interest in Segregation," in G. Franklin Edwards, ed., *E. Franklin Frazier on Race Relations* (Chicago: University of Chicago Press, 1968), pp. 283–91.

5. Drake and Cayton, *Black Metropolis*, pp. 77–98, 214–62, 470–94; Joe William Trotter, Jr., *Black Milwaukee: The Making of an Industrial Proletariat, 1915–45* (Urbana: University of Illinois Press, 1985), pp. 147–95.
6. Drake and Cayton, *Black Metropolis*, pp. 465–66; Lewis, *When Harlem Was in Vogue*, pp. 240–43.
7. Lewis, *When Harlem Was in Vogue*, p. 241.
8. Drake and Cayton, *Black Metropolis*, p. 203.
9. William Julius Wilson, *The Truly Disadvantaged: The Inner City, the Underclass, and Public Policy* (Chicago: University of Chicago Press, 1987), p. 52.
10. Chicago Fact Book Consortium, *Local Community Fact Book Chicago Metropolitan Area* (Chicago: Chicago Review Press, 1984), pp. 98–99.
11. Ibid., pp. 94–95.
12. Wilson, *The Truly Disadvantaged*, pp. 20–92.
13. For studies of poverty's persistence, see Terry K. Adams, Greg J. Duncan, and Willard L. Rodgers, "The Persistence of Urban Poverty," in Fred R. Harris and Roger W. Wilkins, eds., *Quiet Riots: Race and Poverty in the United States* (New York: Pantheon Books, 1988), pp. 78–99; Mary Jo Bane and David Ellwood, "Slipping into and out of Poverty: The Dynamics of Spells," *Journal of Human Resources* 21 (1986):1–23; Mary Corcoran, Greg J. Duncan, Gerald Gurin, and Patricia Gurin, "Myth and Reality: The Causes and Persistence of Poverty," *Journal of Policy Analysis and Management* 4 (1985):516–36; Sara McLanahan, Irwin Garfinkel, and Dorothy Watson, "Family Structure, Poverty, and the Underclass," in Michael G. H. McGeary and Lawrence E. Lynn, eds., *Urban Change and Poverty* (Washington, D.C.: National Academy Press, 1988), pp. 102–147. For studies of the geographic concentration of poverty, see Mary Jo Bane and Paul A. Jargowsky, "Urban Poverty Areas: Basic Questions Concerning Prevalence, Growth, and Dynamics," paper prepared for the Committee on National Urban Policy, National Academy of Sciences, 1988; Mark A. Hughes, "Formation of the Impacted Ghetto: Evidence from Large Metropolitan Areas, 1970–1980," *Urban Geography* 11 (1990):265–84; Douglas S. Massey and Mitchell L. Eggers, "The Ecology of Inequality: Minorities and the Concentration of Poverty," *American Journal of Sociology* 95 (1990):1153–88; William Julius Wilson and Robert Aponte, "Urban Poverty," *Annual Review of Sociology* 11 (1985):231–58.
14. Massey and Eggers, "The Ecology of Inequality"; Douglas S. Massey, Mitchell L. Eggers, and Nancy A. Denton, "Disentangling the Causes of Concentrated Poverty," paper presented at the Conference on the Truly Disadvantaged, Northwestern University, October 19–21, 1989.
15. Douglas S. Massey, "American Apartheid: Segregation and the Making of the Underclass," *American Journal of Sociology* 96 (1990):329–58.
16. See Massey and Eggers, "The Ecology of Inequality."
17. See Michael J. White, *American Neighborhoods and Residential Differentiation* (New York: Russell Sage, 1987), pp. 82–116.
18. Those interested in working through the class-based simulation may consult the original article on which the discussion is based. See Massey, "American Apartheid."
19. Drake and Cayton, *Black Metropolis*, pp. 77–98; Lewis, *When Harlem Was in Vogue*, pp. 240–308; Trotter, *Black Milwaukee*, 147–225.

20. Mitchell L. Eggers and Douglas S. Massey, "The Structural Determinants of Urban Poverty," *Social Science Research* 20 (1991):217–55; Mitchell L. Eggers and Douglas S. Massey, "A Longitudinal Analysis of Urban Poverty: Blacks in U.S. Metropolitan Areas, 1970–1980," *Social Science Research* 21 (1992):175–203; John D. Kasarda, "Urban Change and Minority Opportunities," in Paul E. Peterson, ed., *The New Urban Reality* (Washington, D.C.: Brookings Institution, 1985), pp. 33–68; Frank Levy, *Dollars and Dreams: The Changing American Income Distribution* (New York: Russell Sage, 1987), pp. 74–119, 192–214; Wilson, *The Truly Disadvantaged*, pp. 20–108.
21. Only one study has actually measured the probabilities of in- and out-migration from poor neighborhoods for blacks of different social classes; it found that poor and middle-class blacks had roughly the same probabilities of out-migration from poor census tracts, whereas affluent blacks had the lowest probability of out-movement from poor tracts (possibly because they couldn't sell the homes they owned there). In contrast, Kathryn Nelson measured rates of black out-migration from different urban zones of forty metropolitan areas and found higher rates for middle- and upper-class blacks; but her zones contained in excess of 100,000 inhabitants, making them considerably larger than urban neighborhoods. See Edward Gramlich and Deborah Laren, "Geographic Mobility and Persistent Poverty," Department of Economics, University of Michigan, Ann Arbor Michigan, 1990; and Kathryn P. Nelson, "Racial Segregation, Mobility, and Poverty Concentration," paper presented at the annual meetings of the Population Association of America, Washington, D.C., March 19–23, 1991.
22. See the increases in the black and white poverty rates reported in Massey and Eggers, "The Ecology of Inequality."
23. A description of the index of poverty concentration and its justification are included in Massey and Eggers, "The Ecology of Inequality."
24. Ibid., and Massey, Eggers, and Denton, "Disentangling the Causes."
25. For theoretical discussions of the interaction between individual decisions and collective outcomes see: Otto Davis and A. Whinston, "The Economics of Urban Renewal," *Law and Contemporary Problems* 26 (1961):105–117; Mark Granovetter, "Threshold Models of Collective Behavior," *American Journal of Sociology* 83 (1978):1420–43; Thomas C. Schelling, *Micromotives and Macrobehavior* (New York: Norton, 1978), pp. 135–66; Richard P. Taub, D. Garth Taylor, and Jan D. Dunham, *Paths of Neighborhood Change: Race and Crime in Urban America* (Chicago: University of Chicago Press, 1984), pp. 119–94.
26. William C. Finnie, "Field Experiments in Litter Control," *Environment and Behavior* 5 (1973):123–44; Wesley G. Skogan, "Disorder, Crime and Community Decline," in Tim Hope and Margaret Shaw, eds., *Communities and Crime Reduction* (London: Her Majesty's Stationery Office, 1988), pp. 48–61; Wesley G. Skogan, *Disorder and Decline: Crime and the Spiral of Decay in American Neighborhoods* (New York: Free Press, 1990), pp. 1–84; Taub, Taylor, and Dunham, *Paths of Neighborhood Change*, pp. 119–41; James Q. Wilson, *Thinking about Crime* (New York: Basic Books, 1983), pp. 41–60, 75–94.
27. Skogan, *Disorder and Decline*, pp. 1–84; James Q. Wilson and George L. Kelling, "Broken Windows," *Atlantic Monthly*, March 1982, pp. 29–38; Taub, Taylor, and Dunham, *Paths of Neighborhood Change*, pp. 119–94.

28. See Massey, "American Apartheid."
29. U.S. Department of Housing and Urban Development, *Abandoned Housing Research: A Compendium* (Washington, D.C.: U.S. Government Printing Office, 1973).
30. Ibid., p. 9.
31. Ibid.
32. Massey, "American Apartheid."
33. Deborah Wallace, "Roots of Increased Health Care Inequality in New York," *Social Science Medicine* 31 (1990):1219–27; Rodrick Wallace, '"Planned Shrinkage,' Contagious Urban Decay and Violent Death in the Bronx: The Implications of Synergism," Epidemiology of Mental Disorders Research Department, New York State Psychiatric Institute, 1990; Rodrick Wallace, "Expanding Coupled Shock Fronts of Urban Decay and Criminal Behavior: How U.S. Cities Are Becoming 'Hollowed Out,'" Epidemiology of Mental Disorders Research Department, New York State Psychiatric Institute, 1991.
34. Michael J. Munson and Wallace E. Oates, "Community Characteristics and the Incidence of Fire: An Empirical Analysis," in Chester Rapkin, ed., *The Social and Economic Consequences of Residential Fires* (Lexington, Mass.: D. C. Heath, 1983), pp. 61–78.
35. Winston Moore, Charles P. Livermore, and George F. Galland, Jr., "Woodlawn: The Zone of Destruction," in Chester Rapkin, ed., *The Social and Economic Consequences of Residential Fires* (Lexington, Mass.: D. C. Heath, 1983), pp. 271–88; George Sternlieb and Robert W. Burchell, "Fires in Abandoned Buildings," in Chester Rapkin, ed., *The Social and Economic Consequences of Residential Fires* (Lexington, Mass.: D. C. Heath, 1983), pp. 261–70.
36. D. Wallace, "Roots of Increased Health Care Inequality"; R. Wallace, "Planned Shrinkage"; Sternlieb and Burchell, "Fires in Abandoned Buildings"; Harry L. Margulis, "Rat Fields, Neighborhood Sanitation, and Rat Complaints in Newark, New Jersey," *Applied Geography* 67 (1977):221–31.
37. Rodrick Wallace, "Urban Desertification, Public Health, and Public Order: 'Planned Shrinkage,' Violent Death, Substance Abuse and AIDS in the Bronx," *Social Science Medicine* 32 (1991):1–32.
38. Loic J. D. Wacquant and William Julius Wilson, "Poverty, Joblessness, and the Social Transformation of the Inner City," in Phoebe H. Cottingham and David T. Ellwood, eds., *Welfare Policy for the 1990s* (Cambridge: Harvard University Press, 1989), p. 92.
39. From Massey, "American Apartheid."
40. The number of households equals the number of inhabitants in our hypothetical neighborhood, 8,000, divided by the average U.S. household size of 2.7, which equals 2,963, or approximately 3,000. Our simplifying assumption that the median is the same as the mean is conservative, since the mean income is typically somewhat larger than the median because of the skewed shape of most income distributions.
41. See Wilson, *The Truly Disadvantaged*, pp. 93–106; Eggers and Massey, "The Structural Determinants of Urban Poverty"; Eggers and Massey, "A Longitudinal Analysis of Urban Poverty."
42. See Wacquant and Wilson, "Poverty, Joblessness, and the Social Transformation

of the Inner City"; Loic J. D. Wacquant and William Julius Wilson, "The Cost of Racial and Class Exclusion in the Inner City," *Annals of the American Academy of Political and Social Science* 501 (1989):8–25.

43. Douglas S. Massey and Nancy A. Denton, "Trends in the Residential Segregation of Blacks, Hispanics, and Asians: 1970–1980," *American Sociological Review* 52 (1987):802–825.
44. Chicago Fact Book Consortium, *Local Community Fact Book*, pp. 79–84.
45. Skogan, *Disorder and Decline*, pp. 21–50; Skogan, "Disorder, Crime and Community Decline"; Ralph B. Taylor and Stephen D. Gottfredson, "Attachment to Place: Discriminant Validity, and Impacts of Disorder and Diversity," *American Journal of Community Psychology* 13 (1980):525–42; Wilson and Kelling, "Broken Windows"; James Q. Wilson and George L. Kelling, "Making Neighborhoods Safe," *Atlantic Monthly*, February 1989, pp. 46–52.
46. Lynne Goodstein and R. Lance Shotland, "The Crime Causes Crime Model: A Critical Review of the Relationships between Fear of Crime, Bystander Surveillance, and Changes in the Crime Rate," *Victimology* 5 (1980):133–51; Stanislav V. Kasl and Ernest Harburg, "Perceptions of the Neighborhood and the Desire to Move Out," *American Institute of Planners Journal* 38 (1972):318–24; Martin T. Katzman, "The Contribution of Crime to Urban Decline," *Urban Studies* 17 (1980):277–86; Dan A. Lewis and Michael G. Maxfield, "Fear in the Neighborhoods: An Investigation of the Impact of Crime," *Journal of Research in Crime and Delinquency* 17 (1980):160–89; Marlys McPherson, "Realities and Perceptions of Crime at the Neighborhood Level," *Victimology* 3 (1978):319–28; R. Lance Shotland and Lynne I. Goodstein, "The Role of Bystanders in Crime Control," *Journal of Social Issues* 40 (1984):9–26; Skogan, *Disorder and Decline*, pp. 65–84; Wesley G. Skogan, "Communities, Crime, and Neighborhood Organization," *Crime and Delinquency* 35 (1989):437–57; Wesley G. Skogan, "Fear of Crime and Neighborhood Change," in Albert J. Reiss, Jr., and Michael Tonry, eds., *Communities and Crime* (Chicago: University of Chicago Press, 1986), pp. 203–229; Wesley G. Skogan and Michael G. Maxfield, *Coping with Crime: Individual and Neighborhood Reactions* (Beverly Hills: Sage, 1981); Tom R. Tyler, "Assessing the Risk of Crime Victimization: The Integration of Personal Victimization Experience and Socially Transmitted Information," *Journal of Social Issues* 40 (1984):27–38.
47. Skogan, *Disorder and Decline*, pp. 51–84.
48. See Massey, "American Apartheid."
49. See Christopher Jencks and Susan E. Mayer, "The Social Consequences of Growing Up in a Poor Neighborhood," in Laurence E. Lynn, Jr., and Michael G. H. McGeary, eds., *Inner City Poverty in the United States* (Washington, D.C.: National Academy Press, 1990), pp. 111–86.
50. Wilson, *The Truly Disadvantaged*, pp. 20–62; Lee Rainwater, *Behind Ghetto Walls: Black Families in a Federal Slum* (Chicago: Aldine, Atherton, 1970).
51. From Massey, "American Apartheid."
52. See Jonathan Kozol, *Savage Inequalities: Children in America's Schools* (New York: Crown Publishers, 1991), pp. 2–5.
53. See Mark A. Hughes, "Concentrated Deviance or Isolated Deprivation? The 'Un-

derclass' Idea Reconsidered," Woodrow Wilson School of Public and International Affairs, Princeton University, 1988; Christopher Jencks, "Is the American Underclass Growing?" in Christopher Jencks and Paul E. Peterson, eds., *The Urban Underclass* (Washington, D.C.: Brookings Institution, 1991), pp. 3–27; Frank Levy, "How Big Is the American Underclass?" The Urban Institute, Washington, D.C., 1977; Ronald Mincey, "Is There a White Underclass?" Urban Institute, Washington, D.C., 1988; Robert D. Reischauer, "The Size and Characteristics of the Underclass," paper presented at the APPAM Research Conference, Bethesda, Md., 1987; Errol R. Ricketts and Isabel V. Sawhill, "Defining and Measuring the Underclass," *Journal of Policy Analysis and Management* 7 (1988):316–25; Patricia Ruggles and William P. Marton, "Measuring the Size and Characteristics of the Underclass: How Much Do We Know?" Urban Institute, Washington, D.C., 1986.

54. Douglas G. Glasgow, *The Black Underclass: Poverty, Unemployment and the Entrapment of Ghetto Youth* (New York: Vintage, 1980).
55. Alphonso Pinkney, *The Myth of Black Progress* (Cambridge: Cambridge University Press, 1984), pp. 1–17, 58–80.
56. Ken Auletta, *The Underclass* (New York: Vintage, 1982), pp. xiv–xv.
57. Ibid., p. xvi.
58. Charles Murray, *Losing Ground: American Social Policy, 1950–1980* (New York: Basic Books, 1984), p. 9.
59. Ibid.
60. Lawrence M. Mead, *Beyond Entitlement: The Social Obligations of Citizenship* (New York: Free Press, 1986).
61. Wilson, *The Truly Disadvantaged*, pp. 60–62, 137–38, 157–61.
62. Bane and Jargowsky, "Urban Poverty Areas"; Reischauer, "The Size and Characteristics of the Underclass"; Ricketts and Sawhill, "Defining and Measuring the Underclass."
63. After increasing substantially during the 1960s, the real value of AFDC payments fell during the 1970s and 1980s. Although many states increasingly used the food stamp and Medicaid programs to forestall the effects of declining real AFDC payments, at best this substitution held the value of the total benefits package constant; it did not provide the large increases characteristic of the 1960s. See Robert Moffitt, "Has State Redistribution Policy Grown More Conservative?" *National Tax Journal* 43 (1990):123–42; and Robert Moffitt, "Incentive Effects of the U.S. Welfare System: A Review," Institute for Research on Poverty Special Report no. 48, University of Wisconsin, Madison, 1990.
64. Drake and Cayton, *Black Metropolis*, pp. 379–97; Otis Dudley Duncan and Beverly Duncan, *The Negro Population of Chicago: A Study of Residential Succession* (Chicago: University of Chicago Press, 1957), pp. 237–98; E. Franklin Frazier, "Negro Harlem: An Ecological Study," *American Journal of Sociology* 43 (1937):72–88; Karl Taeuber and Alma Taeuber, *Negroes in Cities: Residential Segregation and Neighborhood Change* (Chicago: Aldine, 1965).
65. Massey and Eggers, "The Ecology of Inequality."
66. Nancy A. Denton and Douglas S. Massey, "Residential Segregation of Blacks, Hispanics, and Asians by Socioeconomic Status and Generation," *Social Science*

Quarterly 69 (1988):797–817; Reynolds Farley, "Residential Segregation in Urbanized Areas of the United States in 1970: An Analysis of Social Class and Racial Differences," *Demography* 14 (1977):497–518; Douglas S. Massey, "Effects of Socioeconomic Factors on the Residential Segregation of Blacks and Spanish Americans in United States Urbanized Areas," *American Sociological Review* 44 (1979):1015–22.

67. Massey and Denton, "Trends in Residential Segregation"; Douglas S. Massey and Nancy A. Denton, "Hypersegregation in U.S. Metropolitan Areas: Black and Hispanic Segregation along Five Dimensions," *Demography* 26 (1989):373–92.
68. For documentation of the close connection between social and residential mobility, see John Bodnar, *The Transplanted: A History of Immigrants in Urban America* (Bloomington: Indiana University Press, 1985); John Briggs, *An Italian Passage: Immigrants to Three American Cities, 1890–1930* (New Haven: Yale University Press, 1978); Frances E. Kobrin and Calvin Goldscheider, *The Ethnic Factor in Family Structure and Mobility* (Cambridge, Mass.: Ballinger, 1978); Douglas S. Massey, "Ethnic Residential Segregation: A Theoretical Synthesis and Empirical Review," *Sociology and Social Research* 69 (1985):315–50; Humbert S. Nelli, *Italians in Chicago, 1880–1930* (New York: Oxford University Press, 1970); Stephen Thernstrom, *The Other Bostonians: Poverty and Progress in the American Metropolis, 1880–1970* (Cambridge: Harvard University Press, 1973); David Ward, *Cities and Immigrants: A Geography of Change in Nineteenth Century America* (New York: Oxford University Press, 1971).
69. Gramlich and Laren, "Geographic Mobility and Persistent Poverty."
70. Massey and Denton, "Trends in Residential Segregation."
71. Douglas S. Massey, "Hispanic Residential Segregation: A Comparison of Mexicans, Cubans, and Puerto Ricans," *Sociology and Social Research* 65 (1981):311–22; Douglas S. Massey and Nancy A. Denton, "Residential Segregation of Mexicans, Puerto Ricans, and Cubans in Selected U.S. Metropolitan Areas," *Sociology and Social Research* 73 (1989):73–83.
72. See Massey and Eggers, "Ecology of Inequality."
73. Douglas S. Massey and Brooks Bitterman, "Explaining the Paradox of Puerto Rican Segregation," *Social Forces* 64 (1985):306–331; "Racial Identity among Caribbean Hispanics: The Effect of Double Minority Status on Residential Segregation," *American Sociological Review* 54 (1989):790–808.
74. Bane and Jargowsky, "Urban Poverty Areas."
75. Massey and Denton, "Trends in Residential Segregation."
76. Massey and Eggers, "The Ecology of Inequality."
77. Thomas F. Pettigrew, "Racial Change and Social Policy," *Annals of the American Academy of Political and Social Science* 441 (1979):114–31.

6. The Perpetuation of the Underclass

1. Epigraph cited in David L. Lewis, *When Harlem Was in Vogue* (New York: Oxford University Press, 1981), p. 306.
2. For classic treatments of status attainment in the United States, see Peter M. Blau and Otis Dudley Duncan, *The American Occupational Structure* (New York: Free

Press, 1967); Robert M. Hauser and David L. Featherman, *The Process of Stratification* (New York: Academic Press, 1977); David L. Featherman and Robert M. Hauser, *Opportunity and Change* (New York: Academic Press, 1978).

3. Ibid.
4. E. Digby Baltzell, *Philadelphia Gentlemen: The Making of a National Upper Class* (Glencoe, Ill.: Free Press, 1958); Peter W. Cookson, Jr., and Caroline H. Persell, *Preparing for Power: America's Elite Boarding Schools* (New York: Basic Books, 1985); Mark Granovetter, *Getting a Job* (Cambridge: Harvard University Press, 1974).
5. Peter M. Blau, *Heterogeneity and Inequality: A Primitive Theory of Social Structure* (New York: Free Press, 1977).
6. John R. Logan, "Growth, Politics, and the Stratification of Places," *American Journal of Sociology* 84 (1978):404–416; John R. Logan and Harvey L. Molotch, *Urban Fortunes: The Political Economy of Place* (Berkeley: University of California Press, 1987), pp. 1–49, 147–99; Mark Schneider and John R. Logan, "Suburban Racial Segregation and Black Access to Local Public Resources," *Social Science Quarterly* 63 (1982):762–70.
7. Michael J. Weiss, *The Clustering of America* (New York: Harper and Row, 1988).
8. Brian J. L. Berry, *The Human Consequences of Urbanization* (New York: St. Martin's Press, 1973), p. 50.
9. Robert E. Park, "The Urban Community as a Spatial Pattern and a Moral Order," in Ernest W. Burgess and Robert E. Park, eds., *The Urban Community* (Chicago: University of Chicago Press, 1926), pp. 3–18; see also Otis D. Duncan and Beverly Duncan, "Residential Distribution and Occupational Stratification," *American Journal of Sociology* 60 (1955):493–505; Albert A. Simkus, "Residential Segregation by Occupation and Race in Ten Urbanized Areas, 1950–1970," *American Sociological Review* 43 (1978):81–93; Duncan W. G. Timms, *The Urban Mosaic: Towards a Theory of Residential Differentiation* (Cambridge: Cambridge University Press, 1971), pp. 1–35, 85–121; Michael J. White, *American Neighborhoods and Residential Differentiation* (New York: Russell Sage, 1987), pp. 82–116.
10. Stanley Lieberson, *Ethnic Patterns in American Cities* (New York: Free Press, 1963), pp. 133–90; Logan and Molotch, *Urban Fortunes*, pp. 17–49.
11. Alan N. Burstein, "Immigrants and Residential Mobility: The Irish and Germans in Philadelphia, 1850–1880," in Theodore Hershberg, ed., *Philadelphia: Work, Space, Family, and Group Experience in the 19th Century* (New York: Oxford University Press, 1981), pp. 174–203; Humbert S. Nelli, *Italians in Chicago, 1880–1930: A Study in Ethnic Mobility* (New York: Oxford University Press, 1970); Stephen Thernstrom, *The Other Bostonians: Poverty and Progress in the American Metropolis, 1880–1970* (Cambridge: Harvard University Press, 1973); David Ward, *Cities and Immigrants: A Geography of Change in Nineteenth Century America* (New York: Oxford University Press).
12. Douglas S. Massey, "Ethnic Residential Segregation: A Theoretical Synthesis and Empirical Review," *Sociology and Social Research* 69 (1985):315–51.
13. Ricahrd D. Alba and John R. Logan, "Variations on Two Themes: Racial and Ethnic Patterns in the Attainment of Suburban Residence," *Demography* 28 (1991):431–53; Douglas S. Massey and Nancy A. Denton, "Spatial Assimilation

as a Socioeconomic Process," *American Sociological Review* 50 (1985):94–105; Douglas S. Massey and Eric Fong, "Segregation and Neighborhood Quality: Blacks, Hispanics, and Asians in the San Francisco Metropolitan Area," *Social Forces* 69 (1990):15–32; Andrew B. Gross and Douglas S. Massey, "Spatial Assimilation Models: A Micro-Macro Comparison," *Social Science Quarterly* 72 (1991):347–60; Douglas S. Massey and Brendan P. Mullan, "Processes of Hispanic and Black Spatial Assimilation," *American Journal of Sociology* 89 (1984): 836–74.

14. Nancy A. Denton and Douglas S. Massey, "Racial Identity among Caribbean Hispanics: The Effect of Double Minority Status on Residential Segregation," *American Sociological Review* 54 (1989):790–808.
15. Douglas S. Massey and Brooks Bitterman, "Explaining the Paradox of Puerto Rican Segregation," *Social Forces* 64 (1985):306–331.
16. See Peter Jackson, "Paradoxes of Puerto Rican Segregation in New York," in Ceri Peach, Vaughn Robinson, and Susan Smith, eds., *Ethnic Segregation in Cities* (London: Croom Helm, 1981), pp. 109–126; Massey and Bitterman, "Explaining the Paradox of Puerto Rican Segregation."
17. Douglas S. Massey, Gretchen A. Condran, and Nancy A. Denton, "The Effect of Residential Segregation on Black Social and Economic Well-Being," *Social Forces* 66 (1987):29–57.
18. Equations are used to predict neighborhood outcomes from education, income, and occupational status. To generate the values in the table, an occupational status score of 40 (skilled blue collar) and an education of 12 years were assumed, and income was varied as shown in the table.
19. Lawrence Biemiller, "Black Students' Average Aptitude-Test Scores Up Seven Points in a Year," *Chronicle of Higher Education*, January 16, 1985, p. 1.
20. The link between segregation and educational inequalities is also discussed by Jonathan Kozol, *Savage Inequalities: Children in America's Schools* (New York: Crown Publishers, 1991), pp. 2–5.
21. Jean Kinsey and Sylvia Lane, "Race, Housing Attributes, and Satisfaction with Housing," *Housing and Society* 10 (1983):98–117.
22. Stephen C. Case, "The Effect of Race on Opinions of Structure and Neighborhood Quality," *Annual Housing Survey Studies No. 5*, Office of Policy Development and Research, U.S. Department of Housing and Urban Development, Washington, D.C., 1980.
23. Mary R. Jackman and Robert W. Jackman, "Racial Inequalities in Home Ownership," *Social Forces* 58 (1980):1221–35; Suzanne M. Bianchi, Reynolds Farley, and Daphne Spain, "Racial Inequalities in Housing: An Examination of Recent Trends," *Demography* 19 (1982):37–51; Franklin D. Wilson, *Residential Consumption, Economic Opportunity, and Race* (New York: Academic Press, 1979), pp. 130–31.
24. Bianchi, Farley, and Spain, "Racial Inequalities in Housing"; Lauren J. Krivo, "Housing Price Inequalities: A Comparison of Anglos, Blacks, and Spanish-Origin Populations," *Urban Affairs Quarterly* 17 (1981):445–62; Wayne J. Villemez, "Race, Class, and Neighborhood: Differences in Residential Return on Individual Resources," *Social Forces* 59 (1980):414–30; Franklin D. Wilson, *Residential Consumption*, pp. 130–31.

25. Reynolds Farley and Walter R. Allen, *The Color Line and the Quality of Life in America* (New York: Russell Sage, 1987), pp. 288–90; Bart Landry, *The New Black Middle Class* (Berkeley: University of California Press, 1987), pp. 141–54.
26. Bianchi, Farley, and Spain, "Racial Inequalities in Housing"; Kinsey and Lane, "Race, Housing Attributes, and Satisfaction"; Lauren J. Krivo and Jan E. Mutchler, "Housing Constraint and Household Complexity in Metropolitan America: Black and Spanish Origin Minorities," *Urban Affairs Quarterly* 21 (1986):389–409.
27. Bianchi, Farley, and Spain, "Racial Inequalities in Housing."
28. See Edward Banfield and James Q. Wilson, *City Politics* (Cambridge: Harvard University Press, 1961); Robert A. Dahl, *Who Governs? Democracy and Power in the American City* (New Haven: Yale University Press, 1961; Robert A. Dahl, *Pluralist Democracy in the United States: Conflict and Consent* (Chicago: Rand McNally, 1967); Thomas H. Gutterbock, *Machine Politics in Transition: Party and Community in Chicago* (Chicago: University of Chicago Press, 1980), pp. 200–215.
29. Thomas L. Philpott, *The Slum and the Ghetto: Neighborhood Deterioration and Middle Class Reform, Chicago, 1880–1930* (New York: Oxford University Press, 1978), pp. 113–45; Stanley Lieberson, *A Piece of the Pie: Blacks and White Immigrants since 1880* (Berkeley: University of California Press, 1980), pp. 253–91.
30. Dianne M. Pinderhughes, *Race and Ethnicity in Chicago Politics* (Urbana: University of Illinois Press, 1987), pp. 12–38.
31. Ibid., pp. 9, 67–108.
32. Ibid., pp. 36–38.
33. Allan H. Spear, *Black Chicago: The Making of a Negro Ghetto* (Chicago: University of Chicago Press, 1967), pp. 186–200; Joe William Trotter, Jr., *Black Milwaukee: The Making of an Industrial Proletariat, 1915–45* (Urbana: University of Chicago Press, 1985), pp. 196–225.
34. Ira Katznelson, *Black Men, White Cities: Race, Politics, and Migration in the United States, 1900–1930, and Britain, 1948–68* (Chicago: University of Chicago Press, 1976), pp. 62–104; Kathleen A. Kemp, "Race, Ethnicity, Class, and Urban Spatial Conflict: Chicago as a Crucial Test Case," *Urban Studies* 23 (1986):197–208; Pinderhughes, *Race and Ethnicity*, pp. 12–38, 228–50; James Q. Wilson, *Negro Politics: The Search for Leadership* (New York: Free Press, 1960).
35. William J. Grimshaw, *Black Politics in Chicago: The Quest for Leadership, 1939–1979* (Chicago: Loyola University Press, 1980), pp. 1–28; Katznelson, *Black Men, White Cities*, pp. 62–85; Spear, *Black Chicago*, pp. 77–126; Wilson, *Negro Politics*, pp. 350–51.
36. Grimshaw, *Black Politics*, p. 7; Katznelson, *Black Men, White Cities*, pp. 102–104.
37. Grimshaw, *Black Politics;* Gilbert Osofsky, *Harlem: The Making of a Ghetto* (New York: Harper, 1963), pp. 162–68.
38. Pinderhughes, *Race and Ethnicity*, pp. 9–10, 181–227.
39. See E. Franklin Frazier, "Human, All Too Human: The Negro's Vested Interest in Segregation," in G. Franklin Edwards, ed., *E. Franklin Frazier on Race Relations* (Chicago: University of Chicago Press, 1968), pp. 283–91; Katznelson, *Black Men, White Cities*, p. 103.
40. Arnold R. Hirsch, *Making the Second Ghetto: Race and Housing in Chicago, 1940–1960* (Cambridge: Cambridge University Press, 1983); Nicholas Lemann, *The*

Promised Land: The Great Black Migration and How It Changed America (New York: Knopf, 1991).

41. William J. Grimshaw, "The Daley Legacy: A Declining Politics of Party, Race, and Public Unions," in Samuel K. Gove and Louis H. Masotti, eds., *After Daley: Chicago Politics in Transition* (Urbana: University of Illinois Press, 1982), pp. 57–87; Gutterbock, *Machine Politics in Transition;* Pinderhughes, *Race and Ethnicity,* pp. 1–11, 236–61.
42. Pinderhughes, *Race and Ethnicity,* pp. 236–61.
43. Thomas B. Edsall and Mary D. Edsall, *Chain Reaction: The Impact of Race, Rights, and Taxes on American Politics* (New York: Norton, 1991).
44. Deborah Wallace, "Roots of Increased Health Care Inequality in New York," *Social Science and Medicine* 31 (1990):1219–27; Rodrick Wallace, "Urban Desertification, Public Health and Public Order: 'Planned Shrinkage,' Violent Death, Substance Abuse, and AIDS in the Bronx," *Social Science and Medicine* 32 (1991):801–813; Rodrick Wallace, " 'Planned Shrinkage,' Contagious Urban Decay, and Violent Death in the Bronx: The Implications of Synergism," Epidemiology of Mental Disorders Research Department, New York State Psychiatric Institute, 1990.
45. Ibid.
46. Ibid.
47. Ibid.
48. Ibid.
49. Ibid.
50. R. Wallace, "Urban Desertification."
51. See Douglas S. Massey and Nancy A. Denton, "Suburbanization and Segregation in U.S. Metropolitan Areas," *American Journal of Sociology* 94 (1988):592–626; and the indices reported in Table 3.3.
52. Daniel T. Lichter, "Racial Differences in Underemployment in American Cities," *American Journal of Sociology* 93 (1988):771–92.
53. William L. Yancey, Eugene P. Ericksen, and George H. Leon, "The Structure of Pluralism: 'We're All Italian Around Here, Aren't We Mrs. O'Brien?' " *Ethnic and Racial Studies* 8 (1985):94–116.
54. Sophie Pedder, "Social Isolation and the Labor Market: Black Americans in Chicago," paper presented at the Chicago Urban Poverty and Family Life Conference, Chicago, Ill., Oct. 10–12, 1991.
55. Ibid.
56. Mark S. Granovetter, *Getting a Job: A Study of Contacts and Careers* (Cambridge: Harvard University Press, 1974); Mark S. Granovetter, "The Strength of Weak Ties," *American Journal of Sociology* 78 (1973):1360–80; Harold L. Sheppard and A. Harvey Belitsky, *The Job Hunt: Job-Seeking Behavior of Unemployed Workers in a Local Economy* (Baltimore: Johns Hopkins Press, 1966); Richard C. Wilcock, *Unwanted Workers: Permanent Layoffs and Long-term Unemployment* (New York: Free Press, 1963).
57. See William Julius Wilson, *The Truly Disadvantaged: The Inner City, the Underclass, and Public Policy* (Chicago: University of Chicago Press, 1987), pp. 58–62.
58. John Baugh, *Black Street Speech: Its History, Structure, and Survival* (Austin: University of Texas Press, 1983), pp. 11–22.

59. Baugh, *Black Street Speech;* William Labov, *Language in the Inner City: Studies in the Black English Vernacular* (Philadelphia: University of Pennsylvania Press, 1972); William Labov, "The Logic of Nonstandard English," in Paul Stoller, ed., *Black American English: Its Background and Its Usage in the Schools and in Literature* (New York: Dell Publishing, 1975), pp. 89–131.
60. William Labov and Wendell A. Harris, "De Facto Segregation of Black and White Vernaculars," in David Sankoff, ed., *Current Issues in Linguistic Theory 53: Diversity and Diachrony* (Amsterdam: John Benjamins Publishing, 1986), pp. 1–24.
61. See Labov, *Language in the Inner City;* Labov, "The Logic of Nonstandard English"; William Labov, ed., *Locating Language in Space and Time* (New York: Academic Press, 1980).
62. Labov and Harris, "De Facto Segregation," p. 2.
63. Ibid., pp. 2, 18.
64. Ibid.
65. Ibid., pp. 5–17.
66. Baugh, *Black Street Speech,* pp. 108–117; William Labov, "Competing Value Systems in the Inner-city Schools," in P. Gilmore and A. Glatthorn, eds., *Children in and out of School* (Washington, D.C.: Center for Applied Linguistics, 1982), pp. 148–71; Labov, "The Logic of Nonstandard English."
67. William Labov, *The Social Stratification of English in New York City* (Washington, D.C.: Center for Applied Linguistics, 1966); Labov and Harris, "De Facto Segregation."
68. Labov, "The Logic of Nonstandard English"; Roger W. Shuy, "Teacher Training and Urban Language Problems," in Paul Stoller, ed., *Black American English: Its Background and Its Usage in the Schools and in Literature* (New York: Dell Publishing, 1975), pp. 168–85.
69. Baugh, *Black Street Speech,* pp. 118–26.
70. Ibid.
71. Ibid.; Joleen Kirschenman and Kathryn M. Neckerman, ' "We'd Love to Hire Them, But . . . ': The Meaning of Race for Employers," in Christopher Jencks and Paul E. Peterson, eds., *The Urban Underclass* (Washington, D.C.: Brookings Institution, 1991), pp. 203–232.
72. Baugh, *Black Street Speech,* pp. 54–67.
73. Kareem Abdul-Jabbar and Peter Knobler, *Giant Steps: The Autobiography of Kareem Abdul-Jabbar* (New York: Bantam Books, 1983), p. 16; Baugh, *Black Street Speech,* p. 55; Bob Blauner, *Black Lives, White Lives: Three Decades of Race Relations in America* (Berkeley: University of California Press, 1989), pp. 77–78, 295–96.
74. James R. Kluegel and Elliot R. Smith, *Beliefs about Inequality* (New York: Aldine de Gruyter, 1986).
75. William Julius Wilson, *The Truly Disadvantaged: The Inner City, the Underclass, and Public Policy* (Chicago: University of Chicago Press, 1987), pp. 63–92; William Julius Wilson and Kathryn M. Neckerman, "Poverty and Family Structure: The Widening Gap between Evidence and Public Policy Issues," in Sheldon H. Danziger and Daniel H. Weinberg, eds., *Fighting Poverty: What Works and What Doesn't* (Cambridge: Harvard University Press, 1986), pp. 232–59.
76. M. Belinda Tucker, "The Black Male Shortage in Los Angeles," *Sociology and Social Research* 71 (1987):221–27; M. Belinda Tucker and Robert Joseph Taylor,

"Demographic Correlates of Relationship Status among Black Americans," *Journal of Marriage and the Family* 51 (1989):655–65; M. Belinda Tucker and Claudia Mitchell-Kernan, "The Decline of Marriage among African Americans: Attitudinal Dimensions," paper presented at the annual convention of the American Psychological Association, New Orleans, August 13–14, 1989; Claudia Mitchell-Kernan and M. Belinda Tucker, "Perceived Mate Availability and Marital/Familial Values: A Cross-cultural Analysis," paper presented at the annual convention of the American Psychological Association, August 13–14, 1989.

77. This argument has been forcefully made by participant observers who have carried out detailed studies of ghetto life, such as Elijah Anderson, *A Place on the Corner* (Chicago: University of Chicago Press, 1976); Elliot Liebow, *Talley's Corner: A Study of Negro Streetcorner Men* (Boston: Little, Brown, 1967); Lee Rainwater, *Behind Ghetto Walls: Black Families in a Federal Slum* (Chicago: Aldine Atherton, 1970); Carol Stack, *All Our Kin: Strategies of Survival in a Black Community* (New York: Harper and Row, 1974); Terry M. Williams and William Kornblum, *Growing Up Poor* (Lexington, Mass.: D. C. Heath, 1990).
78. Kenneth B. Clark, *Dark Ghetto: Dilemmas of Social Power* (New York: Harper and Row, 1965), p. 13.
79. See John U. Ogbu, *Minority Education and Caste: The American System in Cross-Cultural Perspective* (New York: Academic Press, 1978); John U. Ogbu, "Minority Status and Schooling in Plural Societies," *Comparative Education Review* 27 (1983):168–90; Signithia Fordham and John U. Ogbu, "Black Students' School Success: Coping with the 'Burden of Acting White,'" *Urban Review* 18 (1986):176–206.
80. Fordham and Ogbu, "Black Students' School Success," p. 181.
81. Ibid., emphasis in original.
82. Ibid.; see also Signithia Fordham, "Racelessness as a Factor in Black Students' School Success: Pragmatic Strategy or Pyrrhic Victory?" *Harvard Educational Review* 58 (1988):54–84.
83. Fordham and Ogbu, "Black Students' School Success."
84. Ibid.
85. James E. Rosenbaum and Susan J. Popkin, "Economic and Social Impacts of Housing Integration," Center for Urban Affairs and Policy Research, Northwestern University, 1990; James E. Rosenbaum, Marilynn J. Kulieke, and Leonard S. Rubinowitz, "White Suburban Schools' Responses to Low-Income Black Children: Sources of Success and Problems," *Urban Review* 20 (1988):28–41; James E. Rosenbaum and Susan J. Popkin, "Black Pioneers: Do Their Moves to Suburbs Increase Economic Opportunity for Mothers and Children?" *Housing Policy Debate* 2 (1991):1179–1214.
86. Robert Crain and Rita Mahard, "School Racial Composition and Black College Attendance and Achievement Test Performance," *Sociology of Education* 51 (1978):81–101.
87. Susan E. Mayer, "How Much Does a High School's Racial and Socioeconomic Mix Affect Graduation and Teenage Fertility Rates?" in Christopher Jencks and Paul E. Peterson, eds., *The Urban Underclass* (Washington, D.C.: Brookings Institution, 1991), pp. 321–41.

88. See William Ryan, *Blaming the Victim* (New York: Random House, 1971).
89. See Oscar Lewis, "The Culture of Poverty," in Daniel P. Moynihan, ed., *On Understanding Poverty* (New York: Basic Books, 1968), pp. 187–200; Oscar Lewis, *La Vida: A Puerto Rican Family in the Culture of Poverty—San Juan and New York* (New York: Random House, 1965).
90. Clark, *Dark Ghetto*, p. 19.
91. Shelby Steele, *The Content of Our Character* (New York: St. Martin's Press, 1990), p. 60.
92. See Stanley Lieberson, *A Piece of the Pie*, pp. 123–252, esp. 234–37.
93. Ibid.
94. Kenneth L. Kusmer, *A Ghetto Takes Shape: Black Cleveland, 1870–1930* (Urbana: University of Illinois Press, 1976), pp. 235–74; Spear, *Black Chicago*, pp. 51–90.
95. Cited in Dinesh D'Souza, *Illiberal Education: The Politics of Race and Sex on Campus* (New York: Free Press, 1991), p. 239.
96. Robert Moffitt, "An Economic Model of Welfare Stigma," *American Economic Review* 73 (1983):1023–35; Mark R. Rank and Thomas A. Hirschl, "A Rural-Urban Comparison of Welfare Exits: The Importance of Population Density," *Rural Sociology* 53 (1988):190–206; Thomas A. Hirschl and Mark R. Rank, "The Effect of Population Density on Welfare Participation," *Social Forces* 70 (1991):225–36; Thomas A. Hirschl and Mark R. Rank, "Does Urbanism Affect Welfare Participation?" paper presented at the annual meetings of the Population Association of America, Washington, D.C., March 21–23, 1991.
97. Liebow, *Talley's Corner*; Rainwater, *Behind Ghetto Walls*; Ulf Hannerz, *Soulside: Inquiries into Ghetto Culture and Community* (New York: Columbia University Press, 1970); Anderson, *A Place on the Corner*.
98. Anderson, *A Place on the Corner*.
99. Elijah Anderson, *Streetwise: Race, Class, and Change in an Urban Community* (Chicago: University of Chicago Press, 1990).
100. Ibid., p. 69.
101. Ibid.
102. Ibid., p. 72.
103. Ibid., pp. 74–75.
104. Ibid., p. 76.
105. Ibid., pp. 77–111; Philippe Bourgois, "Just Another Night on Crack Street," *New York Times Magazine*, November 12, 1989, pp. 52–53, 60–65, 94; Philippe Bourgois, *Scrambling: Living with Crack in El Barrio* (Boston: Little, Brown, forthcoming).
106. Anderson, *Streetwise*, p. 77.
107. Ibid., pp. 77–111; Wesley G. Skogan, *Disorder and Decline: Crime and the Spiral of Decay in American Neighborhoods* (New York: Free Press, 1990), pp. 29–32, 170–71.
108. Anderson, *Streetwise*, pp. 77–112; R. Wallace, "Urban Desertification."
109. Anderson, *Streetwise*, pp. 112–37.
110. Ibid., p. 114.
111. Ibid., p. 120.
112. Ibid.

113. Ibid., p. 126.
114. Richard P. Taub, "Differing Conceptions of Honor and Orientations toward Work and Marriage among Low-Income African-Americans and Mexican-Americans," paper presented at the Chicago Urban Poverty and Family Life Conference, October 10–12, 1991.
115. Ibid.
116. Anderson, *Streetwise*, pp. 123–28.
117. Ibid., p. 126.
118. N.W.A. and the Posse, "A Bitch Iz A Bitch" (Hollywood, Calif.: Priority Records, published by Ruthless Attack Muzick, 1989, ASCAP).
119. H.W.A., "Livin' in a Hoe House" (Hollywood, Calif.: Drive By Records, published by Thunder Publishing Company, 1990, BMI).
120. Shaharazad Ali, *The Blackman's Guide to Understanding the Blackwoman* (Philadelphia: Civilized Publications, 1990), p. 169.
121. Haki R. Madhubuti, ed., *Confusion by Any Other Name: Essays Exploring the Negative Impact of the Blackman's Guide to Understanding the Blackwoman* (Chicago: Third World Press, 1990).
122. Clark, *Dark Ghetto*, p. 12.
123. Williams and Kornblum, *Growing Up Poor*, pp. 4–14; Anderson, *Streetwise*, pp. 90–97.
124. Linda Datcher, "Effects of Community and Family Background on Achievement," *Review of Economics and Statistics* 64 (1982):32–41.
125. Mary Corcoran, Roger Gordon, Deborah Laren, and Gary Solon, "Effects of Family and Community Background on Men's Economic Status," Working Paper 2896, National Bureau of Economic Research, Cambridge, Mass., 1989.
126. Jonathan Crane, "The Epidemic Theory of Ghettos and Neighborhood Effects on Dropping Out and Teenage Childbearing," *American Journal of Sociology* 96 (1991):1226–59.
127. Datcher, "Effects of Community and Family Background."
128. Corcoran, Gordon, Laren, and Solon, "Effects of Family and Community Background."
129. Crane, "The Epidemic Theory."
130. Dennis P. Hogan and Evelyn M. Kitagawa, "The Impact of Social Status, Family Structure, and Neighborhood on the Fertility of Black Adolescents," *American Journal of Sociology* 90 (1985):825–55.
131. Frank F. Furstenburg, Jr., S. Philip Morgan, Kristin A. Moore, and James Peterson, "Race Differences in the Timing of Adolescent Intercourse," *American Sociological Review* 52 (1987):511–8.
132. Douglas S. Massey, Andrew B. Gross, and Mitchell L. Eggers, "Segregation, the Concentration of Poverty, and the Life Chances of Individuals," *Social Science Research* 20 (1991):397–420. Background characteristics for black males are held constant by predicting the probability of joblessness for a native born man aged twenty-five who speaks English well and is an unmarried high school graduate; background traits for females are held constant by predicting the probability of heading a single-parent family for a native-born woman aged twenty-five who

speaks English well and is an unmarried high school graduate who is not working.

133. A series of papers indicates that levels and trends in black poverty are determined by precisely these changes in the urban economy, specifically the suburbanization of employment, the decline of manufacturing, and the rise of a service economy; see Mitchell L. Eggers and Douglas S. Massey, "The Structural Determinants of Urban Poverty: A Comparison of Whites, Blacks, and Hispanics," *Social Science Research* 20 (1991):217–55; and Mitchell L. Eggers and Douglas S. Massey, "A Longitudinal Analysis of Urban Poverty: Blacks in U.S. Metropolitan Areas between 1970 and 1980," *Social Science Research* 21 (1992):175–203.

7. The Failure of Public Policy

1. Epigraph from Robert G. Schwemm, "The Limits of Litigation under the Housing Act of 1968," in Robert G. Schwemm, ed., *The Fair Housing Act after Twenty Years* (New Haven: Yale Law School, 1989), p. 47; Robert G. Schwemm, "Private Enforcement and the Fair Housing Act," *Yale Law and Policy Review* 6 (1988):375–84.
2. Roger L. Rice, "Residential Segregation by Law, 1910–1917," *Journal of Southern History* 64 (1968):179–99.
3. Ibid.
4. John H. Denton, *Apartheid American Style* (Berkeley, Calif.: Diablo Press, 1967), pp. 40–45.
5. See Thomas Philpott, *The Slum and the Ghetto: Neighborhood Deterioration and Middle Class Reform, Chicago, 1880–1930* (New York: Oxford University Press, 1978), pp. 189–99.
6. Arnold R. Hirsch, *Making the Second Ghetto: Race and Housing in Chicago, 1940–1960* (Cambridge: Cambridge University Press, 1983), p. 30.
7. Kenneth T. Jackson, *Crabgrass Frontier: The Suburbanization of the United States* (New York: Oxford University Press, 1985), p. 208.
8. Denton, *Apartheid*, p. 45.
9. Jackson, *Crabgrass Frontier*, p. 208.
10. Hirsch, *Making the Second Ghetto*, p. 31.
11. See Chapter 4 and Kenneth T. Jackson, *Crabgrass Frontier*, pp. 195–218; George R. Metcalf, *Fair Housing Comes of Age* (New York: Greenwood Press, 1988), pp. 101–114; Karen Orren, *Corporate Power and Social Change: The Politics of the Life Insurance Industry* (Baltimore: Johns Hopkins University Press, 1982), pp. 126–27.
12. John F. Bauman, *Public Housing, Race, and Renewal: Urban Planning in Philadelphia, 1920–1974* (Philadelphia: Temple University Press, 1987); Hirsch, *Making the Second Ghetto;* Jackson, *Crabgrass Frontier*, pp. 219–29; Frederick A. Lazin, "Policy, Perception, and Program Failure: The Politics of Public Housing in Chicago and New York City," *Urbanism Past and Present* 9 (1976):1–12.
13. Arthur S. Flemming, "The Politics of Fair Housing," *Yale Law and Policy Review* 6 (1988):385–92.

14. Ibid.
15. Leonard S. Rubinowitz and Elizabeth Trosman, "Affirmative Action and the American Dream: Implementing Fair Housing Policies in Federal Homeownership Programs," *Northwestern University Law Review* 74 (1979):493–617.
16. Beth J. Lief and Susan Goering, "The Implementation of the Federal Mandate for Fair Housing," in Gary A. Tobin, ed., *Divided Neighborhoods: Changing Patterns of Racial Segregation* (Newbury Park, Calif.: Sage Publications, 1987), pp. 227–67.
17. Ibid.
18. Frederick A. Lazin, "Federal Low-Income Housing Assistance Programs and Racial Segregation: Leased Public Housing," *Public Policy* 24 (1976):337–60; Rubinowitz and Trosman, "Affirmative Action."
19. Lief and Goering, "Implementation of the Federal Mandate."
20. Hirsch, *Making the Second Ghetto,* p. 265.
21. Michael J. Vernarelli, "Where Should HUD Locate Assisted Housing? The Evolution of Fair Housing Policy?" in John M. Goering, ed., *Housing Desegregation and Federal Policy* (Chapel Hill: University of North Carolina Press, 1986), pp. 214–34.
22. Hirsch, *Making the Second Ghetto,* p. 265.
23. Ibid.
24. Robert McClory, "Segregation City," *Chicago Reader* 20 (1991):1, 16, 18–19, 22–23,26, 28–29; Irving Welfeld, "The Courts and Desegregated Housing: The Meaning (If Any) of the Gautreaux Case," *Public Interest* 45 (1976):123–35.
25. Vernarelli, "Where Should HUD Locate Assisted Housing?"; McClory, "Segregation City."
26. Ibid.
27. Hirsch, *Making the Second Ghetto,* p. 265.
28. Ibid.; McClory, "Segregation City."
29. Lief and Goering, "Implementation of the Federal Mandate."
30. Jean E. Dubofsky, "Fair Housing: A Legislative History and a Perspective," *Washburn Law Journal* 8 (1969):149–66.
31. Ibid.
32. Ibid.
33. Ibid.
34. Metcalf, *Fair Housing Comes of Age,* pp. 75–85.
35. Dubofsky, "Fair Housing."
36. Ibid.
37. Ibid.
38. U.S. National Advisory Commission on Civil Disorders, *The Kerner Report* (New York: Pantheon Books, 1988).
39. Metcalf, *Fair Housing Comes of Age,* pp. 84–85.
40. Dubofsky, "Fair Housing."
41. Metcalf, *Fair Housing Comes of Age,* p. 84.
42. Dubofsky, "Fair Housing."
43. Metcalf, *Fair Housing Comes of Age,* p. 85.
44. Ibid.; Dubofsky, "Fair Housing."
45. Metcalf, *Fair Housing Comes of Age,* pp. 85–86; Rubinowitz and Trosman, "Af-

firmative Action and the American Dream"; Schwemm, "The Limits of Litigation."

46. Richard H. Sander, "Individual Rights and Demographic Realities: The Problem of Fair Housing," *Northwestern University Law Review* 82 (1988):874–939.
47. Metcalf, *Fair Housing Comes of Age*, p. 86.
48. Dubofsky, "Fair Housing"; Metcalf, *Fair Housing Comes of Age*, pp. 75–85; Schwemm, "The Limits of Litigation."
49. Metcalf, *Fair Housing Comes of Age*, pp. 85–86; Rubinowitz and Trosman, "Affirmative Action and the American Dream"; Schwemm, "The Limits of Litigation."
50. Metcalf, *Fair Housing Comes of Age*, pp. 3–14, 85–86.
51. U.S. Congress, *Fair Housing Act: Hearings before the Subcommittee on Civil and Constitutional Rights of the House Committee on the Judiciary*, 95th Congress, 2nd sess. (Washington, D.C.: U.S. Government Printing Office, 1978), cited in Metcalf, *Fair Housing Comes of Age*, p. 115.
52. U.S. Congress, *Fair Housing Act: Hearings*, p. 141, cited in Metcalf, *Fair Housing Comes of Age*, p. 6.
53. U.S. Commission on Civil Rights, *The Federal Fair Housing Enforcement Effort* (Washington, D.C.: U.S. Government Printing Office, 1979), p. 5.
54. Schwemm, "The Limits of Litigation."
55. John Yinger, "The Racial Dimension of Urban Housing Markets in the 1980s," in Gary A. Tobin, ed., *Divided Neighborhoods: Changing Patterns of Racial Segregation* (Newbury Park, Calif.: Sage Publications, 1987), pp. 43–67.
56. Ibid.
57. Metcalf, *Fair Housing Comes of Age*, pp. 3–14, 85–86.
58. In the case of *Trafficante v. Metropolitan Life Insurance Company;* see Schwemm, "The Limits of Litigation," p. 44.
59. In the case of *Gladstone Realtors v. Village of Bellwood;* see Metcalf, *Fair Housing Comes of Age*, p. 116.
60. Metcalf, *Fair Housing Comes of Age*, pp. 4–5.
61. Ibid.
62. Ibid., pp. 86–92.
63. Ibid., pp. 101–114.
64. Ibid., pp. 116–24.
65. Ibid., pp. 98–100; Robert Lake and Jessica Winslow, "Integration Management: Municipal Constraints on Residential Mobility," *Urban Geography* 12 (1981): 311–26.
66. Metcalf, *Fair Housing Comes of Age*, pp. 15–16, 94–100.
67. Schwemm, "The Limits of Litigation"; Schwemm, "Private Enforcement."
68. Metcalf, *Fair Housing Comes of Age*, p. 3.
69. Ibid., p. 131.
70. Ibid., p. 132.
71. Schwemm, "The Limits of Litigation."
72. Metcalf, *Fair Housing Comes of Age*, pp. 132–37.
73. Civil Rights Act of 1968, Public Law No. 90–284, Section 801; see Rubinowitz

and Trosman, "Affirmative Action and the American Dream."

74. Ibid.
75. Bauman, *Public Housing, Race, and Renewal;* Hirsch, *Making the Second Ghetto;* Jackson, *Crabgrass Frontier,* pp. 219–29.
76. U.S. Commission on Civil Rights, *The Federal Fair Housing Enforcement Effort,* p. 6.
77. Hirsch, *Making the Second Ghetto,* p. 265; McClory, "Segregation City"; Vernarelli, "Where Should HUD Locate Assisted Housing?"
78. Metcalf, *Fair Housing Comes of Age,* p. 118.
79. Vernarelli, "Where Should HUD Locate Assisted Housing?"
80. R. Allen Hays, *The Federal Government and Urban Housing: Ideology and Change in Public Policy* (Albany: State University of New York Press, 1985), p. 131; Daniel R. Mandelker, *Housing and Community Development: Cases and Materials* (New York: Bobbs-Merrill, 1981), pp. 581–90; Vernarelli, "Where Should HUD Locate Assisted Housing?"
81. Rubinowitz and Trosman, "Affirmative Action and the American Dream."
82. Ibid.
83. Ibid.
84. Lief and Goering, "Implementation of the Federal Mandate."
85. U.S. Commission on Civil Rights, *The Federal Fair Housing Enforcement Effort,* p. 5.
86. Lief and Goering, "Implementation of the Federal Mandate."
87. Ibid.; Lazin, "Federal Low-Income Housing Assistance Programs."
88. Hays, *The Federal Government and Urban Housing,* pp. 137–72; John C. Weicher, *Housing: Federal Policies and Programs* (Washington, D.C.: American Enterprise Institute, 1980), pp. 48–52.
89. See Adam Bickford and Douglas S. Massey, "Segregation in the Second Ghetto: Racial and Ethnic Segregation in American Public Housing, 1977," *Social Forces* 69 (1991):1011–36; John M. Goering and Modibo Coulibably, "Investigating Public Housing Segregation: Conceptual and Methodological Issues," *Urban Affairs Quarterly* 25 (1989):265–97.
90. Rubinowitz and Trosman, "Affirmative Action and the American Dream."
91. "Statement of George Romney, Secretary of Housing and Urban Development," in *Equal Educational Opportunity: Hearings before the Senate Select Commission on Equal Educational Opportunity,* 91st Congress, 2nd sess. (Washington, D.C.: U.S. Government Printing Office, 1970), pp. 2753–55, cited in Rubinowitz and Trosman, "Affirmative Action and the American Dream."
92. Ibid.
93. Rubinowitz and Trosman, "Affirmative Action and the American Dream."
94. Lief and Goering, "Implementation of the Federal Mandate"; Metcalf, *Fair Housing Comes of Age,* p. 87.
95. Ibid.
96. Lief and Goering, "Implementation of the Federal Mandate"; U.S. Commission on Civil Rights, *A Report of the Racial and Ethnic Impact of the Section 235 Program* (Washington, D.C.: U.S. Government Printing Office, 1971).
97. Ibid.

98. U.S. Commission on Civil Rights, *Home Ownership for Lower Income Families* (Washington, D.C.: U.S. Government Printing Office, 1971).
99. Rubinowitz and Trosman, "Affirmative Action and the American Dream," p. 593.
100. Rubinowitz and Trosman, "Affirmative Action and the American Dream," p. 495.
101. Ibid., pp. 595–98.
102. Metcalf, *Fair Housing Comes of Age*, pp. 163–64.
103. Lief and Goering, "Implementation of the Federal Mandate."
104. Bill Dedman, "Banks Denied S&L Loans Twice as Often as Whites," *Atlanta Journal and Constitution*, January 22, 1989, p. 1A.
105. Ibid.; Michael Quint, "Racial Disparity in Mortgages Shown in U.S. Data," *New York Times*, Thursday, November 14, 1991.
106. Metcalf, *Fair Housing Comes of Age*, pp. 103–4.
107. Richard D. Hula, "The Allocation of House Credit: Market vs. Non-Market Factors," *Journal of Urban Affairs* 6 (1982):151–65; Peter Hutchinson, James R. Ostas, and J. David Reed, "A Survey of Redlining Influences in Urban Mortgage Lending Markets," *Journal of the American Real Estate and Urban Economics Association* 5 (1977):467–72; Louis G. Pol, Rebecca F. Guy, and Andrew J. Bush, "Discrimination in the Home Lending Market: A Macro Perspective," *Social Science Quarterly* 63 (1982):716–28; Gregory D. Squires, William Velez, and Karl E. Taueber, "Insurance Redlining, Agency Location, and the Process of Urban Disinvestment," *Urban Affairs Quarterly* 26 (1991):567–88; Harriet Tee Taggart and Kevin W. Smith, "Redlining: An Assessment of the Evidence of Disinvestment in Metropolitan Boston, *Urban Affairs Quarterly* 17 (1981):91–107.
108. Lief and Goering, "Implementation of the Federal Mandate."
109. Metcalf, *Fair Housing Comes of Age*, pp. 15–26.
110. Ibid.
111. Ibid.; Schwemm, "The Limits of Litigation."
112. Metcalf, *Fair Housing Comes of Age*, pp. 15–26.
113. Schwemm, "The Limits of Litigation."
114. Ibid.
115. James A. Kushner, "An Unfinished Agenda: The Federal Fair Housing Enforcement Effort," *Yale Law and Policy Review* 6 (1988):348–60; Metcalf, *Fair Housing Comes of Age*, pp. 15–26; Schwemm, "The Limits of Litigation."
116. Metcalf, *Fair Housing Comes of Age*, pp. 15–26.
117. Ibid.
118. Ibid.
119. Schwemm, "The Limits of Litigation."
120. U.S. Congress, *The Federal Government's Role in the Achievement of Equal Opportunity in Housing: Hearings before the Civil Rights Oversight Subcommittee of the House Committee on the Judiciary*, 92nd Congress, 1st and 2nd sess. (Washington, D.C.: U.S. Government Printing Office, 1972).
121. U.S. Commission on Civil Rights, *Equal Opportunity in Housing* (Washington, D.C.: U.S. Government Printing Office, 1974); U.S. Commission on Civil Rights, *The Federal Fair Housing Enforcement Effort.*

122. Robert G. Schwemm, *Housing Discrimination: Law and Litigation* (New York: Clark Boardman, 1990), pp. 5.6–5.11.
123. Robert W. Lake, "The Fair Housing Act in a Discriminatory Market: The Persisting Dilemma," *Journal of the American Planning Association* 47 (1981):48–58.
124. Metcalf, *Fair Housing Comes of Age*, pp. 15–26.
125. Schwemm, *Housing Discrimination*, pp. 5.6–5.11.
126. Ibid.
127. U.S. Department of Housing and Urban Development, *The State of Fair Housing* (Washington, D.C.: U.S. Government Printing Office, 1989).
128. Schwemm, *Housing Discrimination*, p. 5.6.
129. Ibid., pp. 5.6–5.11; U.S. Department of Housing and Urban Development, *The State of Fair Housing*, pp. 1–3.
130. Ibid.
131. Ibid.
132. Ibid.
133. Steve Kerch, "Housing Bias Laws Hit Home: Courts Awarding Higher Penalties," *Chicago Tribune*, May 13, 1991, pp. 1F–2F.
134. Ibid.
135. Ibid.
136. Howard Schuman, Charlotte Steeh, and Lawrence Bobo, *Racial Attitudes in America: Trends and Interpretations* (Cambridge: Harvard University Press, 1985), pp. 74–75.
137. Farley, Reynolds, Suzanne Bianchi, and Diane Colasanto, "Barriers to the Racial Integration of Neighborhoods: The Detroit Case," *Annals of the American Academy of Political and Social Science* 441 (1978):97–113.
138. Schuman, Steeh, and Bobo, *Racial Attitudes in America*, pp. 74–75.
139. See Philpott, *The Slum and the Ghetto*, pp. 149–53, 163–64.
140. For evidence on the motivations of real estate agents for discriminating, see John Yinger, "Prejudice and Discrimination in the Urban Housing Market," in P. Mieszkowski and M. Straszheim, eds., *Current Issues in Urban Economics* (Baltimore: Johns Hopkins University Press, 1979), pp. 530–68; John Yinger, "Measuring Discrimination with Fair Housing Audits: Caught in the Act," *American Economic Review* 76 (1986):881–93; John Yinger, "A Search Model of Real Estate Broker Behavior," *American Economic Review* 71 (1986):591–605; Yinger, "The Racial Dimension of Urban Housing Markets."
141. Nicholas Lemann, *The Promised Land: The Great Black Migration and How It Changed America* (New York: Alfred A. Knopf, 1991), pp. 74–75.
142. Brian J. L. Berry, *The Open Housing Question: Race and Housing in Chicago, 1966–1976* (Cambridge, Mass.: Ballinger, 1979), p. 27.
143. Vernarelli, "Where Should HUD Locate Assisted Housing?," p. 223.
144. Ibid., pp. 223–24.
145. Ibid., p. 224.
146. Stokely Carmichael and Charles V. Hamilton, *Black Power: The Politics of Liberation in America* (New York: Random House, 1967), p. 54.
147. Frances Fox Piven and Richard A. Cloward, "The Case against Urban Desegrega-

tion," in Jon Pynoos, Robert Schafter, and Chester Hartman, eds., *Housing Urban America* (New York: Aldine, 1980), pp. 112–19.

148. David Danzig, "In Defense of 'Black Power,' " *Commentary* 42 (1966):45–46.
149. Kenneth B. Clark, *Dark Ghetto: Dilemmas of Social Power* (New York: Harper and Row, 1965), p. 63.

8. The Future of the Ghetto

1. Epigraph from "Remarks of the President at Howard University," in Lee Rainwater and William L. Yancey, *The Moynihan Report and the Politics of Controversy* (Cambridge: MIT Press, 1967), pp. 127–28.
2. See Douglas G. Glasgow, *The Black Underclass: Poverty, Unemployment, and Entrapment of Ghetto Youth* (San Francisco: Jossey-Bass, 1980); Alphonso Pinkney, *The Myth of Black Progess* (Cambridge: Cambridge University Press, 1984); Charles V. Willie, "The Inclining Significance of Race," *Society* 15 (1978):10, 12–15.
3. See Theodore Hershberg, Alan N. Burstein, Eugene P. Ericksen, Stephanie W. Greenberg, and William L. Yancey, "A Tale of Three Cities: Blacks, Immigrants, and Opportunity in Philadelphia, 1850–1880, 1930, 1970," in Theodore Hershberg, ed., *Philadelphia: Work, Space, Family and Group Experience in the 19th Century* (New York: Oxford University Press, 1981), pp. 461–91; John D. Kasarda, "Caught in the Web of Change," *Society* 21 (1983):41–47; John D. Kasarda, "Urban Change and Minority Opportunities," in Paul E. Peterson, ed., *The New Urban Reality* (Washington, D.C.: Brookings Institution, 1985), pp. 33–68; John D. Kasarda, "Jobs, Migration, and Emerging Urban Mismatches," in Michael G. H. McCeary and Lawrence E. Lynn, Jr., eds., *Urban Change and Poverty* (Washington, D.C.: National Academy Press, 1988), pp. 148–98; John F. Kain, "Housing Segregation, Negro Employment, and Metropolitan Decentralization," *Quarterly Journal of Economics* 82 (1968):175–97; William Julius Wilson, *The Declining Significance of Race: Blacks and Changing American Institutions* (Chicago: University of Chicago Press, 1978); William Julius Wilson, *The Truly Disadvantaged: The Inner City, the Underclass, and Urban Policy* (Chicago: University of Chicago, 1987).
4. Bart Landry, *The New Black Middle Class* (Berkeley: University of California Press, 1987).
5. Douglas S. Massey and Mitchell L. Eggers, "The Ecology of Inequality: Minorities and the Concentration of Poverty, 1970–1980," *American Journal of Sociology* 95 (1990):1153–88.
6. See Lawrence M. Mead, *Beyond Entitlement: The Social Obligations of Citizenship* (New York: Free Press, 1986); Charles Murray, *Losing Ground: American Social Policy, 1950–1980* (New York: Basic Books, 1984).
7. William Ryan, *Blaming the Victim* (New York: Random House, 1971); Willie, "The Inclining Significance of Race."
8. See David R. James and Karl E. Taeuber, "Measures of Segregation," in Nancy Tuma, ed., *Sociological Methodology 1985* (San Francisco: Jossey-Bass, 1985), pp. 1–32; Douglas S. Massey and Nancy A. Denton, "The Dimensions of Residential

Segregation," *Social Forces* 67 (1988):281–315; Michael J. White, "Segregation and Diversity: Measures in Population Distribution," *Population Index* 52 (1986):198–221.

9. George R. Metcalf, *Fair Housing Comes of Age* (New York: Greenwood Press, 1988), p. 10.
10. Ibid., pp. 1–16, 86–137.
11. Ibid., p. 3.
12. Brian J. L. Berry, *The Open Housing Question: Race and Housing in Chicago, 1966–1976* (Cambridge, Mass.: Ballinger, 1979); Robert McClory, "Segregation City," *Chicago Reader* 20 (1991):1–29.
13. McClory, "Segregation City."
14. Harold Baron, *What Is Gautreaux?* (Chicago: Business and Professional People for the Public Interest, 1990); McClory, "Segregation City"; Michael J. Vernarelli, "Where Should HUD Locate Assisted Housing? The Evolution of Fair Housing Policy," in John M. Goering, ed., *Housing Desegregation and Federal Policy* (Chapel Hill: University of North Carolina Press, 1986), pp. 214–34; Irving Welfeld, "The Courts and Desegregated Housing: The Meaning (If Any) of the Gautreaux Case," *Public Interest* 45 (1976):123–35.
15. Metcalf, *Fair Housing Comes of Age*, pp. 65–72.
16. Ibid., pp. 96–101.
17. McClory, "Segregation City."
18. Ibid.
19. See Carole Goodwin, *The Oak Park Strategy: Community Control of Racial Change* (Chicago: University of Chicago Press, 1979); Juliet Saltman, *A Fragile Movement: The Struggle for Neighborhood Stabilization* (New York: Greenwood Press, 1990); Juliet Saltman, "Maintaining Racially Diverse Neighborhoods," *Urban Affairs Quarterly* 26 (1991):416–41; Juliet Saltman, "Neighborhood Stabilization: A Fragile Movement," *Sociological Quarterly* 31 (1990):531–49.
20. Metcalf, *Fair Housing Comes of Age*, pp. 205–221.
21. Carole Goodwin, *The Oak Park Strategy;* Robert W. Lake and Jessica Winslow, "Integration Management: Municipal Constraints on Residential Mobility," *Urban Geography* 2 (1981):311–26; Saltman, *A Fragile Movement.*
22. Ibid.
23. Lake and Winslow, "Integration Management," p. 323.
24. Metcalf, *Fair Housing Comes of Age*, pp. 208–209.
25. John F. Bauman, *Public Housing, Race, and Renewal: Urban Planning in Philadelphia, 1920–1974* (Philadelphia: Temple University Press, 1987); Adam Bickford and Douglas S. Massey, "Segregation in the Second Ghetto: Racial and Ethnic Segregation in U.S. Public Housing, 1977;" *Social Forces* 69 (1991):1011–36; Ira Goldstein and William L. Yancey, "Public Housing Projects, Blacks, and Public Policy: The Historical Ecology of Public Housing in Philadelphia," in John M. Goering, ed., *Housing Desegregation and Federal Policy* (Chapel Hill: University of North Carolina Press, 1986), pp. 262–89; Arnold R. Hirsch, *Making the Second Ghetto: Race and Housing in Chicago, 1940–1960* (Cambridge: Cambridge University Press, 1983).
26. Bauman, *Making the Second Ghetto*, p. 257.

27. R. Allen Hays, *The Federal Government and Urban Housing: Ideology and Change in Public Policy* (Albany: State University of New York Press, 1985), pp. 137–72.
28. Michael N. Danielson, *The Politics of Exclusion* (New York: Columbia University Press, 1976), pp. 50–106; Metcalf, *Fair Housing Comes of Age*, pp. 149–62.
29. Joan Magagna and Brian Heffernan, "City of Yonkers: A Bitterly Fought Civil Rights Case," *Trends in Housing* 27 (1988):1, 9.
30. Ibid.
31. Ibid.
32. George C. Galster and Heather Keeney, "Subsidized Housing and Racial Change in Yonkers, NY: Are the Fears Justified?" Working Paper, Urban Studies Program, College of Wooster, Wooster, Ohio, 1989.
33. Metcalf, *Fair Housing Comes of Age*, pp. 116–24.
34. McClory, "Segregation City."
35. Franklin James, Betty McCummings, and Eileen Tynan, *Minorities in the Sunbelt* (New Brunswick, N.J.: Rutgers Center for Urban Policy Resesearch, 1984), pp. 125–35.
36. John S. Adams, *Housing America in the 1980s* (New York: Russell Sage, 1987).
37. Bickford and Massey, "Segregation in the Second Ghetto."
38. See Metcalf, *Fair Housing Comes of Age*, pp. 93–94; Berry, *The Open Housing Question*, p. 72.
39. U.S. Department of Housing and Urban Development, Office of the Assistant Secretary for Fair Housing and Equal Opportunity, "Fair Housing Initiatives Program: Final Rule," *Federal Register*, vol. 54, no. 27 (1989):6492–6502, February 10.
40. U.S. Department of Housing and Urban Development, *The State of Fair Housing* (Washington, D.C.: U.S. Government Printing Office, 1989), pp. 1–3.
41. Bill Dedman, "Blacks Denied S&L Loans Twice as Often as Whites," *Atlanta Journal and Constitution*, Sunday January 22, p. 1.
42. Beth J. Lief and Susan Goering, "The Implementation of the Federal Mandate for Fair Housing," in Gary A. Tobin, ed., *Divided Neighborhoods: Changing Patterns of Racial Segregation* (Newbury Park, Calif.: Sage Publications, 1987), pp. 227–67.
43. Metcalf, *Fair Housing Comes of Age*, pp. 103–104.
44. Lief and Goering, "The Implementation of the Federal Mandate for Fair Housing."
45. James E. Rosenbaum, Marilynn J. Kulieke, and Leonard S. Rubinowitz, "White Suburban Schools' Responses to Low-Income Black Children: Sources of Success and Problems," *Urban Review* 20 (1988):28–41; James E. Rosenbaum and Susan J. Popkin, "Employment and Earnings of Low-Income Blacks Who Move to Middle Class Suburbs," in Christopher Jencks and Paul E. Peterson, eds., *The Urban Underclass* (Washington, D.C.: Brookings Institution, 1991), pp. 342–56; James E. Rosenbaum and Susan J. Poplin, "Economic and Social Impacts of Housing Integration," Center for Urban Affairs and Policy Research, Northwestern University, 1990.
46. Robert G. Schwemm, *Housing Discrimination: Law and Litigation* (New York: Clark Boardman, 1990), pp. 5.6–5.11.
47. Reynolds Farley, Suzanne Bianchi, and Diane Colasanto, "Barriers to the Racial

Integration of Neighborhoods: The Detroit Case," *Annals of the American Academy of Political and Social Science* 441 (1979):97–113.

48. John Yinger, "The Racial Dimension of Urban Housing Markets in the 1980s," in Gary A. Tobin, ed., *Divided Neighborhoods: Changing Patterns of Racial Segregation* (Newbury Park, Calif.: Sage Publications, 1987), pp. 43–67.
49. Robert W. Lake, "The Fair Housing Act in a Discriminatory Market: The Persisting Dilemma," *Journal of the American Planning Association* 47 (1981):48–58.
50. Metcalf, *Fair Housing Comes of Age*, pp. 15–26.
51. Testimony of Mr. Robert Butters, Association Counsel, National Association of Realtors, *Hearings before the Subcommittee on the Constitution of the Committee on the Judiciary, United States Senate, One Hundredth Congress, First Session, on S. 558.* (Washington, D.C.: U.S. Government Printing Office, 1988), pp. 108–131.
52. Ibid.
53. George C. Galster, "HUD Could Forbid Affirmative Marketing Strategies," *Trends in Housing* 27 (1988):3.
54. U.S. Department of Housing and Urban Development, "Fair Housing Initiatives Program."
55. The ploy was foiled by Senator Alan Dixon of Illinois, the Chair of the Senate banking subcommittee, who vowed to block any attempt to weaken the law's fair housing provisions; see "Dixon Hits Move to Ease Community Lending Rule," *Chicago Tribune*, May 31, 1991, Sec. 3, p. 1.
56. "Headliners: Agency in Decline," *New York Times*, Sunday, October 13, 1991, Sec. 3, p. 9.
57. See U.S. Commission on Civil Rights, *A Report of the Racial and Ethnic Impact of the Section 235 Program* (Washington, D.C.: U.S. Government Printing Office, 1971); U.S. Commission on Civil Rights, *Equal Opportunity in Housing* (Washington, D.C.: U.S. Government Printing Office, 1974); U.S. Commission on Civil Rights, *The Federal Fair Housing Enforcement Effort* (Washington, D.C.: U.S. Government Printing Office, 1979).

Index